10330202

D0997737

Developments in British
Public Policy

Also by Peter Dorey:

British Politics since 1945
The Conservative Party and the Trade Unions
The Major Premiership: Politics and Policies under John Major, 1990–97 (Editor)
Wage Politics in Britain: The Rise and Fall of Incomes Policies since 1945
Policy Making in Britain: An Introduction
The 1964–1970 Labour Governments (Editor)

Developments in British Public Policy

Edited by
Peter Dorey

SAGE Publications
London ● Thousand Oaks ● New Delhi

SAGE Publications Ltd
1 Oliver's Yard
55 City Road
London EC1Y 1SP

SAGE Publications Inc.
2455 Teller Road
Thousand Oaks, California 91320

SAGE Publications India Pvt Ltd
B-42, Panchsheel Enclave
Post Box 4109
New Delhi 110 017

British Library Cataloguing in Publication data

A catalogue record for this book is available
from the British Library

ISBN 0-7619-4905-4
ISBN 0-7619-4906-2 (pbk)

Library of Congress Control Number: 2005901772

Typeset by C&M Digitals (P) Ltd., Chennai, India
Printed on paper from sustainable resources
Printed in Great Britain by The Alden Press, Oxford

Contents

List of Figures and Tables   vii

Notes on Contributors   viii

Acknowledgements   x

Introduction   1
Peter Dorey

1   Agricultural Policy   7
    Wyn Grant

2   Economic Policy   24
    Colin Thain

3   Education Policy   46
    Clyde Chitty

4   Foreign Policy   67
    Steve Marsh

5   Health Policy   92
    Helen Jones

6   Housing Policy   117
    Peter Malpass

7   Industrial Relations Policy   133
    Peter Dorey

8   Pensions Policy   161
    Stephen Thornton

9   Transport Policy   180
    Nick Robinson

10 Developments in British Public Policy   205
    Peter Dorey

    Bibliography   226

    Index   246

List of Figures and Tables

Figure 2.1   Inflation, 1948–2004   27
Figure 2.2   Annual growth of GDP at market prices, 1948–2004   27

Figure 7.1   Main provisions of the 1971 Industrial Relations Act   146
Figure 7.2   Decline of total trade union membership in Britain since 1979   157
Figure 7.3   Declining trade union density in Britain since 1979   157
Figure 7.4   Strikes in the UK, 1983–2003   159

Figure 9.1   Changing transport orthodoxies over time   181
Figure 9.2   Location of actors on a policy network
continuum (pre-Major period)   184
Figure 9.3   Location of actors on a policy network
continuum (early 1980s)   186
Figure 9.4   Location of actors on a policy network
continuum (Major period)   190
Figure 9.5   Location of actors on a policy network
continuum (Blair period)   193
Figure 9.6   Benson's model of a policy sector   202

Table 5.1   The creation of new NHS Trusts and GP fundholders
each year, 1991–6   107

Table 6.1   House building in Great Britain, 1945–64   123

Table 7.1   Responses to the question: do you agree or disagree that
'trade unions have too much power in Britain today'?   150
Table 7.2   Responses to the question: do you think the trade unions
are becoming too powerful, or are not powerful enough?   150
Table 7.3   Trade union and industrial relations legislation, 1980–93   152
Table 7.4   The decline of trade union membership in Britain, 1979–98,
by selected trade unions (membership rounded to the nearest 1,000)   156

Notes on Contributors

Clyde Chitty is Professor of Policy and Management in Education, at Goldsmiths' College, University of London. His recent publications include: *Education Answers Back* (with Brian Simon, 1993); *Thirty Years On: Is Comprehensive Education Alive and Well, Or Struggling to Survive?* (with Caroline Benn, 1996); *Promoting Comprehensive Education in the 21st Century* (with Brian Simon, 2001); and *Understanding Schools and Schooling* (2002); *Education Policy in Britain* (2004); and *A Tribute to Caroline Benn: Essays in Education and Democracy* (with Melissa Benn, 2004).

Peter Dorey is Senior Lecturer in Politics in the School of European Studies at Cardiff University. His books include: *British Politics since 1945* (1995); *The Conservative Party and the Trade Unions* (1995); *The Major Premiership: Politics and Policies under John Major, 1990–1997* (editor, 1999); *Wage Politics in Britain: The Rise and Fall of Incomes Policies since 1945* (2001); *Policy Making in Britain: An Introduction* (2005); and *The 1964–1970 Labour Governments* (editor, forthcoming). He is currently completing two monographs: *The Labour Party and Constitutional Reform*, and *British Conservatism: The Philosophy and Politics of Inequality*, both scheduled for publication late 2006/early 2007.

Wyn Grant is Professor of Politics at the University of Warwick. His most recent books include: *Business and Politics in Britain* (1993); *Agriculture and the EU* (1995); *The Common Agricultural Policy* (1997); *Agricultural Policy* (co-edited with John Keeler, 2000); *Pressure Groups and British Politics* (2000); and *Economic Policy in Britain* (2002).

Helen Jones is Senior Lecturer in History at Goldsmiths' College, University of London. Her publications include: *Health and Society in Twentieth-Century Britain* (1994); *Social Policy and the City* (co-edited with John Lansley, 1994); *The Politics of the Family* (co-edited with Jane Millar,1996); *Towards a Classless Society?* (editor, 1997); *Social Issues and Party Politics* (co-edited with Susanne MacGregor, 1998); and *Women in British Public Life, 1914–1950* (2000).

Peter Malpass is Professor of Housing Policy at the University of the West of England. He is author of: *Reshaping Housing Policy: Subsidies, Rents and Residualisation* (1990); *Housing Associations and Housing Policy: A Historical Perspective* (2000); *Housing and* *the Welfare State: The Development of Housing Policy in Britain* (2005); *Housing Policy and Practice*, 5th edn (co-authored with Alan Murie, 1999); and *Implementing Housing Policy* (co-edited with Robin Means, 1993).

Steve Marsh is Lecturer in European Politics and International Relations in the School of European Studies at Cardiff University. His recent publications include: *US Foreign Policy since 1945* (co-authored with Alan Dobson, 2001); *Anglo-American Relations and Cold War Oil* (2003); and *The International Relations of the European Union* (co-authored with Hans Mackenstein, 2005). He is currently working on a revised and expanded second edition of *US Foreign Policy since 1945* for publication in 2006.

Nick Robinson is Lecturer in Public Policy at the University of Leeds. His publications include: *The Politics of Agenda Setting: The Car and the Shaping of Public Policy* (2000) and *Transport Policy and the Environment in the European Union* (forthcoming).

Colin Thain is Professor of Politics at the University of Ulster. His books include: *The Treasury and Whitehall: The Planning and Control of Public Expenditure, 1976–1993* (co-authored with Maurice Wright, 1995). He is currently conducting research into economic policy under New Labour, and the role and independence of the Bank of England.

Stephen Thornton is Lecturer in Politics in the School of European Studies at Cardiff University. He has published several articles and chapters on pensions policy in Britain, and is currently writing a book on *The Labour Party and Pensions Policy since 1945*.

Acknowledgements

Introduction
Peter Dorey

This book is intended to provide a companion text to *Policy Making in Britain: An Introduction* (Dorey, 2005), which examines the key characteristics of policy making in Britain, and discusses the roles played by the main policy actors in the British policy process. Although plenty of examples and empirical evidence were provided to illustrate and clarify key points and concepts, it was readily acknowledged that students of British public policy would benefit enormously from a separate text which examined distinct areas of public policy much more specifically and systematically.

This text therefore provides a series of 'case studies' of particular policy areas in Britain, from 1945 to the present day. The policies were selected both for their intrinsic importance, and because they clearly illustrated or exemplified key aspects – either conceptual or empirical (or both) – of policy making and the policy process in Britain, along with the factors which contribute to policy continuity and policy change. Having determined the key policies to be covered, a leading, internationally-renowned, academic expert in each policy, was invited to write the relevant chapter, in which they were asked to identify the main actors, concepts, influences, issues, objectives, paradigms and overall developments in their particular area of policy. The contributors, we are delighted to note, have admirably fulfilled this remit, and we are therefore extremely grateful to them. In so doing, they have provided a collection of essays which should be essential reading for students of British public policy.

In Chapter 1, Wyn Grant analyses the key features of agricultural policy in Britain since 1945, drawing particular attention to the 'productionist' policy paradigm which prevailed until the 1990s, whereafter various crises, scientific evidence, environmental considerations and increasing consumer concern about food safety combined to call into question the impact and efficacy of intensive farming methods and widespread use of agri-chemicals. Grant shows how these developments also served to destabilize the agricultural policy community, which not only obliged the National Farmers' Union to accept the involvement of other groups and interests in agricultural policy making, but culminated in the abolition of the Ministry of Agriculture, Fisheries and Food, and its replacement by the Department of the Environment, Food and Rural Affairs.

Chapter 2 sees Colin Thain surveying the main developments in British economic policy since the Second World War. Not only is economic policy a crucially important topic in its own right, it also impacts upon all of the other policies examined in this book. Thain illustrates how, from the mid-1940s until about 1973, successive governments adhered to Keynesianism, whereby policy makers used a judicious blend of monetary and fiscal tools to maintain (or boost) demand, in order to maintain full employment, and prevent an economic slump. Such governmental regulation of the economy, coupled with the explicit bipartisan commitment to full employment, was in stark contrast to the economic orthodoxy of the pre-war era, characterized by the 'Great Depression' and mass unemployment of the 1930s. During the 1960s, growing concern about low rates of economic growth and relative economic decline led policy makers to supplement Keynesianism with experiments in indicative planning, and a shift towards 'voluntaristic corporatism', entailing the incorporation of trade union leaders and employers into economic policy making. Ministers were particularly concerned to craft policies which improved rates of economic growth and industrial productivity, and maintained full employment, yet which did not fuel inflation.

By the 1970s, though, the 'Keynesian consensus' was crumbling, and the 1980s and 1990s therefore heralded new approaches to economic management, initially in the form of monetarism, and then, when this proved too problematic, the adoption of what Thain terms 'monetary-constrained Keynesianism'. Certainly, during the first half of the 1980s, the Conservative Governments led by Margaret Thatcher were ideologically committed to monetarism, and thus constituted a decisive break with the macroeconomic policies which had prevailed during the 1950s and 1960s. Rather than seeking to reverse economic decline and recession through an expansion of government intervention in the economy and increased public expenditure, the early 1980s witnessed the Thatcher Governments explicitly committing themselves to cutting public expenditure and borrowing (albeit with limited success), curbing the money supply (often via raising interest rates deliberately to make borrowing more expensive, and thus less financially attractive), reducing the economic and industrial role of the state, promoting liberalization and enterprise, and focusing on supply-side reforms (rather than directly seeking to boost demand through reflation). Although the Thatcher Governments' early monetarist experiment itself encountered various problems, and proved difficult to sustain in the long term, it did have profound implications for virtually all other policy areas in Britain.

Education policy is the subject of Chapter 3, in which Clyde Chitty notes the extent to which education provision from the mid-1940s to the late 1980s was shaped by the principles and provisions of the 1944 Education Act. This Act – itself the product of the Wartime Coalition Government – effectively laid the basis for a national education system in England and Wales, free at the point of access, but which was administered through local education authorities (LEAs). Furthermore, although not stipulated or recommended in the Act (which was actually rather ambiguous on issues such as the structure of secondary education and schools) there was an increasing trend towards comprehensive schooling, a trend which was given a considerable and conscious boost by the 1964–70 Labour Governments. Meanwhile, an education policy community was clearly discernible, with the Ministry/Department of Education, the Association of Education Committees, LEAs, and the National Union of Teachers working very closely together with regard to education policy.

By the 1970s, however, there was growing disquiet in a number of quarters about the structure and provision of education in England and Wales, to the extent that in October 1976, the Labour Prime Minister, James Callaghan, publicly called for a 'Great Debate' about education. It was not until the 1980s and 1990s, though, that this growing disquiet was translated into a series of reforms of secondary education in England and Wales, whereupon the former emphasis on partnership between central government, LEAs and the education profession was supplanted by a demand for greater accountability of schools and teachers, and a new emphasis on parental choice. With schools also being encouraged to opt-out of LEA control – and parents granted ballots to express their support for such a move – and central government imposing a controversial National Curriculum (and other related reforms) which was widely denounced by many teaching unions, the 1980s and 1990s heralded a destabilizing of the education policy community. Ministers aligned themselves with parents against the 'education establishment', which was deemed to be characterized by 'trendy Left-wing' ideas and teaching methods – allegedly a product of 1960s liberalism – which placed too much emphasis on 'child-centred learning', at the expense of the 'three Rs' (reading, writing and arithmetic), standards and discipline in schools.

In Chapter 4, Steve Marsh examines British foreign policy since 1945, placing particular emphasis on how policy makers have sought to square the three circles (as Winston Churchill originally characterized them) of post-war British foreign policy, namely empire and Commonwealth, the 'special relationship' with the United States, and Europe. Marsh begins by outlining the context in which post-war British foreign policy has been developed, highlighting such variables as Britain's relative decline, international systemic change, technological developments and globalization. He then analyses Britain's relationships with the empire and Commonwealth, the United States and Europe during the Cold War era (1945–90), before delineating the main features of British foreign policy since the end of the Cold War, to the present day. In spite of the various changes which have occurred since 1945, both in terms of Britain's own relative decline, and in international relations generally, Marsh suggests that perhaps the most notable feature of post-war British foreign policy has actually been its consistency, particularly in terms of Britain's determination to remain a global power, and exercise a significant influence – in partnership with the United States – in international relations.

Health policy is the subject of Chapter 5, in which Helen Jones notes that, until the 1980s, the dominant policy paradigm was that of curative medicine provided by NHS hospitals and general practitioners (GPs), rather than forms of preventative medicine. In other words, health care was generally equated with medical treatment. Moreover, the NHS was funded almost overwhelmingly from general taxation and National Insurance contributions, thereby ensuring that medical treatment was free at the point of access or need. Health policy also provided another good example of a policy community, with the medical profession, most notably through the British Medical Association (BMA) and the Department of Health, usually working very closely together to determine the nation's health needs, and the way that these should be provided for. Furthermore, proposals to expand or improve health care in Britain usually focused on the need to build new hospitals or modernize existing ones.

Since the 1980s, though, the altered politico-ideological climate, coupled with growing concern about the inexorably rising costs of the NHS (an issue lent added resonance by both governmental concern to curb public expenditure generally, and an ageing population), has yielded a number of changes in British health policy. Most notable of these, Jones explains, have been the 1980s' promotion of private health care and medical insurance, with Conservative Ministers encouraging (what economists call) 'exit' from the NHS, a major concern with such criteria as cost-effectiveness, efficiency and value-for-money in the delivery of health care, and a greater emphasis on public and preventative health care, with individuals exhorted to take much greater responsibility for their personal health, and the impact of their life-styles on their physical well-being. The NHS itself has also been subject to internal restructuring and reorganization, with managers ascribed a much greater role. This has reduced the former role and autonomy of doctors and consultants somewhat, and thus weakened the health policy community to some degree, particularly as successive governments have also insisted that patients be granted more rights and choice as 'consumers'.

With regard to housing policy, Chapter 6 provides an account by Peter Malpass which notes how the post-war era has witnessed an inexorable rise in homeownership, a corresponding decline in the private rented sector, and a major shift in the provision of public or social housing by local authorities. Until the 1970s, there was a mixed economy of housing, whereby those who could afford to do so tended to buy their own homes, whilst those on low(er) incomes predominantly rented a house from their local authority. To many observers, this distinction between homeowners and council tenants seemed to symbolize class inequalities and life-styles in Britain.

During the 1980s, however, home ownership was given a significant boost by virtue of the Conservative Governments' policy of selling council houses. With local authorities prohibited from using the revenues to build new council houses to replace those they had sold, the stock of local authority housing diminished considerably. To reduce the role of local authorities further, the Thatcher–Major Governments actively encouraged housing associations and other not-for-profit bodies to take over the management and provision of what became increasingly referred to as 'social housing'.

One other significant change since the 1980s, which Malpass identifies, concerns the various forms of financial support and subsidies previously available to homeowners and tenants, but which have been reduced or removed altogether. Deregulation of the private rental sector has effectively ended rent controls (so that rent controls have been replaced by 'the market' as the primary determinant of levels of rent charged by landlords). At the same time, rent rebates and levels of housing benefit for low-income tenants – private or local authority – have been reduced. Meanwhile, in spite of the active promotion of home-ownership, successive governments since the 1980s have reduced mortgage tax relief, to the point where it was abolished completely in April 2000.

Industrial relations provides the subject matter of Chapter 7, which identifies the various strategies adopted by policy makers to deal with the trade unions since 1945. During the post-war period in Britain, the trade unions' status changed from that of putative partners (with policy makers) to political pariahs, and so during this period of transformation the issue of industrial relations moved steadily up the policy agenda. During the 1960s and 1970s, governmental concern over trade union behaviour and power led to oscillation between two industrial relations policies, namely neo-corporatism, whereby the unions would be treated as partners in economic and industrial policy making (in the hope that this would yield greater responsibility and 'maturity'), and legalism, whereby statutory curbs would be placed on the unions to compel them to behave more responsibly. This latter policy replaced neo-corporatism entirely during the 1980s and 1990s, during which time industrial relations was also transformed by various other policies and wider structural changes.

In Chapter 8, Stephen Thornton examines the evolution of British pensions policy since 1945, during which time, he explains, policy makers have repeatedly sought to address certain deficiencies arising from the basic, flat-rate, old-age pension introduced in 1946. In particular, cognizant of the subsistence level at which the state pension has invariably been set (with many pensioners living in poverty), whilst recognizing the funding problems which would accrue from significantly increasing it (such as having to increase NI contributions or/and tax rates for those in work), policy makers have devised various 'top-up' schemes to supplement the state pension. These have often revolved around occupational or private pensions, but as Thornton explains, none has so far provided a lasting or workable solution. For example, pension schemes which are occupational or 'earnings-related' have generally been of little use to low-paid workers who are at most risk of enduring poverty in their old age: such schemes are likely to replicate socio-economic inequalities into retirement. Furthermore, low-paid workers – even assuming they could somehow afford to contribute to a pension scheme – have often been of little commercial interest to private pension companies. On the other hand, various scandals, controversies and shortfalls in the value of 'payouts' since the 1980s, have made some people wary of private pension schemes. In the context of Britain's ageing population, the need for an attractive and affordable pensions policy is more urgent than ever, but the Blair Government appears to be struggling as much as previous administrations in attempting to formulate such a policy.

Transport policy is the subject of Chapter 9, in which Nick Robinson delineates the three general options available to policy makers since 1945. He explains how one of these options, namely 'predict-and-provide', constituted the dominant transport policy paradigm until the 1970s. This particular policy option reflected the premise that increasing car ownership and ensuing traffic congestion should be addressed through the construction of more roads and motorways. This approach was supported by a corresponding transport policy community comprising the Department of Transport and key organized interests representing road transport users. Wider concerns, such as those pertaining to the environmental and public health impact of increased traffic and road-building, and other interests, such as those of public transport users, were largely excluded. Since the 1970s, however, such concerns and interests have been taken more seriously, thereby yielding challenges to the 'predict-and-provide' policy paradigm, and enabling alternative transport policies to be promoted, with the growing use of congestion charging providing a good example. Meanwhile, the transport policy community – rather like its agricultural counterpart – has been somewhat destabilized by the incorporation of various environmental groups into transport policy making, coupled with public concern over the health problems (particularly respiratory diseases arising from inhalation of exhaust fumes) posed by heavy volumes of traffic in Britain's towns and cities.

Chapter 10 is the concluding chapter, and seeks to extrapolate the main findings of the chapters in this book, so that the main sources of both continuity and change in British public policy can be summarized. The chapter notes that prior to the 1980s, considerable continuity was facilitated, not only by the general political context (entailing a broad consensus between the Labour and Conservative Parties on many key policy issues and objectives, which often led to successive governments pursuing similar policies, or building upon those of their predecessors), but by various conceptual and empirical features, such as the prevalence of policy communities in a number of policy areas, along with dominant policy paradigms which shaped and sustained institutional agendas. Many senior Ministers during this period also adopted a predominantly managerial style of political leadership *vis-à-vis* their Departments, which ensured that attempts at imposing significant policy change tended to be the exception rather than the rule. The cumulative and combined impact of these features was the existence of what Jordan and Richardson (1982) identified as a distinct 'British policy style'.

However, from the 1980s onwards, many of these spheres of public policy experienced considerable change. Many such changes derived from the significantly different ideological and political framework which became established in the 1980s, and which itself both reflected and reinforced trends and transformation in the British economy. Yet changes in public policy from the 1980s onwards are also attributable to the destabilization of a number of formerly closed and highly-conservative policy communities, which were either challenged by new medical knowledge or scientific evidence (which served to challenge or discredit some of their normative principles and policy goals) or confronted by senior Ministers who increasingly adopted an activist or agenda-setting role, and were sometimes willing to invoke 'despotic power' in order to overcome resistance to change by Departments and/or organized interests. This new role adopted by at least some Cabinet Ministers was itself partly attributable to reforms of the civil service (which sought to downgrade the policy advice role of civil servants, and, instead, placed much greater emphasis on 'policy delivery'), and the increasing use of Special Advisers to generate new ideas and innovative policy proposals. Arguably, think-tanks also became a more important source of policy advice for some Ministers. These developments, in turn, served to undermine various policy paradigms – which had previously sustained discernible institutional agendas – so that from the 1980s onwards, a number of 'paradigm shifts' occurred in British public policy; the causes and consequences of these developments in British public policy will become evident in the chapters that follow.

1 Agricultural Policy
Wyn Grant

Introduction

For much of the post-war period, agricultural policy offered the prime example of a policy arena dominated by a stable and exclusive policy community in which policy change occurred only incrementally. Policy was framed around a 'productionist' policy paradigm which emphasized the maximization of domestic production in the interests of food security, a goal that it was thought required and justified the payment of considerable subsidies to farmers. British membership of the European Economic Community (EEC) in 1973 changed the way in which these subsidies were paid, but not their extent. Agricultural policy even survived largely unscathed the shift to a neo-liberal policy paradigm which characterized the Thatcher Governments during the 1980s.

However, by the start of the 21st century, both the form and content of agricultural policy were starting to change in significant ways. In part, this reflected a more general change in society from a politics of production towards a politics of collective consumption (Grant, 2000: Ch. 9). It also reflected a long-term shift in consumer preferences away from price (although that was still important for many consumers) towards quality, value-added and food safety. Indeed, consumers were becoming increasingly concerned about the welfare of the animals that provided the food. A greater emphasis was given to the environmental impact of farming. Although the European Union's Common Agricultural Policy remained largely unreformed, the way in which subsidies were paid was changing, and there was a new emphasis on the 'multifunctional' character of farming as a provider of public goods, including attractive landscapes. The devolved administrations in Scotland and Wales – particularly the former – were able to take new initiatives on agricultural politics. Above all, the Ministry of Agriculture, Fisheries and Food (MAFF), which had been seen – with some justification – as a spokesperson for farming interests within the machinery of government, had been replaced by the Department of the Environment, Food and Rural Affairs (DEFRA) with a new remit.

The 1947 Agriculture Act and the productionist paradigm

The 1947 Agriculture Act, passed by Clement Attlee's 1945–51 Labour administration, provided the basis of British agricultural policy until Britain entered the EEC in 1973. It instituted a comprehensive system of subsidies for farmers which were reviewed each year, through a process of negotiation with the National Farmers' Union (NFU), known as the annual farm price review. As such: 'During the first few years of the recovery period, the output objective comprised the general expansion of agricultural production virtually regardless of either the commodity composition of the extra output, or the costs and efficiency of expansion' (Ingersent and Rayner, 1999: 130).

Post-war agricultural policy generally – not just in Britain – was dominated by the objective of food security, which led to an emphasis on the maximization of production as the principal goal of agricultural policy. Although no one starved in Britain during and after the war, and the diet consumed was generally more nutritious and balanced than in more prosperous times later in the century, food rationing was not popular. In continental Europe, though, starvation was not an unknown phenomenon in the immediate post-war period. There were fears of a recurrence of the post-war slump that agriculture experienced in the years after the First World War, from which it never fully recovered until the outbreak of the Second World War. There were also concerns that scarcity of supply might force up prices at a time when food comprised a much larger part of the average family budget. With Britain still very reliant on imported food, the development of the Cold War raised fears that its sea-lanes might again be vulnerable during armed conflict as they had been during the Second World War.

Tom Williams (later Lord Williams of Bamburgh) was agriculture minister from 1945 to 1951, and therefore the architect of the 1947 Act. His approach to agricultural policy was made clear in his memoirs: '[It] was clear that the world would be suffering a grave food shortage for some years to come … the essential first need was to maintain the momentum of food production achieved during the War' (Williams, 1965: 154). Outlining the Government's plans to the House of Commons in 1945, he explained that: 'the Government propose to establish, as an essential and permanent feature of their policy for food and agriculture, a system of assured markets and guaranteed prices for the principal agricultural products' (Williams, 1965: 156).

The 1947 Agriculture Act included an unusual provision that required the Government, when setting agricultural price support levels, to consult 'such bodies of persons who appear to them to represent the interests of producers in the agricultural industry'. In practice, this was interpreted to mean the NFU and its associated bodies in Scotland and in Northern Ireland, the Scottish Farmers' Union and the Ulster Farmers' Union respectively. A breakaway farmers' union was formed in Wales in 1955 (*Undeb Amaethwyr Cymru*) and received official recognition in 1978. The Country Landowners' Association (CLA), with its basis of support in the traditional big estates, also enjoyed a highly influential position. However, it was the NFU that was uniquely privileged, for it:

> derived considerable political advantage from its symbiotic relationship with MAFF: through the Ministry's single-minded commitment to the farmers' cause, through the NFU's entrenched role in policy making and through its privileged access on a routine basis to centres of decision making, including the highest levels of government. The Ministry and the Union are in constant contact at all levels over the myriad of issues, large and small, that arise in the development and implementation of policy. (Cox et al., 1986a: 185)

MAFF was seen as something of a backwater in Whitehall, not the place where the most ambitious civil servants would wish to go, but there were advantages in being 'an old and unusually inbred department' (Self and Storing, 1962: 78). The position of agriculture was strengthened by the fact that the Scottish Office also functioned as an agriculture department with representation in Cabinet committees, later joined by the Welsh Office. The Ministry of Agriculture in Northern Ireland 'was also integrated into the national policy and Annual Review machinery' (Greer, 1996: 59).

Faced by the formidable institutional weight of this agricultural establishment, the Ministry of Food attempted to act as a champion for consumers, but was finally absorbed into MAFF in 1956. The influence of the Treasury, meanwhile, was 'limited by the established conventions of the price review' (Self and Storing, 1962: 78). Dissident politicians did question the wisdom of a high subsidy agricultural policy from time to time, but quickly found themselves crushed by the weight of the agricultural establishment and its shared assumptions. John Strachey had been Minister of Food from 1946 to 1950 and caused trouble for Williams: 'at heart Strachey was never anything but a free-trader, and I don't believe that he ever really appreciated what we were trying to do at the Ministry of Agriculture in the post-war years'. The official orthodoxy was that the policy was one of consumer subsidies, albeit largely paid to farmers (food subsidies to consumers were pegged in 1949). It is true that the Government had chosen not to follow the option of imposing tariffs on imported food, opting instead to continue with the traditional policy of allowing cheap food to enter the country and compensating farmers for the difference between guaranteed and market prices. Stanley Evans, Parliamentary Under-Secretary of State at MAFF after the 1950 election, nevertheless caused trouble by doing 'everything he could to reduce the taxpayers' contribution towards the settlement of the review' (Williams, 1965: 176–7). Eventually, this unorthodox stance became publicly known and he was dismissed.

The very complexity of agricultural policy helped the farmers to secure good deals from successive price reviews, although this did not stop them complaining about many of the settlements. It has been noted that: 'The record suggests that Cabinets have often made substantial last-minute concessions rather than face an open disagreement with the [NFU]' (Self and Storing, 1962: 79). For example, in 1967, the Labour Cabinet discussed that year's farm price review in the presence of Richard Crossman, whose wife owned a farm. The agriculture minister had asked for an extra two old pence a gallon on milk, but the Treasury had been prepared to concede only 0.75 old pence, a figure gradually increased to 1.5 old pence. The previous weekend Crossman had talked to his wife's farm manager 'who had told me that he thought [1.5 old pence] was very good if only the farmers could get it in ... so I realized that Fred [Peart, the agriculture minister] was demanding a great big bonus' (Crossman, 1977: 238, diary entry for 14 February 1967). Nevertheless, the Cabinet agreed to the 1.5 old pence figure argued for by the chair of the Cabinet's agriculture committee. Apart from Crossman, 'No one knew that the compromise was a very generous concession to the farming industry' (Crossman, 1977: 239, diary entry for 14 February 1967).

These political advantages enjoyed by MAFF persisted until the 1990s, by which time agriculture was coming under increasing pressure on environmental grounds. Gillian Shephard, Secretary of State for Agriculture from May 1993 to July 1994, recalls that MAFF was paradoxically helped by the fact that it had 'almost no clout in Whitehall, being both unfashionable and arcane' (Shephard, 2000: 112). She argued that:

It was regarded by smart political commentators as dull, and by other Departments as incomprehensible. Therefore the Minister was left alone for the most part to get on, which is certainly in its way a form of power. It worked particularly well with the Treasury, whose clever officials knew nothing about agriculture and who usually gave in during public expenditure rounds, simply out of boredom. (Shephard, 2000: 22)

The most important long-term effects of the productionist paradigm were to be found not so much in the policies it produced, for these soon started to be modified: 'Between 1950 and 1954, there was some shift in the objective of production policy away from general expansion regardless of efficiency to expansion combined with improved efficiency' (Ingersent and Rayner, 1999: 131). However: 'Although increased "efficiency" was called for, what exactly was meant by "efficiency" was not generally defined, nor were there any major provisions for achieving it' (Cheshire, 1975: 66). Raising farm incomes and expanding output continued to be the most important aims, reflected in a target to increase production by 1956 by 60 per cent over the average level of the immediate post-war years.

With its emphasis on the importance of taxpayer-funded rewards for increased output by farmers, the most lasting effect of the productionist paradigm was the mindset it produced in many farmers, a mindset that was slow to change. At the risk of some caricature, this mindset was one that emphasized maximizing efficient production, regardless of any negative externalities. The nation should be grateful for the food thereby produced, and express its gratitude in terms of subsidies funded by taxpayers.

In broad terms, the productionist paradigm comprised the following main features:

- Farmers deserved and required substantial subsidies, both to provide the food the nation required, and help the balance of payments (this latter argument became particularly important in the 1960s).
- Government should set out the overall parameters for the future development of agriculture, but do so through a close and intensive dialogue with farming organizations. The task of MAFF was to represent farmers.
- Capital should be substituted for labour with government support, although often grants were diverted into consumption, rather than capital expenditure.
- Intensification of farming was desirable and necessary, including the increased use of fertilizers and agrochemicals, and the enlargement of fields through hedge removal (all activities encouraged at one time or another by government subsidy).
- Government should provide research and advisory services to encourage innovation, supported by a network of specialist educational institutions for agriculture.

Changing economic and political circumstances, including a greater emphasis on the role of markets, more sophisticated consumers and growing pressures from environmental organizations, did little to change these perspectives, although individual farmers challenged the prevalent policy paradigm or modified their own practices. Oliver Walston, an East Anglian grain farmer, made himself unpopular by questioning the need for subsidies and protection. A more typical view was expressed by the chairman of the Devon NFU who complained that: 'There appears to be almost an anti-farmer, certainly an anti-subsidies, culture in the MAFF civil service today. But the fact is that they are responsible for farmers' income' (*Farmers Weekly*, 14 November 1997). One would have thought that by 1997, like other groups in society, they might be responsible for their own incomes. Similarly, notions of the importance of economic planning persisted long after they had disappeared elsewhere. The president of the Scottish NFU commented:

> ... above all, we need a clear statement from government about its view of the future role of agriculture. If government wants fewer farmers then it must come out and say so. Then we can sit down with ministers and plan some orderly approach. (*Farmers Weekly*, 19 June 1998)

Indeed, some farming leaders attempted to revive the productionist paradigm in the 21st century through a use of food security arguments based on the threat of terrorism.

In the 1950s and 1960s, the objective of maximizing production in agriculture remained paramount, with balance of payments starting to assume a greater importance, particularly under Harold Wilson's 1964–70 Labour Governments, which viewed the elimination of balance of payments' deficits as a major economic policy objective. Previously, under the Conservatives in the 1950s, there had been a greater emphasis on selectivity in the support of commodities, although, apart from the case of pigs, this generally meant standstills in guaranteed prices rather than reductions. There was, however, an increased use of deficiency payments, reinstated in 1953 and formally embodied in the 1957 Agriculture Act. This meant that:

> Farmers sold their output at the best market price they could obtain, but any difference between the average market price thus realized and the guaranteed price determined at the annual review was made good in the form of a Government bonus paid retrospectively on each unit of output sold. (Self and Storing, 1962: 70)

Advocates of deficiency payments deemed them to be closer to the market mechanism than other methods of subsidy. Farmers were encouraged to respond to market signals, for markets normally function without the accumulation of 'mountains' or 'lakes' of surplus stocks later evident in the EEC's interventionist purchasing system. Politically, they had the advantage of enabling Britain to continue to import competitively priced agricultural products from the Commonwealth, a practice that both benefited consumers and strengthened traditional political ties.

However, there were two important drawbacks. Firstly, in a net food importing country like Britain, 'if imports are unrestricted the exchequer cost of the deficiency payment bill remains uncontrolled, and is likely to rise unpredictably if there are exogenous downward shocks to the price of imports' (Ingersent and Rayner, 1999: 136). Secondly, Britain did not participate in the formation of the European 'common market' and the discussions that produced the Common Agricultural Policy (CAP). Britain subsequently had substantially to modify its subsidy arrangements when it joined the EEC in 1973.

By the 1960s, there were the first signs that the privileged position of farmers, especially the larger-scale ones who benefited most from the subsidy policies, was coming under challenge. Not only was there a discussion about the income distribution effects of the policies, there was also:

The first shock to farmers' complacency and the belief that the national system of financial support for agriculture was 'gold-plated' came in 1960. ... Prime Minister Macmillan made clear the Government's unease at its open-ended commitment to provide deficiency payments if prices fell as a result of markets being saturated. (Plumb, 2001: 22)

Entry to the European Economic Community (EEC)

Between Britain's first and final application for membership of the European Economic Community, the position of the NFU shifted from outright opposition to broad support. In view of the generous levels of support provided to farmers under the CAP, what did the farmers have to fear? In part, it was a simple fear of the unknown. The annual price review process suited the leadership of the NFU very well. In particular, it allowed them to balance settlements between 'corn and horn' (arable and livestock producers) in such a way as to prevent jeopardizing the unity of the NFU, which was one of the keys to its strength. There were also concerns about the impact of membership on particular sectors of the agricultural economy, notably horticulture.

The concerns of the farmers had a considerable impact on the nature of the first British application for EEC membership in 1961. In its January 1961 White Paper reporting on its talks with the farmers' organizations, Harold Macmillan's Conservative Government pledged that it would seek to achieve membership 'without sacrificing the vital interests of UK farmers and horticulturalists' (Cmnd 1249, 1961: para. 37). In fact, it was difficult to see how membership could be achieved without making some sacrifices in the sphere of agriculture. The CAP was one of the major obstacles to British membership, rather than a reason for it. Applying for membership involved making a strategic political decision that the drawbacks of the CAP were outweighed by the broader economic and political benefits of membership. Britain entered the first set of negotiations especially concerned with three safeguards: a transition period of 12 to 15 years (as against the five eventually achieved), measures to safeguard the standard of living of farmers and special arrangements for horticulture. Even if President de Gaulle had been better disposed to British membership of the EEC, it is difficult to see how these conditions could have been met. For example, there was simply no way that much of British horticulture, as it was then organized, could compete effectively in a wider common market. This was primarily because Britain's climate did not favour the growing of many horticultural crops, although this was eventually offset by the emergence of large-scale growers making sophisticated use of controlled environments in glasshouses.

The second application for British membership of the EEC, submitted by the Labour Prime Minister, Harold Wilson, in 1967, was also unsuccessful, but it adopted a very different approach to that taken in 1961–3, when the British stance had been to a considerable extent shaped by the demands of organized interests like the NFU. With the 'political class' more convinced of the benefits of membership, the matter was treated by Wilson as a political issue of high politics, not subject to pledges to pressure groups.

The farming leadership, and eventually the farmers themselves, became increasingly aware of the benefits of membership. Deficiency payments had worked well for the farmers, but their increasing cost was becoming an issue for government: 'Prior to accession, British farmers believed that producer prices would increase as a result of the CAP, and given the relatively efficient structure of British agriculture, that they would be well placed to compete' (Fearne, 1997: 37). The leadership of the NFU, which had better forward vision than the leaders of many other organized interests, also recognized that it would not be possible to keep agriculture out of international trade negotiations for ever. This had suited the United States in the 1950s, but the comparative efficiency of American agriculture would ultimately lead to demands for greater liberalization, a demand intensified by the distorting effects of CAP subsidies on world trade. Far better, then, to move inside a trade bloc that would be better placed to resist American demands. Britain 'inside would be afforded protection from the trade pressures being increasingly applied by the big power-blocs outside Europe, notably from the far shores of the Atlantic' (Plumb, 2001: 71–2).

The 1970–4 Conservative Government, led by Edward Heath, started to replace deficiency payments by a 'minimum import price' scheme, which was operated through import levies similar to those used by the EEC. The final negotiations concerning British membership were thus able to overcome what had seemed to be intractable difficulties with relative ease: 'The issue of Britain's relations with the Commonwealth which had seemed so intractable in 1961–63 now broke down into a limited number of relatively technical problems' (Tracy, 1989: 287). New Zealand, for example, was granted a special concession over exports of butter.

The one major modification made to the CAP as a result of British accession to the EEC was a Less Favoured Areas directive, which was viewed as a means of continuing the generous levels of assistance provided to hill farmers. As is so often the case with EEC policies, though, this initiative had unintended and perverse consequences. A report from the European Court of Auditors in 2003 made a number of criticisms of the policy, noting, for example, that the areas designated 'less favoured' had expanded considerably, while Luxembourg still had 75 per cent of its farming area designated in this way despite the changes in farming conditions since 1975.

British farmers did not benefit as much as they had hoped in the years after accession in 1973, because of the manipulation of the 'green currency' system. This had originally been devised as a means of dealing with the shift from a fixed to a floating exchange rate system at the beginning of the 1970s. The Labour Government that entered Office in 1974 was faced by very high rates of domestic inflation (peaking at just over 24 per cent in 1975). Green pound overvaluation had the helpful political effect of holding down the price the consumer paid for her food, as intervention prices paid to farmers were lower than they would otherwise have been, while imports were subsidized through a system of monetary compensation amounts applied at national borders. Farmers' organizations pressed for a series of green pound devaluations, but faced opposition from the trade union movement (Grant, 1981).

The management of dissent

The difficulties faced by Britain's farmers over the green pound were one portent of a decline in their influence compared with the immediate post-war period. This loss of influence had already been evident towards the end of the 1960s, when farmers felt aggrieved about the outcome of a series of price reviews. The NFU's influence depended on its status as a key insider group with government, but if it no longer seemed able to control its own members, and thus deliver their assent to any agreement reached with government, that influence could be placed in jeopardy. As the then NFU president recalls: 'It would have been so easy to swing open the floodgates of protest, but I had to consider the end result in the long term, and the effect it would have on future negotiations with the Government' (Plumb, 2001: 64).

Demonstrations by members could, of course, be useful to the NFU leadership as a means of illustrating the strength of feeling of their membership, provided that they could be kept under control. Indeed, this was precisely the strategy that the NFU leadership followed. A distinction was drawn between illegal action which 'would have a negative effect and alienate the public' (such as street demonstrations and traffic disruption of the kind favoured in France) and what was termed 'solidarity' (Plumb, 2001: 64). It was decided to operate a ban on sending livestock to any market, a measure which was highly effective, in the sense that most markets were completely closed as a result.

As the financial situation of farmers deteriorated during the 1970s, however, it became increasingly difficult for the NFU to maintain control of its membership. The 1972 and 1974 miners' strikes, along with other instances of militant industrial action, suggested to some farmers that tactics such as 'flying pickets' could be used to their advantage. A particular problem arose in the livestock sector in 1974, for whilst the old system of guaranteed prices and deficiency payments had been dismantled, the EEC system was not fully operative. The flash-point came with the literal unloading of Irish cattle on the British market, whereupon Welsh farmers massed at Holyhead to prevent the unloading of Irish beef. The demonstrations later spread to Fishguard and Birkenhead, and a 'flying picket' of Midland farmers was reported ready for action. Following clashes between farmers and police, the NFU president called for a suspension of the demonstrations.

The ferocity of these particular demonstrations posed uncomfortable problems for the NFU leadership. On the one hand, they illustrated to the general public the depth and extent of the farmers' fears, leading Sir Henry Plumb to comment that: 'What has been done in Anglesey helps the cause' (*Farmer and Stockbreeder*, 9 November 1974). On the other hand, whilst the demonstrations continued, there was always the risk that the NFU's leadership might lose control of the situation, with consequent damage to their credibility with government. The NFU was placed under 'fearsome stress', for as its own journal remarked: 'The Union's leadership has ... been in a slightly delicate position – unable to advocate anything which could be interpreted as illegal ... but anxious not to discourage spontaneous demonstrations'. Meanwhile, the chairman of the NFU's Welsh Council admitted that: 'In Wales, we have kept the initiative, but only just' (*Farmer and Stockbreeder*, 23 November 1974).

In the 1970s, the NFU was able to maintain a united front. However, the tension between insider strategies and outsider tactics never went away. Indeed, it was to resurface again, with renewed force, at the end of the 20th century, as will be discussed later in this chapter.

The Thatcher era

The significant aspect of 1979–90 Thatcher Governments *vis-à-vis* farming is the lack of impact which they had in terms of advancing a neo-liberal agenda. Whilst Britain was within the CAP, farmers received the subsidies and protection it provided. The Social

Democratic, and Christian Democratic, governments of continental Europe provided continued political support for the CAP, for as far as they were concerned it was the cornerstone of the EEC. When the budgetary cost of the CAP forced reforms, as with the introduction of milk quotas for 1984, they actually provided new benefits for farmers. Milk quotas helped to support prices by limiting output, but they also gave existing farmers a windfall capital gain that made it more difficult for new entrants to start dairy farming. Sales of dairy farms invariably mentioned the associated quota and factored it into the farm price.

Margaret Thatcher had relatively few domestic political instruments at her disposal to influence farming. She deregulated liquid milk prices, but this had the paradoxical effect of strengthening the highly corporatist milk marketing regime. Rather than trying to change the nature of the CAP, Mrs Thatcher's initial strategy was to get 'Britain's money back' by negotiating an adjustment of the situation where Britain contributed considerably to the cost of the CAP, but received relatively few benefits from it. This objective was achieved by the Fontainebleau agreement in 1984, which gave Britain a budget rebate. Thatcher took an active part in the 1988 reform debate that led to the introduction of budgetary stabilizers, probably the least effective reform of the CAP. However, although she tried to present it as a success in her memoirs, she admitted that: 'The CAP was still wasteful and costly' (Thatcher, 1993: 737).

Thatcher's dislike of 'vested interests' did affect her Governments' relationship with the NFU, to the extent that, in 1987, the NFU passed a vote of no-confidence in the Governments' agricultural policy, and called for the resignation of the then Secretary of State for Agriculture, Michael Jopling (he was removed from the government a few months later). Margaret Thatcher was provoked into a typically robust reply, in which she pointed out that her Government was providing £2.5 billion in agriculture and food sector support during the coming financial year. Although two-thirds of this sum was under the CAP, a third came from various national measures. Thus, at a time when subsidies to industries such as coal and steel were being removed, agriculture continued to receive substantial support. Indeed, when Mrs Thatcher considered proposing a reversion to national subsidies for agriculture in 1988, she saw the main disadvantage as being 'that individual countries would have been competing in subsidy and probably our farmers would have lost out in the race to the French and the Germans' (Thatcher, 1993: 732). However, this consideration did not stop her reducing subsidies to manufacturing industry, and it is clear that she envisaged continuing governmental support for agriculture, if the CAP had been abolished.

Nevertheless, in 1989, the NFU president, Sir Simon Gourlay, launched a strong attack on the Thatcher Governments' agricultural policy, accusing a 'hostile' Government of pushing the industry to the brink of recession (*Farmers Weekly*, 8 February 1989). Farmers were particularly annoyed that the pound had been allowed to 'float' downwards, while the green pound rate was maintained because of concerns about the impact on food prices. Rumours subsequently circulated that the government was planning to abolish the Ministry of Agriculture. The Conservative Party had become a far more urban party under Mrs Thatcher (for a disparaging account of this change by a then Conservative MP, see Critchley, 1990: *passim*) and attendance at the Conservative backbench committee on agriculture had fallen. Thatcher felt obliged to appear at that year's Royal Show to reassure farmers that they were 'the backbone of society' and that she had no intention of abolishing the Ministry of Agriculture (*Farmers Weekly*, 7 July 1989).

When John Major succeeded Thatcher in November 1990, he judged it necessary to reassure farming supporters of the Conservatives, appearing at the Oxford Farming Conference and becoming the first Prime Minister to address the NFU's annual conference. He also instructed Gillian Shephard, when she became Secretary of State for Agriculture, 'to work to bring the farmers back on side' (Shephard, 2000: 107).

The emergence of new agendas

The politically protected position of agriculture and its policy community – based around the close relationship between the NFU and MAFF, and the shared commitment to the productionist policy paradigm – has been most effectively challenged by the emergence of new agendas. Three such agendas are discussed here: environment and conservation; food safety and quality; international trade. These have brought new actors into the policy process, and generated new ways of thinking about agriculture which have challenged the traditional productionist paradigm. Nevertheless, it must be emphasized that the agricultural policy community has shown considerable resilience in the face of these new challenges. It has resisted some of them, and adapted others for its own purposes, and as such it is possible to observe an interesting interaction between new ideas and established policy interests.

Productionist perspectives had little place for environmental concerns, except as a hobby for wealthy landowners often motivated by sporting priorities. In the name of maximizing production, field boundaries were stripped out, monoculture grew at the expense of mixed farming, and fertilizers and pesticides were applied with little concern about environmental impact. The dominant 'expansionist ideology was so widely held that few voices could be raised against it'. Indeed, 'for much of the post-war period, the environmental effects of intensive agriculture were excluded from the primary decision-making arena – a classic example of non-decision-making' (Garner, 2000: 198).

With the growth of the environmental movement from the 1960s onwards, an alternative perspective emerged and gathered strength. Rachel Carson's best-selling book, *Silent Spring*, published in 1962, drew attention to the damaging consequences of the unrestrained use of pesticides, and: 'By the mid-1970s, considerable evidence about the adverse impact of modern agricultural technology on wildlife habitats had accumulated' (Cox et al., 1990: 35). It quickly became evident that the designation of nature reserves for threatened species did not offer a simple solution.

What was also required were broader changes in the nature of farming. The farming organizations fell back on traditional characterizations of farmers as trustees who acted as stewards of the countryside, and who insisted on voluntary co-operation rather than legislation. Nevertheless, studies by the Nature Conservancy Council and the Countryside Commission, 'established the parameters for a wide-ranging debate, that gathered momentum during the following years, on how the forces intensifying production might be moderated in the interests of conservation' (Cox et al., 1990: 37). Marion Shoard's (1980) book on *The Theft of the Countryside* popularized this debate and attracted extensive media coverage. Long-running disputes, such as that concerning the draining and ploughing of

Halvergate marshes, on the Norfolk broads, attracted further publicity, and provided a locus for direct action by Friends of the Earth.

Nevertheless, the influence of the conservation policy network on agricultural policy remained limited. For example, 'only the [Royal Society for the Protection of Birds] of the conservation network had any input into the Wildlife and Countryside Bill before it was put before Parliament in the early 1980s. Even the state conservation agencies were excluded' (Garner, 2000: 198). An underlying problem was that: 'The policy community for rural conservation is … large, diverse and pluralistic; that for agriculture … small, tightly-knit and corporatist' (Cox et al., 1986b: 16). The various conservation and environmental groups – more properly categorized as an issue network than a policy community – had different agendas. One of the longest established and most influential lobbies, the Council for the Protection of Rural England (CPRE), was preoccupied with the aesthetic of the rural landscape, whereas newer and more wide-ranging groups such as Friends of the Earth had a more radical agenda.

However, it is the transformation of the Royal Society for the Protection of Birds (RSPB) into a mass membership organization that is probably the most significant development in the emergence of a countervailing conservationist policy network. By the beginning of the 21st century, it had more than one million members – significantly more than the combined membership of Britain's three main political parties – and in 2003 it was given an award for agenda-setting by the UK Political Studies Association. It was noted for its sophisticated critiques of agricultural policies, proceeding from the argument that declining bird populations were a good indicator of environmental stress. From being perceived as a 'harmless eccentricity' (Newby, 1979: 251), bird-watching had developed into a major leisure occupation. Even more important, the RSPB has emerged as a major definer and articulator of conservationist values and of alternative agricultural policies.

Some legislation was passed as a result of the activities of the conservation lobby, although they regarded it as far from adequate. The measures included the Wildlife and Countryside Act, 1981, the Agriculture Acts of 1986 (which gave MAFF a duty to promote conservation) and 1988, and some parts of the 1990 Environmental Protection Act. Although the 1981 Act was, in many respects, a disappointment for conservationists, Winter argues that: 'It marks a watershed in post-war agri-environmental policies'. The narrowly defined agricultural policy was opened up to outside influences, producing 'a defeat for agricultural exceptionalism' (Winter, 1996: 208).

Further progress was made with the more stringent enforcement of existing regulations. Dairy farming was a major source of water pollution, because more intensive methods of production, including the switch from hay to silage, produce a liquid slurry when concrete floors are washed down, and this can easily pollute rivers and streams. A typical (English) West Country dairy farm with some 50 cows has a pollution potential equivalent to that of a community of around 500 human inhabitants. Through a mixture of exhortation, grants and prosecution, dairy farming practices have been considerably changed (Lowe et al., 1997).

More recently, the debate over genetically modified (GM) crops has linked the environmental and food safety discourses. This debate is a complex one, in which polarized positions have been adopted by the protagonists, but in general it can be said that evidence of human health effects is at best speculative. There are more grounds for concern about the environmental effects of such crops. For example, if they reduced insect populations, this would in turn have an effect on the bird population. There is also concern about possible impacts on organic farming. Although the Blair Government states that it wants to have an open public debate over the subject, there is a perception that it favours the commercial use of GM crops. Its main motivation seems to be to prevent a trade dispute with the United States, and also, in part, to foster the development of the biotechnology industry in Britain.

Even before GM crops became an issue, MAFF's response to the bovine spongiform encephalopathy (BSE) crisis of the mid-1990s suggested that 'the department's primary motivation is to support the producers rather than the protestors or consumers' (Garner, 2000: 201). Nevertheless, the link that the BSE crisis revealed between intensive farming practices and threats to human health produced a fundamental challenge to the agricultural policy community. Without the BSE crisis, traditional policy arrangements might have survived for much longer. It had been foreshadowed by the 1988 crisis about salmonella in eggs, which had led to the resignation of Edwina Currie as a junior agriculture Minister, an outcome interpreted at the time as a victory for a producer lobby searching for a scapegoat. However, Smith argues that

> the reality is more complex. The *salmonella* crisis was indicative of a general weakening of the position of the farmers partly as a result of long-term changes in the policy community. The farmers failed to keep the *salmonella* in eggs issue off the agenda. (Smith, 1991: 244)

Food policy ceased to be the adjunct of a conventional agricultural policy and became increasingly politicized.

One consequence of the salmonella crisis was the passage of a new Food Safety Act in 1990, which 'enhanced hygiene control in the downstream industry (retail and processing) but … had little effect on the primary industries because farming was regarded as a food source, and was largely exempt' (Meat and Livestock Commission, 1997: 2). Meanwhile, MAFF was reorganized internally to create a new Food Safety Directorate in 1993.

However, food safety problems were not just the result of inadequate legislation or enforcement, but had a systemic relationship with more intensive and industrialized forms of agriculture. Animals kept in high densities, often among their own faeces, allowed bacteria to be spread more widely. The extensive use of antibiotics to keep animals healthy increased the risk of resistant strains of bacteria entering the human food chain. For example, there has been an increase in food poisoning from a particular type of salmonella that is resistant to five antibiotics. In short, the 'intensification of agriculture, and its exposure to world markets, increased the risk of consumers being exposed to potential hazards' (Meat and Livestock Commission, 1997: 2).

The crisis triggered by the revelation of a link between BSE and a new variant of the invariably fatal Creutzfeldt–Jakob disease (vCJD) dramatized all these concerns. The immediate consequence was that 'British food policy and the role of the state in relation to food has been scrutinised to a level not seen since World War II' (Lang et al., 1996: 1). BSE was initially discovered in 1986, and although the subsequent official inquiry concluded that the origin of the disease will never be known with certainty, it probably originated in the early

1970s, possibly from a cow or other animal that developed the disease as a consequence of gene mutation. However, the reason that BSE turned into an epidemic was the consequence of intensive farming practices, whereby traditional methods of raising cattle on grass were partially displaced by recycling animal protein, making carnivores out of ruminants.

The public was assured, in 1990, by the then Chief Medical Officer of Health that beef was absolutely safe to eat. In what came to be recalled as an unfortunate gimmick, the then Agriculture Secretary, John Gummer, publicly fed his young daughter a beefburger in an attempt to reassure the public. It was only in 1996 that a link was discovered between BSE and vCJD. Why more people were not affected with this disease is not clear, but the people most at risk were those who had eaten poor quality beefburgers containing tissue from BSE-infected brain and spinal cord. It is also probable that there was a genetic predisposition or resistance to the disease. There were 28 deaths in the UK from nvCJD in 2000, 20 in 2001, and 17 in 2002.

The handling of the BSE crisis by MAFF revealed a number of policy failures. According to the subsequent BSE inquiry, the measures taken were not always timely or adequately enforced and implemented. There was sometimes a lack of rigour in considering how policy should be turned into practice, whilst at times, bureaucratic processes resulted in an unacceptable delay in implementing policy. One consequence was that the incoming Labour Government, having commissioned a report on the subject whilst in Opposition, established a new Food Standards Agency that removed a large part of MAFF's work and much of its rationale.

MAFF's problems were then compounded by the serious outbreak of foot-and-mouth disease (FMD) which occurred in the early months of 2001. FMD is not normally a human health problem, but the sight of burning pyres of culled animals provided dramatic media images. Certainly, 'In the early weeks of the crisis, FMD was the lead news story day after day. As the spread of the disease appeared to accelerate, so the competence of MAFF to deal with it increasingly came under question' (Winter, 2003: 49). There was particular criticism of its inability to appreciate the impact of FMD on the wider rural economy, especially tourism, whose losses far outweighed those of agriculture. Following the 2001 general election, MAFF was abolished and replaced by the Department of the Environment, Food and Rural Affairs (DEFRA).

The third driver of change, international trade, operated mainly at the European level where trade policy is conducted, but its impact on the CAP affected domestic agriculture. In the 1980s, a political coalition based around agribusiness developed in the United States that exerted political pressure for agricultural trade liberalization. This was reflected in the Uruguay Round of trade negotiations, which became stalemated on the subject of agriculture. In order to break the stalemate, the then Agriculture Commissioner, Ray MacSharry, introduced, and won support for, a package of CAP reforms in 1992.

These reforms are generally seen as the most significant attempt to change the nature of the CAP, their key feature being the introduction of an element of 'decoupling' into agricultural subsidies, although confined to arable products. Decoupling in this context means that farmers no longer have to produce a food product to be sold, in order to claim their subsidy. Instead, in the case of arable farming, aid was paid on a per hectare basis. In the 2003 reforms, this was extended to partial decoupling in the livestock sector. In the long run, the fact that farmers do not have to produce to claim their subsidy (although they still have to farm the land) could lead to the questioning of the need for subsidies at all. It could result in subsidies being phased out and being replaced by some kind of agricultural bond, a capital asset that farmers could use for investment or to generate an income.

The policy community disintegrates

Two events in the opening years of the 21st century have suggested that the hitherto tightly-knit agricultural policy community was starting to disintegrate, although, as we have already noted, there had been signs for some time that agriculture was becoming less 'exceptional' (Grant, 1995b). The special state-sponsored arrangements for providing credit to farmers were dismantled. The Agriculture Mortgage Corporation had been established by legislation in 1928, but in 1991 it was removed from its statutory framework and in 1993 it was acquired by the then Lloyds Bank. Funding for the Agricultural Training Board was reduced, whilst specialist agricultural educational institutions were either closed, or merged into more broadly-based institutions of further and higher education. Particular controversy was aroused by proposals to transfer agricultural education at the Seale Hayne campus of the University of Plymouth, to the main campus, ending the tradition of what had once been an independent agricultural college. The provision of free technical advice to farmers through ADAS (the Agricultural Development Advisory Service) was replaced by a system of charges in 1986. The Agriculture and Food Research Council was subsumed within a new Biotechnology and Biological Sciences Research Council. The milk marketing boards were abolished. Specialist television and radio programmes for farmers were increasingly displaced by programmes with a 'countryside' theme – such as the BBC's Sunday lunchtime *Countryfile* – which were often more critical of farming practices.

However, until its abolition, MAFF, and the NFU, continued to form the core of the agricultural policy community. As long as MAFF survived, farmers retained a privilege granted to no other industry, a Whitehall ministry focused on their special problems. The replacement of MAFF by DEFRA is, therefore, potentially a very significant development. At around the same time, new breakaway groups have posed an increasing challenge to the hitherto hegemony of the NFU.

Nevertheless, one has to be aware of the limits of this process. The NFU is still a very influential pressure group, as was evident during the FMD dispute. As long as the CAP remains largely unreformed, farmers will continue to receive substantial financial support. Leaders of farming groups have proved themselves adept at developing new justifications for the continuation of agricultural support. As well as using the perceived terrorist threat after September 2001 to revive discourses about food security, the language of 'multi-functionality' has been used to provide a new set of justifications for the continuation of agricultural support. The argument is that farmers produce public goods, such as maintaining heritage landscapes and preventing land abandonment that can undermine bio-diversity as scrub replaces supportive habitats. According to this perspective, they should therefore be financially rewarded for public good provision, a term that is interpreted in a rather elastic fashion.

Meanwhile, DEFRA has proved something of a disappointment for, as Greer notes, 'to the frustration of government, DEFRA has not yet shed some of the problems inherited from MAFF' (Greer, 2003: 535). Not surprisingly, farming organizations complained that the new department had not given a sufficiently high priority to agriculture, that the economic sustainability of agriculture had not been given enough weight compared to sustainable development, and that the agriculture portfolio in DEFRA had been given to a junior minister. It was often said in farming circles that the department's initials stood for the 'Department for the Elimination of Farming and Rural Activity'. The new department was not supposed to replicate the clientilistic orientation of MAFF towards farmers. However, there have been more serious doubts about its capacity to manage change. Following complaints from the House of Commons environment, food and rural affairs select committee about the ability of DEFRA management to oversee change, it was announced that all senior mainstream civil servants in the department would undergo a 'leadership review'. They would be graded on their leadership ability and willingness to manage change, and early retirement was expected to follow for a number of senior managers.

The organizational design of DEFRA in any case reveals deeper flaws, for as Winter observes:

> … the formation of DEFRA, while clearly a more radical step than the incremental shifts that might have occurred in the absence of FMD, retains a rather narrow focus on agriculture. DEFRA's broader remit, in terms of both its environmental focus and rural development … remains largely rooted in the land-based sector. Rural development is equated with diversifying agriculture rather than with any sense of a highly diverse rural economy and society in which farming per se is no longer the economic linchpin. (Winter, 2003: 51)

DEFRA's policy strategy has been based around the report of the Curry Commission, which was established to examine the future of food and farming. Considerable emphasis is placed on the efficiencies to be achieved in a 'joined-up' supply chain. A new Food Chain Centre has been established. There is a considerable emphasis on competitiveness and efficiency, and on bringing farmers closer to the consumer and the market. Such efforts, however, come up against the reality of a food supply chain dominated by a small number of retailers, where there is already 'a clear asymmetric monopoly in the UK market' (Clarke et al., 2002: 152), and where further consolidation and concentration seems likely. One of the most significant changes in the position of farmers, therefore, has been the way in which power has seeped down the supply chain to retailers.

One of the traditional strengths of the NFU has been its ability to maintain a united front. Whereas in other countries, farmers have been divided between different commodity groups, or between large and smaller farmers, the dominance of the NFU in Britain was not really threatened by the formation of a Tenant Farmers' Association or by the existence of a breakaway union in Wales. However, it has faced an increasing challenge from a group pursuing an 'outsider' strategy, Farmers for Action (FFA), a body formed at a meeting at a motorway service station in March 2000. The farmers present were annoyed at being excluded from the Downing Street summit on agriculture, claiming that they would be poorly represented by the main farming unions. Some of FFA's leaders were prominent in the fuel price protests in September 2000.

At the other end of the spectrum, support emerged in 2002 for a breakaway organization to represent arable farmers. This was something of a paradox, given that affluent arable farmers have always been well represented in the NFU leadership, as they are best able to spare the time for NFU activities. Nevertheless, arable farmers had become discontented, because they felt that the FMD crisis had led to some neglect of very low prices experienced by arable farmers. The advocates of a breakaway organization had been directly influenced by the more commodity-based structure of farm representation in the United States, and a perception that single-issue groups outside farming are becoming more successful. There was also a subtext about arable farmers being better able to adapt to a life without subsidies, but not wanting environmentally-linked subsidies that might be more acceptable to live-stock farmers. With prices staging something of a recovery, not least because of currency movements, no more was heard of the breakaway organization, but it was a warning to the NFU leadership about the level of discontent among its core support.

Meanwhile, the FFA's blockades of milk depots and retailers appeared to be having some success, particularly in preventing reductions in milk prices. The FFA emphasized that it was not seeking to destroy the NFU, but to reform it. There was some support for such a stance among the NFU's members who thought that the organization, with its system of indirect election of the leadership, was insufficiently internally democratic. In June 2003 the chair of the NFU's milk committee sought a meeting with the FFA to seek common ground. It is not clear whether the NFU leadership had approved this move, but becoming too closely associ-ated with an outsider group might damage the NFU's credibility with government. Even so, in July 2004 the FFA and the NFU joined together with four other organizations in what was described as a loose alliance to support dairy farming.

As the farming industry has shrunk, so the NFU has seen its farming membership decline from 100,000 to around 67,000. The NFU carried out an internal review to see if it was offering members value for money. Other leading rural organizations have also encountered financial difficulties, with the CLA, for example, faced with financial diffi-culties, making 10–15 of its 98 staff redundant in 2003, and reported to be considering leaving its London headquarters. Both moves would undermine its effectiveness as an insider group.

Conclusion

For most of the period since 1945, discussion about British agricultural policy was domi-nated by a largely unchallenged productionist paradigm. Discussion of agricultural policy formation largely took place between MAFF and the NFU, with the latter then playing a major role implementing the agreed policy. Parliament was a relatively marginal player in the agricultural policy process. Continuity was further encouraged by a lack of understand-ing, by other policy actors, of the technicalities of agricultural policy. The high political entry price any outsider had to pay to enter the debate was reinforced by the complexities of the CAP.

However, during the last two decades, a great deal has changed, both institutionally and in terms of the dominant discourses. MAFF has been replaced by DEFRA. The NFU's grip on farmer representation has been weakened. New discourses about conservation and the environment, food safety and quality, and trade liberalization have reshaped the policy debate, although the last discourse is often at odds with the first two, as is illustrated by the case of GM crops. Margaret Beckett, the first Secretary of State at DEFRA, declared that she would like to see all subsidies eventually phased out. She has also declared that 'Farming is a major polluter' (*Farmers Weekly*, 4 October 2002). Such statements from a Minister responsible for agriculture would previously have been unthinkable.

However, there are also limits to the changes that have occurred. This is evident in the mindset of many farmers and their representatives. A *Farmers Weekly* editorial praised Mrs Beckett for a stance she took in the farm council in Brussels for putting up a fight 'for those she represents' (*Farmers Weekly*, 31 January 2003). Environmental regulations have proliferated, but the annual cost of agriculture to the environment in 2003 was still estimated by the Environment Agency at about £1.4 billion a year. New Labour's policy seems to lack 'a recognition of the social dimension to the food supply chain' (Barling and Lang, 2003: 14), particularly in terms of food policy and its link to social exclusion.

Above all, farmers continue to be more heavily subsidized and protected than any other group in society. OECD figures suggest that the average EU farmer is paid 36 per cent of his or her income from subsidies or protection. The actual sums received vary considerably from farmer to farmer, but there are a number of farmers in Britain who receive over one million euros a year in subsidies. In an era in which neo-liberalism has supposedly triumphed elsewhere in the economy, if not in social policy too, agriculture remains a conspicuous exception.

2

Economic Policy
Colin Thain

Introduction

How can we link the policies and issues of a period that takes us from the exuberance of VE celebrations in 1945 – mixed with all the trauma and devastation of a long war – through to the early years of the 21st century; from an era of total war to one in which there is an ongoing war on terror?; from an era of utility furniture to one of modern retro- and post-modernism?; from an era of rationing to one of avid consumption and wide consumer choice?; from an era of Empire to one of European integration? Clearly much has changed; the past has the appearance of another country. Yet there are also many themes which weave through the period. In this chapter, we explore six recurring and interlocking themes in a post-war analysis of British economic policy: adjusting to intellectual and ideological shifts; coping with decline; managing foreign economic policy; seeking frameworks for stability; crisis management; and institutional experimentation.

Intellectual and ideological shifts

Much of public policy is about continuity. No history of economic policy can be divided neatly into eras or paradigms; there are often gradual changes. Occasionally there are clear junctures, points of profound change. In retrospect, 1945 and 1979 stand out as significant: the clear emergence of a more collectivist and then less collectivist approach to policy respectively. In broad terms, the period from 1945 is marked by three main phases of dominant 'ideas in good currency' about the conduct of economic policy. From the end of the war until the early 1970s, economic policy was conducted in a way termed 'Keynesian'. The late 1970s to the mid-1980s constituted an experiment in monetarism. From 1992, British economic policy could be described as monetary-constrained Keynesianism. It remains to be seen whether the post-1997 period represents a new era – one of the 'Third Way' (Blair, 1998a; Giddens, 1998) – or more of an incremental adjustment to the 1993–7 economic policies of John Major and his Chancellor during this period, Kenneth Clarke. During these phases, economic policy has been influenced, but not absolutely determined, by dominant ideas in economics itself. Economics is always tempered by political ideologies, the exigencies of the electoral cycle, personality clashes and institutional and structural influences.

Coping with decline

Coping with, or attempting to reverse, Britain's relative economic decline has been a constant theme from the 1960s onwards. Why did Britain slump from being the leading industrial nation in Europe after the Second World War to one of the poorest in the 1980s? Most of the debate was based on the assumption that Britain *was* in decline, but this was not immediately apparent. Indeed, Britain's economic growth since 1945 has actually been higher than in earlier periods. For most people, living standards have risen faster than at any time in history, and social provision has been extended and improved (Gwyn and Rose, 1980; Dahrendorf, 1982). However, that there was *relative* economic decline, there is no doubt. Pollard described this process graphically by comparing economic performance to the movement of a convoy of ships. By 1980, Britain had been overtaken by most European nations (ranked by output per head). From 1960, comparable economies out-paced Britain, not just in rates of economic growth, but also in almost all the conventional measures of economic success (Pollard, 1982). In response to this decline, there have been successive waves of experimentation by British economic policy makers. Coping strate-gies have alternated between three approaches: attempts to manage social democracy better through incremental modernization (most associated with the post-war 'Butskellism'); an attempt at using the State as an agent of enterprise through collectivist policies (the early policies of the 1974–9 Labour Governments); and an agenda that deemed markets to be sovereign, with dramatic policies to shift away from State intervention in the economy (the Thatcherite agenda of rolling back the frontiers of the State) (see Gamble, 1994; English and Kenny, 2000). It was not until the early years of the 21st century that talk of decline had been replaced by assertions of relative British improvement, as Britain over-took France as the fourth largest industrial economy.

Managing foreign economic policy

Successive British governments have struggled with a series of linked problems associated with Britain's integration into the international economy, struggles which have involved politics as much as economics. Through the 1940s and 1950s, decisions were taken to cling on to great-power status by maintaining overseas investment and military expenditure, and protecting the interests of the holders of 'sterling balances' (mainly in the old Commonwealth and former imperial preference countries) (Shonfield, 1958). However, this was problem-atic because it involved the psychological trauma of adjusting to the loss of Empire. Some analysts associated lack of attention to the needs of the domestic economy as a long-run failure in British economic policy making (Strange, 1971; Blank, 1982). Foreign economic policy took a significant turn away from an Anglo-American perspective in 1972, when Edward Heath negotiated entry into the European Economic Community (commonly referred to as the Common Market, and which has now developed into the European Union).

The debates of the 1980s and early 1990s under the Conservative administrations of Margaret Thatcher and John Major over the Exchange Rate Mechanism (ERM) of the European Monetary System, and Britain's opt-out from the euro, followed by a wait-and-see policy under both Major and (from 1997) Tony Blair, suggest that this controversial aspect of economic policy remains one clouded in concerns about sovereignty and Britain's 'proper' role in the world. Should Britain look to the USA or the EU for its models of economic policy and social structure, or should it be a bridge between two power blocs?

Seeking panaceas or frameworks of stability

The creeping realization that relative decline was a serious issue led British policy makers to seek various solutions or panaceas. Recent academic research would term this the politics of policy learning or policy transfer (Rose, 1993; Dolowitz and Marsh, 2000; James and Lodge, 2003), whereby alternative policies, instruments or institutions from abroad are adopted or 'imported' in order to solve particular problems (Hall, 1993; Oliver, 1997), and which policy makers then learn to adjust as policy is implemented. The period has a number of examples of this trend. In the 1960s, both Labour and Conservative Governments became impressed with the French success story and sought to import economic planning. This culminated in the Labour Government's *National Plan* in 1965. Meanwhile, German corporatism – the inclusion of representatives of employers and trade unions in discussions with Government on macroeconomic goals and incomes policy – led to a rash of initiatives in the 1960s and 1970s aimed at creating a tripartite partnership in Britain, a process heralded by the 1962 establishment, by Harold Macmillan's Conservative administration, of the National Economic Development Council (NEDC). The 1974–9 Labour Governments extended tripartite partnership by pursuing planning agreements with employers and a social contract with trade unions. Subsequently, in the 1980s, German success in creating low and stable inflation became one impetus behind the attempt to shadow the German currency prior to joining the ERM, whilst in the 1990s, Gordon Brown became convinced of the need to give greater independence to the Bank of England and looked to the model provided by the United States Federal Reserve.

Policy frameworks have also followed the ebbs and flows of economic orthodoxy. We will discuss later the way in which the Medium-Term Financial Strategy in the 1980s and the monetary and fiscal frameworks of the post-1997 era have sought to constrain and limit government room for manoeuvre in order to provide certainty and stability.

Crisis management

Almost every book written since 1945 about British economic policy has included obligatory chapters on crisis and failure, these invariably focusing on the exchange rate, balance of payments, inflation, lack of growth and loss of control of public expenditure. Clement Attlee's 1945–50 Labour Government faced a convertibility crisis in 1947, when the UK was required by the US administration – as part of the conditions of an American loan – to allow full convertibility of the pound for dollars. This was followed in 1949 by a devaluation crisis, when a deteriorating balance of payments and outflow of reserves forced a devaluation of sterling by nearly 30 per cent (Cairncross, 1985). This was followed in the 1960s by a further devaluation in 1967 after much resistance by Harold Wilson, Labour's Prime Minister. As we discuss later, the 1976 and 1992 crises, while focusing on the role of the exchange rate, were at heart symptomatic of underlying problems in the economy.

Figures 2.1 and 2.2 show this graphically. The marked peak of inflation in the mid-1970s and collapse of growth in 1976 attest to the severity of the problems faced by the Chancellor, Denis Healey. Negative economic growth in the early 1980s and early 1990s provides the background to the economic difficulties faced by Prime Ministers Thatcher and Major, respectively. Since 1997, Gordon Brown's period as Chancellor has been noteworthy for its lack of crisis and for steady growth and low inflation.

Figure 2.1   Inflation, 1948–2004

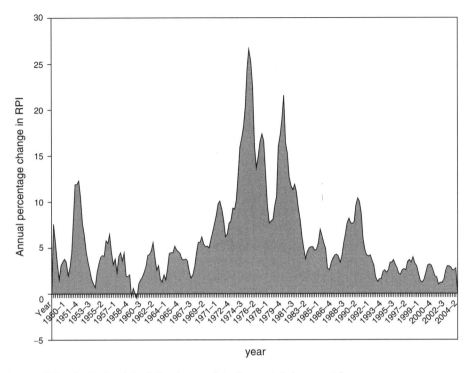

Source: Office for National Statistics dataset (http://www.statistics.gov.uk/)

Figure 2.2   Annual growth of GDP at market prices, 1948–2004

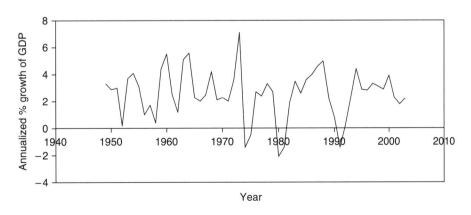

Source: Office of National Statistics dataset (http://www.statistics.gov.uk/)

Institutional stability punctuated by innovation

Britain is unique among comparable advanced economies in having an economic policy managed by a closed and select policy network. Unlike France, Germany or the USA, two institutions and an office manage Britain's economic policies: HM Treasury, the Bank of England and the Prime Minister of the day, with very little active involvement by the Cabinet. Of these three policy actors, the Treasury has held sway (see Thain, 2004). In terms of what might be called the modern British state, the Treasury acts as the guardian of departmental authority stretching back to Orders in Council (cleverly extracted from King Charles II by Sir George Downing) in 1668, establishing Treasury control of public expenditure, and then of the civil service 'establishments'. Its constitutional power resources have been enhanced throughout the succeeding 350 years.

The story is of a ministry of finance. It was not until the accident of Sir Stafford Cripps – then Minister of Economic Affairs and rival to the Treasury – inheriting the Exchequer after Hugh Dalton's resignation, that the Treasury assumed responsibility for broader economic management of the economy (Greenleaf, 1987; Clarke, 2002). This involved control of the multiple levers of economic policy, namely managing demand, the positive use of fiscal policy, supply-side or microeconomic policies, the setting of interest rates, attempts at planning and control of pay levels, through incomes policy, and the control of pay and numbers in the civil service. It was not until 1998 that the Treasury ceded control of monetary policy to the Bank of England, reversing a process of Treasury dominance over the Bank which had been codified in 1947 with the Bank's nationalization.

Stability should not be seen as denoting lack of conflict or tension. Throughout the post-war period there has been a battle for control and ascendancy over economic policy, a battle most evident in the relationships between various Prime Ministers and Chancellors. The former Labour Cabinet Minister, Tony Benn, once asserted (in a parliamentary debate) that a Chancellor of the Exchequer is just number two in economic policy making; the Prime Minister is First Lord of the Treasury. This does get to the heart of the problem for Chancellors, for their next-door neighbour has a direct constitutional role in the affairs of their department.

It is one of the pivotal relationships in Whitehall (Jenkins, 1998; Holt, 2002). Prime Ministers, it is said, are either their own Foreign Secretary or Chancellor. As economic crises have dominated the domestic agenda, Prime Ministers from Attlee to Blair have perforce become concerned with economic management. Prime Ministers frequently intervene in disputes between the Treasury and departments over public expenditure. In 1957, this led to the resignation of the Conservative Chancellor, Peter Thorneycroft, and his two Treasury Ministers (Hennessy, 1989).

There have been both policy differences and personality clashes between Prime Ministers and Chancellors. Whilst being in Number 11 (Downing Street) is not necessarily a stepping stone to the top of the greasy pole – only four of the eleven post-war Prime Ministers have also previously served as Chancellor (Churchill, Macmillan, Callaghan and Major) – they can appear as rivals for office, and for ideological and policy leadership. Attlee was suspicious of the Treasury, and tried to minimize its power through the creation of the Ministry of Economic Affairs, which was in charge of planning and general economic management. Wilson likewise, haunted by the memory of the convertibility and devaluation crises when he was President of the Board of Trade in the latter half of the 1940s, and concerned about the rivalry of Callaghan, created the Department of Economic Affairs (DEA) in 1964 as a counterbalance to the Treasury (although, as if to confirm the power of the Treasury, the DEA was abolished just five years later). During the late 1980s, the close marriage of minds between Chancellor Lawson and Prime Minister Thatcher ended acrimoniously as the Prime Minister sought to use her economic adviser (Alan Walters) as a means of reducing Treasury influence and disagreements over European policy, leading, eventually, to the resignation (or effective sacking) of Nigel Lawson, and the following year, the fatal resignation – as Leader of the House (of Commons) and Deputy Prime Minister – of Thatcher's former (prior to Lawson) Chancellor, Geoffrey Howe – the latter precipitating the leadership challenge which heralded the end of Thatcher's premiership. Much has been – and continues to be – written of the Blair–Brown 'marriage', but as can be seen, such a close political relationship is not entirely new.

The rest of the chapter looks at a narrative of policy making which seeks to show how these six themes played out during the 1944 to 2004 period.

The dominance of Keynesian social democracy, 1944–73

The first phase of the Keynesian system, from the end of the Second World War to the beginning of the 1960s, can be described as 'pure and simple Keynesianism' (Longstreth, 1984). The period was characterized by the acceptance by governments of duties in the economic sphere, hitherto unknown, to stimulate and maintain employment, but this fell short of major changes in the nature of the capitalist system. It was Keynesianism as Keynes had intended – to protect the system from its own defects (Skidelsky, 1979; 1992; 2000). The 1944 White Paper on Employment Policy was a landmark in British economic policy. The mindset of policy makers was changed dramatically from that of the 1930s, because for the first time, government accepted 'as one of their primary aims and responsibilities the maintenance of a high and stable level of employment after the War' (Cmd 6527, 1944). The White Paper established the general framework of economic policy for a generation.

Meanwhile, three basic assumptions underpinned the Keynesian system. Firstly, international co-operation was considered essential, so that the types of external constraints evident in the 1920s and 1930s would not prevail and blow policy off course, necessitating the abandonment of full employment. The Bretton Woods fixed exchange rate system, the creation of the International Monetary Fund (IMF) to provide short-term support to currencies, and the General Agreement on Tariffs and Trade (GATT) to reduce trade protection and expand trade, were seen as key components of this new order of international economic planning and co-ordination. Britain played a leading role in the creation of the system, along with the USA. Sterling was to remain the second reserve currency after the dollar, until the collapse of the fixed exchange rate system in the early 1970s.

The second component was the commitment of governments to take action 'at the earliest possible stage to avoid a slump'. Various policy tools were outlined in the White Paper, most notably setting interest rates to ensure adequate investment, tax changes to maintain consumption, and the acceptance of short-run budget deficits. Although the language was guarded, and stressed the need for a balanced budget over time, it represented a major departure from practice in the 1920s and 1930s, when a balanced budget was an article of faith.

The third component was the pivotal role assigned to co-operation between government, employers and trade unions. The White Paper was clear about the inflationary consequences of any lack of 'moderation on wage matters' by unions and employers, and thus emphasized that 'action taken by government to maintain expenditure will be fruitless unless wages and prices are kept reasonably stable'. This was a theme that would return to haunt successive governments after 1945.

It was clear from the subsequent actions of the 1945–51 Labour Governments, and of the subsequent Conservative Governments during the 1950s, that the White Paper constituted a treaty or settlement between the main parties on the shape of economic management; it was the fruit of debate and dialogue within the wartime coalition. Leading liberal Conservative figures, such as Rab Butler and Harold Macmillan, were influential in moving the party towards acceptance of what was essentially a social democratic programme.

Equally significant, however, was the approach of the Labour leadership, for after initially flirting with the concept of full-blooded national planning and social control of the economy, nationalization was restricted to key strategic industries (see Cairncross, 1985; Morgan, 1985). Yet the intra-party debates about the degree to which the State should control and direct industry and the economy would re-emerge in the 1960s and 1970s, as this consensus was challenged by both the Left and the Right.

Economic policy was pursued broadly on the lines of Keynesian demand management (Mosley, 1985; Tomlinson, 1985). Full employment became the linchpin of economic policy, and was maintained by the use of monetary policy (interest rate changes and adjustments to credit controls) and fiscal policy (tax and expenditure changes). As this first phase of British Keynesianism progressed, criticisms were voiced about the logic and conduct of policy. Indeed, three critical themes emerged in the 1950s. Firstly, that foreign economic policy was damaging economic performance, as weaknesses in sterling and the balance of payments were compounded by decisions to continue maintaining great-power status abroad. Secondly, far from stabilizing output and demand, government action was seen as destabilizing. The time lags between the need for action and the decision to use the levers of monetary or fiscal policy were so great that, critics argued, policy either accentuated booms or deepened slumps (Dow, 1964). This was seen, in part, as a reflection of technical problems in forecasting and designing policy tools. However, the harshest critics of Keynesianism saw this as evidence of inherent defects – a theme which was to re-emerge in the 1970s with the revival in classical economic theory.

The most damaging criticism of early Keynesianism, as applied by British governments in the 1940s and 1950s, was that it was not arresting Britain's relative economic decline. Economic policy makers became aware that growth was significantly lower than in competitor nations, whereupon frantic efforts were made to isolate the major causes, with institutional as well as policy weaknesses highlighted (Ham, 1981; Pollard, 1982; Gamble, 1994). The 'moving consensus' (Rose, 1984), which formed the basis of economic policy from 1944 to the mid-1970s, was thus modified. Both major parties looked to emulate French indicative planning. Demand management had to be supplemented by more direct government intervention in the supply side of the economy (Young, 1974). Ideas-in-good-currency changed to allow for a new 'voluntaristic corporatist' phase of economic policy (Longstreth, 1984).

The concern to improve economic performance through co-operation between government, unions and employers was not confined to one political party. The tripartite forum – the National Economic Development Council (dubbed Neddy) – was sponsored by the Conservative Chancellor Selwyn Lloyd in 1962, whilst the Labour Government elected in 1964 continued with the NEDC, and used it to debate its major planning experiment, the *National Plan* published in 1965. The National Plan boldly asserted that 'the publication by the government of a plan covering all aspects of the country's economic development for the next five years is a major advance in economic policy-making in the United Kingdom' (Cmnd 2764, 1965: iii). However, its ambitious target of 25 per cent economic growth in the period to 1970 was not fulfilled. Once again policy was blown off course by the exchange rate. The failure to devalue sterling in 1964 signalled that priority was to be given to the defence of the exchange rate and balance of payments equilibrium rather than the growth objective embodied in the National Plan (Brittan, 1971).

Despite the difficulties in implementing the macroeconomic goals of the plan, the 1964–70 Labour Governments (Labour was re-elected with a comfortable majority in 1966, having been elected in 1964 with a parliamentary majority of just four seats) continued its policies of intervention at the micro level. The statutory mechanisms for achieving this were the Science and Technology Act and the Industrial Expansion Act, both of which gave the Government the powers to restructure large parts of manufacturing industry. The executive agency responsible for the policies was the Industrial Reorganisation Corporation (IRC), through which British competitiveness was to be improved.

At the same time, the post-war goal of maintaining full employment was under increasing strain as policy makers became more concerned about wage inflation. It became a major preoccupation of the Labour Governments, as it had been in the late 1950s and early 1960s for the Conservative Chancellors Selwyn Lloyd and Reginald Maudling. A central element of the National Plan was the need to develop machinery to administer prices and incomes policy. Increasingly both parties saw the remedy for high wage inflation as tackling the perceived weaknesses of the trade union movement. Unofficial or 'wild cat' strikes suggested that the leadership of the unions – closely tied to the Labour Party leadership – could not control the more militant shop stewards. By introducing the White Paper, *In Place of Strife*, in 1969, the Labour leadership signalled the first significant breach in the post-war consensus, by seeking to place legal restrictions on trade unions and the conduct of industrial relations. The policy deeply divided the Labour Government (at both Cabinet and backbench levels) and was shelved (see Morgan, 1990; Dorey, forthcoming). It returned in modified form during the subsequent Heath Government, when the Conservatives attempted a more radical programme to reduce the power of the trade unions. Although this too failed at the time – Heath hastily sought a return to tripartism during 1972 and 1973 – it none the less presaged the almost complete abandonment of tripartisanship in economic policy during the 1979–83 Conservative Government, led by Margaret Thatcher.

Internationally, the post-war consensus was crumbling too. The Bretton Woods fixed exchange rate regime could not survive the impact of multiple pressures. The dollar's weakness – as the linchpin of the international system – resulted in its demise. The large

US balance of payments deficit, in significant part the product of social spending at home and the costs of the Vietnam War, put pressure on the dollar, and led to a worldwide surge of inflation as the supply of dollars increased. In addition, governments were finding it increasingly difficult to defend the parities of exchange rates against rising levels of private sector capital flows, which had become a key feature of the internationalization of finance (Walters, 1990).

The combination of these real-world changes and intellectual paradigm shifts led to a resurgence of interest in classical economics. The combination of the perceived failures of Keynesianism, rising inflation, stop–go growth and the revived interest in the role of money, stimulated by the research of Milton Friedman and the Chicago School of monetary economics, began to influence policy makers in the USA. In Britain, this centred on the Money Study Group at the LSE led by Harry Johnson. Other key figures included Alan Walters, David Laidler and Michael Parkin (see Smith, 1987).

The crumbling of consensus and the crises of the 1970s

By the early 1980s, the 'Keynesian Social Democratic' system which had dominated economic policy making since the end of the Second World War had been overturned. One by one, the pillars of this consensus had crumbled. The decline of the 'Keynesian' system was gradual, presaged in the 1960s by problems with inflation. A combination of changes in the international economy, the long-term relative weakness of Britain's economy, policy failure by British governments, and concern about the role of the trade unions, led to the crises of the 1970s. At first there was an attempt to shore up the consensus and adopt innovatory policy tools, but finally a 'monetarist' system briefly supplanted the Keynesian system through the radicalism of the early Thatcher years. By 1985, economic policy had shifted towards a more eclectic approach, yet still with a rhetorical bias firmly rooted in 'New Right' thinking (Bosanquet, 1983).

Coincident with the breakdown in the Keynesian system was the increased salience to policy makers of the issue of Britain's long-term economic decline. Through the 1970s and 1980s, the issue of tackling decline moved up the political agenda. The early approach in 1970–2 of the Heath Government involved an experiment with what Harold Wilson dubbed 'Selsdon Man' policies, a 'quiet revolution' in which the dynamism of the economy would be unleashed through tax cuts, less state intervention, and reform of industrial relations. Heath was not an advocate of social market economics; rather he was an advocate of the selective use of free market solutions if those promised to improve economic growth. Negotiating membership of the European Economic Community in 1972 was also part of a modernizing strategy aimed at increasing the competitive challenge and opportunity for British industry. The subsequent (1974–9) Labour Governments' attempt to reverse decline, against a mounting economic crisis, involved a much diluted and modified version of the Left's Alternative Economic Strategy, with nationalization, the creation of a National Enterprise Board and 'planning agreements', and a more traditional tripartite 'industrial strategy' bringing together the TUC and CBI in an effort to remove barriers to economic growth (Coates, 1980).

Even allowing for the unprecedented shock administered to the world economy by the 1973 oil price rise, Keynesian economic policies had become progressively less successful. In each successive boom, inflation and unemployment were higher. The advent of 'stagflation' – simultaneously high inflation with low growth and high unemployment – was something with which traditional Keynesian theory could not cope. Policy makers throughout the Organisation of Economic Co-operation and Development (OECD) countries therefore began a search for techniques which would better deal with the phenomenon; and the control of inflation was to dominate the policy agenda (OECD, 1979).

In Britain, Denis Healey, as Labour's Chancellor, presided over a major shift in the emphasis of macroeconomic policy, but one which fell short of an outright repudiation of the post-war consensus. His approach was to use whatever means were at hand to shore up that consensus while responding to the particular crises of the time (see Healey, 1989). Under his direction, the Treasury began to attempt to deal with the inflationary and deflationary consequences of the oil crisis by using traditional Keynesian techniques. Wage inflation was to be moderated by the 'social contract' with the trade unions, which involved Ministerial commitments on a whole range of social policies, and reform of industrial relations legislation, in return for 'restraint' on wage demands by the unions. The public sector borrowing requirement (PSBR) was to be allowed to rise as a proportion of GDP, as output fell due to the recession. Internationally, Healey attempted to obtain a co-ordinated response by the major industrial nations to avoid deflationary action, in response to the oil crisis, exacerbating the world recession. The Treasury tried to obtain an international agreement to support, with loans, those countries (including Britain) with major balance of payments problems, and, in concert with the pro-Western members of OPEC, to introduce an active policy to 'recycle' the surpluses being generated by the oil-exporting countries.

Most of these policies were to prove untenable. The raft of international agreements Healey hoped for did not materialize. Yet the increasingly interdependent nature of the world economy was a constraint on domestic policies (Wass, 1978). In 1975 the Treasury engineered a 'controlled depreciation' of sterling in an attempt to revitalize domestic production and ease the deficit on the balance of trade. However, lack of confidence in British economic policy by the financial markets turned the depreciation into a free fall. Market confidence in domestic policies was undermined by both the size of the budget deficit, and the failure of the 'social contract' to cope with the surge of inflation in 1974–5 (which peaked at just over 24 per cent in 1975).

The sterling crisis in 1976 led to the Labour Government to request a loan from the IMF. Following the subsequent negotiations, the Treasury agreed, in December 1976, to adjustments in both the techniques and objectives of economic policy. Targets for domestic credit expansion were publicly announced, the PSBR was to be reduced, and public expenditure cut back. Earlier, in July 1976, the Treasury had introduced cash limits on public expenditure in response to the 'crisis of control'. Economic policy was in disarray. All the features of a classic British economic policy crisis were abundantly evident – crisis Cabinet discussions, public expenditure cuts, concern about the foreign exchange markets – together with a politically damaging and demoralizing submission to the IMF (see Burk and Cairncross, 1992).

These changes in macroeconomic policy, introduced in response to the exigencies of crisis, have been cited as evidence for the proposition that the real change of direction in economic policy occurred under Chancellor Healey, rather than under the Conservatives after 1979 (see Brittan, 1983; Congdon, 1989). Certainly, there is plenty of evidence to support the view that the period from 1976 to 1979 involved a significant shift in macro-economic policy towards a monetarist system, with the goal of full employment suspended. In his 1975 Budget speech, Healey noted that the Budget judgement would not be based on an estimation of the amount of demand which the Government should put into the economy. In 1977, the Treasury dropped the medium-term assessment (MTA) – which had been used to ensure policies maintained full employment – in its public expenditure planning. There was an element here of the Government responding to the inevitable, since unemployment was rising against difficult circumstances of higher inflation and a poor balance of payments. Nevertheless, the British Government had joined other industrialized nations in giving priority to the control and reduction of inflation.

Economic policy actions during the mid-1970s show how the objective of full employment became less sacrosanct. In the period from 1945 to 1973, governments of both major parties had usually reacted to rising unemployment with an active fiscal policy (increasing public expenditure or reducing taxation) and relaxing monetary policy. From 1975, an increase in unemployment produced a virtually neutral policy response. Not until the 1990s was the PSBR as a proportion of GDP as large as it was in 1974–5, despite the fact that unemployment rose to (and remained) at post-war historically high levels. In addition, during the Healey Chancellorship, the PSBR was given a pivotal role in linking fiscal and monetary policies. In 1978, Healey took action to reduce the PSBR when the financial markets became concerned that fiscal policy was out of step with monetary policy, as the large PSBR was adding to monetary growth. The Bank of England began setting internal, unpublished monetary targets in 1973, and this was followed, during the rest of the 1970s, by increasing emphasis on monetary policy in general, and broad money aggregates in particular, by both the Bank and the Treasury.

Monetary policy was pursued in a way which supported the view that Labour Ministers were 'reluctant' or 'unbelieving' monetarists. In reality, policy was 'monetarily constrained Keynesianism' rather than monetarist (Fforde, 1983; Smith, 1987). While domestic credit expansion targets were set several years ahead, money supply targets were announced on an annual basis, rather than set in a medium-term context.

The loss of confidence by policy makers in their ability to manage economic crises produced changes in public statements. However, rhetoric can be misleading. The statements of senior Labour Ministers have to be judged against the particular political and economic background of the time. For example, Callaghan made a famously 'monetarist' speech to the 1976 Labour Party Conference, when he declared that:

> We used to think you could spend your way out of a recession and increase employment by cutting taxes and boosting spending. I tell you in all candour that this option no longer exists, and in so far as it ever did exist, it only worked by injecting a bigger dose of inflation into the system. (Labour Party, 1976: 188)

However, this speech was a tactical political attempt to achieve multiple objectives: to appease the financial markets, to frighten the Labour Party into accepting the need for tough economic measures, and to make the right impression on the US Treasury Secretary whose support would be vital for Britain to obtain IMF support (Keegan, 1984).

'Believing monetarism', 1979–85

By contrast, the approach of Margaret Thatcher and her economic team was motivated by a more wholehearted commitment to the monetarist system. The Medium-Term Financial Strategy (MTFS), which set economic policy making in an explicit medium-term framework, replaced the short-term approach previously adopted by Healey. It represented a far more 'rational' co-ordinated response than previous policies: limits to governmental action were incorporated into economic policy making as a first principle. Changes and adjustments in policy there certainly were in the 1976–9 period, but we must look to the 1979–82 era for the real decisive break with the Keynesian system, and the change in those attitudes towards the use of public spending as a tool of economic management which had underpinned the Treasury's PESC (Public Expenditure Survey Committee) system of planning and control from 1961 onwards.

This commitment to a monetarist project also involved a concerted and deliberate attempt to give priority to reversing Britain's economic decline. The responsibility for this decline was firmly placed with the governments of the post-war consensus. Chancellor Geoffrey Howe's first Budget speech, in June 1979, set the tone when he argued that Britain's poor economic performance was due to intervention by governments which had stifled enterprise. He committed the new Conservative Government to a strategy aimed at strengthening individual incentives through tax cuts, reducing the role of the state and liberating the private sector, and reducing public spending and borrowing. Howe's successor from 1984, Nigel Lawson, pursued economic policies (in particular from 1985 to 1988) which sought to accelerate economic growth through tax cuts and supply-side reforms. Throughout the 1980s and early 1990s, the Conservative Governments of Thatcher and Major emphasized the way in which their policies had established an 'enterprise culture' and 'popular capitalism', the fruits of which were said to be the creation of a more competitive economy.

Meanwhile, in other OECD countries during the late 1970s and 1980s, policy makers developed economic strategies based on medium-term financial and economic frameworks (Chouraqui and Price, 1984; OECD, 1987). These reflected their loss of confidence in the ability of Keynesian policies to reduce unemployment, the tendency to high or volatile levels of inflation, or low growth, and the difficulties of funding public-spending programmes. By contrast, in Britain from 1979, the framework adopted was the result of *ideological* commitment, and sprang from a combination of political, economic and intellectual factors.

The late 1960s witnessed the resurgence of interest in neo-classical economics, initially in the USA and later in Britain. In the years when the Conservatives were in Opposition during the latter half of the 1970s, numerous policy advisers and think-tanks – most notably the Institute of Economic Affairs, the Adam Smith Institute, and the Centre for Policy Studies (CPS) – were influential in shaping the policy positions of Thatcher, Sir Keith Joseph and their closest supporters. Indeed, the CPS had actually been established by Joseph and Thatcher in 1974, as part of their own search for an alternative to the political economy of post-war Keynesian social democracy. This network – growing both in numbers and confidence – was drawn from the academic world, the City, journalism and business (Keegan, 1984; Smith, 1987; Young, 1989). Together, it moved the Conservative Party towards a policy position which was an amalgam of various schools of monetarism and right-wing populism. Yet it was this, in combination with the failures of the Labour Government's attempts at maintaining consensus politics, which was to provide Thatcher and her supporters with the opportunity to win the policy debate. The creation of what has been called 'Mrs Thatcher's domestic statecraft' (Bulpitt, 1986) was thus the product of a mixture of events and their consequences, slowly changing ideas-in-good-currency nourished by the contributions of intellectuals, accident and opportunity.

The Medium-Term Financial Strategy unveiled in 1980 was the clearest signal that the economic policy regime had changed (Buiter and Miller, 1983), representing as it did an attempt to impose discipline on government policy making by deliberately limiting the range of options open to the Treasury on monetary and fiscal policies. Money-supply targets were paramount, supported by projections for the PSBR and an unprecedented set of plans to cut public spending in real terms. The MTFS was explicitly counter-inflationary: governments, it was stated, could only influence output over the medium term by supply-side (or microeconomic) reforms (Lawson, 1992). Initially these reforms were limited, but nevertheless included the significant act of abolishing exchange controls in November 1979, the abolition of credit controls, some reduction in personal taxation, and a series of Acts reducing the power of trade unions. After 1983, the supply-side element of the strategy became more prominent, with large-scale privatization, the deregulation of financial markets and tax-reforming measures.

The Medium-Term Financial Strategy
The MTFS was intended to influence the expectations of a whole set of institutions and markets. For the first time, the Treasury was deliberately reducing the scope for discretionary macroeconomic policy. Financial markets were given a clear, public statement of the Treasury's policies over the medium term. Whitehall departments and agencies in the public sector were presented with a framework deliberately set to restrain resources available for public policies. Business leaders and trade union wage-bargainers were reminded that the Treasury would not act to reduce unemployment; inflationary wage demands would not be covered by money-supply increases (Thain, 1985).

Most of the tenets of the monetarist revolution failed and were abandoned. Economic policy was not led by clear, transparent medium-term rules; stop–go policies were not replaced by a stable regime predicated on 'sound finance', consistent non-inflationary monetary policy, and by government limiting itself to what it could influence. Since the late 1980s, there has been the emergence of an ever more powerful European dimension to policy, most notably with the Maastricht Treaty and its goal of Economic and Monetary Union (EMU). British economic policy has been influenced intermittently by the economic convergence criteria which emerged as part of the EMU process. British politics has been (and continues to be) sharply divided on the response to trends in the EU and how to manage foreign economic policy.

In the course of the 13 years from 1980, the MTFS evolved and changed. The single target for broad money was later replaced by multiple targets for both broad and narrow aggregates, and then finally abandoned altogether in favour of an objective for money

GDP. It became less and less a rigorous medium-term framework, providing clear guidelines to financial markets and other economic actors, and increasingly an annually updated set of financial figures consistent with the broad thrust of the Government's policies. However, annual decisions continued to be taken against the background of an explicit medium-term framework, including goals for public expenditure. The MTFS survived partly because of the political embarrassment its shelving would have created, partly because it proved to be a useful vehicle for changing the substance of policy actions whilst maintaining the aura of consistency, and partly because the annual exercise in setting out PSBR, public expenditure and revenue figures provided the Treasury with a useful weapon in containing public-spending pressures.

Until 1991, it was on the fiscal side of the MTFS that the Treasury could claim the most success. The PSBR declined as a proportion of GDP from the crisis levels of the mid-1970s, and the generation of a budget surplus in the four financial years from 1987–8 to 1990–1 had last been achieved by Roy Jenkins in 1969–70. Yet the economic growth which helped to generate these surpluses proved unsustainable. The recession which followed the Lawson boom proved so long-lasting that the public-sector financial position has swung dramatically into deficit, with the public sector's finances moving from a budget surplus (PSDR) equivalent to 1 per cent of GDP in 1989–90 to a deficit (PSBR) of 3 per cent in 1991–2; it was projected to rise to 8 per cent of GDP in 1993–4.

Just as the crisis of public expenditure control and economic turbulence in the mid-1970s produced a reassertion of Treasury control, so the looming fiscal crisis implied by the 1992–3 forecasts pushed the Treasury into instituting a 'new' top-down control on public spending and a medium-term review of spending priorities. In macroeconomic terms, the level of public-sector borrowing led Chancellor Norman Lamont to adjust one of the emergent orthodoxies of the 1980s – the achievement of an annual balanced budget – to the aspiration of achieving budget balance at the end of the economic cycle.

Measured against the original objectives in 1980, the MTFS failed as a precise monetary framework for four main reasons. Firstly, economic relationships were not as clear and stable as assumed by the Treasury in 1980 (Goodhart, 1989). Secondly, there was an intellectual problem, brought sharply into focus as Conservative Governments attempted to implement the MTFS. What was the most appropriate measure of the money supply? The aim of controlling spending and cutting direct taxation could be more easily packaged as examples of 'sound' and 'prudent' finance consistent with Conservative rhetoric. The problems over monetary aggregates also explain the desire of Chancellor Lawson to ground anti-inflation policy in a firmer framework, hence the increasing focus on the exchange rate and desire to enter the ERM (see Keegan, 1989; Lawson, 1992). Thirdly, conflicting policy objectives were not eliminated by the simple act of publicly announcing a clear economic policy agenda. Monetary policy was complicated by the abolition of exchange controls because sterling was prone to rapid inflows (and outflows) of capital. The deregulation of financial markets, and in particular the abolition of credit controls in 1980–2 and the lifting of restrictions on building societies and banks allowing customers to use 'equity withdrawal' as a means of adding to purchasing power, paved the way for a massive explosion of credit in the late 1980s (discussed by Congdon, 1989, and Keegan, 1989). Finally, the original 1980 MTFS largely ignored the exchange rate, which was said to be determined by market forces. But in 1981 the exchange rate was accepted as an indicator, and the Treasury acknowledged its importance in economic decision making.

The pursuit of the ERM, 1985–92

It was with Chancellor Lawson's conversion, in 1985, to the view that the exchange rate was the most appropriate guide to monetary policy that the debate about joining the Exchange Rate Mechanism of the EMS was joined in earnest in Whitehall (see Walters, 1990; Lawson, 1992). Lawson became convinced of the need to supplement (and effectively replace) the MTFS with a clearer and more easily understood exchange rate rule through linking sterling to the Deutschmark. Indeed, the initial success of John Major, who succeeded him as Chancellor, in obtaining Prime Minister Thatcher's agreement to ERM membership looked as if it was going to be one of the most significant macroeconomic policy decisions of the last two decades, and a decision supported by the British political, industrial and commercial elites. If the MTFS had represented the high noon of a British brand of monetarism, ERM membership appeared to represent the fuller integration of Britain into the European Community (it had not become the European Union at this stage), and with it a commitment to long-term non-inflationary growth.

Within the ERM, the overall goals of economic policy remained very similar to those of the 1980 MTFS document: the reduction of inflation and the introduction of supply-side reforms which would create the conditions for sustainable economic growth. Public expenditure played a key role in this. In terms of the mechanisms for achieving this, the official position was that macroeconomic policy since 1990 was effectively based on two legs: maintaining sterling's position in the ERM, using interest rates if necessary; and a fiscal policy set in order to achieve a balanced budget over the medium term. The latter represented a further change in the Conservative Government's formal public expenditure objectives. A balanced budget over the medium term was intended to constitute a clear and simple rule ensuring that a prudent fiscal policy supported monetary policy in the fight against inflation.

In the event, the 'experiment' of locking Britain into a Deutschmark-dominated exchange-rate system proved even less long-lasting than the failed attempt at national planning in the 1960s or the MTFS in the 1980s. ERM membership had contributed to a reduction in the underlying level of inflation from an annual rate of over 9 per cent in 1990 to under 4 per cent by the autumn of 1992. However, this was at the price of setting domestic monetary policy so tightly that the recession was prolonged as output continued to fall and unemployment to rise. The decision to suspend sterling's membership of the ERM in September 1992, effectively leaving the system for the indefinite future, was as significant a blow to the prestige and confidence of Britain's economic policy makers as the devaluation of sterling in 1967 and the recourse to an IMF loan in 1976.

Britain's withdrawal from the ERM was the result of a complex interplay of at least four factors (discussed by Stephens, 1997; Treasury and Civil Service Select Committee, 1992). Firstly, the foreign exchange markets were unsettled by the uncertainty about French ratification of Maastricht, and the continuing problem of the Danish rejection of the Treaty. Secondly, sterling was particularly vulnerable to the subsequent pressures in the system because Britain's domestic economy was in deep recession. Thirdly, there remained an underlying lack of confidence in the financial markets that the British authorities would defend sterling's position in the grid, confirmed by the decision not to follow the Bundesbank's raising of interest rates because of concerns about Britain's economic conditions. Fourthly and finally, in the absence of any collective decision to realign currencies in the ERM, influenced in the main by the desire of one group led by France not to jeopardize the role of the ERM as a vehicle for monetary union, the system was ripe for speculative moves against weaker currencies by foreign exchange market leaders. Even the concerted action of Central Banks could not match the volume of private capital flowing in such an environment.

Economic policy post-ERM

After the suspension of Britain's ERM membership, British macroeconomic policy moved back to an eclectic mix of responses reminiscent of Chancellor Healey in the 1970s, with some changes in policy tools and presentation. Control of inflation remained the core aim of policy with, for the first time, an explicit 1–4 per cent target range set for the retail price index (RPI) (excluding mortgage interest payments). In order to achieve this target, and achieve inflation at the lower end of the range by 1996, monetary policy would be set after assessing a wide range of indicators: narrow money, M0, broad money, M4, the exchange rate, market interest rates, asset prices and the state of the real economy. Implicitly, policy became more concerned with domestic output and employment within an overall anti-inflation constraint. Discretion had replaced policy rules.

Fiscal policy was set in a medium-term context, with the aim of balancing the budget over the cycle, but with no explicit policy to reduce the PSBR or reduce public debt as a proportion of GDP. Given the continued public commitment to reducing taxation in order to contain the pressures on public borrowing, the Treasury announced in July 1992 (pre-dating the ERM crisis) a further modification to the public spending control system. In the aftermath of the ERM débâcle, the Treasury announced a number of potentially significant presentational changes. These changes were motivated by awareness that the Treasury's credibility had been damaged by the ERM episode, and by the failure to predict the scale of the boom and the length and depth of the recession. They also pre-empted demands for granting statutory monetary policy independence to the Bank of England; and, more prosaically, were an attempt to reassure financial markets that removing the ERM constraint and returning to a more judgement-based policy would not lead to a repeat of the mistakes made in the mid- and late 1980s. The first set of changes was termed greater 'openness'. The Treasury committed itself to publishing monthly monetary reports, following the regular meeting between the Governor of the Bank of England and the Chancellor. The Bank would be charged with producing a quarterly report on the progress towards the inflation target; after each interest rate change the Treasury would explain the detailed reasoning behind the policy change. A panel of seven independent economic advisers/forecasters (the 'seven wise men'), under the chairmanship of the Chief Economic Adviser, would produce quarterly reports on forecasts on the economy and provide policy advice.

Prudence with a purpose: New Labour since 1997

It is difficult to judge whether the policies of (New) Labour's Chancellor, Gordon Brown, represent a further paradigm shift in economic management or incremental changes to the post-ERM regime. The assessment is complicated by the multiple paradoxes of policy since 1997. Despite having an unassailable majority of 179 seats in the House of Commons and with it the capacity to adopt a more activist macroeconomic policy, the Chancellor has removed from the Treasury's control a key instrument of economic policy management – monetary policy – and handed it to a reconstituted Bank of England. Chancellor Brown has gone further by creating a series of fiscal policy rules designed to restrict the room for manoeuvre in that area of economic policy remaining. Such orthodoxy has extended into a domain previously reserved for the Conservative Party – commitment to liberating markets and an active competition policy. Yet this orthodoxy hides the start of a process of modest wealth and income redistribution by stealth, coupled with the return of the goal of full employment as a cornerstone of economic strategy.

The second paradox is that an administration committed, in some policy areas, to decentralization and devolution, has presided over a growth of Treasury power and influence quite unprecedented in the post-war era. Gordon Brown has wrought a quiet revolution in economic policy and in the role of the Treasury in British central government. He has been given free rein to transform the Treasury as a Ministry of Finance and engine of economic and social policy reform. Giving power resources to the Bank of England has freed the Treasury to focus on other policy areas and here Brown has shaped the Treasury in his image, to perform roles suited to his agenda for reform across the range of government policies (see Keegan, 2003).

The final paradox involves external economic policy making. Under Brown's Chancellorship, the Treasury has been a leading advocate of increased labour market flexibility and deregulation in a European Union dominated by Social Democrat governments still committed to the Rhine Social Market model. A practical and ideological battle has been joined between the Blairite/Brown version of the Third Way (Blair, 1998a; Giddens, 1998), a transatlantic concept (Blumenthal, 1997) which attempts to square social democracy and liberalism, versus the rearguard defence of the Social Market model, championed in Europe by the French. At the same time, Blair and Brown have tentatively moved Britain closer to joining the single European currency (the euro) by stating a commitment in principle to joining, outlining a set of policy tests, and formulating a national changeover plan. The same Treasury has led an emerging international consensus to give debt relief to the world's poorest developing nations.

Policy rules – limiting the room for manoeuvre

There are significant elements of continuity between the macroeconomic policies of the 1992–7 Major administration and those of the post-1997 Blair Government. What is different is that the Treasury under Gordon Brown has moved to codify and consolidate an economic framework which seeks deliberately to limit the room for manoeuvre in large areas of policy. Rules have replaced discretion in ways not seen since the early years of the MTFS in 1980. Policy learning has taken place with the Chancellor determined to remove policy makers' responsibility for accentuating economic cycles. Chancellor Brown's policy statements have stressed the need for long-termism, avoiding 'stop–go' policies and providing stability and predictability (see Treasury, 2002).

Technocratic solutions to policy problems are preferred. Brown's version of medium-term financial planning involves three elements: creating a new permanent monetary policy framework; setting out fiscal policy rules; and a new medium-term public expenditure-planning regime. The core rationale for this is to promote policy stability and transparency in a way designed to regain financial market confidence that Britain's economic policy makers are locked into a long-term anti-inflation strategy. It represents a further move by (New) Labour to accept an economic orthodoxy previously championed by governments of the Right. Policy goals for reducing unemployment, redistributing income and investing in public services have to be achieved within the constraints imposed, or by using microeconomic tools.

Immediately following its landslide election victory in May 1997, the first Blair Government began its term of Office with the most radical and unexpected revolution in the way in which British economic policy is managed. Within four days of moving into the Treasury, Gordon Brown announced that he was ceding operational control of setting interest rates to the Bank of England. For the first time in its history the Bank would be given responsibility for achieving an inflation target set by the Chancellor, and would be free to adjust interest rates in order to achieve this. However, the decision to change the balance of power between the two institutions had a long gestation period. The Chancellor's economic team had discussed it during the previous three years, whilst in Opposition. The intellectual guiding light was the Chancellor's economics adviser and former *Financial Times* journalist, Ed Balls. The then Shadow Chancellor had a seminal meeting with the Chairman of the Federal Reserve in March 1997 at which Brown had been 'impressed again by the arguments for an independent central bank on the American model' (Pym and Kochan, 1998). The decision was subsequently enshrined in legislation amending the Bank of England Act of 1946. The arrangements involved changing the framework within which monetary policy would be set and changes in the Bank's objectives and structure (Bank of England, 1997; Treasury, 2002).

The Bank of England was given the objective of ensuring price stability, as defined by an inflation target set by the Chancellor, currently 2.5 per cent. The target is symmetric, meaning that the Bank is required to act as robustly if inflation is likely to undershoot, as it is if inflation is rising. Without prejudicing this overall objective, the Bank was expected to support the Government's other economic objectives for growth and employment. This moved the arrangements closer to the US model than that of the German Bundesbank. In order to discharge this new responsibility, the Bank was reconstituted, and a new Monetary Policy Committee (MPC) created. The Governor, two Deputy Governors and six additional members would take decisions on interest rate policy, whilst the Treasury would have the right to send an observer with non-voting rights. The Chancellor appoints the non-Bank members of the MPC, which meets on a regular, monthly, basis. In a further move to ensure that the new arrangements were transparent, the Chancellor announced that the Bank would be accountable to the House of Commons through regular reporting to the Treasury (Select) Committee.

Most of the anomalies of British economic policy making have revolved around the way in which the Bank of England's historic role has left it as the Government's banker, responsible for managing borrowing and debt, the regulator of the financial system, responsible for the stability of the financial system, the agent for the Treasury in adjusting interest rates, and intervening in the foreign exchange markets. Many of these roles are seen as potentially in conflict, especially regulating the financial system whilst being the guarantor of its stability. These were ended. The Bank's responsibility for supervising the banking system was transferred to a new Securities and Investment Board, and the Treasury took over responsibility for managing the government's debt, selling gilts and managing cash in the economy. Determining the exchange rate regime would remain one of the roles of the Treasury, although the Bank would be allowed some foreign exchange reserves which it might use in pursuit of its monetary objectives. Taken together, these changes represented a major shift in British economic policy making. The Chancellor had simultaneously taken monetary policy out of party political control and moved Britain closer to the stipulation of the Maastricht Treaty to give independence to the central bank. The rationale was that by removing the control of interest rates from the Treasury, economic policy would be transparent and open and consistent. This would provide a stable background for business to plan and invest. Gordon Brown was, by implication, accepting the prevailing wisdom that independent central banks are trusted by financial markets, and therefore likely to produce lower rates of interest than would prevail if political control remained with the Treasury.

Fiscal policy rules

Without the pressures of a financial crisis or a collapse of economic strategy, the Chancellor announced a Code for Fiscal Stability (Treasury, 2002). This was a further example of embedding into policy making the emergent Anglo-Saxon consensus on economic orthodoxy. The code set out five principles governing the conduct of fiscal policy: transparency (in the setting of objectives and the reporting of progress); stability in policy processes and in the degree to which fiscal policy impacted on the real economy; responsibility in the management of public finances; fairness between generations (that is, not allowing current borrowing to be paid for by future generations); and efficiency in the design and implementation of fiscal policy. The code committed the Treasury to producing a pre-budget report and an Economic and Fiscal Strategy Report (EFSR) in addition to the usual budget documents. The EFSR crucially was intended to set out long-term strategy, assess short-term developments, assess the degree to which these were consistent with EU commitments, and produce long-term economic projections. For the first time, the National Audit Office was charged with auditing the assumptions and conventions underlying projections made.

In practical terms this represented an incremental development of the approach previously adopted by Chancellor Kenneth Clarke, constituting a codification of previously implicit rules. Substantively the Treasury committed itself to abiding by the 'golden rule' (Treasury, 2002) whereby current expenditure is covered by taxation (and the revenues obtained therein), and any borrowing is only to fund investment. Two qualifications further constrain economic policy: namely, that investment is sustainable over the economic cycle (through public debt, as a proportion of GDP, being held stable and 'prudent') and that the policies are consistent with the EU Growth and Stability Pact (the component of EMU which stresses the importance of Finance Ministries containing their borrowing).

When New Labour's first Comprehensive Spending Review was published (Treasury, 1998), it was notable for four reasons. Firstly, the Treasury was reinstituting medium-term planning. The totals for expenditure for the three years of the cycle, 1999–2000 to 2001–2, were intended to be firm, unlike the incremental drift which characterized the PES (Public

Expenditure System) as it had evolved to 1997 (see Thain and Wright, 1995). Secondly, departments were to be closely monitored to see that any increases in expenditure were linked to the achievement of modernizing programmes, with a new 'public service agreement' established between departments and the Treasury, overseen by a Cabinet Committee (PSPX). This represented a significant shift in power from departmental discretion to greater centralized control. Yet another paradox among many: the review itself showed the Treasury continuing with a less intrusive, more strategic role begun under Clarke, yet the spending plans which resulted would be used to ensure that the Treasury could attach more strings to resources assigned than at any time since the crisis of control in 1976. Thirdly, the review talked the language of targeting, the Treasury being more concerned than ever with the outputs of expenditure – what was bought in terms of improved services – than the inputs of resources. Fourthly, there were headline figures of increased spending in priority areas. Here the Treasury continued a long-standing approach of producing politically clever statistical tricks to show the agreed plans in the best light. In the past this had been used as subterfuge for increases which were supposed to be decreases under the mantra of Thatcherite 'public expenditure is bad'. Now the process was reversed.

The Treasury under Brown and the Blair–Brown Axis

The relationship between a Prime Minister and their Chancellor of the Exchequer is the most vital in any administration (see Jenkins, 1998), and there is no better example of the veracity of this axiom than the Blair administration. Tony Blair's relationship with Gordon Brown cannot be described as a conventional power battle, or a clear and sharp ideological struggle. There are elements of both dual-executive power and managed competition. It is unique in post-war political administration. The Blair/Brown axis has a pedigree of a close personal friendship (Routledge, 1998), and close political views from the period when they were chosen by John Smith to spearhead the further modernization of the Labour Party after he succeeded Neil Kinnock as leader in 1992. At one level this has been a singular driving force behind the rise of 'New' Labour: Blair the popularizer of the 'Third Way', acceptable to middle-class 'middle England'; Brown the engine of economic and social policy reforms giving substance to the claim to philosophical cohesion. Nevertheless, behind this coincidence of view and symbiosis, there is a personal battle built on some bitterness on Brown's part, derived from having given way to Blair in the leadership election to replace John Smith (Pym and Kochan, 1998; Routledge, 1998). What has resulted is a fascinating mix of personal rivalries, battles for control of key elements of the core executive and co-operation and co-ordination (Naughtie 2001; Rawnsley, 2001; Peston, 2005).

Blair gave Brown unprecedented dominance in economic policy making in Opposition, and then in Government. More than any other post-war Chancellor, except perhaps for the short tenure of Sir Stafford Cripps in the Attlee Government, Brown has been given enormous amounts of constitutional and political power resources. He chairs the two key economic committees of the Cabinet – Economic Affairs (EA) and Public Services and Public Expenditure (PSPX) Committee, and all the sub-committees of the EA committee. A second element in growing Treasury power has been in public spending. Gordon Brown has continued the trend begun under his Conservative predecessors, Norman Lamont and Kenneth Clarke, of turning the Treasury into more of a strategic controller of spending, but with the proviso that Departments now have a public service agreement with the Treasury. Increases in spending are dependent on departments delivering value-for-money and policy improvements aimed at modernizing the public sector. The PSPX committee – chaired by the Chancellor – is charged with monitoring these achievements. This represents an unprecedented increase in Treasury involvement in departmental policy making.

A further manifestation of the Treasury's significantly enhanced role is that it plays a major role in driving the core domestic policy-making agenda of the New Labour Government, rather than its more traditional participant and veto roles. Welfare-to-work is a Brown initiative; it is the Treasury – not the Department of Social Security – which has shaped social security reform since 1997. For example, the 'new deal' for the young unemployed is seen as representing the Chancellor's brand of radicalism. Similarly, the drive to increase industrial productivity and economic competitiveness comes not so much from the Department of Trade and Industry (DTI), but from the Treasury.

Nor has the Treasury's greatly enhanced role been confined to domestic policies. The Treasury has also been instrumental in shaping Britain's stance on such issues as Third World debt relief, reform of international financial institutions and, crucially, British policy towards the European single currency (the euro). The Treasury's National Changeover Plan imbues it with the role of advising business and the public sector on preparations for the ECU (European Currency Unit), a role which would traditionally have been the responsibility of the DTI. More broadly still, Gordon Brown has an effective veto on whether Britain joins the Euro, as he is the guardian of the five economic tests which must be passed in order for the Government to recommend entry. In both 1997 and 2003, he used this veto power to postpone a decision (Treasury, 1997; Cm 5776, 2003).

The five tests indicate the remarkable consistency of British economic policy makers' attitude towards 'the euro'. The débâcle of 'black Wednesday' in September 1992, when sterling was forced out of the ERM, has had a profound effect on the 'assumptive worlds' of policy makers. The fear is that the British economy is on a different economic cycle to the continental European economy, and that the interest rates prevailing in the euro-zone will thus be inappropriate for economic conditions in Britain. The criteria stipulated via the five tests could be viewed as a permanent block on British membership if Britain's economy continues to be at a different stage of the economic cycle, and if the level of domestic inflation demands a higher level of interest rates than those set by the European Central Bank (ECB). However, such economic considerations appear less pressing than the fundamental fear of Blair and Brown that a referendum on British membership of 'the euro' would be lost, in the context of a campaign (waged by eurosceptic opponents of British membership) based on the loss of national identity and sovereignty, and wrapped in the concept of an 'independent' currency, with the British people exhorted to 'save the pound'.

The sheer breadth of the Treasury's involvement in almost every aspect of governmental policy ironically gives substance to the charge of 'Treasury power' that in the past was claimed amid great fanfare, but was in fact more rhetorical than real. Historically, the Treasury has always been a typically British institution – evolving and adapting in incremental fashion. However, the core role of protecting the public purse has been expanded and augmented by broader macroeconomic responsibilities. Although primarily an economic (and finance) Ministry, it is also a highly political beast, adapting to the personalities of its Chancellors. In some respects, the changes effected under Gordon Brown are no more than a continuation of this evolutionary trend. What is different, though, is the expansion of the Treasury into direct policy making and agenda control in a way that does not reflect accepted structural responsibilities, but the interests of its Chancellor.

Conclusion

We have seen that, during the 60 years since the end of the Second World War, British economic policy makers have been struggling with the difficulties of transition from Imperial power to European State, coupled with the reality of relative economic decline and attendant economic crises. Until the late 1990s, there was a relentless quality about the nature of the problems facing British governments, so much so that Harold Wilson gave this as a reason why he should leave office in 1976: he had seen the same crisis before (Pimlott, 1992). With the ever-present fear of crisis have come many attempts to provide a permanent or workable 'solution' – from tripartite co-operation, to National Planning, to alternative new left and then new right experimentation, medium-term financial planning and exchange rate rules. All have ended with less achieved than had been promised or planned. From his position of dominance in economic policy making since 1997, Gordon Brown has shown signs of social and policy learning, and of digesting the lessons of previous economic policy failures. There has been institutional change, in the guise of (greater) Bank of England independence, medium-term frameworks and a highly activist Treasury. It remains to be seen if this bout of British economic policy experimentation achieves the economic holy grail, which has eluded previous holders of his office from Hugh Dalton to Kenneth Clarke, that of long-term embedded stability, high growth and low inflation.

3

Education Policy
Clyde Chitty

Introduction

Despite recurring talk of crisis and a remarkably negative image in large and influential sections of the popular media, it needs to be recorded at the outset that the story of state education in Britain since the end of the Second World War is one of considerable advance. Before 1945, nearly 90 per cent of young people left school to enter the labour market at the age of 14, having largely attended 'all-age' 5-to-14 elementary schools; very few older students were entered for public examinations; and less than 5 per cent of 18- or 19-year-olds went into some form or other of higher education. Today, by contrast, all young people are entitled to 11 years of full-time state education from 5 to 16, around 50 per cent of 16-year-olds gain at least five GCSE passes at grades A* to C, 95 per cent of Advanced Level entries achieve at least an E grade, and it is anticipated that by the year 2010, participation in higher education will embrace at least 50 per cent of those aged 18 to 30.

Yet none of this progress has prevented governments – both Labour and Conservative, and particularly since 1976 – from seeking to exert greater control over the education system and to make teachers and local authorities more accountable for their performance. At the same time, economic uncertainty, a changing moral climate and increasing parental power and influence have combined to place unprecedented demands on schools and teachers, now regularly called upon to help solve a host of society's problems.

This essay looks in detail at the changing social and economic climate in which policy decisions have been made since 1945, and seeks to show that the chief decision makers today do not come from the same bureaucratic groups that wielded enormous power 50 years ago.

The 1944 Education Act

For over 40 years, from the mid-1940s to the end of the 1980s, the education system of England and Wales was dominated by the philosophy and provisions of the 1944 Education Act, often referred to as the Butler Act. Scotland had separate legislation, but there were to be parallel developments during this period, particularly with regard to the organization of secondary schooling.

Although the 1944 Act was a product of the wartime Coalition Government, and was piloted through Parliament by the Conservative politician R.A. (Rab) Butler – who had become President of the Board of Education in the summer of 1941 – it was the 1945–51 Labour Government, led by Clement Attlee, which was ultimately responsible for its initial implementation, whereupon it soon established itself as a cornerstone of the Welfare State.

It was widely seen as part of that post-war programme of reconstruction and renewal, designed to ensure that the country would not return, in the words of historian Brian Simon, to 'the stagnant, class-ridden depressing society of the 1930s' (Simon, 1991: 35).

The 1944 Education Act contained a number of very significant provisions, including:

- The establishment of secondary education for all young people as an integral part of a new education structure that was to be seen as a continuous process – ranging from the primary sector through to further education.
- The recognition of a clear distinction between primary and secondary education, with the proposed phasing out of the former 'all-age' 5-to-14 elementary schools.
- The stipulation that state secondary education would in future be free, with the proposed elimination of fees charged for 11-year-olds attending publicly-provided or grant-aided secondary schools.
- The delegation of a duty to all local education authorities to contribute to 'the moral, mental and physical development of their community' by making 'sufficient and satisfactory provision' for the three main stages of education.
- The proposed raising of the school leaving age to 15 in 1947, with the stipulation that this was to be extended to 16 once the Ministry of Education was satisfied that it had become 'a practical proposition' (something that did not, in fact, happen until 1972–3).

There was a particular complication regarding the legal position of religious schools, and here the system established in 1944 was largely the outcome of lengthy negotiations between R.A. Butler and Archbishop William Temple in the period from 1942 to 1944. The final version of the Act created a unified framework which brought the church schools under state control but left them with varying degrees of independence according to how much financial support the church continued to provide. Those schools owned and run by the local authorities were named 'county' schools; those owned by the churches and run in partnership with the local authority became 'voluntary' schools. Of this latter category, there were to be two main types: 'aided' and 'controlled'. Voluntary aided schools were set up by voluntary bodies or trusts, mainly the churches. They provided their own premises and met some of the maintenance costs in exchange for a degree of control, which included control over the curriculum. Voluntary controlled schools were set up by voluntary foundations, usually the Church of England or the Roman Catholic Church, but sometimes it was a non-denominational private-supported body. They also provided their own premises, but all the running costs were to be met by the local education authority, and governing bodies had control over the religious education provided.

A recent reappraisal of the Act argued that

> 1944 assumed great significance because it commanded cross-party support; enjoyed the patronage and benefaction of the wartime coalition [and] became entrenched in folklore as benevolent and accommodating; as a grand occasion of consensual celebration; as a golden moment of history. (Batteson, 1999: 5, 7)

Yet despite the praise heaped upon it, both at the time and subsequently, and its remarkable longevity, the 1944 Act had a number of serious ambiguities and shortcomings which increasingly undermined its effectiveness over time.

For example, it provided no guidance as to the actual *content* of primary or secondary education. The word 'curriculum' does appear in the Act (on page 20), but only in passing – and at the end of a section (Section 23) giving responsibility for secular instruction in state schools (though not in voluntary-aided secondary schools) to local education authorities.

At the same time, the 1944 Education Act was extremely vague on issues relating to the *structure* of the proposed new secondary sector. The wording of the legislation – and of the 1943 White Paper *Educational Reconstruction* (Board of Education, 1943) which preceded it – appeared to recommend a *divided* system of secondary schools (consisting presumably of grammar, technical and secondary modern schools), but experiments with multilateral or comprehensive schools were not officially proscribed. Section 8 of the Act stipulated that:

> The secondary schools available for an area shall not be deemed to be sufficient unless they are sufficient in number, character and equipment to afford for all pupils opportunities for education, offering such variety of instruction and training as may be desirable in view of their different ages, abilities and aptitudes, and of the different periods for which they may be expected to remain at school, including practical instruction and training appropriate to their respective needs. (Ministry of Education, 1944: 5)

One interpretation of this Section ensured that secondary reform of a radical nature was deferred for many years. Yet it is also true that the curious ambiguity in the wording of the Section meant that when grassroots pressure for reorganization became almost irresistible in the mid-1960s, it could be addressed by simply *reinterpreting* the formula without the need for further legislation. Attention was, in fact, drawn to the possibility of having just one secondary school serving a given area or neighbourhood even while the Education Bill was making its way through Parliament. Speaking in April 1944, J. Chuter Ede, the Labour Parliamentary Secretary to the old Board of Education, made the case for local autonomy:

> I do not know where people get the idea about *three* types of school ... because I have gone through the Bill with a small toothcomb, and I can find only one school for our senior pupils – and that is a secondary school. What you like to make of it will depend on the way you serve the precise needs of the individual area in the country. (*The Times*, 14 April 1944)

Meanwhile in Scotland, the Education (Scotland) Acts of 1945 and 1946 applied the principles of the 1944 Education Act for England and Wales to Scottish circumstances, though it is rather misleading to put it this way, since two of the major innovations – the provision of secondary education for all and the raising of the school leaving age to 15 – had already been enacted in Scotland in 1939 and had then been suspended owing to the outbreak of the Second World War (see McPherson and Raab, 1988: 73). As we shall see later in this chapter, Scotland was to be particularly active in the 1950s in exploring the possibilities and opportunities offered by the adoption of a unified system of secondary schooling, so that by the time comprehensive education became official Labour Government policy in the mid-1960s, the door in Scotland was already in a sense 'half-open'.

A national system, locally administered

Organizationally, the 1944 Education Act established what is usually referred to as 'a national system, locally administered'. What this amounted to, in England and Wales, was a tripartite 'partnership' between central government, local government and the individual schools and colleges (with the *third* element in this 'partnership' sometimes replaced in studies of the period by the organized teaching profession). The same model of 'partnership', with a clear implication of a genuine dispersal of power and responsibility, also existed in Scotland, although it has been argued (see, for example, McPherson and Raab, 1988: 29) that from the 1940s onwards, the Scottish system was somewhat more centralized than that existing in England and Wales.

According to the constitutional expert, Vernon Bogdanor, writing in the *Oxford Review of Education* in 1979, the 'efficient secret' of the education system operating in Britain, and the main reason why conflict and tension surfaced only periodically, was that no one individual participant could enjoy a monopoly of power in the decision-making process, and this meant that

> power over the distribution of resources, over the organisation and over the content of education was to be diffused amongst the different elements and no one of them was to be given a controlling voice. … Such a structure … offered clear and obvious advantages, not only for the administrator concerned primarily with the efficient working of the system, but also for the liberal, anxious to avoid the concentration of power in a few hands, and the pluralist insistent that different interests should be properly represented. For parallel to the formal relationships between central and local government, embodied in statute and convention, there grew up a network of professional communities whose role it was to soften the political antagonisms which might otherwise render the whole system unworkable. … The diffused structure of decision-making led, it could be argued, to better decisions because it ensured a wide basis of agreement before any changes were made. (Bogdanor, 1979: 157–8)

It is worth pointing out that a number of significant factors contributed to the prevailing mood of co-operation and consensus in the 1950s and early 1960s. The relative absence of damaging political conflict was facilitated not only by the general climate of expansion, but also by the availability of sufficient financial resources to ensure the successful implementation of expansionist policies. At the same time, the post-war period was one when the number of powerful interest groups was fairly small, and it was comparatively easy to secure consensus among a cosily restricted network. As Vernon Bogdanor goes on to argue:

> The system of consultation worked best when only a small number of interests were involved whose rank and file were content to defer to elites, and could, therefore, always be relied upon to act 'sensibly'. This process of elite accommodation reached its apogee during the post-war period, when, or so it was believed, many important policy decisions in education were taken over lunch at the National Liberal Club by a troika consisting of Sir William Alexander, Secretary of the Association of Education Committees, Sir Ronald Gould, the General Secretary of the National Union of Teachers, and the Permanent Secretary at the Ministry of Education. If these three agreed on some item of educational policy, it would

more often than not, be implemented. Such at least was the general belief; and even if it was a caricature, it is at least significant that it was widely held. (Bogdanor, 1979: 161)

The position of the local education authorities was certainly fairly secure in the post-war period, and they were entrusted by Ministers to undertake several functions specified in the 1944 Act (see Chitty, 2002). Section 23 of the Act stipulated that such matters as dates of terms, length of the school day and secular instruction in all except voluntary-aided secondary schools, were to become the responsibility of LEAs, unless otherwise provided for in the school articles of government:

> In every county school and, subject to the provisions hereinafter contained as to religious education, in every voluntary school except an aided secondary school, the secular instruction to be given to the pupils shall, save in so far as may be otherwise provided by the rules of management or articles of government for the school, be under the control of the local education authority. (Ministry of Education, 1944: 19)

In reality, the majority of Local Education Authorities (LEAs) in England and Wales failed to exercise even a *nominal* control over the curriculum and related policies of their primary and secondary schools. The absence of curriculum guidelines meant that, in practice, and despite the wording of Section 23 of the 1944 Act, day-to-day decisions about the content and timetabling of the school curriculum were invariably taken by head-teachers and teachers under the perfunctory oversight of the school governing body. Indeed, when, at the end of the 1970s, James Callaghan's Labour Government asked LEAs for information about their curriculum policies, many of the responses that arrived at the Department of Education and Science were politely-worded 'nil returns' (see Maw, 1988: 51). As we shall see below, it was, in fact, in the mid-1970s that a general emphasis on trust and co-operation was replaced by a new and more demanding culture of accountability and sanctions.

For all the cosy rhetoric of the post-war period, there were, of course, occasions when the model of consensus and partnership broke down. In 1954, for example, the Conservative Minister of Education Florence Horsbrugh refused to allow the then London County Council (LCC) to close Eltham Hill Girls' Grammar School and transfer these 'selected' pupils to Kidbrooke School, London's first new *purpose-built* comprehensive. Her successor, Sir David Eccles, was anxious to reassure the grammar-school lobby that comprehensive reorganization was not part of the Conservative Party's education agenda. Shortly after taking office in October 1954, he emphasized:

> One has to choose between justice and equality, for it is impossible to apply both these principles at once. Those who support comprehensive schools prefer equality. Her Majesty's present Government prefer justice. My colleagues and I will never allow local authorities to assassinate the grammar schools. (*The Schoolmaster*, 7 January 1955)

Yet although the Conservative Governments of the 1950s were generally hostile to local experiments in comprehensive schooling, the concept of 'a national system, locally administered' was not seriously ruptured even by such a potentially explosive issue as the pattern of secondary education. As we shall see in the next section, there were divisions of opinion in both major political parties, and attitudes towards the comprehensive reform were often quite complex, both at a local and at a national level.

New trends in secondary education, 1951–64

Although the Labour Party of the 1950s and 1960s is often associated with the campaign to reorganize secondary schools along comprehensive lines, for much of the 13-year period when the Party was in Opposition at Westminster, from 1951 to 1964, its official attitude towards the merits of reorganization was somewhat ambivalent and confused. It was certainly very nervous about tackling the position of both the direct grant schools, which received a grant direct from central government in return for offering a number of free grammar-school places to complement the fee-paying element, and the so-called public schools, which were wholly independent and fee-charging and the majority of which were boarding establishments. One reason for this ambivalence was that the Leaders of the Labour Party often harboured a nostalgic preference for the more privileged forms of education: Clement Attlee (Leader of the Party from 1935–55) had fond memories of his days at Haileybury Public School, whilst his successor, Hugh Gaitskell (1955–63), wanted to retain 'an educated elite learning Latin verse' (Benn, 1994: 172, diary entry for 2 October 1953).

At the same time, the Labour Party found it very difficult to clarify its position with regard to grammar schools. Although a commitment to the comprehensive school was endorsed by the Labour Party Conference in 1952, there existed a degree of confusion about the precise meaning of common, unsegregated secondary education. As Michael Parkinson argued in a study of Labour Party policy making published in 1970 (Parkinson, 1970), the problem originally lay with sorting out the implications of a policy of 'secondary education for all'. This had, after all, been formulated in the period *before* 1939 when the grammar school was the principal kind of state school providing a proper secondary education. Not surprisingly, the grammar school had implicitly become the Party's model for the development of secondary education, despite the selective nature of its entry. It was also true that the grammar school was seen by many as playing an important *practical* role as the main avenue of occupational and social mobility for working-class children. For both these reasons, many Labour Party members were emotionally attached to them and were not prepared to see them discarded or assimilated into a new type of school. The thinking of many Labour politicians was summarized by the late Emanuel (Manny) Shinwell in a letter sent to *The Times* in June 1958:

> We are afraid to tackle the public schools to which so many wealthy people send their sons, but, at the same time, we are ready to throw overboard the grammar schools, which are for many working-class boys the stepping-stones to universities and then a useful career. I would rather abandon Eton, Winchester, Harrow and all the rest of them than sacrifice all the advantages of the grammar school. (*The Times*, 26 June 1958)

Despite such reservations, it was clear that the case for change was building throughout the country; and this was particularly true after the 1959 general election which was won by the Conservative Party for the last time for just over a decade. One aspect of the post-war arrangements that attracted particular criticism was the 11-plus selection examination, consisting of tests of intelligence and tests of attainment in English and arithmetic, which was employed in most parts of the country as the principal means of allocating children to different types of secondary school.

It needs to be emphasized at this point that the post-war (divided) system of secondary schools was based on the widely-held belief that it was possible to say, from the results of tests administered at the age of 10 or 11, what a child's future accomplishments would be. And this was itself based on the extraordinary view that every child was born with a given quota of 'intelligence' which then remained constant throughout his or her life – and that this key quality was a direct product of genetic endowment and not, therefore, susceptible to any educational influence. Needless to say, human intelligence was thought to relate closely to social class, with the highest social (or occupational) groupings possessing the highest intelligence (or IQs).

Although the structure of secondary education that emerged during the 1940s and 1950s was officially a tripartite one, comprising grammar, secondary modern and technical schools, it was effectively a *bipartite* system, comprising grammar schools on the one hand and modern schools on the other – the former taking, in the 1950s, around one in five of all children at the age of 11 – and 'failure' in the 11-plus exam was often a cause of great distress both for a child and its parents. Writing in 1965, Stewart Mason, Director of Education for Leicestershire, looked back on the previous decade when the life-chances of so many young people were destroyed as part of the process of preserving an elite education for the few:

> A sense of success in a few was being paid for by a sense of failure in the many; primary school friendships were severed, brothers and sisters artificially separated. A sense of social injustice was being engendered while reservoirs of talent were doomed to remain untapped. More and more people were coming to see that the eleven-plus reflected an outmoded 'we/they' society. (Mason, 1965: 52)

The 11-plus selection process certainly had a harmful effect on the curriculum and ethos of many primary schools. In the 1965 essay cited above, Stewart Mason spoke of the need to remove 'the deadening backwash' of the 11-plus upon the nation's primary schools (ibid.: 52), and this involved aspects of grouping and pedagogy as well as the nature of the curriculum on offer. With their reputation among both working-class and middle-class parents largely dependent on the acquisition of an impressive number of grammar-school places each academic year, many primary schools, if they were large enough, began to stream their pupils from the age of seven onwards, with the 'brightest' children in the 'top' streams, thereby being specially 'groomed' for success in the 11-plus. So that selection at *eleven* became, in effect, selection at *seven*. And such a process was always bound to be arbitrary and unfair. Describing his experience of working with ten-year-old boys in a streamed (A, B, C) primary school, Brian Jackson wrote in 1961 that the more he had got to know these boys ('of the grammar-school type'; 'of the C type', etc), the more he had became convinced that 'they had not been "given" to us in these neat categories: *we had manufactured them*'. In Jackson's view, 'these boys were simply the product of the educational society that we had established. That society demanded that they be selected or rejected at eleven; therefore we pre-selected at ten, nine, eight, seven, even six (Jackson, 1961: 6, 8). All this began to change only when local authorities in various parts of the country began the process of abolishing the 11-plus and reorganizing their secondary schools along comprehensive lines.

Somewhat paradoxically, it was the development of the *bipartite* system itself that served to challenge and undermine the theoretical justification for 11-plus selection. In particular, the successes secured by many secondary modern school candidates in the new GCE (General Certificate of Education) Ordinary Level Examination introduced in 1951 had the unforeseen effect of exposing the fallibility of the whole process. It became increasingly difficult to sustain the argument that a child's intellectual capacity was a fixed quantity that could not be influenced by social policy and educational approaches.

One secondary modern school for girls serving a working-class district in a large industrial city, which took in only those children who had failed to secure a place at either a grammar or a selective central school, entered a number of pupils for the O Level Examination in 1954. Of those who gained five or more passes, one had had an IQ of 97 on entry to school five years earlier, another an IQ of 85. (This was at a time when an IQ of 115 or over was widely considered to be essential in order to embark on examination courses.) And other secondary modern schools were soon in a position to tell similar success stories, thereby emphasizing the importance of *education* as the key to human development (see Simon, 1955: 64–6).

Yet despite the efforts of a number of local authorities to develop 'academic' work in their secondary modern schools, parental dissatisfaction with the 11-plus was definitely growing in the second half of the 1950s, so that a social movement of some significance was under way which could not be ignored. Historian David Crook has emphasized that 'the drive for comprehensive education in England and Wales was a "bottom up", rather than a "top down" initiative' (Crook, 2002: 257), with the limited experiments of the 1950s providing the essential background to what Brian Simon has termed the 'breakout' of the following decade (Simon, 1991: 198). The local elections of May 1963 resulted in sweeping victories for the Labour Party and provided a vital catalyst for the growing comprehensive movement. Bristol, Liverpool and Manchester LEAs swiftly produced city-wide schemes for comprehensive reorganization, while the London County Council finally felt able to abandon the 11-plus, replacing it in those areas where grammar schools continued to exist by a combination of teacher assessment and parental choice. A number of rural counties, including Devon, Dorset and Shropshire, none of them Labour-controlled, also declared themselves in favour of comprehensive education.

The grassroots movement that was in progress in the early 1960s demanded a new approach to education from a Conservative government that seemed to be losing popular support on a wide range of issues. Minister of Education Edward Boyle (1962–4) did not share the hostility of the majority of his parliamentary colleagues towards comprehensive schooling and began encouraging LEAs to look at strategies for softening their selection procedures – in a vain attempt to forestall more drastic solutions. In a private briefing paper to Harold Macmillan, dated 3 July 1963, he recommended that the Conservative Government should 'make an end of the strict neutrality which my Department has maintained in public towards local selection methods' (quoted in Crook, 2002: 251).

The Labour Party for its part was devising various propaganda techniques designed both to respond to grassroots pressure and, at the same time, remove all lingering doubts about the 'merits' of reorganization. It was, for example, emphasized by Hugh Gaitskell and others that comprehensive education meant 'grammar schools for all', and, as this author has argued elsewhere, this somewhat disingenuous message was not without its appeal to voters:

> The slogan of 'grammar schools for all' ... served a number of useful functions: it helped to silence the opponents of reorganization within the Party itself; it appealed to growing demands for a more meritocratic system of secondary education; and it dispelled the fears of those parents who placed their trust in the traditional grammar-school curriculum. (Chitty, 1989: 36)

A second line of attack was opened up by Harold Wilson (Gaitskell's successor as Party Leader from February 1963) in his now famous 'Science and Socialism' Speech to the 1963 Labour Party Conference. Here the new Leader laid great stress on the point that the Party opposed a segregated, elitist secondary system, not only because it was unjust and socially divisive, but also because, by failing to capture talent at the point of entry to secondary education, it held back Britain's technological development and militated against her success in economic affairs.

Circular 10/65 and 'comprehensivization'

Soon after Harold Wilson's Labour Party was returned to power in the October 1964 General Election, Ministers decided that implementation of the policy of secondary reorganization in England and Wales should take the form of a Circular to be issued to all 163 local education authorities. This was still the period when the education system could be fairly described as 'a central service, locally administered'. We know that after Anthony Crosland became Education Secretary in January 1965, there was a fierce debate within the Department of Education and Science as to whether the new Circular should *require* or *request* the local authorities to prepare plans for reorganization, although most Cabinet Ministers felt that compulsion at this stage was likely to prove counter-productive (see, for example, PRO: PRO CAB 129/120, Part One, C (65) 4, 'Comprehensive Secondary Education', 14 January 1965; PRO CAB 128/39, Part One, C (65) 2nd Conclusions, 19 January 1965). Interviewed by Professor Maurice Kogan at the end of 1970, Crosland claimed that, in deciding to back those of his officials opting for 'request', he had been strongly influenced both by his meetings with the Association of Education Committees and by his judgement of 'the general mood of the local authority world' (Kogan, 1971: 189). Many Labour and Conservative local authorities were broadly sympathetic to what the Government was proposing, and hence there seemed little point in risking widespread alienation by adopting a policy of compulsion.

In a speech delivered at the end of May 1965, Crosland defended his conciliatory policy by reminding his audience that almost two-thirds of the secondary school population already lived in areas where the local authority was implementing or planning a comprehensive schools policy:

> The fact is that there has been a growing movement against the eleven-plus examination – and all that it implies. This movement has not been politically inspired or imposed from the Centre. It has been a spontaneous growth at the grass-roots of education, leading to

widespread conviction that separatism is an offence against the child as well as a brake on social and economic progress. ... The whole notion of a selection test at the age of eleven belongs to the era when secondary education was a privilege of the few, and this is now generally understood. (Quoted in Kerckhoff et al., 1996: 28)

Crosland recognized the unique local knowledge that LEAs possessed, and respected the fact that, where the planning and oversight of reorganization were concerned, there was undoubtedly more expertise in the localities than existed within his own Department. Here, then, was a Cabinet Minister openly acknowledging the signal importance of 'street level bureaucrats' and local-level policy actors.

In its final form, Circular 10/65 began by declaring the intention of the Government 'to end selection at eleven-plus and to eliminate separatism in secondary education'. Local authorities were *requested* to submit, within a year, 'plans for reorganizing secondary education in their areas on comprehensive lines'. No single pattern of comprehensive organization was laid down; and, instead, the Circular described the 'six main forms' that had so far emerged from 'experience and discussion'. Two of these would be acceptable only as 'interim solutions', while the most favoured type was the 'all-through' 11-to-18 comprehensive school as pioneered in London, Coventry and other large cities.

The two patterns regarded as 'acceptable' only as 'interim solutions' involved the use of separate schools for pupils over the age of 13 or 14 and the continuance of some form of selection. In one, for example, older pupils had to choose between a senior school catering for those who intended to stay at school *beyond* the statutory leaving age and a less prestigious school catering for those who did not.

The four patterns accepted as 'fully comprehensive' were:

- The orthodox comprehensive school for pupils aged 11 to 18.
- A two-tier system whereby *all* pupils transferred automatically at the age of 13 or 14, *without any form of selection*, to a senior comprehensive or upper school.
- A two-tier system comprising non-selective schools for the 11-to-16 age range, combined with sixth-form colleges for those over the age of 16.
- A two-tier system comprising new 'middle schools' for pupils aged 8 to 12 or 9 to 13, followed by 'upper schools' with an age range of 12 or 13 to 18.

It was accepted in the Circular that the most appropriate system would depend on 'local circumstances' and that a local authority could decide to adopt 'more than one form of organization' in a single area. It was emphasized that the Government was *not* seeking to impose 'destructive or precipitate change' on existing schools and that 'the evolution of separate schools into a comprehensive system must be a constructive process requiring careful planning by local education authorities in consultation with all those concerned' (Department of Education and Science, 1965: 1, 2, 11).

Whereas the system of secondary schools established by Circular 10/65 resembled a patchwork quilt of uneven quality, the implementation of comprehensive schooling in Scotland was remarkably uniform (see Kerckhoff et al., 1996: 6). Circular 600, issued in 1965 by the Scottish Education Department, specified only *one* acceptable form of comprehensive organization: the six-year, 'all-through', 'fixed-catchment' comprehensive school for 12–18-year-olds. Some variant of a two-tier system *might* be necessary in outlying rural areas, but only as 'an unavoidable interim arrangement' (SED, 1965: paras 10 and 11). Interviewed at the end of the 1980s about the effectiveness of Circular 600, former Scottish Minister Bruce Millan argued that the *official* start of reorganization in Scotland was a relatively straightforward affair because the previous 20 years had already witnessed a considerable amount of experimentation and change towards comprehensive education north of the border (see McPherson and Raab, 1988: 374).

The backlash begins, 1968–76

The general mood of co-operation and consensus, which was such a prominent feature of the post-war system, began to turn sour in the years following the publication of Circular 10/65; and this was to have an adverse effect on future developments in both primary and secondary education. The late 1960s was also the period which saw the beginning of a slow but perceptible erosion of trust between central government and local administrators.

A small number of Conservative LEAs indicated from the beginning that they would defy Circular 10/65, while others preferred to opt for reorganization plans that involved minimal and half-hearted change. For example, Buckinghamshire County Council pledged its support for comprehensive schools, 'provided that any such comprehensive school does not prejudice the continuance of any existing selective secondary school' (quoted in Crook, 2002: 252). Most of the large, Labour-controlled urban authorities, including Leeds and Birmingham, shared the preference of Bristol, Liverpool, London and Manchester for 'all-through' 11-to-18 comprehensives; but in each of these cities, rapid progress was hampered by the absence of adequate buildings, the need to consult with powerful church authorities and uncertainties about the future of local direct grant grammar schools. There was no shortage of carefully-articulated long-term plans; but the absence of additional Department of Education and Science (DES) funding to implement reorganization meant that ideal solutions often had to be temporarily sacrificed. As David Crook has observed, 'compromises invariably took the form of "interim" arrangements, the phased abolition of the eleven-plus and school amalgamations that created comprehensive schools on two or more sites' (Crook, 2002: 252).

Another factor which contributed to the steady disintegration of the cross-party alliance on education issues was the exposed nature of Edward Boyle's position on the 'liberal' wing of the Conservative Party – a position which eventually became untenable as large groups of Right-wing backbenchers and constituency activists mobilized against the beleaguered shadow Education Minister (see Knight, 1990: 22–60). Matters came to a head at the Conservatives' 1968 Annual Party Conference, where Boyle was challenged to concede that the Party was hopelessly divided on such issues as secondary planning, the future of the grammar schools and reorganization, and where he made a passionate plea for moderation and consensus:

I will join with you willingly and wholeheartedly in the fight against Socialist dogmatism wherever it rears its head. But do not ask me to oppose it with an equal and opposite Conservative dogmatism, because in education, it is always dogmatism itself which is wrong. (Quoted in Corbett, 1969: 785)

Boyle's plea was unsuccessful and the official motion on education was defeated. The following year (1969), Boyle was replaced as Shadow Education Secretary by Margaret Thatcher, who was far more in tune with traditional grassroots opinion.

It was also at this time that the first three Black Papers were published (Cox and Dyson, 1969a; 1969b; 1970) and these were enormously successful in tapping into a public mood that was disillusioned with change. The contributors to these documents were seen as wanting to put the clock back: to the days of formal teaching methods and streaming in primary schools; of academic standards usually associated with a grammar-school education; of well-motivated, hard-working and essentially conservative university students.

Yet theirs was *not* to be the voice of the future as far as Conservative education policy was concerned. In August 1974, six months before replacing Edward Heath as Leader of the Conservative Party, Margaret Thatcher joined Sir Keith Joseph and Alfred Sherman in setting up the Centre for Policy Studies (CPS), a Right-wing think-tank designed to come up with radical new ideas in all areas of social policy. Meanwhile, the last two Black Papers, published in 1975 and 1977 (Cox and Boyson, 1975; 1977), gave support to the introduction of new and untried ways of organizing education, principally the idea of the voucher, whereby all parents would be issued with a free basic coupon, fixed at the average cost of schools in their area, to take along to the school of their choice. Here were the first signs that, now that Margaret Thatcher was in charge, the politics of *reaction* would give way to the politics of *reconstruction*.

The end of the 'welfare capitalist consensus'

The Conservative Party was not alone in wishing to challenge existing ideas in the 1970s, though for the Labour Party – and specifically for the 1976–9 Labour Government of James Callaghan – the chief concern was to increase the accountability of schools, teachers and local authorities as part of the drive to improve standards. All politicians were aware of extreme public disquiet, justified or otherwise, about the state of the nation's schools.

As far as secondary education was concerned, stories were frequently appearing in the media indicating that many of the new comprehensive schools – and especially those situated in tough inner-city areas – were actually 'out of control'. According to Stephen Ball, writing a decade later, 'by the mid-1970s, fuelled by press and television "horror stories", the level of "public concern" about the state of the nation's schooling – and particularly its secondary schooling – had reached the level of a moral panic' (Ball, 1984: 6). The picture that was painted was one of incompetent, unaccountable and often 'trendy-Lefty' teachers, delivering an increasingly irrelevant curriculum to bored teenagers who were poorly motivated, illiterate and innumerate. For many employers and industrialists, the majority of these teenagers were totally ill-equipped to enter the world of work; and, to this extent, schools could actually be held responsible, at least in part, for the rising rate of youth unemployment.

As far as the primary sector was concerned, much blame for the current malaise was laid at the door of the Plowden Report, published in 1967 (Department of Education and Science, 1967), which had important things to say about the curriculum and internal organization of primary schools in England. While initially welcomed for its warm humanity ('at the heart of the educational process lies the child'), the Report soon came to be attacked for its promotion of 'child-centred' learning and for its rejection of the traditional didactic teaching methods associated with the dogged preparation of primary-school pupils for the 11-plus selection examination. Evidence that many primary-school teachers did not automatically embrace the soft-centred progressivism associated with Plowden (see Simon, 1991: 379–82) did not trouble those who were anxious to demonize the 1960s as a decade when 'progressive education' and the abandonment of standards destroyed the life-chances of thousands of children.

The event which seemed to confirm the traditionalists' worst fears was the so-called William Tyndale Affair which occupied several column inches in the London and national press in the mid-1970s. It seems clear that William Tyndale Junior School in Islington in north London was beset with serious conflicts between late 1973 and the autumn of 1975, which had a damaging effect on its standing in the local community. A group of teachers (including the Head) found themselves in conflict with parents, managers and then finally the ILEA (Inner London Education Authority) for persisting with a progressive curriculum which apparently ignored or at least 'down-played' proficiency in reading, writing and arithmetic. The ILEA set up an inquiry into the running of the School; and the Auld Report published in 1976 found that a group of 'politically-motivated' primary-school teachers had indeed been allowed to continue for far too long in what could be described as a gross violation of their teaching duties (Auld, 1976). In the eyes of the media and of many Right-wing politicians, the story of William Tyndale was conclusive proof that irreparable harm could be done by a group of 'progressive' teachers in a state school when parents were kept out of the decision-making process, and where managers and inspectors were clearly guilty of failing to carry out their statutory duties. What was true of one badly-managed primary school in north London might well apply to significant numbers of primary (and secondary) schools in other parts of the country.

Underlying a concern about all these immediate issues, which affected politicians of all parties in the mid-1970s, was a preoccupation with the worsening economic situation which signalled an end to the post-war period of optimism and expansion, and ushered in a new obsession in all areas of social policy with 'value for money', and the monitoring of performance.

It was, in fact, the economic recession of the early 1970s that fundamentally altered the map of British politics and caused politicians and their advisers to challenge a whole range of existing practices. The collapse of fixed exchange rates in 1971–2, followed by the quadrupling of the oil price in 1973, resulted in a general world recession and thereby undermined all the somewhat complacent assumptions about growth and expansion that had been made in a period of relative prosperity. In Britain, the economic downturn exposed all the underlying weaknesses of what has been described as 'the post-war welfare capitalist consensus'. That consensus relied on an increasing prosperity for any success it might have had in promoting a sense of social unity; and when that prosperity disintegrated, so, too, did the consensus (for an overview of this period, see Dorey, 1995a: Ch. 4).

The famous speech on education that James Callaghan delivered at Ruskin College, Oxford, on 18 October 1976 contained a number of themes that were considered relevant to the changed and chastened circumstances of the period: the need to challenge some of the assumptions underlying teacher autonomy; a concern for central government to assume greater control of education in general, and of the secondary-school curriculum in particular; above all, the need to make more effective use of the money – roughly £6 billion a year – that the Government was spending on education. It was at this time that 'accountability' definitely replaced 'partnership' as the dominant metaphor in discussions about the distribution of power in the education system.

New patterns of policy making

Coinciding with the breakdown of the post-war welfare capitalist consensus, with its direct effect on the concept of a national educational service, locally administered, came the beginnings of new patterns of decision making at the Centre. It was at this time that the Government's political advisers began to take the lead in determining education policy, with the key role in this respect being played by the Downing Street Policy Unit, which, over the past 30 years, has contained some of the Prime Minister's most trusted political aides.

The creation, in March 1974, of a new Policy Unit (renamed Policy Directorate in 2001), separate from the Central Policy Review Staff (CPRS) created by Edward Heath at the beginning of his 1970–4 Government, has been described by Professor Peter Hennessy as 'Harold Wilson's most important and, to date, durable innovation'. Certainly, under the strong leadership, from 1974 to 1979, of Dr Bernard (now Lord) Donoughue, then a political scientist from the London School of Economics, it rapidly became, in Hennessy's words, 'a prime-ministerial cabinet in all but name' (Hennessy, 1986: 82; see also Donoughue, 1987: 20; Kavanagh and Seldon, 1999: Ch. 4).

By 1976, the Policy Unit already felt strong enough to challenge the orthodox thinking of a number of government departments; and this was particularly true in the case of education. Shortly after taking over from Harold Wilson as Prime Minister in April 1976, James Callaghan received a lengthy memorandum from Dr Donoughue suggesting that it might well be appropriate, given the widespread anxiety being expressed, for the new occupant of 10 Downing Street to make the issue of standards in state schools an important feature of his public pronouncements. It was the Policy Unit which wrote the education section of Callaghan's Speech to the 1976 Labour Party Conference, and then proceeded to play a major role in drafting the Speech delivered at Ruskin College, Oxford. Relations between the Unit and the DES bureaucracy were not always harmonious, but Donoughue was determined that central government should adopt a more positive and interventionist role in educational policy making.

The 1979–90 Thatcher administrations

Initially, when Margaret Thatcher replaced Callaghan as Prime Minister in May 1979, her first inclination was to rely for policy advice on her newly-appointed ministers and their departmental teams. She reduced the number and seniority of her political aides at Number 10 and cut down the size of the Policy Unit. It was the frustration of working with a predominantly cautious set of ministers and their attendant bureaucracies (see King, 1985: 101–7) that led her to reverse this judgement and give the Policy Unit greater authority than it had ever wielded before. For the major part of the 1980s, Mrs Thatcher came to rely for advice, encouragement and a steady stream of radical new ideas on a growing number of young, committed Right-wing analysts who occupied all the key positions in the Policy Unit. Indeed, there were only *two* major educational issues where DES civil servants could claim 'victory' over the Policy Unit's idealists in the 1980s: the rejection of the idea of 'educational vouchers', and the incorporation of the clauses creating a broad-based national curriculum into the 1987 Education Reform Bill.

Throughout her 11 years as Prime Minister, Margaret Thatcher made little secret of her determination to undermine and eventually destroy *both* the comprehensive system of secondary schooling *and* the post-war concept of a national system of education, *locally* administered. The first could be achieved by establishing new types of school within the secondary system and by reintroducing (or reinforcing) the principle of selection. The second would involve ensuring that parents were given far greater control over the choice of secondary school for their children, that any new type of secondary school would be independent of local authority control and that existing schools could exercise the right to 'opt out of' the control of the local authority.

As far as Margaret Thatcher and her advisers were concerned, the decline in educational standards which had begun in the mid-1960s had been caused by a corrupt alliance between misguided local education authority inspectors, Left-wing educationists in the universities and politically-motivated classroom teachers. What was needed was a profound change in the whole culture of education whereby professional autonomy was no longer regarded as sacrosanct. The cosy relationships of the post-war world had no place in this new and more brutal world of heightened accountability and the zero tolerance of failure.

Yet in spite of such trenchant views, the first (1979–83) Thatcher Government's only radical measure in the sphere of education policy was the introduction of the Assisted Places Scheme, designed, in the words of the 1979 Conservative Party Manifesto, to enable 'less well-off parents to claim part or all of the fees at certain independent schools from a special government fund' (Conservative Party, 1979: 24). According to Mark Carlisle, the Education Secretary who formally introduced the Assisted Places Scheme, its purpose was 'to give certain children a greater opportunity to pursue a particular form of academic education that was regrettably not otherwise, particularly in the cities, available to them' (quoted in Griggs, 1985: 89). Overall, however, as Margaret Thatcher herself subsequently admitted – and in spite of her own strong views – education was not really a priority for the Conservative Government elected in 1979, due largely to the more pressing need to reduce inflation and curb public expenditure, and also the greater priority ascribed by the Cabinet to confronting organized interests, most notably the trade unions (Thatcher, 1993: 339–78). Even Carlisle's successor as Secretary of State for Education, Sir Keith Joseph (1981–6), made little significant impact on education policy. Although he was an ideological soul-mate and close political ally of Margaret Thatcher, and a keen supporter of 'education vouchers' – which would enable parents to 'shop around' for the school of their choice, and thereby remove from LEAs their role in allocating children to schools – Joseph was unable to overcome the fierce opposition from his own civil servants at the DES, and was eventually persuaded that even the introduction of a pilot scheme was politically impracticable.

Here was a clear example of a reform-minded Minister proving unable successfully to challenge the deeply-entrenched 'in-house' philosophy of a Government Department and its senior officials. As Smith et al. (2000) noted, a significant and successful challenge to a prevailing Departmental ethos often requires a succession of reform-minded Ministers before sufficient momentum is developed to effect a significant change in policy, and instil a new intellectual approach – a 'paradigm shift' – inside the Department (Smith et al., 2000: 151; see also Smith, 1999: 133–7).

It fell to Kenneth Baker (Education Secretary from 1986 to 1989) to effect such a 'paradigm shift', and thereby introduce the most radical and far-reaching educational reforms of the 1979–90 Thatcher Governments. The 1988 Education Reform Act was described by journalists Peter Wilby and Ngaio Crequer as 'a Gothic monstrosity of legislation' (*The Independent*, 28 July 1988). It actually covered England and Wales only, although parallel bills with many similarities had also been prepared for Scotland and Northern Ireland. With its 238 clauses and 13 schedules, covering everything from the 'spiritual welfare' of the next generation to the definition of a 'half day', it took up nearly 370 hours of parliamentary time and gave the Secretary of State for Education 451 new powers. In setting out to redesign the education service from top to bottom, it attracted more bitter and widespread professional opposition than any piece of legislation passed since Aneurin Bevan's introduction of the National Health Service in the 1940s.

Despite its enormous breadth and scope, the main purpose of the 1988 Education Act can be summed up quite simply: to erect (or rather reinforce) a hierarchical system of schooling, particularly at the secondary level, subject both to market forces and to greater control from the Centre.

The first 25 sections of the Act legislated for a subject-based national curriculum and its assessment. In England, this would consist of 10 subjects to be taken by all pupils during their compulsory education: English, maths, science, a modern foreign language (except in primary schools), technology, history, geography, art, music and physical education. Of these, English, maths and science would form the 'core' of the curriculum, and the majority of curriculum time at primary level would be devoted to these three subjects. Children would be assessed at the end of four key stages, at ages 7, 11, 14 and 16, Key Stage Four ending with the General Certificate of Secondary Education (GCSE), which had been introduced as a single system of examining at 16 in 1986. A National Curriculum Council and a School Examinations and Assessment Council would oversee the arrangements, but the Secretary of State would have considerable power to decide ultimately on actual curriculum content.

It can be argued that this was a key occasion when the civil servants of the DES (with the support of Kenneth Baker himself) scored a notable victory over the neo-liberal faction advising the Prime Minister. Mrs Thatcher herself disliked the idea of a detailed national curriculum on the grounds that it was inimical to the underlying philosophy of the Act which laid great stress on choice and diversity and on the right of all schools, especially at secondary level, to develop a distinctive ethos in order to attract as many pupils as possible. In his autobiography, Kenneth Baker subsequently revealed that as late as October 1987 – only *three* weeks before the introduction of the Education Reform Bill into the House of Commons – he had felt obliged to use the threat of his resignation to prevent his broad-based curriculum being sabotaged by the Prime Minister (Baker, 1993: 197).

Another major provision of the Act introduced a new system of school management whereby school budgets for staffing, premises and services would be delegated to individual schools. This new delegated budget would be determined by a formula largely reflecting the number of pupils on the school roll. At the same time, there would be significant changes to admissions regulations obliging all schools subsequently to admit pupils to their full capacity.

The third major change introduced in the late 1980s involved the creation of a new tier of secondary schooling comprising city technology colleges (CTCs) and grant-maintained (GM) or 'opted-out' schools. With their emphasis on technical and practical work, CTCs were to be completely independent of local authority control. Similarly, GM schools were those secondary and large primary schools where a requisite proportion of parents voted to remove the school from the control of the local authority.

The politics of choice, 1990–7

Having replaced Margaret Thatcher as Conservative leader and Prime Minister in November 1990, John Major had the difficult task of coping with the many shortcomings and unforeseen consequences of the 1988 Education Act. (For an overview of education policy under Major, see Dorey, 1999a) With regard to the National Curriculum, for example, there was much professional opposition to the cruder forms of testing of 7-, 11- and 14-year-olds, and Ron Dearing's 1993 Review was confidently expected to find ways of 'slimming down' the Curriculum, particularly at Key Stage Four.

Meanwhile, a White Paper entitled *Choice and Diversity: A New Framework for Schools*, published in July 1992, painted a glowing picture of the new education system that the Conservatives were creating. It claimed that since Margaret Thatcher's election victory in May 1979, five great themes had characterized educational change in England and Wales: quality, diversity, increasing parental choice, greater autonomy for schools and greater accountability (Department for Education, 1992: 3).

Yet this was to ignore the many obstacles that the reform programme was facing. An important aspect of the CTC initiative, launched in 1986, was the expectation that private sector sponsors would be forthcoming to contribute to the heavy capital and running costs. Yet this did not prove to be the case, and whereas it had been anticipated that 20 such colleges would be open by 1990, only 15 eventually got off the ground.

It had also been hoped that large numbers of schools, and particularly those in Labour-controlled local authorities, would rush to opt for 'grant-maintained' status. Yet by the time of the April 1992 general election, there had been only 428 decisive 'opt-out' ballots in England and Wales, with voters in only 331 schools voting in favour, and parents in the remaining 97 schools voting against. In Scotland, no school had opted to go 'grant maintained'.

Choice and Diversity: A New Framework for Schools tried to tackle this lack of enthusiasm for the Government's changes. For example, to build on the work of the 15 CTCs, there was to be a new network of secondary schools with enhanced technology facilities, to be known as either 'technology schools' or 'technology colleges'. Moreover, any institution wishing to become one of these new-technology establishments would do so as a 'grant-maintained' school. At the same time, new 'grant-maintained' schools could be created in response to parental demand, and on the basis of local proposals, thereby paving the way for the establishment of state-funded schools aiming to foster, for example,

Muslim, Buddhist or evangelical Christian beliefs, or wishing to promote particular educational philosophies.

This was also the time when the idea of specialist schools was being promoted by the Major Governments as a means of circumventing the comprehensive principle. The need for all Socialists to come to terms with the concept of specialization at the secondary level was, in fact, the theme of an article by Education Secretary John Patten in *New Statesman and Society* published in July 1992:

> Selection is not, and should not be, a great issue for the 1990s as it was in the 1960s. The S-word for all Socialists to come to terms with is, rather, 'specialisation'. The fact is that children excel at different things; it is foolish to ignore it, and some schools may wish specifically to cater for these differences. Specialisation, underpinned by the National Curriculum, will be the answer for *some* – though not *all* – children, driven by aptitude and interest, as much as by ability. (Patten, 1992: 20)

By the time of the 1997 general election, the national picture at the secondary level was one of extraordinary diversity and confusion, with many local authorities unable to operate anything resembling a coherent admissions strategy. There were still 164 grammar schools in England and Wales, together with 1,155 opted-out schools, accounting for 19.6 per cent of pupils in the secondary sector, 15 CTCs as originally conceived in the late 1980s, 30 new Colleges specializing in modern languages and 151 new Colleges specializing in technology. At the same time many 'comprehensive' schools, and particularly those situated in inner-city areas, were hardly worthy of the appellation.

Education and New Labour

On 1 May 1997, Tony Blair's 'New' Labour Party gained a landslide general election victory which brought to an end 18 years of Conservative rule in Britain. Securing 43 per cent of the national vote, its 419 MPs gave it a remarkable House of Commons majority over all other parties of 179. With just 31 per cent of the national vote and only 165 MPs, the Conservatives put up their most dismal general election performance since their defeat at the hands of Sir Henry Campbell-Bannerman's Liberal Party in January 1906.

Throughout the election campaign, Tony Blair had repeatedly stressed that 'education, education, education' were to be 'the top three priorities' of a New Labour government; and this was also the message that the Party was anxious to put across in the 1997 New Labour Election Manifesto *Because Britain Deserves Better* (Labour Party, 1997).

In the course of a five-page introduction to the Manifesto by Tony Blair himself, it was argued that Britain *could* and *must* be better: with 'better schools, better hospitals, better ways of tackling crime, of building a modern welfare state, of equipping ourselves to be a new world economy'. With education as 'the number one priority', the Party would 'increase the share of national income spent on education', while decreasing it on 'the bills of economic and social failure' (Labour Party, 1997: 1, 5).

While admitting that Tony Blair's Government had a difficult inheritance where education was concerned, it also has to be conceded that the new administration was unable or unwilling to make a *decisive* break with the past. Even before the election, it was emphasized that, in the event of a Labour victory, several key personnel would remain in their posts at the major education quangos set up by the Conservatives: Anthea Millett at the TTA (Teacher Training Agency), which back in 1994 the Labour Party had promised to abolish on coming to power; Nicholas Tate at the QCA (Qualifications and Curriculum Authority); and, most controversially of all, Chris Woodhead, an outspoken figure commanding, it must be said, very little respect within the teaching profession, at Ofsted (Office for Standards in Education), which had been established by the 1992 Education Act as a new independent body responsible for contracting teams to inspect all state primary and secondary schools. In his 2002 book *Class War*, Mr Woodhead attacked the notion that, under his leadership, Ofsted inspections invariably placed an intolerable strain on schools and teachers: 'If Ofsted has a fault, it is not that it has been too critical of schools and teachers; it is that too often it has bent over backwards to be too kind' (Woodhead, 2002: 20).

In July 1997, just 67 days after the general election, the Department for Education and Employment published an 84-page White Paper *Excellence in Schools*, setting out the education programme for the lifetime of a parliament (Department for Education and Employment, 1997), and here the main emphasis was on primary-school standards. There would now be challenging national targets for the performance of all 11-year-olds in English and maths. By the year 2002, 80 per cent of the age group would have to reach the standards expected for their age in English and 75 per cent the required standards in maths. Each primary school would be expected to devote a structured hour a day to literacy from September 1998 and a similar hour a day to numeracy from September 1999. While many teachers welcomed this new commitment to the raising of standards, there were genuine fears that this new emphasis on basic skills could easily result in the marginalization of the more aesthetic and creative areas of the primary curriculum.

As far as the secondary sector was concerned, it was *not* the Government's policy to abolish the remaining grammar schools; and the 1997 White Paper made it clear that the fate of individual selective schools would be decided by ballots of local parents, and not by LEAs. This naturally angered those comprehensive-school campaigners who had confidently expected that there would be no 11-plus selection under a Labour Government. When the first ballot on the future of a grammar school was, in fact, held in March 2000 with reference to the long-term future of Ripon Grammar School in north Yorkshire, the parents eligible to vote decided by a majority of around two to one to reject the proposition that 'henceforth, the School be required to admit children "of all abilities"'. And just two days after the announcement of these voting figures, Education Secretary David Blunkett gave an interview to *The Sunday Telegraph* in which he left his readers in no doubt that it was time to 'bury the dated arguments of previous decades' and reverse 'the outright opposition to grammars' that had regrettably been 'a touchstone of Labour politics for at least 35 years':

I'm not interested in hunting the grammar schools. ... I'm desperately trying to avoid the whole debate in education once again, as was the case in the 1960s and 1970s, concentrating on the issue of selection, when it *should* be concentrating on the raising of standards. ... Arguments about selection are part of a past agenda. (*The Sunday Telegraph*, 12 March 2000)

It was the policy of the new Government that there should, in fact, be *three* types of secondary school: community, aided and foundation. Community schools would be based on the existing county schools; aided schools would be based on the existing voluntary-aided schools; and foundation schools would offer a new 'bridge' between the powers available to secular and those enjoyed by church schools. These three categories were designed to embrace all local authority and grant-maintained schools; and it was confidently expected that foundation-school status would have a particular attraction for most, if not all, GM establishments.

Most important of all as far as the structure of the new system was concerned, the Government decided to continue with the Conservative policy of fostering specialist secondary schools. The 1997 White Paper emphasized that there would be an extensive network of such schools developing their own distinctive identity and expertise. These would initially focus on technology, languages, sports or arts, and would be expected to act as a resource for local people and neighbouring schools to draw on. A later White Paper with the title *Schools Achieving Success*, published in September 2001 (Department for Education and Skills, 2001), predicted that there would be at least 1,000 specialist schools in operation by September 2003 and at least 1,500 by the year 2005. Four new specialisms that such schools would be able to offer comprised: engineering, science, business and enterprise, and mathematics and computing.

The latest major government policy document covering all sectors of education, entitled *Five Year Strategy for Children and Learners*, was published on 8 July 2004 (Department for Education and Skills, 2004a). Here it was emphasized that choice and diversity at the secondary level would be enhanced by the rapid expansion of *two* types of school: specialist schools and city academies. The number of specialist schools and colleges had already increased from 196 when New Labour came to power to 1,955 in the summer of 2004; and it was envisaged that there would be a further massive expansion over the following four years. The specialisms available to these specialist schools now covered 10 main curriculum areas: technology, arts, sports, sciences, languages, maths and computing, business and enterprise, engineering, humanities and music, with by far the largest number of schools (545) specializing in various forms of technology. Meanwhile five types of specialist school – those specializing in technology, arts, sports, languages and music – could select up to 10 per cent of their pupils on grounds of aptitude. With regard to city academies, it was anticipated that the number of these schools – 17 in September 2004 – would have increased to 200 by the year 2010. These academies, clearly modelled on the Conservatives' City Technology Colleges Project, were designed to be sponsored by business entrepreneurs, faith groups or private schools. Taken together, specialist schools and city academies would account for at least 95 per cent of all state secondaries by the year 2008.

One important area where there have been signs of interesting and positive developments in recent years concerns provision for the 14-to-19 age group. There was much regret that, following the recommendations of the 1993 Dearing Review and more recent amendments, Key Stage Four of the National Curriculum came to consist of only English, maths and science of the original 10 subjects, with the later addition of ICT, citizenship, religious education, sex education, careers education and PE. Yet, to set against this, we had the prospect of radical proposals emanating from a major review of qualifications for older students launched in January 2003 and carried out by Mike Tomlinson, a former

Chief Inspector of Schools. When the Final Report of the Working Group was published on 18 October 2004, it recommended the introduction of a broad 'baccalaureate-style' diploma designed to replace GCSEs and A levels, improve parity of esteem between academic and vocational courses and broaden access to higher education (Department for Education and Skills, 2004b). Unfortunately, the White Paper on the 14–19 curriculum, *14–19 Education and Skills*, published by the newly-appointed Education Secretary Ruth Kelly on 23 February 2005, rejected the Tomlinson Report's main proposal for a four-tier overarching diploma embracing all academic and vocational qualifications and opted instead to retain GCSEs and A levels largely in their present form. It did accept the need for a rationalization of vocational qualifications, with the replacement of the existing 'alphabet soup' of 3,500 separate qualifications by a three-tier system of 'specialized' diplomas in just 14 occupational areas (Department for Education and Skills, 2005).

Conclusion

There have been four Education Secretaries over the period of the two Blair administrations (1997–2005): David Blunkett (1997–2001), Estelle Morris (2001–2), Charles Clarke (2002–4) and, since December 2004, Ruth Kelly. Blunkett and Clarke are clearly politicians of considerable stature, though it is fair to say that at all times under New Labour, as was the case with previous Labour and Conservative administrations, the Downing Street Policy Unit has had a very important role to play in long-term policy making. Here the key figure is now Andrew Adonis who was appointed to advise the Policy Unit on education matters in 1998, became Head of the Unit after the 2001 general election, and, while stepping down from that position in 2003, has continued to take a keen interest in education policy formulation in particular, together with the wider issue of ensuring diversity of provision in all areas of the public sector. In a recent article in the *Education Guardian* (1 March 2005), Professor Ted Wragg has argued that Andrew Adonis and his colleagues in the Policy Unit even played a key role in persuading the Prime Minister of the need to reject the Tomlinson Report. Following Labour's 2005 election victory, Adonis was appointed as a junior (Education) Minister.

At the end of an admittedly brief survey of some of the main issues, it is not easy to summarize the fundamental set of beliefs underpinning New Labour's education agenda over the past eight years. Despite the occasional use of the rhetoric of 'inclusion', there is really very little that distinguishes New Labour policy from that of John Major's Conservative Party so decisively beaten in the 1997 general election. There is the same emphasis on teacher accountability, on the overriding importance of fostering choice and competition and, at the secondary level, on a form of selection by specialization. Above all, the importance attached to standards, targets and examination results encourages a view of schooling which is obsessed with outcomes, and has very little to say about ways of enhancing the quality of the learning process for all children.

4 Foreign Policy
Steve Marsh

Introduction

After the Second World War, Britain had to make practical and psychological adjustments to accelerated relative decline, whilst contending also with the implications of deepening interdependence, and a rapid transition from wartime 'victory' to the cold peace of the bipolar era. The challenges therein for British foreign policy makers and the foreign policy-making system can scarcely be overstated. Commitments far outweighed capabilities. Traditional trade routes had been distorted or lost. Rising nationalism in the developing world challenged British imperial possessions. The emergence of the United States (US) and Union of Soviet Socialist Republics (USSR) as two superpowers overtly reduced Britain's stature as a Great Power. Europe was too close to ignore but integration with Europe potentially threatened British sovereignty and foreign policy autonomy. Meanwhile, the process of globalization, and the rising influence of non-state actors, challenged traditional 'realist' foreign policy perspectives and blurred divisions between high and low politics, and between the realms of domestic and foreign policy.

This chapter aims to provide insights into the key trends and transformations in post-war British foreign policy. In doing so it acknowledges the compelling explanatory power of the declinist thesis, but seeks also to consider the influence of structural changes, along with the impact which policy makers' perceptions of the world had on foreign policy, and of Britain's role therein. The first of three sections consequently delineates some broad structural factors that impinged significantly on British foreign policy and policy making. The second section examines Britain's foreign policy during the Cold War in the context of Churchill's famous three circles, namely Britain's relationships with the US, the Commonwealth/Empire and Europe. The final section assesses the main themes of post-Cold War British foreign policy. How far have globalist foreign policy traditions survived Britain's demotion from the top table to medium-sized power, and has Britain found a post-imperial role?

British foreign policy and challenges from without

British foreign policy and policy making since 1945 have been moulded by a variety of forces that have lain largely beyond the control of policy makers themselves. Consideration is given here to four of them: relative decline, international systemic change, technology, and processes of globalization and deepening interdependence. Of these, Britain's relative decline has dominated the discourse of post-war British foreign policy.

Britain's relative decline

Britain's relative supremacy arguably peaked in the mid-Victorian era, when it accounted for 40 per cent of world trade in manufactured goods, around 20 per cent of Europe's GNP and about 50 per cent of the world's iron and steel production. The advantages of Britain's early industrialization, coupled with an era in which sea-power was supreme, also enabled it to control one-fifth of the world's land surface backed by a fleet that comprised half of the world's warships. This position was never likely to be sustainable in the long term, given Britain's dependence on overseas trade, deficiencies in key natural resources, physical distance from its empire and the industrialization of other countries (Reynolds, 1991: 9–12). The latter reduced relative British power, raised the costs of maintaining empire and, by challenging British maritime power and control over the sea-lanes, threatened to sever the arteries to Britain's industrial heart.

The impact of the Second World War on Britain's relative decline was actually equivocal. The cost and implications of Britain's sustained war effort were enormous, especially for a country traditionally dependent on overseas trade and investment. By 1945 its exports were 30 per cent of the 1939 total, import prices had risen 50 per cent and there were acute shortages of raw materials, industrial equipment and labour. Britain's war campaign had forced the Government to liquidate £1,118,00 million of overseas assets, incur huge debts (including £2,143 million to the Sterling Area alone) and allow its gold and dollar reserves to be more than halved. Britain was economically dependent on another power for the first time in its history, and following the abrupt termination of Lend–Lease, the Attlee Government had to accept the humiliating 1946 US loan, which lent Britain over $3.5 billion at 2 per cent interest. Indeed, the war dramatically weakened Britain's relative position *vis-à-vis* the US, which emerged from the conflict with a monopoly on the atomic bomb, and the most advanced military–industrial complex in the world (Dobson and Marsh, 2001: 46).

However, Britain's relative decline was neither a linear nor a necessarily inexorable process. Despite all its hardships, and America's rise to superpower status, Britain actually emerged from the Second World War in a stronger relative position than before it. British military power and political stability were second only to the US in the West, and the same was true of Britain's economic position. For instance, in 1950 Britain accounted for 25.5 per cent of world exports of manufactured goods, a market share that was up from 21.3 per cent in 1937 and equivalent to more than two-and-a-half times that of France and three times that of West Germany (Chalmers, 1985: 126). Moreover, by the end of the war, Britain had redeemed most of the losses incurred to its empire during the early years of conflict (Darwin, 1988: 43–4).

Blessed with hindsight and the assiduous work of diplomatic historians, it seems almost delusional for Foreign Secretary Ernest Bevin to have believed, in October 1948, that 'if we only pushed on and developed Africa, we could have the United States dependent on us, and eating out of our hand, in four or five years …' (Gallagher, 1982: 146). Yet policy makers view events through the prisms of their own experience and precepts, and for those overseeing post-war British foreign policy this generally meant Britain as a Great Power along with its traditions of empire and a global role. This expectation was reinforced by an Executive endowed with considerable constitutional independence in external relations, general bipartisanship in British foreign policy and a career civil service largely impervious to the rise and fall of governments.

In addition, there were the difficulties in addressing an unpredictable process of relative decline on the basis of incomplete and fragmented information. The latter afflicts all foreign policy makers but posed British policy makers greater problems given a fragmented bureaucracy and the enormity of British overseas activities. For instance, the Foreign Office was responsible for Britain's relations with foreign states and international organizations, but until 1947 the country's imperial relationships were divided between the India Office, the Dominions Office and the Colonial Office. The eventual rationalization of responsibilities through the creation of the Foreign and Commonwealth Office in 1968 symbolized Britain's dwindling empire, but the management of external affairs was concomitantly complicated by the growing number of government departments involved therein – especially after Britain's entry into the European Communities in 1973.[1]

Understanding British foreign policy since 1945 also requires an appreciation of the international context in which relative decline had to be managed and British interests pursued. Allied planning for the post-war international order was predicated on continued co-operation between, in particular, the US, Britain and the USSR. International security was to be provided through the United Nations (UN), the idealistic collective security apparatus which was underpinned by a Security Council that reflected realist power politics. Britain, France, China, the US and USSR were permanent veto-wielding members, and there was an unwritten concession to spheres of interests in that each was expected to have primary responsibility, working through the UN, for its own area. However, the wartime Allied triumvirate of Roosevelt, Stalin and Churchill was quickly broken and mutual suspicions about post-war intentions deepened. The Soviets resented exclusion from the occupation of Japan, feared the contagion of Western capitalism, felt insecure on account of US monopoly of the atomic bomb and objected to Western interference in what they regarded as justifiable efforts to establish a security perimeter in Eastern Europe. Britain and the US feared Kremlin-inspired communist subversion across Europe, regarded Soviet handling of Poland as reneging on agreements made at Yalta in early 1945, and were alarmed by Stalin's truculent call for Soviet rearmament in February 1946, coupled with his initial refusal to withdraw from northern Iran. In fact, Britain was quicker than the US to adopt a strong line against the Soviet Union; something epitomized by Churchill's famous speech at Fulton, Missouri, on 5 March 1946, in which he warned of an iron curtain having descended from Stettin in the Baltic to Trieste in the Adriatic. (For an account of Britain's central role in the development of the Cold War, and recognition of this after an initial tendency to portray it as an exclusively US–Soviet affair, see Deighton, 1990, and Maier, 1996).

The onset of this Cold War helped determine the contours of British foreign policy for decades to come. It delimited Britain's geo-strategic sphere of action and provided a beguiling rationale for a continuing global role that maintained Britain's traditional sense of special status, and allowed the containment of communism to be seen as synonymous with the

---

1 This was the collective name, following the entry into force in 1967 of the Merger Treaty, for the European Coal and Steel Community, European Economic Community and the European Atomic Energy Community.

preservation of British overseas interests and commitments. In some respects, it also accorded British foreign policy more influence, especially *vis-à-vis* the US, than would have been the case had the envisaged post-war peace been co-operatively established and successfully maintained. For instance, Germany's potential power was limited following its division after the 1948 Berlin crisis, and the spectre of the Soviet threat enabled successive British governments to justify to the electorate the peacetime allocation of considerable proportions of stretched resources to rearmament and military strength. Moreover, British foreign policy became locked into maintaining commitments well beyond Britain's capabilities by the combination of genuine concern about the Soviet threat, and the need to convince allies and enemies alike of British determination to uphold their interests and honour their overseas obligations. As was observed in a Cabinet paper in the summer of 1952, 'once the prestige of a country has started to slide, there is no knowing where it will stop' (PRO CAB 129 C(52) 202, 'British Overseas Obligations', 18 June 1952).

International systemic change

International systemic change again re-shaped the contours of British foreign policy when the implosion of the USSR and the 'velvet revolutions' that swept across Europe 1989–91 signalled the end of the bipolar/bipolycentric era. British foreign policy had thereafter to be devised and implemented in an incipient multipolar international order that was significantly less predictable than that of the bipolar era, the latter having dramatically reduced potential conflict dyads and provided stability through Mutually Assured Destruction. For a start, Britain needed a new rationale to underpin a continuing global foreign policy, and to pursue this in recognition that it had been reduced to a medium-ranking state in an international system dominated by the US hyper-power. The radically different geo-strategic topography invited and demanded that Britain develop foreign relations with countries of the former Soviet bloc whilst protecting established alliance structures. This was especially true of the North Atlantic Treaty Organisation (NATO), which was the premier vehicle for tying the US to Europe but for which the collapse of the Soviet Union seemingly denied a *raison d'être*. Furthermore, the new security agenda affected the appropriate instruments of British foreign policy in terms both of their application and sustainability. Military force, for instance, became less easy to deploy once stripped of anti-communist legitimization and as the focus switched to soft security, which emphasized the importance of economic and diplomatic tools to promote a New World Order. In addition, political difficulties increased in justifying expenditure to sustain military capabilities and replace obsolete Cold War platforms in the absence of an identifiable military threat.

Technology

Technology is another factor that impacted significantly upon post-war British foreign policy, of which perhaps the most obvious example is the development of weapons of mass destruction (WMD). Anglo-American wartime collaboration produced the first atomic bomb, but Britain was denied possession of it by the US 'nuclear betrayal', whereby it reneged on the 1943 Quebec Agreement to share the bomb, and terminated all meaningful Anglo-American atomic co-operation upon the authority of the 1946 McMahon Act. Britain's decision in 1947 to develop its own nuclear deterrent was thus unsurprising, but its reasons ran much deeper than pique, and are revealing of technology's impact on British foreign policy. Atomic weapons potentially offset deficiencies in British conventional forces and were a source of great prestige. As Bevin put it, 'We've got to have the bloody Union Jack flying on top of it [the atomic bomb]' (Bullock, 1983: 352). Being in the elite club of atomic powers, which it achieved in October 1952, was a way of retaining Britain's Great Power ranking, and projecting the expectation of British supremacy in its efforts to maintain its overseas interests. Also, British officials quickly perceived the diplomatic advantages of possessing the atomic bomb and of restricting access to atomic technology. Churchill, for instance, had argued, during the Second World War, for Anglo-American monopoly of the bomb, and rejected notions that international control over atomic energy could be used as a cornerstone for a peaceful post-war order (Sherwin, 1994: 85). Furthermore, the development of even more powerful WMD, coupled with Britain's nuclear strike force of long-range V-bombers, began to negate the strategic disadvantages of Britain's small size and dense population clusters. Herein, Britain's becoming the third thermonuclear power in May 1957 was seen as a great leveller, as the destructive power of the H-bomb increased massively to the two continent-wide superpowers the risks of nuclear war.

British diplomacy and relative influence within the Western Alliance were also affected significantly by atomic weaponry. Atomic capability reinforced Britain's ranking second only to the US, and British influence in Washington was enhanced by their importance in making the West's atomic arsenal a credible threat – at least until such time that missile technology phased out the necessity of aircraft delivery of nuclear weapons (see Bell, 1964: 8; Manderson-Jones, 1972; Campbell, 1984). Hence the Foreign Office argued, in January 1950, that the stationing of American B-29 bombers equipped with atomic weapons on British soil was fully consonant with the primary objective of keeping the US firmly committed to Europe: 'We must face the fact that this island is strategically well placed as an advanced air base and that we must accept this role' (quoted in Reynolds, 1991: 180–1). Unsurprisingly, Britain's consequent increased vulnerability to nuclear attack inclined British diplomacy towards the USSR to minimize East–West tension and seek opportunities for dialogue, which frequently put Britain at odds with the US. For instance, in 1951 American policy makers detected 'a basic difference in our points of view'. The US wanted to establish a position of overwhelming strength *vis-à-vis* the USSR before negotiating but, with Britain being what Churchill described as an 'aircraft carrier' (cited in Colville, 1985: 636), British policy makers were unwilling to forgo either negotiations with the Soviets, or efforts to restrain aggressive American posturing (for examples of British concerns, see Moran, 1966: 410, 444, diary entries for 25 June and 25 July 1953).

Globalization and deepening interdependence

Finally, post-war British foreign policy had to adapt to processes of globalization and conditions of deepening interdependence. Herein, traditional realist perspectives of international relations were challenged by, amongst other things, the development and growing influence of international organizations, international regimes and non-governmental actors such as multinational corporations. Consider, for example, foreign policy makers' sensitivity about the importance of British international oil companies. It was estimated in

1944 that a failure to control oil imports would require Britain to find approximately a further $100 million per year of foreign exchange, and six years later the Economic Relations Department concluded that 'we depend upon the British oil industry to an alarming extent to maintain our favourable balance of payments ...' (Harry S. Truman Library (HST), R.K. Davies papers, box 13, folder 2, Anglo-American Oil Treaty 1945–7, Summary of the Minutes of the Joint Subcommittee, 26 July to 1 August 1944; PRO, FO 371/82377, minute by P.E. Ramsbotham, 22 November 1950; Darby, 1973: 25). It is thus striking that when the Anglo-Iranian Oil Company became embroiled in a bitter nationalization dispute with Iran in 1949, government officials sprang to its defence and demonstrated extreme reluctance to interfere in its management of the issue, despite provision for this in its Articles of Association (for details, see Marsh, 2001).

British control over foreign relations under conditions of interdependence has also been affected by Britain's membership of international organizations. For example, obligations under the General Agreement on Tariffs and Trade (GATT), and subsequently the World Trade Organization (WTO), set parameters of British international trade policy, and impacted significantly on domestic economic policy, such as growing restrictions on measures to protect sunset or infant industries.

The effects of Britain's membership of European Communities (EC)/European Union (EU) have been even more significant and wide-ranging. Many aspects of British foreign economic policy have been pooled at the supranational EC level and, although many other external relations activities remain largely intergovernmentally controlled, they are increasingly co-ordinated with fellow EU members through common procedures and interface with EC institutions, especially the European Commission. In Development Policy, for instance, there is parallel competence whereby British and EC policies run alongside, and are complementary to, one another (with the EC contribution to development policy amounting to approximately 4 per cent of its budget). British foreign policy itself, whilst resisting communitaurization, has been progressively 'Brusselized' through first European Political Co-operation (EPC) and then the EU's Common Foreign and Security Policy (CFSP). The latter continued the EPC practice of non-binding declaratory diplomacy, issuing common statements, declarations and *démarches,* but also developed potentially stronger and legally binding instruments such as Common Positions and Joint Actions.

British foreign policy making has also been significantly changed by Britain's EU membership, the communications revolution and the blurring of the foreign and domestic policy realms. Agenda-setting, for example, has become subject to considerations of multilateral fora to which Britain is party, and to the so-called CNN effect, the idea that a press endowed with real-time communications technology is partially able to drive foreign policy responses (for an interesting discussion of this, and a guide to further reading, see Robinson, 1999). Also, the balance of power and number of actors involved in British foreign policy making has changed significantly. Studies in the 1960s and early 1970s emphasized the dominance of a core of institutions comprising the Board of Trade, Ministry of Defence, the FCO and the Treasury. Today, though, there is a sense in which everything has become internationalized, and the policy process more permeable. Lying at the confluence of the foreign and the domestic, the Cabinet Office has wrested significant power from the FCO, whilst a multiplicity of formerly domestic departments have become players in external relations. Consider, for instance, the increasing international role of the former Ministry of Agriculture, Fisheries and Food (replaced in 2001 by the Department of the Environment, Food and Rural Affairs – DEFRA) that developed not least due to the EC's Common Agricultural Policy (CAP) and Common Fisheries Policy (Vital, 1968; Wallace, 1975; Murphy, 2001; Richards and Smith, 2002: 152–3).

British Cold War foreign policy

The Anglo-American 'special relationship'

The most immediately important of Churchill's three circles in the aftermath of the Second World War was the so-called Anglo-American Special Relationship, within which co-operation during the war had been unprecedented for nation-states – ranging from intelligence collaboration and command over each other's troops and through to ground-breaking research on the atom bomb. For some British foreign policy makers, notably Churchill, the term 'Special Relationship' was both prescriptive and descriptive (Reynolds, 1988–9: 95). It was rooted in shared values, historical experiences and a common language, which in turn meant that there should be close transatlantic collaboration in combating common enemies and pursuing common objectives. Others were more instrumental in their calculations of 'specialness', but were equally convinced of the importance of close Anglo-American relations. National security demanded that the US remain militarily entangled in Europe, especially given the parlous state of West European continental forces, the size of the Soviet army and precipitate post-war American demobilization. Close Anglo-American co-operation could likewise discourage White House manipulation of what was initially assumed to be Britain's temporary economic weakness, and assist attempts to manage the mismatch between Britain's overseas commitments and capabilities – commonly termed 'overstretch'. Herein the US would ideally tolerate British discriminatory practices, such as the Sterling Area, support established British overseas interests and allow British policy makers quietly to offload unsustainable burdens without giving the impression of British weakness.

These aspirations initially seemed unrealistic when Anglo-American relations cooled in the immediate aftermath of the Second World War. Reasons for this include the US loan, unbridled American pursuit of international free trade, severe differences over the Palestine question and the 'nuclear betrayal'. More generally, Britain was a declining Great Power resolved upon a broadly status quo foreign policy, whilst the US was an emergent superpower keen to expand its economic interests and emboldened by its new-found dominance within Anglo-American relations. It has, for example, been argued that nuclear relations, if taken in isolation, 'would present a depressing picture of a superpower playing with a satellite' (Gowing, 1974: 320). (For analysis of early post-war Anglo-American atomic relations, see also Pierre (1972) and Gormly (1984)).

The eventual viability of Churchill's first circle therefore owed much to the Cold War. George Kennan's famous Long Telegram in 1946 (the text is in Kennan, 1968: Appendix C, pp. 547–59) provided an ideological and a *realpolitik* basis for a US policy of containing communist expansionism, and the subsequent Truman doctrine signalled American determination to do so. The European Recovery Programme (Marshall Aid) and passage of the Vandenberg Resolution followed in quick succession, and National Security Council

Resolution 68 in 1950 shifted containment policy from a primarily European to a global level. Crucially for British foreign policy, this persuaded American policy makers once more to acknowledge that Britain, of all US allies, was 'in a special or preferred position – the facts of the world situation require it' (Washington National Archives (NA), RG 59, box 2768, H.R. Labouisse Jr to Perkins, 27 February 1950, p. 4). (For an overview of containment see Dobson and Marsh, 2001: 18–45. For interpretations of NSC-68, see May, 1993. For details of containment, see especially Leffler, 1972; Yergin, 1977; Gaddis, 1982.) After all, British production far exceeded that of other European countries, its military power remained substantial, it occupied a strategically vital position, and it exercised crucial political and economic influence in Western Europe, the Near East and Southeast Asia, and through the Commonwealth and the Sterling Area.

The reaffirmation of the Special Relationship as the single most important relationship within the Western Alliance enabled Britain to regain some of its lost influence in Washington and created opportunities to harness American might to British ends. The centrality of Britain and America in devising the post-war international order meant that their power, and therefore potentially also their bilateral relationship, was institutionalized through mechanisms such as the UN Security Council, NATO, the Bretton Woods system and the GATT. This partnership was reinforced by their economic interdependence. For example, sterling was a reserve currency for the Bretton Woods system, the US overtook Australia in 1956 as Britain's biggest export market and concern for Anglo-American economic relations was an important factor in the US subordinating 'the immediate enforcement of multilateralism to the political and economic interests of the western world' (Gardner, 1980: 346).

However, the keystone of Anglo-American co-operation was the defence alliance. This was wide-ranging, multilayered and often exclusive, especially in the sharing of intelligence and military technology. For instance, the July 1958 US Atomic Energy Act restored the special nuclear relationship previously curtailed by the McMahon Act. Also, Britain afforded the US key and sometimes controversial bases and facilities – both in the homeland, such as the Fylingdales (North Yorkshire) early warning centre and the Polaris submarine base at Holy Loch (Scotland), and abroad, including Ascension Island and Diego Garcia. Such closeness was mirrored by Macmillan unexpectedly securing, from President Kennedy, Polaris missiles in 1962, the deployment of cruise missiles in Britain in 1984 and Margaret Thatcher's stance on the Westland affair in 1986 (for an account of the latter, see Leigh and Linklater, 1986; Oliver and Austin, 1987; Dunleavy, 1995b).

Britain undoubtedly benefited significantly throughout the Cold War from the Anglo-American relationship. The US provided repeated economic relief, not least because interdependence calculations often left American policy makers little alternative. For instance, Brien McMahon, Chairman of the Joint Committee on Atomic Energy, noted in December 1951 that: 'Mr Churchill says publicly that he is not coming over here to seek American funds. This is, of course, nonsense – he has no choice but to solicit more money, and we have little choice except to give it to him' (*FRUS* 1952–54, 6, part one, Chairman of the Joint Committee on Atomic Energy (McMahon) to President, 5 December 1951, pp. 695–8).

Britain was also able to transfer discreetly to American shoulders onerous and unsustainable burdens, such as responsibility for Greece and Turkey in the late 1940s. This was important both because the US was Britain's foremost ally, and because it helped to maintain the impression of continuing international power and prestige, especially when backed by overt demonstrations of Anglo-American solidarity. As a Cabinet paper acknowledged in 1960, the US would be the only power capable of supporting British interests, and Britain's international status would be increasingly contingent upon American willingness to treat Britain specially (cited by Rees, 2001: 36). Furthermore, the Special Relationship sometimes secured for Britain practical American assistance even where there was no clear rationale for the US to provide it. For example, the Reagan administration afforded Britain vital military and intelligence assets during the Falklands War in 1982, despite the risk of alienating Galtieri's Argentina and other Latin American countries in the fight against communism (Thatcher, 1993: 226–7; see also Weinberger, 1991: 203–17; Richardson, 1996). This was, in part, due to the close personal relationship between Reagan and Thatcher, but also to the traditions of co-operation that made assistance seem almost automatic, one commentator noting that '[s]ome of the most crucial assistance came clandestinely on the Old Pals network between senior members of the Intelligence Service' (Dickie, 1994: 5).

Yet for all the advantages Britain secured from the Special Relationship, it was rarely an easy foreign policy option. The closeness of the relationship ebbed and flowed depending on personal relationships between Anglo-American leaders, the ideological similarity or otherwise of the political parties in power, the priorities pursued by both sides and specific issues. For instance, Thatcher prioritized the Special Relationship and developed a personal friendship with Reagan 'which was as close as any imaginable between two major leaders' (Shultz, 1993: 153–4; see also Young, 1990: 561), whereas Edward Heath looked first to Europe, and had an awkward relationship with Nixon. Britain's overwhelming concern about its economic weakness and overstretch frequently encountered American willingness to sacrifice British economic interests upon the altar of anti-communism. Examples of this include the Anglo-Iranian oil crisis, China policy, strategic embargo policy, and the application of extra-territorial sanctions – such as the Siberian oil pipeline crisis in the early 1980s, about which Thatcher 'continuously harangued the President and his advisers' (Dobson, 2002: 267; for further details of the pipeline crisis, see Blinkin, 1987; Thatcher, 1993: 253–6). There were also numerous specific issues of great tension, not least the Skybolt affair, Britain's refusal to commit to the Vietnam War, and Attlee's rush to Washington in 1950 following Truman's intimation that the US might use the atomic bomb in Korea.

Moreover, it was sometimes at American hands that Britain suffered major embarrassment and/or turning points in its retreat from empire. American economic pressure was instrumental in Britain's ignominious abandonment of Anglo-French military intervention in Suez in 1956, initiated in response to the nationalization of the Suez Canal by Nasser's Egypt (for one of the many accounts of the Suez episode, see Louis and Owen, 1989). The 1976 sterling crisis likewise saw Britain incur severe damage to its prestige when American refusal to help Callaghan's Labour Government compelled the latter to issue an infamous letter of intent in order to secure a £2.3 billion loan from the IMF, which was granted only on condition that the Cabinet impose a range of public expenditure cuts. Even the Thatcher–Reagan relationship was not immune from America embarrassing Britain, the most obvious example being the US invasion of Grenada in October 1983. How was

Thatcher supposed to explain that a Commonwealth member had been invaded by Britain's closest ally: '[a]t best, the British Government had been made to look impotent; at worst we looked deceitful' (Thatcher, 1993: 330–2; Howe, 1994: 327–36).

The Anglo-American relationship was not an inexpensive option either. British policy makers wanted a quantitatively as well as qualitatively Special Relationship with the US, which demanded that Washington should need to consult London as often as possible. However, this helped to lock Britain into a 'Great Power illusion' that has since been criticized for unduly slowing economic reform and the downsizing of commitments sufficient to correct over-stretch (see, for example, Barnett, 1987: 304). Firstly, British influence in Washington was believed to depend significantly on Britain maintaining its overseas interests and obligations. This helps explain, for instance, British sacrifices during the 1960s to try to maintain a strong pound sterling in line with its reserve currency function within the Bretton Woods system. It is also reflected in differential British influence over American foreign policy, ranging in the 1950s and 1960s, for instance, from significant in the Middle East and Europe through to very limited in the Far East. Secondly, as former British Ambassador to the US Robert Renwick observed, for Britain '[t]he price of consultation has always been presence and participation' (Renwick, 1996: 394). This included the deployment of troops alongside US forces, such as in Korea and in the Lebanon in 1982, the provision of military bases and intelligence and a willingness to support the US even in the face of international opinion – as Thatcher did for Reagan during 'Irangate'.

The Commonwealth and empire

While British policy makers accepted the substantial economic and political costs of pursuing the American 'circle' during the Cold War, it was to the Commonwealth/empire that many initially looked as the means to secure Britain's long-term economic well-being, and even to restore Britain to the top table of global powers. This was an instinctive response given Britain's imperial past, but also a pragmatic one given extant trade patterns, established overseas British bases and influence, the potential resources of the Commonwealth/empire and the emerging Cold War importance of the constituent territories. Equally pragmatic were the different methods that Britain adopted by which to exchange the formal trappings of empire for influence, including nation-building, British-supervised constitutionalism, the granting of independence and reform of the Commonwealth. Gradual decolonization has been portrayed as a British 'duty to spread to other nations those advantages which through the course of centuries they had won for themselves' (Macmillan, 1972: 116–17), but in reality it was an erratic process geared above all to protecting British overseas bases and influence as best possible. Britain supported colonial nationalists sympathetic to British interests, such as Nkrumah in the Gold Coast, influenced constitutional processes and broke uncooperative elements – such as the Enotists in Cyprus. It also used military force where the stakes were high enough, including in Malaya, where Britain forcibly resettled 400,000 Chinese, and fought a major counter-insurgency war against a communist-inspired insurrection among ethnic Chinese Malays (for details, see Short, 1975).

Britain's first priority was to transform the Middle East into the 'new keep and stronghold' (Reynolds, 1986: 6) of informal empire, not least because of its established regional predominance and America's relatively weak position there. Thus did Labour's Foreign Secretary, Ernest Bevin, deem the Middle East to be 'an area of cardinal importance to the United Kingdom' (PRO CAB 129, CP(50) 264, 'Memorandum for the Cabinet', 8 November 1950). Britain had numerous treaties and agreements with Middle Eastern countries, and the hub of its power was the huge Suez base in Egypt, which in the early 1950s covered 200 square miles and served as home to more than 70,000 troops. In addition, the Royal Navy enjoyed a presence in Malta, Bahrain, Cyprus, Aden and the Suez Canal; and the Royal Air Force had headquarters in Ismailia, and established bases in Bahrain, Sharjah, Masirah, Amman, on the Shatt-el-Arab border and in Iraq at Habbaniya and Shaibah. All of this guarded substantial British economic interests – especially oil, the Suez Canal and air landing and transit rights. For instance, in 1950 sterling oil from Iran and Kuwait was crucial to Britain's balance of payments, industrial growth and defence programmes. In addition, Cold War considerations accorded the Middle East extra strategic significance. It was the link between strong points in the containment perimeter fence in the North Atlantic area and the Pacific Rim of Asia. Moreover, geography and Soviet failure to develop buffer defences in the Middle East akin to those in Europe made the region potentially ideal to host Western military bases.

This combination of economic, Cold War, Great Power and 'special responsibility' considerations provided a beguiling rationale for maintaining as much as possible of the Commonwealth/empire elsewhere too. A macro-consideration was the Sterling Area, which as late as 1960 accounted for over 60 per cent of all British foreign investment. Comprising the dominions (excluding Canada), the colonies and certain associated states, this was effectively an extensive British-led club that openly discriminated against the dollar by collectively excluding dollar imports through dollar rationing, fostering non-dollar trade between members and limiting capital transfers outside of the club (Strange, 1971: 620). As such, the Sterling Area underpinned British claims to continued world economic power and to an autonomous role within an international economy organized around the pre-eminence of the dollar. It also served as a cohesive force within the Commonwealth/empire, reaffirmed British leadership, protected British imperial trade preferences and was potentially invaluable in offsetting Britain's dollar requirements and balance of payments pressure (Holland, 1984: 167–8; Darwin, 1988: 304).

British officials also saw the Commonwealth/empire and the Sterling Area as key elements in their ambitions to operate some sort of autonomous foreign policy, and to influence the White House. Britain's overseas assets provided potentially bountiful supplies of raw materials, which could be used both for Britain, and to influence the US. For instance, in 1948 Malaya had net dollar earnings of $173 million and provided the US with over half of its imported rubber, and nearly all of its tin imports (Reynolds, 1991: 188). The Commonwealth/empire could also counterbalance US preferences for Britain becoming a European power and secure American assistance for wavering British overseas positions. If the Americans wanted Britain to maintain expensive overseas commitments for Cold War purposes, then they would have to make doing so worthwhile – a connection that Churchill explicitly made in 1952 when arguing for an American military presence in the internationally important Suez Canal zone. Furthermore, the Commonwealth/empire was expected to provide troops, bases and facilities for the Cold War in much the same way that they had throughout the Second World War, in spite of India's attainment of independence in 1947. Indeed, arguments were advanced to the effect that '[t]he Commonwealth taken as a unit if, and only if, organised to act quickly together, is perhaps better placed defensively – because of geographical land dispersal – than either Russia or America' ('British Defence Brief', cited by Devereux, 1989: 331).

In the event, Britain's use of its colonies and informal empire to extract American concessions delivered ambiguous results. It ran up against both US anti-colonialism, which was an ongoing sore in Anglo-American relations, and heightened American fears that US association with imperialism would make more difficult the fight for the Cold War allegiance of the developing world, where communist movements were seemingly adept at hijacking national liberation movements. Inviting the US to burden-share in areas of established British interest also required an extraordinarily difficult balancing act, for the US was a competitor as well as an ally. It was, as R.J. Campbell of the British Eastern Department noted, 'a matter of getting the mixture right' ('Memorandum by R.J. Campbell', 9 June 1945, cited in DeNovo, 1976–7: 934; see also Nachmani, 1983). All too often, the US slowly supplanted British interests and contributed to Britain's retreat from empire. For instance, exclusion from ANZUS in 1951 symbolized Britain's Far Eastern decline and the weakening bonds of the Commonwealth (for details, see Williams, 1987).

Nevertheless, the Commonwealth/empire strategy did secure some important American concessions, not least because the US believed that the Commonwealth provided a ready-made structure in the organization of the 'Free World' and that it was of greater political, economic and strategic significance than any other existing group (Marsh, 2003: 35). For instance, the US tolerated the inherent dollar discrimination of the Sterling Area despite the rules of GATT, the IMF and Article VII of the Anglo-American loan agreement. In the early 1950s, it also – given Britain's Middle Eastern military pre-eminence and American fears of over-commitment – largely supported British defence initiatives in the region 'in lieu of a better idea'. It was even argued that part of the rationale for ANZUS was to free-up Commonwealth troops to assist British defence of the Middle East (Devereux, 1990: 250; *FRUS* 1952–4, 9, minutes State-Joint Chiefs of Staff Meeting, 18 June 1952, pp. 237–47; ibid., State Dept. minutes State-Joint Chiefs of Staff Meeting, 28 November 1952, pp. 319–26).

Until the late 1950s, Britain's Commonwealth/empire strategy appeared to work relatively well. Despite Indian independence having since been seen as setting the British empire inexorably on the road to dissolution (Chamberlain, 1999: 3), between 1948 and 1960 only three British colonies became independent. Yet by the end of the 1960s, decolonization was progressing apace, and the Commonwealth/empire 'circle' was shrinking dramatically. Harold Macmillan's famous 'wind of change' speech, in Cape Town in February 1960, partially explained this in its reference to the need to adjust to the rise of national consciousness in Africa (Macmillan, 1972: 156). Britain's over-stretched forces could neither hold this nationalism at bay nor control its assertion, particularly as the Sharpeville massacre and fighting in the Congo indicated probable widespread bloodshed. However, this was just one of a concatenation of factors underlying Britain's retreat from empire. Others included a shift in British trade patterns towards Europe and an equivocal economic balance sheet regarding maintaining Britain's colonies, the knock-on effects of the Suez crisis and France's decision in 1959 to cede independence to its African colonies. Still more important were the interconnected factors of resource constraint, sterling's recurrent weakness and the 1957 Defence Review, which switched British resources from conventional to nuclear programmes. To this end, the Defence Review aimed to reduce the manpower of Britain's armed services from 690,000 to 375,000 (with conscription abolished in 1960). This rendered unlikely any future sustained military campaign to defend colonial possessions – something reflected in Britain's inability to react militarily to Ian Smith's Unilateral Declaration of Independence (UDI) in Rhodesia in 1965 (for the significance of such resource constraint, see, for example, Coker, 1986; Baylis, 1989; Ovendale, 1994). Although none of this meant British abrogation of a world role, announcement in 1968 of Britain's withdrawal from East of Suez symbolized the increasingly obvious relative poverty of the Commonwealth/empire 'circle' within British foreign policy.

Britain's relationship with Europe

This left Britain's relationship with Europe, which began as the least favoured of the three circles, but finished the Cold War vying for pre-eminence with the Special Relationship. Britain's foremost European concern was security, first for fear of a revanchist Germany, but quickly focusing instead on the USSR. Soviet conventional military superiority was staggering. In 1949 American intelligence estimated that the Red Army had 175 divisions at its disposal whilst Western Europe had just 12 (Sanders, 1990: 62). The fear of communist subversion was also strong. Communists were in coalition governments between 1945 and 1947 in France and Italy, national Communist Party membership in these countries exceeded 1 million and 1.7 million respectively in 1946, and widespread economic distress was thought liable to lead to the accession to power of communist elements elsewhere too.

Crucially for both Britain's policy towards Europe, and its overall post-war foreign policy, Europe's plight promoted a coincidence of strategic interests between Whitehall and Washington. Britain stood to gain considerably from leading Europe to demonstrate its determination to do as much as possible for itself. This was a prerequisite to securing American commitments, and offered Britain an opportunity to develop an Anglo-American partnership, whilst also influencing the ways in which US assistance was administered. In March 1948, Britain duly led the formation of the Brussels Treaty Organisation – a mutual defence agreement comprised of Britain, France and the Benelux countries (for British calculations about the BTO, see Baylis, 1984). Although this was in part targeted against a future German threat, it was also designed to encourage American peacetime security guarantees to Europe. Anglo-American military co-operation in Europe quickly deepened. Their joint airlift eventually defeated the Soviet blockade of Berlin, and US stationing, during the crisis, of US B-29 bombers in Britain indicated a strengthening of the Special Relationship in Europe. Not until October 1951 was a formal agreement made for the presence on British soil of the B-29s, long after they had been modified to carry atom bombs (Dobson, 1995: 95). In April 1949, Britain finally secured an American security guarantee to Europe through the creation of NATO, the intergovernmental military alliance that provided for mutual defence, and which subsequently dominated Western Europe's hard security arrangements throughout the Cold War.

In the economic sphere, British policy makers viewed post-war Europe as an unattractive prospect. British trade patterns lay more with the Commonwealth/empire and the US, and its wartime devastation rendered continental Europe a potentially formidable financial drain. Conversely, however, European economic rejuvenation was essential to resist communist subversion, and Britain's relative strengthening *vis-à-vis* France and Germany in particular offered it both an unchallenged leadership role, and an opportunity to exploit inherent short-term economic comparative advantages during the reconstruction process. In addition, Anglo-American relations could be further strengthened, transatlantic interdependence deepened and additional economic aid for Britain garnered. Anglo-American policy towards Germany was one of the first indications of these objectives. In January 1947, Britain and the US merged their zones of occupation and subsequently introduced a new currency: the Deutschmark. Shortly afterwards, the announcement of $17 billion of Marshall aid portended significant economic aid for Britain, and a key role in designing the stipulated collective European apparatus for its administration (see Wexler, 1983; Mee, 1984; Hogan, 1987).

Given the chequered history of post-war British relations with Europe, and with integration in particular, it is important to recognize that there were limits to the mutually supportive nature of Britain's European and US policies. American policy makers favoured remaking 'the Old World in the likeness of the New' (Hogan, 1987: 52). Strength and prosperity could be returned to Europe by applying to it the American model of interstate trade and a single market. Moreover, supranational integration might override the collective European memory such that recent adversaries could co-operate in political and economic reconstruction and psychological reconciliation. British policy makers were prepared to see this on the continent, but balked at it being applied to Britain. Britain was a global power and would not be reduced to guarantor of Europe, especially if that meant the US reducing its commitment to European security. As Averell Harriman, a leading figure in the Truman administration, once observed, '[t]he British didn't want to be treated as "another European country". We had endless arguments with Bevin and others, trying to convince them that their job was to build a strong Europe ...' (quoted in Gelb, 1988: 201).

Much retrospective criticism has been made of Britain's decision to stand aloof from continental functional integration during the 1950s, and to withdraw from the negotiations which led to the Treaty of Rome and the creation of the European Economic Community (EEC) (see, for example, Denman, 1996; Lord, 1996). At the time, though, there appeared to be valid reasons for this stance. The Suez crisis had yet to expose the frailties of British power, and the three circles of British foreign policy were both widely supported and seemingly successful. Trade with the Commonwealth/empire remained strong, and there was genuine concern that Britain's imperial preference would be jeopardized by entering a European Common Market with a common external tariff. The political risks of pooling British sovereignty were also potentially grave, both in terms of domestic politics, and with regard to the international message this might send about Britain's Great Power status and commitment to its overseas interests. Furthermore, Britain's relative importance to the US, and its strength *vis-à-vis* Europe, enabled it at this time to steer a course commensurate with these convictions and concerns. This explains why Britain was able both to opt out of the European Coal and Steel Community and of a proposed supranational European Defence Community, whilst also ensuring that the Organisation for European Economic Co-operation, which was created to administer Marshall aid, was intergovernmental rather than supranational in nature. It also explains Britain's initial attempts to deter the development of the EEC, and then to establish the European Free Trade Association (EFTA) in 1960 as a potential rival organization.

Britain reconciled itself to pursuing its European policy primarily within the EEC only once the Commonwealth/empire option began to implode, the US demonstrated declining willingness to treat Britain 'specially' and the economic growth of EEC members outperformed those outside of the Community. Shorn of options and with Washington pushing Britain towards membership, the Conservative Prime Minister, Harold Macmillan, tendered Britain's first application to join the EEC in 1961 – the same year that Britain, for the first time, exported more goods to Europe than to the Commonwealth/empire (Young, 2000: 71). Thereafter Britain's European policy was dominated by a struggle first to gain EEC membership, and then to push the Community in directions better suited to British interests. This was no easy task. For a start, Britain's European credentials were far from impressive: a general preference for its relationship with the US, its attempt in the 1950s to derail integration and an application born not of enthusiasm but for want of alternatives. It is therefore unsurprising that, particularly when coupled with lacklustre British negotiating and a series of demands for special treatment, French President de Gaulle vetoed successive British applications for EEC membership in 1963 and 1967.

Further subsequent negotiations for membership in 1970–1 were marked by considerable difficulties in reconciling British Commonwealth preferences and, once Britain was finally allowed to join the EEC in 1973, it quickly established for itself the reputation of the 'awkward partner' (for the classic account of Britain's 'awkward partner' relationship with the EC/EU, see George, 1998). For instance, when Harold Wilson's Labour Government succeeded Heath's in February 1974, it immediately – against a backdrop of rising unemployment, industrial unrest and international economic turmoil following the collapse of Bretton Woods and the onset of the Arab–Israeli war – demanded re-negotiation of the terms on which Britain had entered the Communities.

Margaret Thatcher's Bruges speech of 20 September 1988, her stance on the British Budgetary Question (BBQ) and her clear preference for a revitalized Anglo-American relationship, provided further evidence of Britain's 'awkwardness'. Thatcher viewed Europe in ways that resonated of de Gaulle, but which also reflected New Right thinking that ran against notions of 'social Europe'. Her Bruges speech was an accordingly impassioned advocacy of a Europe that eschewed federalist ambitions and instead organized itself around sovereign states and a Single European Market that embraced free market economics. As for the BBQ, Thatcher waged a truculent five-year battle to again renegotiate Britain's budgetary contributions, arguing that Britain still contributed too much to Brussels' coffers and castigating the profligacy of the CAP. Britain eventually secured an improved deal at the Fontainebleau summit in 1984, but not before the issue had dominated EC business for five years and combined with Thatcher's enthusiastic Atlanticism to reaffirm impressions of Britain as a reluctant European. Indeed, although the Thatcher Governments were keen to develop intergovernmental foreign policy co-ordination within EPC, times of crisis revealed that their primary allegiance lay across the Atlantic. For example, Thatcher resolutely supported Reagan's 'Second Cold War' and the deployment of cruise missiles in Europe regardless of the reservations of most EC members. Likewise, Britain supported US action against Libya in 1986 despite the failure of the EPC to do so and the decision by France and Spain to deny their airspace to American aircraft launching – from British bases – military strikes in retaliation for alleged Libyan terrorist activities.

That said, the European 'circle' of British foreign policy still assumed ever-increasing significance, driven as it was by changing trade patterns, pragmatic adjustment to Britain's relative decline, the need to recover economic stability and begrudging acceptance, under changed conditions, of the longstanding US argument that Britain's being inside the EC would strengthen Anglo-American relations. Moreover, Britain's difficulties in attaining, and then adjusting to, EC membership too often obscure the relative success and positive impact of its European policy. Its substantial military commitment to Western Europe was instrumental in maintaining the peace during the Cold War, binding the US to an indefinite peacetime military commitment, the orchestration of NATO and the creation of an environment in which recent enemies were able to develop integration. All of this enhanced British security, underpinned and to an extent institutionalized Anglo-American co-operation, and encouraged a level of economic interdependence with Europe that proved more sustainable than with the Commonwealth/empire. Britain's eventual EC membership also brought significant benefits, both for itself and the Community. For example, Britain provided a potential counterpoise to the Franco-German axis, boosted the EC's international weight and, despite differences with EC partners, developed an implementation record stronger than some 'euro-enthusiast' member states. Similarly, accommodation of British interests forced EC reform, encouraged new policies from which Britain benefited, including the European Regional Development Fund, and allowed British policy makers to promote both the Single European Market (SEM) and a more outwardly-looking Community, through EPC and initiatives such as the Lomé Conventions.

Post-Cold War British foreign policy

If ever there was an opportunity for a fundamental rethink of British foreign policy and of Britain's place in the world, then it came with the collapse of the Cold War. The 1989–91 implosion of the USSR left British territorial integrity unthreatened by any other power for the first time in over 50 years. There was an opportunity to deliver a meaningful peace dividend to the British people, downsize the armed forces and overseas commitments, and re-orientate political attention towards pressing domestic issues. The Sterling Area was long gone, the Commonwealth safe, British dependent territories few and the prelude to the Maastricht Treaty demanded that Britain tend its deepening relationship with Europe. Also, the relationship with the US was weakening. NATO entered an existential crisis following the dissolution of the Warsaw Pact and Britain's self-appointed role as transatlantic intermediary faced a two-fold challenge from a potential geo-strategic divorce in Europe–US relations and the emergence of 'alternative bridges' across the Atlantic, notably a reunified Germany. President George H. Bush resolutely supported German reunification regardless of private and public British reservations. The most visceral expressions of British anxiety over German reunification were articulated by Nicholas Ridley, while he was Secretary of State for Trade and Industry, in a July 1990 interview he gave to *The Spectator*, and Margaret Thatcher's own (leaked) comments during the same month concerning the 'German Question'. (For Ridley's defence, see Ridley, 1991: 223–6. For the text of Thatcher's comments, see Charles Powell's leaked Chequers memorandum in James and Stone, 1992: 233–9.) Thatcher herself publicly expressed her desire to 'curb German power' (Thatcher, 1993: 760). In spite of such concerns over German reunification by senior British Ministers (including the Prime Minister herself), the American President also hailed Kohl's new Germany as a 'partner in leadership' of a New World Order and, according to Thatcher, deliberately downgraded the special position she had formerly enjoyed with Reagan (Thatcher, 1993: 783).

Yet despite all of this, the basic tenets of post-war British foreign policy remained unchallenged. Foremost herein is the bipartisan and popular support for a British foreign policy geared to Britain's continued global engagement. This derives in part from traditions of empire and special responsibility, but also from pragmatic calculations of British interest in maintaining the predominant neo-liberal international order. Indeed, it is striking that ever since Dean Acheson's famous indictment in December 1962 of Britain's having lost an empire and failed to find a new role, British governments have consistently sought to counter his charge (for details, see Snyder, 1964: 3–4). Thatcher cited the victorious Falklands campaign as evidence that 'we have ceased to be a nation in retreat' (Thatcher, 1993: 253), whilst Conservative Foreign Secretary Douglas Hurd declared in March 1995 that Britain's decline had ended in the 1980s and that it had almost completed all its necessary adjustments, including the transformation of the empire, membership of the EU and addressing the economic weaknesses that had formerly plagued the country. Then, in November 1999, Tony Blair responded directly to Acheson's barb:

> [s]uccessive generations of British politicians tried – unsuccessfully – to find a way back, from Churchill's three concentric circles to Mrs Thatcher's call to repel a European federal state. However, I believe that search can now end. We have got over our Imperial past – and the withdrawal symptoms. ... We have a new role. ... It is to use the strengths of our history to build our future not as a superpower but as a pivotal power, as a power that is at the crux of the alliances and international politics which shape the world and its future'. (Speech by Tony Blair to the Lord Mayor of London's Banquet, 22 November 1999, http://www.fco.gov.uk)

The leitmotif of post-Cold War British foreign policy has been of Britain as a medium-sized power 'punching above its weight' in international affairs. True, the Thatcher/Major and Blair governments have differed in their relative enthusiasm for certain aspects of foreign policy, such as European integration, development policy, human rights and Robin Cook's 'ethical dimension'. But these reflect differences of style and emphasis rather than about Britain maintaining a high-profile and active global foreign policy. Moreover, although continued overstretch is indicated by equipment deficiencies during the 2003 Iraq War, the foundations of this foreign policy are arguably stronger than at any time since the 1950s. In 2002, Britain stood fourth in the World Bank's GDP rankings, and in recent years its economy has been largely stable, maintained low inflation and generally outperformed the big eurozone countries. Also, in 2001 Britain was the fifth largest military spender and the fourth largest exporter of conventional weaponry. Moreover, it has considerable institutionalized power through its membership of most key international financial and security organizations. Consider, for instance, its memberships of NATO, EU, Western European Union (WEU), Organisation for Security and Co-operation in Europe, UN, Council of Europe, Commonwealth, International Monetary Fund, Organisation for European Co-operation and Development, WTO and the G8.

Britain's increasing use of multilateral fora, NGOs and so forth, reflects a pragmatic adjustment to the implications of relative decline, a broader post-Cold War security agenda and the reconfiguration of power in terms of both its distribution and application. Yet the hallmark of British foreign policy has been continuity. For instance, Britain has continued its traditional determination to maintain and use considerable military power for foreign policy objectives much wider than territorial defence. The nuclear deterrent has remained sacrosanct and the 1998 Strategic Defence Review reaffirmed the need for British conventional armed forces to be able to perform a range of tasks – including regional conflict resolution, peace support missions, global interventions and even to tackle organized crime. Britain has also been instrumental in pushing NATO reform and enlargement, the development of rapid deployment units and, from the St Malo agreement in December 1998, the creation of an EU military capability. Moreover, British foreign policy activism is reflected in a series of post-Cold War military engagements and peacekeeping operations, most notably the 1990–1 Gulf War, Sierra Leone, Kosovo, Afghanistan, Iraq and contributions to UNPROFOR, IFOR, SFOR, KFOR, the enforcement of no-fly zones in southern Iraq and NATO's *Operation Essential Harvest* to collect weapons from Albanian insurgents in the Former Yugoslav Republic of Macedonia (FYROM).

It is also evident that the couching of British foreign policy in post-Churchillian rhetoric scarcely veils continued preferences for the three circles, albeit that the balance between them has changed substantially, and the revised objective is influence through interdependence rather than autonomy by Great Power action. The relative importance of the Commonwealth has declined significantly: the empire has been transformed, the Commonwealth officially ceased being British in 1965, and Britain's reduced influence therein was demonstrated by the Blair Government's inability to orchestrate the suspension of Mugabe's Zimbabwe before the rigged elections of March 2002. (Zimbabwe subsequently gave official notice of its decision to withdraw from the Commonwealth on 11 December 2003.) Nevertheless, Britain has continued to work with and through the Commonwealth and to exploit 'the strengths of our history'. For example, the Commonwealth has long been an important promulgator and protector of democracy and human rights. It formally established its standards of democracy, good governance and social justice in Harare in 1991, and made them a condition of membership in 1993. Britain's historical connections have also been important in both promoting specific foreign policy objectives, and in influencing other actors. Military action against the Taleban in 2001, for example, demonstrated the importance of Britain's residual influence in the Middle East and around Afghanistan in securing intelligence and airspace for the allied military campaign from key countries such as General Musharraf's Pakistan.

Britain has also continued to pursue concomitant relationships with the EU and US and its traditional self-appointed role as 'Atlantic intermediary' (Dumbrell, 2001). Perhaps unsurprisingly, questions have been raised about the viability of these strategies. Britain's deeper integration within the EU, especially its commitment to CFSP (Common Foreign and Security Policy), has been seen by some as precluding 'any prolongation of the Special Relationship on foreign policy co-ordination' (Dickie, 1994: 242). Others have contended that pursuit of the Special Relationship has unduly undermined Britain's relationship with the EU and/or stranded British foreign policy in a bygone era. For them, the painful asymmetry in Anglo-American power and the loss of cohesion following the collapse of the Cold War dissolved what was left of the functional dimension of 'specialness'. What remained was an empty and largely non-reciprocated political construct that both provided an illusion of continuity for a nation experiencing 'a profound sense of powerlessness', and a delusion of power used to legitimize and justify an erroneous mixed commitment to Europe (Coker, 1992: 409, 416; see also Danchev, 1998). Even during the Cold War, some argued that the Special Relationship was a dangerous intellectual concept which 'gave us a distorted perception of our power and influence in the world' (Owen, 1979: 63).

Furthermore, there has been extensive debate about the viability, even desirability, of Britain's transatlantic bridging function. John Major and Tony Blair have echoed the likes of Macmillan and Callaghan in seeing Britain's 'straddl[ing] the divide' as facilitating influence disproportionate to British power (see, for example, Major, 1999: 578). Critics, however, contend that '[a] bridge is not needed, and … runs a very real risk of jeopardising our relations with our European partners …' (Warner, 1997: 157). Moreover, there has been considerable debate about whether the transition to a post-Cold War era has initiated an inevitable process of strategic divorce between the EU and US (Marsh and Mackenstein, 2005: Ch. 4; see also Nye, 2000: 59; Walt, 1998–9; Newhouse, 1997; Lieber, 2000; W. Pfaff, 'The US Campaign is Skirting Key Foreign Policy Issues', *International Herald Tribune*, 15 January 2000; Blinken, 2001), in which case Britain's bridging of a widening gap between two far more powerful entities becomes increasingly unrealistic.

Britain and Europe since 1990

The ambiguous record of post-Cold War British foreign policy suggests that these debates will continue for some time. Britain's relationships with the EU and the US have waxed and waned in accord with specific issues, government preferences and personal relationships. Conservative and Labour governments alike claimed their desire and determination to put Britain at the heart of Europe, and emphasized a more constructive tone towards Europe than that adopted by their predecessors. The first (1990–2) Major Government was initially welcomed in Europe for a less adversarial negotiating style, having also dropped the anti-German rhetoric that pervaded Thatcher's last year in power, but improvements in Anglo-German relations failed to survive Black Wednesday (see, for example, Glees, 1994).

The New Labour Government elected in 1997 was similarly fortunate in that it could condemn the euroscepticism within the Conservative Party which had become increasingly open, and had progressively pushed Major towards a harder line on Europe. In addition, Blair's large parliamentary majority in 1997 made it a more attractive potential partner, and its political philosophy further enabled a quick and symbolically important *rapprochement* with the EU through reversing Britain's opt-out of the Social Charter.

In terms of policy substance, post-Cold War Conservative and Labour Governments have in many aspects been almost indistinguishable from one another. They have consistently pushed for CAP reform, EC/EU enlargement, completion of the SEM, the promotion of wealth creation and employment through deregulation and flexible labour markets, and for more vigorous EU action against poor implementation and wasteful use of resources. They have also self-excluded Britain from the third stage of EMU, promised a referendum on British membership of the single currency and, in line with traditional British policy, sought a more outward-looking Europe committed to international free trade and to foreign policy co-operation.

For example, John Major's first Conservative Government, working in tandem with its Italian counterpart, was largely responsible for the initiation of CFSP in the format adopted within the TEU (Treaty on European Union), whilst the 1998 British EU Presidency – during the first full year of Tony Blair's premiership – oversaw the creation of the Transatlantic Economic Partnership. Blair's drive for employment and for a knowledge-based economy in Europe also complemented his joint job-creation initiative with the then American President, Bill Clinton, through the G8. Neither have the Major nor Blair Governments shown any greater reticence than their Cold War predecessors in asserting British interests, even if this has led at times to their being a minority of one within the EU. For example, Major vetoed the appointment of Jean-Luc Dehaene as Commission President, and, in 1996, waged the 'beef war' – vetoing any EU decision requiring unanimity – in an attempt to weaken an EU export ban placed on British beef as a consequence of the BSE crisis. Likewise, Blair has staunchly defended the British budgetary rebate, and insisted upon maintaining the national veto in areas of key national interest – such as tax policy.

That said, there has been some significant evolution in British European policy, yielding discernible differences between the Major and Blair Governments. The latter, for instance, has acquiesced in the extension of QMV (Qualified Majority Voting), been more enthusiastic about internationalism and shown a willingness to accept greater communitaurization, such as on asylum policy. Particularly interesting has been Britain's interest in enhancing the EU's foreign affairs capabilities. This was encouraged by the geo-strategic changes brought about by the end of the Cold War and evident EC weakness during the collapse of the Yugoslav Federation.

Britain's enthusiasm also reflected several key calculations and aspirations. A leadership role in foreign and security policy offered a potential counterbalance to self-exclusion from EMU and, by taking the initiative, Britain might forestall more radical ideas requiring the pooling of sovereignty. Also, if the EU were to serve as a power-enhancing mechanism for British foreign policy, then it had to be better equipped and co-ordinated, which in turn could lead to useful cost-cutting opportunities. Furthermore, there were significant potential advantages with regard to Britain's relations with other countries. Firstly, Britain might court influence with the US and Atlanticist-oriented EU members through ensuring the compatibility of EU and NATO ambitions. Secondly, foreign and security policy was an area in which Britain could potentially break the Franco-German axis, especially given Germany's post-war civilian power disposition and the continuing constraint of historical memory.

British ambitions were reflected in the Major Governments' support for CFSP and acceptance in the Maastricht Treaty (subject to recognizing the primacy of NATO) of Article J.4. This stated that CFSP 'shall include all questions related to the security of the Union, including the eventual framing of a common defence policy, which might in time lead to a common defence'. The potential hard security issues arising from this aspiration were seemingly pushed the way of the WEU, which was regarded as an 'integral part of the development of the Union'. The Blair Governments subsequently supported a series of reforms that created new tools, such as common strategies, and increased flexibility within CFSP, including the introduction of constructive abstention in the Amsterdam Treaty and enhanced co-operation in the Nice Treaty.[2] Still more significant was the first Blair Government's acceptance, in the Amsterdam Treaty, of the EU assuming responsibility for the Petersberg tasks and its *volte-face* in the 1998 St Malo agreement with France over continuing the Major Governments' opposition to the merging of the WEU into the EU. This had formerly been seen as a bulwark against a creeping integration of defence and safeguard of a strong NATO alliance ('Joint Declaration on European Defence', 3–4 December 1998, www.fco.gov.uk). This 'revolution in military affairs' (Howorth, 2000: 33) provided the genesis of the European Union Rapid Reaction Force (EURRF) and enabled the EU to absorb all but the mutual defence obligations of the WEU in the Nice Treaty. It was particularly telling of the clash between new and old British thinking that Margaret Thatcher condemned Blair's commitment to the EURRF as 'an act of monumental folly' taken 'to satisfy political vanity' (quoted in Harris, 2001: 34).

Anglo-American relations in the post-Cold War era

Neither the Major nor the Blair Governments accepted that their ambition to put Britain at the heart of Europe was either contradictory with, or required, a lessening commitment to the Special Relationship. The Bush–Major relationship was warm and cordial (Dobson, 1995: 163), not least because Major continued his predecessor's staunch support for George H. Bush's leadership of the Gulf War – Thatcher having famously advised the President in August 1990 that 'this is no time to go wobbly' (cited in Renwick, 1996: 374). Britain subsequently provided the largest European component of the military force assembled to repel the Iraqi army and its solidarity stood in stark contrast to the disarray that characterized EPC and led Belgium's Foreign Minister to describe the EC as 'an economic giant, a political dwarf, and a military worm' (quoted in McCormick, 2002: 197). As for Blair, he developed a relationship with Clinton reminiscent of the Reagan–Thatcher years. This derived in part from stalwart British support of Clinton at both the personal and policy level. Blair stood by him during the Monica Lewinsky débâcle, sided with Clinton – and against France's President Chirac – in limiting the first round of NATO enlargement to Poland, Hungary and the Czech Republic, endorsed unilateral US bombings of Afghanistan and Sudan in 1998 and, despite holding the EU presidency at the time, immediately committed to Operation Desert Fox in December 1998, which entailed Anglo-American military strikes against Iraq in response to Saddam Hussein's obstruction of UN weapons

---

2 Under constructive abstention a member state is not obliged to apply a decision by the EU on the proviso that it refrains from any action that might conflict with the Union's action under that decision, which itself must have a minimum of two-thirds of the weighted Council votes. Enhanced co-operation applies to the implementation of a joint action or common position in circumstances where they have no military or defence implications, no member state objects or applies the so-called 'emergency brake' (a call for a unanimous decision in the European Council) and where there exists a threshold of eight member states in favour.

inspections. Anglo-American closeness at this time owed also to ideological affinities between New Labour and the Democrats and to a series of strong personal relationships that helped to convey the appearance of renewed transatlantic vigour (Dumbrell, 2001: 119). For instance, Blair and Clinton were 'joined at the hip' as practitioners of 'Third Way' politics and shared a fascination with the opportunities and problems presented by accelerating globalization, the importance/utility of multilateral fora, and the blurring both of foreign and domestic policy, and of national and international interests (Campbell and Rockman, 2001: 36).

It was widely expected that Anglo-American relations would cool upon the arrival of George W. Bush at the White House. The New Labour Government nevertheless continued its commitment to Anglo-American relations. It quickly invoked the imagery of the Special Relationship, which Bush reciprocated. Blair was the first European leader to visit Bush at Camp David in February 2001 and declared confidently that they would 'strengthen still further the special friendship between Britain and the United States' ('Blair Congratulates Bush on Presidential Victory', 14 December 2000, www.fco.gov). Bush subsequently publicly endorsed the Anglo-American Special Relationship and, in a phrase reminiscent of Margaret Thatcher's pledge to Reagan in February 1981, declared 'I can assure you that when either of us get in a bind, there will be a friend on the other end of the phone' (transcript of Bush–Blair press conference at Halton House, 19 July 2001, www.fco.gov; transcript of Bush–Blair press conference at Camp David, 23 February 2001, www.fco.gov). In February 1981, Thatcher told Reagan that, 'The message I have brought across the Atlantic is that we in Britain stand with you.... Your problems will be our problems and when you look for friends we will be there' (Thatcher cited in Dickie, 1994: 175).

Undoubtedly, the 11 September 2001 ('9/11') terrorist attacks infused the Blair–Bush personal relationship with new vigour and shared aspirations (for a much fuller discussion of this, see Marsh, 2003). The two have since seemingly substituted for the ideological bond of the Clinton years an apparent Christian missionary zeal in their defence of values to which both subscribe strongly, and that have long been a binding agent in the Anglo-American relationship. For instance, both have emphasized that the terrorist attacks were against a way of life rather than just against America (speech by Blair at the George Bush Senior Library, 7 April 2002, www.fco.gov; State of the Union Address, 29 January 2002, www.whitehouse.gov/news/releases; President's address to joint session of Congress, 20 September 2001, http://usinfo.state.gov), and indulged in increasingly moralistic rhetoric that couches foreign policy in terms of 'good versus evil'. Hence Blair labelled Saddam Hussein 'a serial sinner' on CNN in February 2001 and Bush invoked the 'axis-of-evil' in his 2002 State of the Union Address, itself reminiscent of Ronald Reagan's 'Evil Empire' speech of March 1983 (edited transcript of Tony Blair interview for CNN, Washington, 23 February 2001, www.britainusa.com). (For an introduction to the discourse of the war on terrorism see Silberstein, 2002.)

More importantly, the impact of 9/11 re-aligned Anglo-American relations somewhat, and allowed Britain to demonstrate that substance still underpinned the image of the Special Relationship. Blair's immediate promise of support was powerfully reinforced by his presence in the gallery as Bush addressed a joint session of Congress on 20 September – something later hailed by US officials as 'a major symbolic gesture to the American people that we would not be alone in the months ahead' (remarks of Charles P. Ries, US Principal Deputy Assistant Secretary of State for European and Eurasian Affairs to the Southern Center for International Studies annual seminar on Europe, 23 October 2001, www.usembassy.org.uk/europe). His high-profile shuttle diplomacy in building the coalition prior to *Operation Enduring Freedom* in Afghanistan undoubtedly won Britain friends in Washington, as did British military participation in Afghanistan and willingness to assume initial responsibility for the International Stabilisation Force in Kabul. Indeed, rather as the Gulf War did, intervention in Afghanistan demonstrated that British and American armed co-ordination was easier and more effective than with any other country, due to long-established habits of co-operation, integrated command structures and access to the same real-time intelligence (McGhie, 2002: 2). Likewise, Anglo-American civilian counter-terrorist measures saw an intensification of intelligence exchange, and in April 2002, US Treasury officials cited Britain as a model of co-operation in its assiduous freezing of suspected terrorist assets (Alden, 2002: 3). Most significant of all, though, was Britain's steadfast support for the US over Iraq, both in the UN over Security Council Resolution 1441 and in the military campaign launched against Iraq in March 2003. This set it apart from all of America's other allies and was seen by some as confirming a British reversion to 'a brand of unconditional Atlanticism which many in Europe (and even in Britain) had assumed to be anachronistic' (Howorth, 2002: 1).

None of this is to suggest that British foreign policy makers have found Anglo-American relations any easier to maintain in the post-Cold War era than during the Cold War. The EU's increasing prominence and capability as an international actor has further challenged Britain's transatlantic bridging function, and the asymmetry in Anglo-American relations has prompted repeated British protestations that '[w]e are not a tail being wagged by the dog' (speech by John Battle in a House of Commons adjournment debate, 10 January 2001, www.fco.gov). There have also been doldrum periods and sharp Anglo-American differences. The Major–Clinton relationship was run on a 'grin-and-bear-it' basis (Seitz, 1998: 322), and Anglo-American relations cooled for a time amid a series of problems, including the 'running sore' (Major, 1999: 497) of the Balkans and the Clinton administration's policy on Northern Ireland. Similarly, Blair and Clinton were deeply divided over whether to deploy ground troops in Kosovo, and the initial Blair–Bush period was marked by British fears of Bush administration unilateralism, and disagreements on issues as diverse as the Comprehensive Test Ban Treaty (CTBT) and the Kyoto Protocol.

The key point, however, is that post-Cold War British governments have continued to look consistently across the Atlantic as well as to Europe and to pursue Britain's traditional, self-designated role as mediator between the two. This two-fold determination is at the heart of repeated declarations that not only will Britain not choose decisively between the EU and US, but that this is actually a false choice: Europeanism and Atlanticism are compatible and mutually supportive elements of Britain's foreign relations. Moreover, it has been reflected in the careful balancing by British foreign policy makers of Britain's transatlantic and European relationships. Hence, Britain has stood alongside the EU in opposition to US positions on Kyoto, the CTBT, the Ottawa convention, International Criminal Court and over various trade disputes, such as the George W. Bush administration's imposition in March 2002 of 'safeguard' tariffs of up to 30 per cent on steel imports.

Conversely, Britain has lent the US consistent and enduring support over issues such as the primacy of NATO in European security, military action in Afghanistan and, most controversially, the military enforcement of regime change in Iraq and subsequent administration of the country.

Conclusion

British foreign policy has undergone something of a revolution in terms of how it is made, the key actors therein, its scope and its principal objectives. Some of these changes are similar to those encountered by most states, for they are the product of common phenomena: international systemic change, processes of globalization and deepening interdependence, the communications revolution, massive evolution in technology, the growing influence of NGOs, the impact of international organizations and regimes, and so forth. National and international interests have blurred, the foreign and domestic realms merged, and the dimensions, application and ownership of power all become much more complicated. Other changes, however, are either shared only by Britain's partners within the EU or are unique to Britain, especially its particular response to relative decline from Great Power to medium-sized power.

Given the enormity of change, though, perhaps the most striking feature of post-war British foreign policy has been its consistency. As a power in relative decline, Britain has demonstrated considerable attachment to the status quo and preservation of the predominant neo-liberal international order that largely reflects British values, facilitates Britain's interests in international free trade and within which Britain enjoys significant institutionalized power. From the Cabinet through to the general British populace, there has also remained a largely unchallenged assumption that Britain has a special responsibility as an international actor, the right to intervene and assert its interests worldwide, and that British foreign policy and armed forces should be equipped to operate globally. British post-war adjustments can thus be best seen not as an attempt to redefine Britain's established self-perception as a global actor, but as pragmatic efforts to facilitate its continuation in radically changed circumstances. Stripped of any claim or pretension to Great Power status, 'punching above its weight' has become the hallmark of British foreign policy that simultaneously allows for a sense of continuity with the past and justifies ongoing global engagement.

Britain's empire may be long gone, and its foreign policy couched increasingly in internationalist language, but the strategies and problems of British foreign policy have consistently resonated of Churchillian preferences. The 'three circles' aimed originally at securing British autonomy through Great Power action. The Anglo-American relationship would provide immediate security and lasting partnership; the Commonwealth/empire would be the bedrock of Britain's return to the top flight of powers; and leadership of Europe would help repel communism, bring some economic advantages and reaffirm Anglo-American co-operation. Britain's membership of each of these circles would support its influence within the others, and counterbalance American preferences in particular for Britain to become a primarily European power. The three circles were subsequently adapted, rather than abandoned, in the face of relative decline, to the pursuit of influence through interdependence. Today Britain still emphasizes its relationships with the EU, US and the Commonwealth, albeit that the latter is greatly diminished and much more use is made of multilateral fora as power-enhancing mechanisms.

Finally, it is interesting that two key tensions in Britain's foreign policy today are similar in nature, if not in context, to those that afflicted it throughout the post-war era, namely the risk of overstretch and the difficulties of 'squaring circles'. Britain's 'punching above its weight' and continued determination to pay the price of participation in return for consultation in Washington has led it into an escalating series of post-Cold War commitments that threaten once more to exceed its capabilities. Bosnia, Kosovo, the FYROM, Afghanistan and Iraq are just some of the operations with which the British military have struggled to cope. This risk of overstretch is particularly salient given the global scope of the post-9/11 war on terrorism and dearth of exit strategies from many interventions. As for 'squaring circles', Britain's post-war pursuit of relationships with the US, Europe and the Commonwealth/empire was never without friction as the circles frequently overlapped and the interests of each often conflicted with the others. Today the success of British foreign policy seems predicated on tensions between the EU and US circles not becoming overly pronounced; that is a situation in which in its role as 'Atlantic intermediary' Britain has a potentially vital role to play but limited ability to control.

5 Health Policy
Helen Jones

Introduction

Since 1945, health policy in Britain has operated within a framework of improving standards of living and health, and in the context of rising expectations of what a health service should deliver. There have been public admiration and electoral support for health services, but criticisms of specific aspects of the delivery of health care. For most of this period, the media, in particular television, have played an important role in projecting images of health care to the public. The funding of the NHS has been a constant and unresolved dilemma throughout, adding to – and to some extent underpinning – the problem of staff shortages, and difficulties in attracting appropriate personnel. At key moments, individual Health Secretaries – most notably Aneurin Bevan and Kenneth Clarke – have played highly influential roles in the shaping of policy, while occasionally, other senior Ministers – such as Margaret Thatcher and Gordon Brown – have also played a prominent role in health policy. The medical profession has generally enjoyed a powerful role in the health policy process, even if Ministers have occasionally attempted to curb its power. There has also often been a rhetoric of 'inclusion' that has usually fallen short in the delivery of health care, while health policy has constantly had to adapt to social changes.

Against these constant themes, there have been significant changes in the cultural milieu of the health policy process. Deference has declined dramatically in British society, and many citizens are less judgemental of others than was previously the case. This, in turn, has facilitated greater public openness in the airing of health issues, disability, illnesses and differences. Furthermore, there is now far greater emphasis on individual choice and empowerment, and arguably a greater diffusion of power generally.

Academic analysis of health policy in Britain typically focuses on the National Health Service (NHS), although it has long been recognized that standards of health are affected by wider social influences, not by particular health system configurations. Here we will be focusing on the NHS, not because these wider influences are not thought to be important but for three reasons: the main concern of policy makers for health has been with the NHS; many health-related interest and pressure groups focus on the NHS; and the organization, funding and delivery of health care have been a major preoccupation of the health policy community since the NHS's inception.

Michael Hill has underlined the importance of understanding the policy process as a political one (Hill, 1997), with 'political' broadly defined as encompassing power struggles within and between professionals and other organized interests, while also subject to local pressures and circumstances (see Newman, 2002). Health policy is undoubtedly a multi-layered lasagne of people, places and processes.

Health policy is influenced by social and cultural factors that stretch far beyond clearly identifiable actors in the policy community. Whitehall (the senior civil service), the British Medical Association (BMA), and other organized groups concerned with health issues can be clearly identified, and evidence collected to assess their direct influence (what Lukes characterizes as the first or most visible face of power (Lukes, 1974: Ch. 2). Assessing the influence of less direct, and wider, social influences, such as the changing position of women in society, the growing proportion of the elderly in the population, the current interest among the better-off in personal health – as witnessed by diets, health clubs, self-help books and exercise regimes – as well as a decline in unsympathetic and condemnatory attitudes towards groups such as those with mental health problems, mental handicap or homosexuals, is far more problematic.

Similarly, broader cultural changes, such as the role of the media, are also harder to evaluate. In the mid-1990s, Michael Cahill noted that television has a direct impact on the presentation of social problems, whether in dramatic or documentary form, and that news and current affairs programmes are relevant to the formation of social policies (Cahill, 1994: 53). Therefore, in discussing post-war health policy in Britain, we need to be mindful both of the direct and clearly identifiable, as well as the indirect and less obvious, influences on health policy.

Constructing a National Health Service, 1940–48

The history of health policy in Britain since 1945 must begin with the Second World War itself, for its circumstances, experiences, the individuals it brought to prominence, and its social and political milieux, strongly influenced the nature of post-war health care provision, and thus the assumptions and structures with which policy makers subsequently dealt from 1945 onwards.

In the years immediately preceding the outbreak of the Second World War, many policy makers had been preoccupied with maintaining civil order in the event of war, and had therefore drafted plans for evacuating the cities, providing emergency treatment following bombing, and disposing of the deceased. None of these measures had long-term implications for health policy, except in one important aspect, that of hospital provision. The Ministry of Health ensured that all hospitals, local authority (old poor law) and voluntary (private) ones, were co-ordinated on a regional basis. The temporary incorporation of voluntary hospitals into a national system breathed new financial life into a system creaking under the burden of increasing demands on its resources.

The labour demands of war, however, meant that there was a permanent shortage of nurses and doctors to work in the hospitals, and there was a clear order of priorities that related closely to patients' contribution to the war effort. As a result of this prioritizing of patients according to their national usefulness, rather than their health needs, the already low priority accorded the elderly, who were not in the workforce, was reinforced. Within five years of the war's end, Richard Titmuss (1950) argued that the welfare measures of the war and immediate post-war years were the direct result of wartime experiences. In particular, the brave co-operation of civilians with the navy in evacuating soldiers from the beaches of Dunkirk in the wake of advancing German troops, 'the Dunkirk spirit' as it was dubbed, and the subsequent air raids in which everyone – whatever their class – was a potential victim, led to a sense of social solidarity. Meanwhile, the evacuation of working-class children from the cities to more prosperous (and safer) rural areas made many aware for the first time of the extent of poverty and ill health among the urban poor. Moreover, the 1940–5 Coalition Government, sensitive to the need to sustain social morale and workplace efficiency, introduced measures to bolster standards of health. Titmuss believed that the wartime hospital service, despite its shortcomings for civilians, provided the blueprint for the future. Titmuss had provided a highly attractive and influential thesis for wartime policy making. Most historians subsequently accepted his version and explained the creation of the NHS in terms of wartime experience and consensus. Although some historians have more recently questioned the extent of wartime social solidarity and commitment to 'fair shares' and 'equality of sacrifice', there were specific aspects of wartime experience which were important to the way in which policy for health care subsequently developed.

The actual experiences of war influenced health policy making in a number of interrelated ways. Firstly, the Emergency Hospital Service's improvized provision gradually extended ad hoc to include an increasing number and range of social groups. Secondly, despite the increased risks and stresses of war, there was full employment, governmental price controls and dietary supplements for vulnerable groups, all of which contributed to rising standards of health. Thirdly, on the one hand, there was probably a loosening of sexual morals, but on the other hand, a resurgence of society's double standards, so that sexual health was viewed from the point of view of controlling VD among the troops, but not in terms of helping women protect themselves against unwanted pregnancies. Certainly, unmarried mothers continued to attract social opprobrium, and thus receive harsh treatment, from society at large and government institutions.

Although men were able to buy contraceptives more easily than in the past, policy makers still failed to heed calls that had been made publicly for at least a quarter of a century for women, especially poorer women, to control their fertility. Whitehall continued to be dominated by men for whom the health needs of working-class women barely registered. However, whilst women's reproductive health needs did not find a place on the institutional agenda, various other aspects of ordinary people's health were granted more serious attention by policy makers.

The Beveridge Report on Social Insurance and Allied Services made a national health service an explicit part of its overall package. The committee from which the Report emanated had been established to review the question of unemployment and health insurance, as well as workmen's compensation. The Report recommended a comprehensive social security system of which a health service would form an integral part (Beveridge, 1942). Beveridge grasped the importance of integrated services; and thus the public debate on the future of welfare provision that intensified following publication of his Report kept a national health service firmly in the public arena – the systemic agenda – and ensured that it would be central to any post-war welfare settlement. Beveridge had not only presented a cogent case for the broad aspirations of the public, but did so publicly and from a semi-official platform, yet in so doing, he had made life rather uncomfortable for a number of politicians. His Report, and the enthusiastic reactions to it, surprised the Ministry of Health and obliged it to speed up its deliberations. Thus were civil servants and government ministers influenced by wider cultural changes taking place. They rowed the policy-making boat only slowly, but were pushed on their way by the tide of public opinion.

Changing attitudes in British society, coupled with the success of State intervention during the war itself, raised expectations of what government could – and should – provide, and thereby fuelled demands for improved health provision. Throughout the war, those who were most at risk of enemy bombs lived in urban, dock and industrial areas, and were therefore disproportionately working class. From the summer of 1940, when the first bombs fell, there was public discussion of the government's role in raising the working class's standard of living when the war was over, and health care provision was integral to the debate. As early as January 1941, for example, the popular but serious photographic magazine, *Picture Post*, carried a series of articles on future plans for Britain that included a call for a state medical service with a full range of services as a right for everyone. Through the use of images accompanied by text, the magazine highlighted the inadequacies of the existing system, such as the huge numbers who waited in hospital out-patient departments for free treatment because they had no national health insurance cover. It also highlighted the way in which health could be promoted through health centres, communal feeding and family allowances in order to eradicate poverty. Here was a call for a state health care system with access to health care as a right not a privilege, and for the state to recognize that health depended on more than a health care system (*Picture Post*, 4 January 1941).

Although dragging its heels behind wider cultural changes, a shift in thinking within the Ministry of Health meant that it was less self-satisfied and defensive, and more willing than hitherto to recognize the extensive range of health problems that needed tackling. Other areas of Whitehall, along with the main political parties and organized interests, were constantly placing the Ministry under pressure. Furthermore, it was clear to the Ministry (from the Ministry of Information's weekly home intelligence reports), that the public wanted health reforms. In this respect, it is apparent that the Ministry followed – it did not lead – public opinion on health provision, and for much of the war it was attempting to maintain control over the shape of future services. As Charles Webster, the NHS's official historian, noted, the Ministry had to hold the ring between competing interests, although this suggests that he sees the Ministry as a disinterested body (Webster, 1988: 28), whereas the Ministry actually had its own (institutional) agenda, albeit one that was not static.

At the outbreak of the Second World War, Ministry mandarins were drawing up plans for a future hospital system, but in the spring of 1941 the Minister of Health would not countenance a free state medical service for everyone, either during the war or in the long term. Ministry civil servants praised the national health insurance scheme that had been in place since 1911 and the voluntary hospitals. There was no sense within the Ministry at this stage that the health care system should be completely overhauled and integrated, although in the autumn of 1941 the Ministry did commit the Government to a national hospital system after the war, albeit with local authorities exerting a good deal of influence over voluntary hospitals.

While there is much evidence of changing attitudes within society as a whole during the Second World War and immediately afterwards, two highly influential groups, the British Medical Association (BMA), and the bulk of the parliamentary Conservative Party, were determined to uphold pre-existing views about the future of health care, clearly indicating a lack of consensus in health policy making at this time. Kevin Jefferys has argued that there was controversy on party political lines both before and after the publication of the 1944 White Paper on *The Future of the Health Services* (Jefferys, 1987; 1991). The White Paper was vague on various contentious issues, so it was actually relatively easy for the Coalition Government and other relevant policy actors to endorse it, due to their very different interpretations of its details.

Following the White Paper's publication, Henry Willink, the (Conservative) Minister of Health, embarked upon long negotiations with the BMA and reached agreement on various issues which watered down the White Paper's proposals. Consequently, when the main political parties promised a national health service in the 1945 general election, they had very different health services in mind. For example, the Conservative Party – as articulated by Henry Willink and the bulk of the Party in Parliament – wished to ensure that a mixture of state and private provision in hospital care would be maintained, with doctors continuing to enjoy independence from the state.

The views of Conservative voters are virtually impossible to gauge, though, because the Party organization was so run down, and for this reason it is almost meaningless to talk about Conservative Party activists during the war, although the 1945 Conservative Party annual conference did endorse a comprehensive system available to all. As Willink later admitted, however, the health service that a Conservative government would have introduced would have been very different from that subsequently established by Clement Attlee's Labour Government.

It was in the wartime context of raised public expectations, protracted negotiations with organized interests, and detailed Ministry of Health plans, that Aneurin Bevan, Minister of Health in the Labour Government elected in 1945, shaped the new national health service, one which was rather different to that envisaged by the Conservatives during the election campaign. There was no doubting the Labour Government's desire to establish a new health service, for since the 1930s the Party had been committed to a comprehensive health service, and now it had a landslide parliamentary majority, underpinned by heightened public expectations, upon which it could develop one. Bevan was a formidable political fighter, with a clear vision of what he wanted to achieve, which, above all, was a unified health service not under the control of local authorities. It was this aspect of the new service, the 'nationalization' of the hospitals, that bore Bevan's personal stamp.

Health policy making under the 1945–51 Labour Governments was different from that of its Coalition predecessor in a number of crucial respects: Bevan might have been a Ministerial novice, but what he lacked in experience he made up for in strategic vision and determination. These qualities included a willingness to confront both the medical profession (the Conservatives' proposals had entailed keeping the medical profession 'on board'), and Cabinet colleagues, such as Herbert Morrison, who argued for hospitals to be placed under local authority control. While Bevan's predecessor in the wartime Coalition had been immersed in negotiations with doctors, Bevan would only consult with them, a subtle yet important difference in policy-making style.

However, despite the 1945–50 Labour Government's huge parliamentary majority, which meant that it could effectively ignore criticisms from the Opposition benches, Bevan needed to ensure that the doctors, who had expressed considerable hostility (through the BMA) to the new scheme, were willing nonetheless to work in the new system (a clear indication that the power of key organized interests or 'street-level bureaucrats' has often been of much greater influence on public policy than parliamentary politics). Thus, right from the outset, at the policy formulation stage, he was forced to make concessions to the medical profession in order to ensure that the scheme could be implemented. The BMA, as a special organized interest, possessed great power, because without its support the NHS could not be fully or effectively established. Considerations about how the policy would be implemented were thus central to the 'making' of health policy in this respect – rather than a separate and subsequent stage – and this, in turn, was as much about relationships as processes.

Yet the problems with which Ministers grappled in establishing the NHS paled almost into insignificance when compared to the almost immediate funding crisis which arose. Costs remained far higher than expected, and the Korean War diverted money that urgently needed to be spent on domestic problems. The short-term, controversial and inadequate answer was the introduction of some limited charges, which were then extended or increased by subsequent governments. Almost right from the outset, therefore, the principle of a free national health service was compromised somewhat by the introduction of charges for certain types of health care. In this respect, we can also see how the original goals of the NHS were immediately compromised by external factors – derived from unforeseen circumstances – which deprived the new health service of adequate resources right from the outset. These difficulties symbolize two of the factors militating against 'perfect implementation', as discussed in Chapter 7 of *Policy Making in Britain* (Dorey, 2005).

Extending the structures, 1948–79

Although the Conservative Party had originally envisaged a somewhat different health service to that established by the Attlee administration, the health policy-making process was not discernibly affected when the Conservatives returned to Office in 1951 (where they remained for the next 13 years), and the preoccupation with funding continued throughout the 1950s. While the 1945–51 Labour Governments had been somewhat constrained by a particular organized interest – the BMA – in the precise manner that it established the NHS, the Conservatives themselves were subsequently restrained from making radical changes to the NHS by the weight of public opinion. The NHS thus became a prime example of what Rose and Davies have termed 'inheritance in public policy' (Rose and Davies, 1994). The Conservatives could, it appeared, do nothing that might be construed as anything less than a total commitment to what was, by now, the most popular legacy of Labour's six years in Office.

Following the Conservatives' heavy defeat in the 1945 general election, the Party had overhauled and modernized its policies, often explicitly acknowledging that there could be no return to the politics or policies of the 1930s, characterized as they were by economic depression and social deprivation. The 'progressive' outlook of the post-1945 Conservative

Party reflected the extent to which its political perspective during this period, along with many of its senior figures – Edward Boyle, Rab Butler, Iain Macleod, Harold Macmillan, Walter Monckton – derived from the 'one nation' Conservative tradition.

To the extent that the Conservatives did question the NHS in any way, some in the Party sought to find independent data or statistical evidence which would illustrate that the NHS was wasteful or over-funded. Indeed, in an effort to find independent support for savings, the Conservative Government established, in 1953, the Guillebaud Committee, whose remit was

> to review the present and prospective cost of the National Health Service, and to suggest means, whether by modifications in organisation or otherwise, of ensuring the most effective control and efficient use of such Exchequer funds as may be made available; to advise how, in view of the burdens on the Exchequer, a rising charge upon it can be avoided while providing for the maintenance of an adequate Service; and to make recommendations. (Guillebaud Committee, 1956)

In setting up this committee, Conservative Ministers were effectively loosening their grip over the way in which policy could be framed, and, certainly, when the Guillebaud Report was published in 1956, it gave the Conservatives no hope for cutbacks, arguing instead for more, not less, to be spent on the NHS (Guillebaud Committee, 1956). Determined to make savings regardless, Conservative Ministers extended the previous Labour Governments' provision for prescription charges, and increased spectacle and dental charges (in 1964, Labour abolished prescription charges, only to reintroduce them in 1967 in the context of a wider economic crisis presaging cuts in public expenditure). Thus, there was no break in principle with the founders of the NHS, because Labour itself had abandoned the principle of a free NHS by virtue of introducing prescription charges. Indeed, having established the principle that such charges could either be used to make savings or raise additional revenues, subsequent governments were inclined periodically to increase prescription charges in an incremental manner: the precedent had already been established by the founders of the NHS themselves.

Meanwhile, rising public expectations, competing job opportunities in an era of full employment, and uncompetitive pay and conditions, meant that it was difficult for the NHS to recruit and retain staff. An unwillingness to devote a substantially larger proportion of government spending to the NHS, and a tradition of poor remuneration for nurses, meant that instead of improving pay and conditions, governments were inclined to look overseas for sources of cheap labour, initially in Europe and then to countries of the old empire. The NHS was only able to deliver its services because of circumstances thousands of miles away: poverty and poor prospects in their own country drove many to take up the offer of work in Britain. In the Caribbean there was a tradition of migration, mainly to the USA, but when the USA clamped down on immigration, Britain became an alternative destination.

When the NHS was created, Bevan's concessions to the medical profession meant that many features of the old health care system were untouched. Certainly, the old power structures and the strong influence of the doctors remained. The medical profession had ensured that teaching hospitals were granted a special status, and benefited from a disproportionate allocation of resources. Furthermore, private practice and pay beds in NHS hospitals were permitted, while doctors – but no other health workers – were permitted to sit on management bodies. Meanwhile, the proposed health centres, which would have played a major role in preventative work and the co-ordination of services, were shelved because of doctors' fears that they would become subject to local authority control. Regional inequalities were built into the system by allowing teaching hospitals to continue to hold a special status. The emphasis on a hospital service, rather than on primary and preventative community care, co-ordinated through health centres, meant that, virtually from the outset, the NHS was increasingly out of step with changing societal health needs, such as better quality of life for the elderly in their own homes and easily available contraception for women.

Yet for many years, the NHS enjoyed enormous popularity, and an idealized image of the medical profession was widespread in popular culture. The way in which television programmes presented doctors invested them with great authority. For example, in programmes such as *Your Life in Their Hands* (1958), the doctors lectured the audience; there was no challenging their words and the medical discourse which they deployed. In the 1960s, meanwhile, *Dr. Finlay's Casebook* emphasized the importance of the character of the doctors, in this case two country GPs. The structures, funding and priorities of the health service were not questioned, and *Dr. Finlay's Casebook* presented the health service primarily in terms of relationships. It was already outdated by the time it was broadcast, but the British public clung to a nostalgic image of country GPs, which the programme both reflected and reinforced.

In reality, the bulk of NHS funding went into hospitals, not general practice, the latter continuing to hold a relatively low status within medicine, and care in the community fell woefully behind need. Pressure from a well-entrenched medical profession, primarily via the BMA, which effectively formed – with the Department of Health – a classic policy community, and a population still deferential to doctors (and in awe of medical advances) meant that there was little critique of the structures of the NHS among those most closely involved in health policy making. As such, expansion of health care usually focused on the hospitals, rather than other institutions or means of providing health care. This also meant, in effect, that curative medicine was privileged and prioritized over preventative health care and the tackling of the socio-environmental conditions which caused or contributed to poor health and disease in the first place.

Indeed, in the 1960s, a new hospital-building programme, coupled with the development of new drugs and medical technology, reinforced the idea that the NHS was central to rising standards of health, and an essential part of the British way of life. Critical voices demanded more, not less, NHS provision as the basis of health care in Britain. By contrast, academic criticisms of inequalities in standards of health – related to the social and economic structure of British society – were disregarded by the health policy community, and effectively kept off the institutional agenda.

Rudolph Klein, (1983) has emphasized that the NHS was a national *hospital* service, and although hospitals received the lion's share of health expenditure, the constant pressure on funds meant that in the early years of the NHS, maintenance and capital development were subject to cutbacks. Even though concern over the shortage of hospital facilities had long been expressed, the creation of the NHS did not, initially, inaugurate a hospital-building programme. Consequently, the NHS inherited old, poorly-maintained, hospitals, with rather antiquated services and poor staffing arrangements.

By the mid-1950s, though, and then throughout the 1960s, the emphasis within NHS planning did shift towards a building and modernization programme for hospitals. In

1955, Iain Macleod (Conservative Minister of Health, 1952–5) announced a hospital-building programme which was to become the focus of both Conservative and then, from the mid-1960s, Labour health policy. The Conservatives' subsequent 1962 'Hospital Plan' was supported by the Labour Opposition, and duly maintained when Labour returned to Office in 1964. Within the context of prioritizing the building of more hospitals, the 1962 'Hospital Plan' recommended ratios of beds to population in different regions, in accordance with the use of the beds: for example, it distinguished between beds for acute, maternity, geriatric and mentally handicapped patients. The 'Hospital Plan' was especially concerned with the location of hospitals, and recommended large District General Hospitals, providing comprehensive, up-to-date treatment. The interdependence of many branches of medicine, and the breadth of modern facilities, required large catchment areas for the smaller specialisms. Similarly, in-patient and out-patient treatment for maternity, short-stay psychiatric units and geriatric units, could all be embraced by District General Hospitals.

Meanwhile, developments in medical technology neatly corresponded with health policy makers' assumptions that the bulk of funding should go to hospitals. During the 1960s, intensive care units were developed in which all the bodily functions could be performed artificially by machines. From the 1960s kidney dialysis was available as well as kidney transplants, while since the 1970s, heart transplants have been undertaken. Then, from the 1990s, liver transplants were performed.

Mental health treatment

Throughout this time, an increasing range of drugs became integral to hospital treatment. One of the key areas in the development of drugs was in the sphere of mental illness, which had the effect of shifting the treatment of mental health patients away from hospitals. Mental health was one of the issues which became more openly discussed in the post-war era, thereby making it easier for mental health charities to present the interests of those with mental health problems to the public. A ground-breaking American film released in 1975, *One Flew Over the Cuckoo's Nest*, did much to focus wider attention on those in mental health institutions, and place the issue more firmly on the health policy agenda.

The motives for the scaling-down of mental hospitals, and for trying to keep those with mental health problems outside institutions, have been much debated. One view is that the development of tranquillizers in the 1950s meant that it was no longer necessary to keep people in institutions, while more enlightened attitudes in British society towards those with mental health problems meant that it was regarded as more humane *not* to keep people behind closed doors. In this context, doctors placed greater emphasis on rehabilitation of those diagnosed with mental health problems.

Others, however, argued that the scaling-down of mental hospitals, when there was no comprehensive or systematic support for vulnerable people outside hospitals, was primarily a cost-cutting exercise. As noted above, increasing political concern about the apparently escalating costs of the NHS prompted the establishment of the 1953 Guillebaud Committee of Inquiry, but the ensuing Report noted that expenditure on the NHS had actually declined slightly – as a proportion of GDP – during the first half of the 1950s, and that there was no evidence of profligacy or waste.

In spite of this conclusion, the 1950s witnessed a trend away from long-stay hospitals for the mentally ill, towards domestic and residential services (provided by local authorities), a shift reinforced by the 1957 Royal (Percy) Commission on Mental Health. This presaged the 1959 Mental Health Act, which explicitly signalled a move towards community-based care for those suffering from mental illness (Webster, 1998; Ham, 1999: 90). This contraction of long-stay hospitals occurred before the effective use of drugs, leading to the promotion, by policy makers, of 'care in the community', although this policy has frequently been criticized for merely leaving both vulnerable people and their carers without adequate support, be it professional or financial.

During the 1970s there was a general shift in all areas of health and medicine towards care in the community and shorter hospital stays (a shift which was promoted even more vigorously during the 1980s, in the context of curbing public expenditure and reducing dependency on the state). The elderly, by now constituting a growing proportion of the population, were seen as especially in need of help to live independently outside institutions, but the response to their needs was slow and reflected the still dominant hospital orientation of health policy makers. This tardy response to the needs of elderly people reflected a policy-making process that was dominated by a particular institutional agenda and its policy paradigm. This, in turn, was sustained by the health policy community, comprising the Department of Health (and Social Security) and the medical profession, the latter primarily represented by the British Medical Association (see, for example, Ham, 1999: 126–31).

During the Thatcher Governments of the 1980s, 'care in the community', although inextricably linked to neo-liberal concerns to reduce public expenditure, and reduce the role of both the state and local government, was also often linked, directly or indirectly, to the promotion of 'family values', whereby the family – which *de facto* usually meant women – was expected to look after relatives (especially the elderly) who could no longer look after themselves, but for whom there were no longer publicly-funded institutions in which they could be placed. This policy also constituted a partial 'privatizing' of the health service, as the care of certain vulnerable individuals was transferred from public institutions to the private sphere of the family, or, for those who could afford them, private residential/ nursing homes.

Public and environmental health

The strength of the health policy community, and the concomitant emphasis on medical treatment (as opposed to preventative measures concerning health) effectively meant that, for much of the post-war period, those who pointed to influences beyond the NHS which impacted on people's health were largely ignored: such influences – and thus those who sought to draw attention to them – remained part of the systemic agenda. Consequently, important aspects of public and environmental health were not addressed.

Environmental pollution and public health

For example, the effects of smog were ignored, until a crisis in London in 1952 that killed thousands of people (the exact figures are disputed but range between roughly 2,000 and 8,000), compelled Ministers and senior civil servants to develop a policy which resulted in the 1956 Clean Air Act, itself extended in subsequent legislation. Here is an example both of the difficulty of getting a problem from the systemic agenda on to the institutional policy agenda, and also of how a crisis can often provide the prompt for policy change or innovation. Certainly, the 1952 London smog fulfilled two of the criteria which Solesbury (1976) – in his study of the environmental agenda – identified as vital to imbuing an issue with sufficient importance or urgency to elicit action from policy makers, namely 'generality' (in terms of the number, or potential number, of people affected) and 'particularity' (whereby a specific or dramatic event makes an issue highly visible, thereby focusing public and political attention on the problem) (for an account of the move towards clean air, see Ashby and Anderson, 1981).

By contrast, other pollutants, in particular those emanating from vehicle exhaust emissions, remained absent from the policy agenda, reflecting both the lack of scientific knowledge about the impact of such emissions at this juncture, and the strength of the transport policy community, and its 'policy paradigm' which privileged car (and lorry) transport – and road-building – over public transport (see Chapter 9 by Robinson, in this volume).

It was not until the 1980s that other health and environmental issues, such as those pertaining to food, and the recycling of household waste, became much more widely and seriously discussed, although academics are not agreed over the reasons for the arrival of environmental issues on the policy agenda. One view is that it was the result of a groundswell of public opinion that strengthened the power of the environmental lobby. More consumers wanted organic food, ratepayers wanted local authority recycling schemes, and more car drivers used unleaded petrol, reflecting growing awareness of, and hence concern about, global warming. Others have suggested that changes within the core executive, such as the personalities and actions of key politicians, and changes of party ideology, were important. The Green Party has never enjoyed the success or influence of its counterparts in some other European countries, although some of its policies have been adapted – rather than adopted – but diluted by the mainstream ones. The nature of British party politics and the electoral system in Britain have, therefore, also played a part in the type and extent of environmental policies adopted in Britain.

In addition, policies in one area can have a knock-on effect in another. For example, in the late 1980s, plans to privatize water supply and electricity brought forth a range of concerns about pollution and helped to make the problem more prominent (see McCormick, 1991, and Robinson, 1992, for environmental policy issues). Certainly, during the 1980s and 1990s, issues surrounding public health were increasingly being linked to other concerns about environmental pollution and modern farming methods *vis-à-vis* food production (for the latter, see Grant's chapter in this volume).

Cigarette smoking and public health

Another policy that has closely followed changing social attitudes and emerging scientific knowledge – which Virginia Berridge has pertinently analysed – is that of smoking. In the 1950s and 1960s, smoking was socially acceptable and even encouraged, even though, as early as 1950, Richard Doll had illustrated the link between smoking and cancer, and yet uncertainty remained. Even after a 1957 report by the Medical Research Council had accepted the link, governments failed to act. Berridge offers a raft of explanations for governments' tardy response, both then and later (Berridge, 2003). She points out, for example, that politicians and their scientific advisers themselves smoked, and that money raised from tobacco tax was an important source of revenue for the Treasury. Besides, the issue was overshadowed by the main public health issue at the time, coal smoke pollution (in an era before central heating became the norm). Furthermore, smoking was not deemed to be the usual kind of public health issue, and governments were wary of interfering in a private activity. So, in spite of the scientific or medical evidence already available during the 1950s, governments were extremely slow to act, to the extent that it was not until 1965 that cigarette adverts were banned from television. A strong anti-smoking policy was unpopular with politicians who feared a backlash from those who would accuse them of attacking working-class culture. Governments therefore followed a softly, softly approach with health education campaigns, voluntary agreements with the tobacco industry and some limits on advertising.

While governments tiptoed around the issue, an increasingly vocal anti-smoking lobby campaigned against the well-resourced, global tobacco industry, and by the 1980s, no one in Britain could have been unaware of the health risks of smoking. Consequently, the division by the 1980s was no longer, as it had been in the 1950s, between those who accepted the evidence and those who did not, but between those who wanted to reduce the risk and those who wished to eliminate it. During the 1990s, health policy with regard to smoking was based primarily on the need to prevent and treat the addiction (with more than 80,000 deaths in England each year attributable to smoking (Meikle and Wintour, 2004: 13). However, because of growing concern over 'passive smoking' – the inhalation by non-smokers of other people's cigarette smoke – as the decade progressed (concern again fuelled by various medical and scientific evidence), health policy in this area also increasingly sought to tackle the social or wider public health consequences of smoking (Berridge, 2003), an issue to which we return later.

Women's reproductive health

Women's reproductive health was another area of policy where cultural changes prompted health policy changes. While reproduction was increasingly medicalized (which was not necessarily a retrograde step), it was accompanied by concern, among many women, about a lack or loss of control: for example, contraceptives and legal abortion remained difficult to obtain. It was not until the 1960s that significant changes in attitudes over personal choice, the need for greater personal freedom and more openness in the discussion of personal behaviour (especially for women), enabled legislation to be passed that made contraceptives and abortion more easily available to women. Certainly, from the late 1960s, the health policy process operated in a society that was more affluent, more consumer-oriented, in which attitudes towards social class (although not the structures) were changing, where there was a preoccupation with youth, greater equality between women and men, and more personal freedom (Marwick, 1991).

Remodelling health care since 1979

From the 1980s onwards, the ideological context in which health policy making occurred was rather different from that which had previously prevailed since 1945. With the election of Margaret Thatcher's Conservative Party in May 1979, strongly influenced by the political philosophy of the New Right, government policy in general strongly promoted business and private enterprise, and sought to discourage individuals and families from succumbing to 'welfare dependency'. Reliance on the market (not the state), increased competition, and greater choice for individuals – consumer sovereignty – were the principles which underpinned a plethora of policies during the 1980s and 1990s. Individualism was lauded over collectivism.

Yet in the sphere of health policy, there was no immediate overhaul of the NHS in order to render it compatible with, and complementary to, these new values. Indeed, as Ham notes: 'In the case of the NHS, the Thatcher government did not come to power in 1979 with a comprehensive and coherent programme of reform' (Ham, 1999: 28). Instead, Thatcher's Conservative Governments moved cautiously at first, pursuing predominantly piecemeal changes with regard to health policy and the NHS. For example, from 1979, Ministers encouraged greater use of private health care, while from 1983, health authorities were required to contract out domestic, catering and laundry services. At the time, these reforms generated bitter opposition, with trade unions anxious about the job losses which were likely to follow the transfer of such services to the private sector, while the Labour Opposition portrayed 'contracting out' as an attack on the foundational principles of the NHS, and as the first stage of 'privatization by the back door'.

While robustly denying such allegations, Conservative Ministers were nonetheless sensitive to such charges, for they recognized that the NHS was extremely popular – probably the most popular element of the welfare state – so that any perceived attack on it was likely to be electorally damaging. Indeed, during the 1980s, a whole-hearted commitment to the NHS – with which it was indelibly identified – was one of the few issues on which the Labour Party retained any credibility with the public (in sharp contrast to its policies on key issues such as defence – this being the decade of intensified Cold War and fear of the alleged military threat posed by the Soviet Union – and economic management). With hindsight, however, the contracting-out of ancillary services is no longer viewed as a fundamental change.

Recognition of the need for reform

Despite the British people's commitment to the NHS, it was also widely acknowledged that some sort of reform was essential. The NHS faced mounting problems (not unique to Britain) arising from cultural, social and scientific changes: the costs of the NHS were escalating as a result of rising expectations, ever more costly and feasible medical interventions, and an ageing population. Problems specific to Britain, such as the balance between preventative and curative medical treatment, the integration of services and management structures, had existed from the outset, but had become more acute since the 1970s, and were now openly and widely discussed.

It is important to understand not only the political context within which health policy developed during the 1980s, but also the cultural context, for this too affected the political viability of certain health policies. Even those with no direct experience of the NHS were confronted with various images of its problems in their living rooms. For example, in 1985, the hugely popular BBC soap series *EastEnders* portrayed a single mother and her baby, both with bronchitis, living in damp accommodation. When their GP tried to get them rehoused, he had difficulty locating the appropriate person in the local authority, and when he did finally speak to that person, it became apparent that the mother and baby's plight was already known about, but nothing had been done for them. This sequence highlighted a number of issues: the lack of co-ordination between health and social services; the problem of dealing with social services; and the influences on health that were beyond the control of the NHS. Also during the 1980s, the BBC drama series *Casualty* regularly addressed a range of hospital problems, most notably a lack of resources, while in 1988, the comedy programme *Don't Wait Up* dealt with issues such as operations that were repeatedly cancelled; waiting times; the advantages of private medicine; and NHS shortages. Britain had experienced a dramatic decline in deference by this time, and in these and other programmes, the authority of the medical profession was increasingly questioned or challenged.

Furthermore, television and radio documentaries now allowed the general public to speak for themselves, rather than medical experts, on health issues; by allowing a range of voices to be heard, traditional hierarchies were undermined, and alternative – often opposing – views were frequently aired. By homing in on the plight of particular individuals, the personal and very human effects of health policy priorities, governmental resource allocation and NHS structures, were highlighted. Individual, small-scale and local stories illustrated major, national themes. Other programmes, such as chat shows, depicted doctors with differing experiences and views, thereby indicating that the 'medical profession' was no longer monolithic and all-powerful, but subject to internal disagreement and division. Such programmes indicated, and probably contributed to, a new willingness to criticize health policy that, despite a strong popular commitment to the NHS, eventually helped make its reconstruction possible, although the manner in which the new policy developed was neither open nor popular.

It was not until Margaret Thatcher's Conservative Government had won (in 1987) a third successive general election that Ministers felt sufficiently secure and emboldened to attempt to dislodge the jewel in the post-war socialist crown. By early 1987, Thatcher's patience with the NHS had been exhausted, for while she recognized that much of the NHS's work was of a high quality, she was also cognizant that the caveats were, by now, longer than the praises. In particular, the NHS was not deemed sufficiently sensitive either to people's wishes or to increasing costs. It was also adjudged to be inefficient. Furthermore, hospitals and local health authorities performed with inexplicable variations.

The new health policy process
The policy-making process for the reforms that were introduced in the early 1990s was somewhat different from that which had prevailed previously, as was the ensuing health policy itself. The distinctive features of the new health policy process were: the role played by the Prime Minister (Prime Ministers had not traditionally concerned themselves closely with 'social' policies, preferring – or feeling obliged – instead to focus primarily on economic and foreign affairs); the sudden decision to introduce policy changes; the tiny group that formulated these policies; the absence of any negotiations outside Whitehall; and the huge public outcry that the ensuing reforms prompted. However, in spite of this departure from the traditional mode of health policy making, there remained some similarities with

previous policy making in this sphere, most notably with regard to internal Whitehall conflict and departmentalism, opposition from doctors, and the extent to which one dominant health Minister was politically responsible for the reforms.

It was well known that Margaret Thatcher wanted to see a flourishing private health care sector, for this was integral to her political beliefs and ideological outlook (as well as that of the New Right generally). Indeed, on one particular and highly-publicized occasion, her own choice of private treatment had personalized a public debate in the 1980s when she declared that she had not used the NHS because of her desire and determination to be treated where she wanted, when she wanted and by whom she wanted. Although there had been growing financial pressures on the NHS, demonstrations from nurses and a highly publicised case of a baby dying after his hole-in-the-heart operation was cancelled five times, when Mrs Thatcher used an interview on the BBC current affairs programme *Panorama* to announce a fundamental review of the NHS, she did so without having first discussed it with Ministerial colleagues. Needless to say, her announcement certainly took them all by surprise.

She then headed a small Ministerial review team recruited from the Treasury and the Department of Health, which secretly – and without wider consultation – considered various options that revolved around an increased role for private health care. Given their *a priori* premise that 'private is best', any wider involvement or consultations would probably have stymied the reforms before they left the drawing board. No one who worked in the NHS (or possibly who used it) took part in the discussions, although the review group did seek the views of a few doctors who were active in the Conservative Party.

The manner in which the new health policy was devised, entailing the conscious exclusion of the medical profession, provided a good example of a policy community being deliberately disregarded by Ministers willing to invoke 'despotic power', in order to impose policy change on those individuals and/or organizations deemed too conservative or concerned with their own institutional interests voluntarily to accept change or a reorientation of policy in their particular subsystem. Ideological conviction and Ministerial activism were melded together to force through a change in health policy, without the involvement or endorsement of the medical profession, as primarily represented by the BMA, at the formulation stage.

While a shift away from a state service was popular with the politicians serving on the reform committee, they were somewhat divided on how to achieve it. Margaret Thatcher and her Secretary of State for Health, John Moore, both favoured encouraging private health insurance by offering tax relief on private health care plans. The Chancellor of the Exchequer, Nigel Lawson, on the other hand, led the Treasury's opposition to tax relief, and instead argued for extending charges to include direct payment for doctors and hospitals. Such a thought horrified both Thatcher and the Ministers from the Department of Health, for they recognized that such a policy was likely to be deeply unpopular with the electorate. There was deadlock, particularly as John Moore was unable to persuade his Treasury colleagues to relent in their opposition, whereupon Thatcher divided the DHSS into two separate Departments, with Moore becoming Secretary of State for Social Security, and Kenneth Clarke appointed Secretary of State for Health instead. Certainly, Clarke was widely viewed as someone who thrived on political fights.

Kenneth Clarke did indeed find a way through the impasse, by drawing on the ideas of an American economist, Professor Alain Enthoven (1985), which yielded a proposal for an

**Table 5.1   The creation of new NHS Trusts and GP fundholders each
year, 1991–6**

Year	Number of new NHS Trusts	Number of new GP fundholders
1991	57	306
1992	99	288
1993	136	600
1994	140	800
1995	21	500
1996	–	1,200

Source: Ham, 1999: 41. Ham, *Health Policy in Britain*, 1982, Macmillan reproduced with
permission of Palgrave Macmillan.

internal market within the NHS. Clarke now proposed self-governing hospitals that would
compete with each other for patients, while some GPs would be given their own budgets
to buy services and treatment for their patients. The Treasury was appalled at this latter
suggestion especially, but Clarke's proposals – backed by Thatcher as Prime Minister –
prevailed (BBC2, 1996).

When Clarke's plans were published in a White Paper *Working for Patients*, in 1989, they
triggered a political storm. Doctors, nurses, the general public and Opposition politicians were
aghast, and in the ensuing propaganda war, both the Government and its critics spent unprecedented sums of money on publicizing their arguments for/against the proposed reforms. The
BMA urged a pilot project at the very least, but Clarke, suspicious that this was a ruse to scup-
per the project, refused, whereupon the National Health Service and Community Care Act was
passed the following year (1990). However, the implementation of some of the key reforms
enshrined in the Act – most notably the establishment of NHS Trusts and GP fundholders –
was phased in over a number of years 'in recognition of the complexity of the changes and
political anxiety about their feasibility' (Ham, 1999: 41), as illustrated by Table 5.1.

The key change was that an internal market would operate within the NHS, creating a
clear distinction between 'purchasers' and 'providers' of health care. Hospitals could opt
out of District Health Authority control and become self-governing Trusts, selling their
services in the public and private sectors. GP practices of a certain size could control their
own budgets if they chose to opt-out (Thatcher, 1993: 571, 606–17).

However, while GPs were to be granted the opportunity to acquire greater independence
by opting-out, doctors and nurses in the NHS were to be subject to much greater managerial control and monitoring, in the name of accountability and efficiency. Thatcher and
Clarke evidently recognized that clinical expertise and medical knowledge imbued health
professionals with considerable power and autonomy, which – from the perspective of the
New Right – needed to be weakened and undermined. Hence the need to increase both the
number and the power of NHS managers *vis-à-vis* the medical profession, which would,
in turn, serve to weaken a previously strong policy community. The enhanced role of managers was also intended to imbue the NHS with much greater 'business sense', with more
emphasis on such objectives as cost-effectiveness, efficiency, performance indicators, setting (and meeting) targets and value for money.

Yet the Government was adamant that these proposals did not threaten the basic founding principles of the NHS, which would thus continue to be financed almost entirely from taxation,[1] and free to patients at the point of access: there was no intention to introduce charges for patients in NHS hospitals. In other words, access to the NHS would continue to be based on medical need, not income or ability to pay (Ham, 1999: 37). Furthermore, Ministers were emphatic that the type of reforms they were introducing into the NHS would yield an improvement in the choice and quality of care received by patients themselves.

One other important point to note here is that having deliberately excluded the medical profession when formulating their NHS reforms, the Conservatives did, during the 1990s, re-incorporate them somewhat during the implementation 'stage'. In other words, while the NHS reforms were being developed by the Ministerial review team:

> The established rules of conduct in the health policy community were suspended (but not abandoned) and in place of bargaining and negotiation with key groups, ministers decided among themselves what they wanted to do and acted accordingly. Notwithstanding this, pressure groups were closely involved in the implementation of the policy, and on many issues ... they continued to exert influence ... the impact of political ideology was modified by managerial pragmatism and judgement of what was likely to be acceptable to the public and the health professions. (Ham, 1999: 49–50)

As with various other policy communities in the 1980s and early 1990s, therefore, the health policy community found itself subject to a deliberate process of destabilization and weakening, whereby exclusion from the Ministerial discussions about the reform of extant policies and/or development of new policies was followed by an invitation to become involved at the implementation 'stage', and a return to dialogue. Having been subject to such 'despotic power', though, their subsequent return to the policy community was either less exclusive than previously – with other policy actors now sharing 'insider' status (thereby raising a conceptual question about whether it was still sufficiently close-knit and cohesive to constitute a policy community *per se*) – or their subsequent influence was largely confined to the practical implementation, or some of the administrative details, of the policy, but with Ministers emphatic that the original principles or objectives remained non-negotiable: if the 'excluded' organized interest or professional body wished to be re-admitted to the policy community/ network, it would henceforth have to be on the Government's terms and conditions.

Public health issues in the 1980s and 1990s

Since the 1980s, there has been much more open discussion of specific illnesses, especially those that in the past were barely mentioned by name. For example, in 1983, a British film, *Champions*, was made of (the jockey) Bob Champion's experience of testicular cancer; following treatment, he went on to win the Grand National.

---

1 At the end of the Conservatives' 18 years in Office, 82 per cent of NHS finance still emanated from general taxation, while a further 12 per cent accrued from NI contributions. Only 6 per cent was derived from charges and other receipts (Department of Health, 1998a).

Meanwhile, the openness with which HIV/AIDS was discussed was unprecedented. Indeed, during the mid-1980s, the Thatcher Governments found themselves endorsing a national advertising campaign to promote 'safe sex', involving the use of condoms, to curb the spread of AIDS. This caused some unease among 'moral traditionalists' who felt that the campaign was somewhat at odds with the New Right's hostility to 'permissiveness' and advocacy of family values; for such Conservatives, 'safe sex' ought to be about heterosexual-sex-within-marriage only, whereas the exhortation to 'use a condom' seemed, tacitly at least, to condone sexual activity more generally, including homosexual acts. In other words, the anti-AIDS campaign seemed – to moral traditionalists – to promote safety and 'taking precautions' when engaging in sexual activity, rather than encouraging abstinence and self-restraint.

Public awareness of the experience of coping with various diseases and disabilities, along with the seeming obsession with promoting personal health through health clubs, exercise regimes, and endless television programmes devoted to every conceivable aspect of health and illness, have been paralleled with a greater policy focus on reducing particular diseases. For example, the 1992 White Paper, *The Health of the Nation: A Strategy for Health in England*, set targets for reducing: coronary heart disease and strokes; cancer; mental illness; HIV/AIDs and sexual ill-health; and accidents. The strategy for meeting these targets involved the creation of 'healthy alliances' between various organizations and individuals, thus further promoting a mixed economy of health care and provision. The White Paper envisaged that improvement in these areas of health would emanate from changes in the behaviour of individuals and social groups; it made no reference to the structure or organization of society (Department of Health, 1992). Yet, many attempts have been made over the years to draw attention to class (and later, gender and ethnic) inequalities in standards of health, most notably in the 1979 Black Report (1979) and in a 1988 report by the Health Education Council (1988); see also Jones (1994: 172–92). During the early 1990s, there was some recognition in Whitehall that inequalities in health needed to be addressed by governments, although generally, recommendations arising from studies by academics are awkward for governments – irrespective of ideological hue – because of their far-reaching implications (Department of Health, 1991; 1994). Instead, governments have generally deemed it far safer to focus on rearranging health service delivery or to argue about national or local pay bargaining agreements.

New Labour and a health policy: a 'moving consensus' emerges

During the early 1990s, while still in Opposition, the Labour Party had established a working party – the Commission on Social Justice – to conduct a wide-ranging review of its policies, and the title was certainly indicative of the main principle underpinning future Labour policies. By the time 'New Labour' won its landslide victory in May 1997, the originally controversial reforms which had been introduced at the beginning of the decade were now well-entrenched, and the Labour Government, so hostile to the changes at the time of their introduction, now accepted them, albeit with some adaptations which it claimed were a matter of principle (but which some of Labour's critics regarded as little more than minor tweaking). Certainly, the Blair Government's White Paper, *The New NHS: Modern. Dependable*, published in December 1997, insisted that:

> In paving the way for the new NHS, the Government is committed to building on what has worked but discarding what has failed. There will be no return to the old centralised command and control system of the 1970s. ... But nor will there be a continuation of the divisive internal market system in the 1990s. ... Instead, there will be a 'third way' of running the NHS – a system based on partnership and driven by performance ... what counts is what works. (Department of Health, 1997: 10, 11)

Yet – as in various other areas of public policy – New Labour's emphasis on a 'Third Way', which purports to constitute a clear alternative both to Old Labour and Thatcherite Conservatism, has not prevented an ongoing debate about just how distinctive the Blair Governments are when compared to their predecessors. For some critics, the much-vaunted 'Third Way' is not a clear alternative to Thatcherism, but a continuation of many of its features and principles, albeit in a somewhat gentler or less acerbic guise: Thatcherism with a human face.

For example, the Conservatives originally introduced the principle of using private finance to build hospitals, but it was actually implemented by Labour, thereby further blurring the line between public (state) and private health care. When Labour entered Office in 1997, one of its first actions was to strengthen and make operative the Private Finance Initiative (PFI), whereby health care trusts are required to seek private finance for development schemes before bidding for government money. Private consortia build and run new hospitals, leasing them back to the trusts. Like their Conservative predecessors, the Blair Governments – and Tony Blair especially – have insisted that the use of private consortia to finance and build new hospitals (or modernize existing ones) in no way undermines the underlying principle that treatment for patients remains 'free at the point of access', and that the NHS remains funded overwhelmingly from general taxation. As far as Tony Blair and his 'Third Way' disciples are concerned, patients do not lie in their hospital beds fretting about whether or not the hospital was built by a private company or consortium.

Criticisms that such private sector involvement represented another example of 'creeping privatization' of the NHS had originally led the then Conservative Secretary of State for Health, Stephen Dorrell, to claim that no such scheme would apply to clinical services, only to health facilities. However, further evidence of an increasingly entwined state and private health care system appeared in the autumn of 1996, when it emerged that, as a result of the growth of pay beds in Trust hospitals, the NHS was the chief provider of private health care.

While both the Blair Governments and the Conservative Opposition accept a role for private finance and private companies in the provision of health care – not least because demand for health care is infinite while resources are finite – alternative proposals from beyond the party political spectrum suggest that there may be alternative ways of meeting health care needs, most notably the development of Evidence-Based Medicine (EBM), which involves collating evidence on which treatments do, and do not, work. Certainly, New Labour has repeatedly insisted that the 'Third Way' is primarily concerned about 'what works', thereby formally eschewing ideological debates and disagreements. Furthermore, as was noted in Chapter 2 of *Policy Making in Britain* (Dorey, 2005), the Blair Governments have themselves apparently embraced evidence-based policy making in a number of areas, sometimes in tandem with experimentation via local-level pilot schemes to gauge 'what works'.

While the Labour Party had, in Opposition, attacked the Conservative Governments' health policies as they unfolded during the 1980s and first half of the 1990s, the approach to the 1997 general election saw the differences between the two main parties become less distinct. 'Old' Labour's promises to scrap the NHS internal market were modified, while an earlier commitment to reintroduce free eye tests and dental check-ups disappeared altogether. The most radical pledge in New Labour's manifesto, though, was that 'Labour will set new goals for improving the overall health of the nation which recognise the impact that poverty, poor housing, unemployment and a polluted environment have on health' (Labour Party, 1997: 21). Here was an early example of what was subsequently to constitute 'joined-up government', deriving from a clear recognition that certain objectives and policies could no longer be treated as the sole responsibility of just one department. A multi-departmental, cross-sectoral approach would henceforth be needed to tackle problems which were themselves multi-causal in origin.

During the late 1990s, the Blair Government and the Conservative Opposition both displayed, superficially at least, strikingly similar priorities in their health policies. Both professed their commitment to a 'modern' National Health Service that was not burdened by excessive bureaucracy, and in which the interests of the patients were paramount. Both parties claimed to want the provision of greater public information, devolved powers and partnerships between public and private organizations. There was also an apparently bipartisan emphasis on preventative health care, and raising living standards (Jones, 1998).

However, there was discernible divergence between New Labour and the Conservatives in the details of their respective health policies. Although the Labour Party had, as already noted, previously been highly critical of the internal market in the NHS when established by the Conservatives, the Blair Governments have chosen to build upon it, rather than demolish it. The aforementioned December 1997 White Paper *The New NHS: Modern. Dependable*, stipulated that individual fundholding by GPs, who each negotiated annual contracts, was to be replaced by a system in which all practices were brought together, along with community nurses, in primary care groups, which would commission health services on a three-yearly cycle. This change was intended to reduce the volume of paper generated, and to remove the inequalities that manifested themselves between fundholding and non-fundholding practices. Every three years, health authorities were to produce health improvement programmes in order to provide the framework for health services within their area. The services were to be provided by health authorities, local authorities, hospital trusts and primary care groups. Health authorities then allocated funds on the basis of these plans to primary health groups. In other words, while the division between purchaser and provider remains, the Blair Governments have sought to change the rules of the competition and attack inequalities.

Since 1997, the manner in which health policy is framed and presented has followed a formula that is consistent across government departments. There is a template for explicit statements of aims and objectives; there is a Public Statement Agreement (PSA), and there is now internet access to departmental documents on web pages; these are all part of Whitehall 'best practice' in order to comply with the guiding mantra of modernization, not only in the policy that is developed for health but also in the policy process *per se*.

Health policy has gradually evolved since 1997, partly reflecting the Blair Governments' view that modernization of the NHS is a ten-year programme, whereby 'evolutionary change rather than organisational upheaval' should be pursued (Department of Health, 1997: 5). In 1998, the Department of Health set out its aims and objectives in the Public Service Agreement which the Treasury then published as a White Paper, *Public Services for the Future: Modernisation, Reform, Accountability* (DoH, 1998d). Two years later, after extensive consultation, the Prime Minister and Secretary of State for Health announced *The NHS Plan* (DoH, 2000). Tony Blair, like Margaret Thatcher in the late 1980s, closely identified himself with the presentation of policy, although she had also taken a much closer day-to-day interest in the formulation of such policy. In the case of New Labour, it was the Treasury which played an integral part, for the new health policy involved such a substantial increase in resources that it could never have proceeded without close Treasury involvement. *The NHS Plan* entailed a staged implementation, integral to which was Gordon Brown's announcement in 2002 of substantial increases in real terms of 7.4 per cent every year between 2003–4 and 2007–8. The Blair Governments have cited such increases in health expenditure ('investment') as further evidence – against those who complain about 'creeping privatization' – of New Labour's commitment to a world-class, publicly-funded NHS. However, as in other areas of public policy under the Blair Governments, increased expenditure is invariably linked to demands for, or evidence of, improved efficiency, and the attainment of a plethora of targets and performance indicators.

Meanwhile, as if to illustrate the extent to which the Blair Governments are now setting the terms, and determining the terrain, of debate over health policy, the Conservative Opposition, since 1997, has repeatedly pledged to match Labour's planned expenditure on the NHS, even while committing itself to public spending cuts elsewhere. Needless to say, New Labour Ministers have taken great delight in 'welcoming' the Conservatives' professed commitment to matching the Blair Governments' planned spending on the NHS, while ridiculing the Opposition's overall expenditure pledges on the grounds that 'their sums do not add up'.

In 2002 (the year after the Blair Government had been re-elected by another enormous parliamentary majority), the six core ideas behind Labour's health policy were enshrined in *Delivering the NHS Plan* (DoH, 2002): increased patient choice; greater plurality in health service provision; encouraging better working between health and social care; devolving power to frontline staff; strengthening local accountability; and changing the way in which money flows through the NHS. All of these ideas were part of the Blair Government's professed overall aims of helping people not only live longer, but also live healthier (itself a prerequisite of living longer) and more independent lives, and in order to achieve this, the Government aimed to provide faster, fairer services that delivered better health care, and reduced health inequalities. All these aims are so laudable that they appear bland when listed, yet the interpretation and delivery of almost every detailed aspect of policy has been contested, and the subject of local and national, popular and academic debate.

During Tony Blair's first administration, the reduction of inequalities was the centre-piece of the New Labour Government's rhetoric about health. While the Conservatives had previously emphasized the importance of individual responsibility for raising standards of health, and had set specific – and largely unrealistic – targets for reducing illness, New Labour resurrected an Old Labour concern by explicitly acknowledging that inequalities in health resulted from factors which are often beyond an individual's control. Echoing the manifesto commitment to reducing inequalities in standards of health, on 5 February 1998, Frank Dobson, Secretary of State for Health, told the House of Commons that: 'This Government recognises that poverty, poor housing, low wages, unemployment, air pollution, crime and disorder can all make people ill in both body and mind' (Department of Health, 1998b). Launching the Green Paper *Our Healthier Nation*, he promised that the Government would co-ordinate policies across departments, while simultaneously encouraging contracts between central government, local government, individuals and local agencies to improve health. The Government was establishing 10 Health Action Zones and would invest money – accrued from National Lottery revenues – into healthy living centres. The Government scrapped many of the Conservatives' targets, presumably because it realized that they were only hostages to fortune, and, instead, Dobson claimed that the Government would support local strategies with local targets. He linked the attack on health inequalities with other Government policies for reducing inequality, such as the Social Exclusion Unit, the minimum wage, employment creation programmes under welfare-to-work, and the release of money from the past sale of council houses to be spent on new and improved housing (Department of Health, 1998c). For New Labour, therefore, health policy is itself integral to the avowed goal of achieving 'joined-up government'.

Public health issues in the 21st century

Since the Blair Government's re-election in 2001, three particular aspects of public health, albeit inextricably linked to individual behaviour or life-styles, have risen to the top of the health policy agenda.

Smoking

Firstly, the issue of health risks associated with smoking – while not in itself new or novel – has risen to prominence, but this time in the context of growing concern about 'passive smoking'. As we noted earlier, this refers to the involuntary and unavoidable inhalation of cigarette smoke and fumes by non-smokers who are none the less in close proximity to cigarette smokers. By the beginning of the 21st century, medical and scientific evidence was claiming that 'passive smokers' were themselves at risk of developing lung cancer and other smoking-related diseases, as a consequence of repeated or consistent exposure to other people's cigarette smoke.

It was in this context that the issue of banning smoking in certain public places – such as restaurants and pubs – was placed on the institutional agenda, with Ministers seriously discussing whether they should invoke legislation to this effect, or leave it to individual retailers, owners of 'public' premises or businesses and local authorities, to decide whether they wished to prohibit smoking in their establishments or public spaces. Certainly, by this time, many workplaces – particularly offices – and most forms of public transport had already adopted a no-smoking policy.

One reason for Ministerial hesitancy over whether or not to introduce legislation to ban smoking in certain designated public places or establishments, was concern that such a measure would inevitably lead to allegations that Tony Blair's 'New Labour' Governments were turning Britain into a 'nanny state', and in so doing, whittling away individual liberty and people's right to choose how to live their lives. Yet if Ministers did not endorse such legislation, they were equally likely to be criticized for failing to do enough to protect 'passive smokers' and further improve public health. They would also be vulnerable to allegations that the Government was afraid to 'take on' the well-resourced and highly-vocal tobacco industry. None the less, that a debate about banning smoking in public places was taking place at all was indicative of how far the health risks of smoking (and the associated impact on non-smokers) had moved up the policy agenda.

Binge drinking

The second Blair Government also presided over growing concern about 'binge drinking' in Britain, particularly by young people, and especially among young women (see, for example, *The Observer*, 21 December 2003). A report published by the Royal College of Physicians, in early 2005, revealed that since the 1970s, the number of young and middle-aged people dying from alcohol-derived liver diseases had increased by 700 per cent. The issue of excessive or heavy drinking in general, and 'binge drinking' in particular, was lent added resonance by the Government's own proposals for a major reform of Britain's licensing laws, which would effectively permit '24-hour drinking' (by virtue of pubs' opening hours no longer being confined to 11.00–23.00). Opponents deemed this madness, alleging that it would greatly exacerbate binge drinking, alcohol abuse and public disorder arising from drunkenness, with a number of senior police chiefs expressing their concern or opposition to the proposal (*The Guardian*, 21 January 2005). By contrast, pro-reformers argued that it would enable drinkers to 'pace' themselves more, and would end the hitherto tendency to drink quickly in order to finish before closing time. Furthermore, pro-reformers argued, by liberalizing Britain's licensing laws, so that pubs did not all have to close at 23.00, there would no longer be a mass exodus of drunken youths simultaneously congregating in town-centre high streets, fast-food takeaways or taxi ranks. This, in turn, it was envisaged, would actually facilitate a reduction in alcohol-related crime and violence.

Although 'binge drinking' was primarily a health issue, it also had serious implications for the Home Office, due to the public disorder – crime, violence and vandalism – deriving from drunkenness in Britain's towns and cities at weekends, and the consequent extent to which police forces were becoming overstretched in trying to maintain order. This implied that, as in other areas, 'joined-up government' was required, entailing a co-ordinated, cross-departmental, multi-agency, partnership approach, involving – among others – the Department of Health, the Home Office, representatives from the medical profession and police, local authorities (who granted licences to premises selling alcohol), local police authorities and representatives from the brewing industry.

As with smoking, however, Ministers found themselves facing something of a dilemma, for lack of decisive action was likely to be condemned as vacillation or pusillanimity, and possibly an unwillingness to 'take on' the brewing industry, yet any action to curb 'excessive' drinking was equally liable to invite (further) allegations about turning Britain into a 'nanny state' and mollycoddling individuals through overprotective paternalism.

Obesity and poor diet

The third public health issue which rose to the top of the health policy agenda at the beginning of the 21st century concerned dietary trends in Britain, particularly the growing proportion of the population suffering from obesity. Ironically, this was part of a more general trend towards *less* healthy eating habits and food consumption, in spite of apparently greater discernment among consumers over such issues as food safety, and increased sales of 'health foods' and the like. Many people were becoming more reliant on 'fast' or 'convenience' food (partly linked, perhaps, to longer working hours, with less time for the cooking of healthier or more nutritious meals). For example, one study revealed that up to 33 per cent of British citizens had increased their consumption of fried foods in the last decade, while a similar proportion were taking less exercise (partly, perhaps, because longer working hours left many adults with insufficient time or energy for keeping fit). The same study revealed that consumption of (healthier) brown bread had declined – in favour of white, processed bread – as had consumption of fruit and vegetables. These trends were in spite of record levels being spent, by various agencies and governmental bodies, on health campaigns pertaining to both food and exercise (*The Sunday Times*, 19 December 2004).

Meanwhile, an increasing number of teenagers – and even younger children, to some extent – now spend much of their leisure time either watching television (many children now have a television in their bedroom, something almost unimaginable 20 or 30 years ago) or playing computer games – or both – which means that they too are not benefiting from enough exercise. Some parents would also claim that concern over child safety makes them reluctant to let their children play outside in the way that previous generations would have done.

In response to these various trends, the Blair Government published a White Paper in November 2004, *Choosing Health* (Department of Health, 2004), whose proposals included a ban – by 2008 – on smoking in pubs selling food, while smoking would also be banned in the immediate bar area of all pubs. Pubs not selling meals would be free to decide for themselves whether or not to become no-smoking establishments. With regard to food consumption and diet, the White Paper envisaged a system of labelling on food packaging, which would provide clear information about such factors as fat, salt and sugar content, while also indicating which food products ought only to be eaten in moderation. Food manufacturers themselves would be encouraged to reduce fat and sugar levels in their products. Guidelines would be issued concerning the advertising of certain foods – most notably 'junk food' – to children. Failure to adhere to these (by food manufacturers) might lead, ultimately, to legislation. For its part, the Government intended to ensure that school meals were healthier and more nutritious, with the Office for Standards in Education (Ofsted) to play a role in monitoring the provision of school meals.

The Blair Government's main initiatives concerning alcohol abuse and 'binge drinking' were announced separately, at the beginning of 2005. It was proposed that local councils be granted new powers concerning the granting, amending and – most importantly in this context – revoking of licences to sell alcohol. The police were also granted increased powers, to deal with public drunkenness and associated disorder. Most interestingly of all, perhaps, were two other proposed measures. Firstly, pubs which were repeatedly the source of 'alcohol disorder' could, as a last resort, be closed. Secondly, individuals apprehended or fined by the police on three occasions for alcohol-related offences would be liable to a ban on drinking for a specified period of time.

Conclusion

Health policy occurs in a political context that makes smooth, linear, logical, staged developments and rational choices based on a carefully considered range of options highly unlikely. It also has to operate in a culture of contradictions. On the one hand, British people overall are healthier and live longer than ever before, and yet, on the other, there is widespread and growing concern about the nation's health (most notably with regard to obesity, but also concerning alcohol abuse and 'binge drinking'). There is great concern about the safety of food, GM crops and eating disorders associated, on the one hand, with fast food and obesity, especially among children, yet on the other hand, popular culture is obsessed with unhealthily thin celebrities, apparently leading to an increase in anorexia, particularly among young women. In addition, there are growing fears about the safety of children in public spaces which has partly contributed to a polluting car culture that is attacking everyone's health (*viz.* increasing cases of asthma and other respiratory illnesses) and itself contributing to obesity, even though the far greater threat to children's safety lurks in their own homes and comes from adults that they know. The media is saturated with healthy images of sports, which, in fact, are mainly spectator ones; in many cases, wearing designer sports clothes and premiership (replica) football team kits has replaced actually playing sport. So, the need for a 'joined-up' policy process, to which Labour committed itself when it entered Office, has never been greater: the health policy process and health policy outcomes are not only themselves inseparable, but cannot be separated from wider socio-economic and cultural factors and forces which impact upon the nation's health.

<table>
<tr><td>**6**</td><td># Housing Policy
Peter Malpass</td></tr>
</table>

Introduction

Housing policy means different things to different people, and at different points in time, but a general definition would embrace the measures taken by governments to influence the quality, quantity, price and ownership of residential dwellings. British governments have always resisted direct involvement in the provision and ownership of houses, preferring instead to work through a variety of actors and organizations, often locality-based organizations. For much of the period after 1945, successive governments, both Labour and Conservative, relied on local authorities to ensure a regular supply of new rented housing, subsidized by the Exchequer and local taxpayers. Since the 1980s, however, the emphasis has switched to the idea that local housing authorities should concentrate on their strategic functions, working as enablers of housing provision through other organizations, principally housing associations and other types of registered social landlords (Department of the Environment, 1987; Department of the Environment, Transport and the Regions, 2000). These are not-for-profit organizations registered with the Housing Corporation in England (slightly different arrangements pertain in Scotland and Wales) (Cope, 1999; Malpass, 2000). However, most people in Britain (about 80 per cent at the beginning of the 21st century (Wilcox, 2002)) buy or rent their homes in the private market, and so our definition of housing policy must also include the measures taken by governments to influence market conditions and behaviour. In this sense, housing policy shades into, and becomes an aspect of, broader macroeconomic management – certainly, from the point of view of mortgaged homeowners and would-be purchasers, the most important task of government, with regard to maintaining a healthy housing market, is to sustain steady economic growth, low interest rates and reasonably full employment (Kleinman, 1996: 2).

Since the Second World War, housing policy priorities and instruments have changed, and there are many different ways to construct histories of the period. Any account that seeks to span a period of 60 years must involve difficult choices about what to include, and what to omit. Fortunately many of the details are available elsewhere (Holmans, 1987; Harloe, 1995; Malpass and Murie, 1999; Malpass, 2000; 2005), and here it is possible to concentrate on a number of themes and issues. These include the importance of both change and continuity. When compared with the late 1940s, housing policy in Britain in the early 21st century differs in almost every particular, and yet there are some underlying continuities. The emergence of housing policy in the first half of the 20th century, and the rapid growth of public housing after 1945, cannot obscure or diminish the significance of the underlying commitment of all governments to the idea that the market will provide for most people most of the time. This has had a profound impact not only on the manner in which we 'consume' housing, and its significance as a means of wealth accumulation, but also on the form and content of housing policy. The housing market is dynamic, and one of the continuities in housing policy throughout the period since the early 1950s has been political support for the growth of owner-occupation, replacing private renting as the predominant mode of residence in the modern housing market. Public housing played a role in facilitating the restructuring of the private housing market, as well as fuelling the growth of homeownership during the 1980s and 1990s, after the introduction of the council tenants' right-to-buy their houses at deeply discounted prices. Tenure restructuring has been one of the constants of the post-1945 period, and continues today in the form of the large-scale transfer of local authority housing stocks to new not-for-profit organizations.

Changes in housing policy can be understood both in terms of changes in the nature of the problem itself, and in ideas about the role of the state in society and the economy. The housing conditions of the British population as a whole have been transformed since 1945, although how much of that improvement can be attributed to housing policy as such is highly debatable – it is clear that changes in housing are driven by both public policy and private market factors, and that considerable long-term changes in the quality and quantity of housing would have occurred even in the absence of deliberate governmental action. In the immediate aftermath of the Second World War, the housing shortage was the worst ever (Holmans, 1987: 93) and about 80 per cent of households were living in accommodation that was unfit, substandard, overcrowded or shared with other families (Department of the Environment, 1977: 10). At this time, the emphasis was on building as many houses as possible to reduce the shortage, using the local authorities as the key instruments of housing policy. Since then, the general improvement in both the quality and quantity of housing has inevitably helped to reshape policy, as has the changing pattern of homeownership.

Changing ideas about the role of the state have helped to transform the governance of housing. One of the framing ideas for this chapter is that Britain has moved from a highly regulated and subsidized housing system to a less regulated and freer market, with much less subsidy. For most people, housing has become a commodity distributed through the market mechanism, just like any other, although, for reasons of both electoral and macro-economic management, governments are not indifferent to the operation of the housing market. This is an important indicator of the specificity of housing policy as compared with, for example, health or education: because the market is the main supplier, government policy has to work with, and through, organizations whose main purpose is the generation of profit rather than the achievement of public policy objectives. In this context, the command and control techniques traditionally used within public bureaucracies were not available, therefore necessitating the use of different, often incentive-based, policy instruments, which reflected the independence of key stakeholders.

At the same time, it is important to remember that, from the perspective of the providers of social housing (both local authorities and housing associations), central government has become much more interventionist than it was half a century ago – in spite of the 1980s' Thatcherite discourse about 'rolling back the state'. Moreover, this top-down monitoring and regulation co-exists with a requirement that social housing organizations are more accountable to service users and customer-oriented in their approach. One dimension of change in housing governance is the relatively recent (post-1987) growth of the idea that local authorities should transfer their housing stocks to new, non-municipal organizations. Another is that since the devolution of housing to the Scottish Parliament and the Welsh Assembly in 1999, it is no longer correct to speak of British housing policy (and it is worth remembering that housing law and policy in Scotland has always differed to some extent from that in England and Wales).

In a discussion of housing policy since 1945, it is appropriate to consider the relationship between housing and the welfare state. Housing is conventionally counted as one of the five core services of the post-war welfare state, albeit one that is acknowledged to differ in certain important respects. Having been targeted for cuts and retrenchment by the 1979–97 Conservative Governments, housing is now widely seen as the 'wobbly pillar' under the welfare state (Torgersen, 1987; Harloe, 1995). The right-to-buy has been characterized as 'selling the welfare state' (Forrest and Murie, 1988), and others talked of the 'amputation' of the housing arm of the welfare state (Cole and Furbey, 1994: 2). The argument to be developed here, however, is that in the period of the 'classic' welfare state (1945–75) (Digby, 1989; Lowe, 1994a), housing was annexed by political and academic discourse around social policy, but that its development is best understood in terms of market modernization rather than welfare state thinking. More recently, though, housing policy has become divided into two (Kleinman, 1996), and in some respects it is more closely linked to the modernized welfare state; indeed there is a case for saying that housing is actually the exemplar for the remodelled welfare state of the 21st century.

Assessing the impact of the Second World War on housing

The two great wars of the first half of the 20th century are almost irresistible break points in the construction of historical accounts, not least because of the notion of the 'post-war settlement' – the way in which the transition from war to peace was managed through a series of social reforms. After the First World War (1914–18), the commitment to a state-subsidized housing programme was a response to political promises by the Prime Minister, David Lloyd George, to build 'a land fit for heroes'. During the 1940s, housing was again a pressing social and political issue, but this time embedded in a wider reform programme subsequently interpreted as the creation of the welfare state. In the development of social policy as a whole, the significance of the Second World War and its aftermath is not in question, but for historians of housing policy there is scope to debate the importance of this period. Ginsburg (1999), for example, has argued that there is a consistency about housing policy throughout the period from 1915 right through to the 1970s, and none of the four continuities that he identifies derives from the 1940s. Similarly, the argument that housing policy throughout much of the 20th century was a response to the market-driven replacement of private renting by owner-occupation demands a longer-term perspective (Harloe, 1981; 1985; 1995; Malpass and Murie, 1999). According to this view, the Second World War interrupted a process that was well under way before 1939, and which continued apace after 1945; indeed, the 25 years after the end of the war are often seen as a kind of golden age for the growth of homeownership, before the onset of the boom–slump cycle that has been such a feature of the housing market since the early 1970s.

What is clear is that the years of the Second World War had cost the country around 2 million dwellings, in the sense that over 450,000 were destroyed or rendered uninhabitable by bombing, and the number of new houses built during 1939–45 was arguably 1.5 million less than might have been expected (Holmans, 1987: 91). Moreover, the suspension of the slum clearance programme meant that some people were still living in dwellings that had been condemned as unfit for human habitation 15 years earlier. In 1945, housing was a priority issue for the voters (Hennessy, 1993: 85), and a key performance indicator for governments for at least the next decade. One measure of the relative importance of housing at this time is that during the 1950s the Minister of Housing and Local Government was a senior member of the Government (Harold Macmillan went from housing to become Chancellor of the Exchequer and Prime Minister within the space of three years), while the Minister of Health was not even in the Cabinet from 1952 to 1962 (Butler and Sloman, 1980: 36–40). At one level, then, the Second World War was of immense significance for housing: it raised the profile of housing policy and created the conditions that led to the only sustained period in which local authorities were the main providers of new houses. Around 80 per cent of all council houses were built after 1945, and it is reasonable to argue that without the Second World War, the overall total would have been very significantly less. The implications of this achievement continue to shape housing policy and public debate to this day: without the construction of so many council houses the right-to-buy would not have become such a significant political issue, nor would the current transfer of local authority housing stock to non-municipal owners.

However, at another level, it is arguable that the Second World War had very little impact on the long established and deeply held view within British government as to the proper form of housing policy. Appreciation of this point depends upon constructing the narrative from early in the war rather than from its conclusion. It is well known that there was a considerable public debate about post-war reconstruction (Calder, 1969; Barnett, 1987), and the importance of the Beveridge Report (December 1942) setting out plans for social reform is routinely acknowledged. However, existing accounts tend to say very little about policy planning for housing during the war itself, preferring to start from the election of Clement Attlee's Labour Government in July 1945. This focuses attention on the incoming government's difficulties in restarting house building in a shattered and virtually bankrupt economy, while underplaying the extent to which the new government was building on extensive preparatory work undertaken by the wartime coalition government since 1942 (Malpass, 2003). The story of Labour's achievements in the late 1940s makes for fascinating reading (Foot, 1973; Morgan, 1985), but it can lead to an over-emphasis on change.

However, by starting the analysis in 1942 we get a better understanding of the underlying continuities in housing policy. In marked contrast to other programmes of public policy, such as health, social security and education, where wartime planning responded to widespread perceptions of a need for radical reform, in housing the advice of the civil service was that pre-war policy had worked reasonably well, and could be expected to do so in the future. To put it more bluntly, in the other main fields of social policy, post-war planning was based on the rejection of the market, but in housing it was based on the perceived success of private enterprise in meeting need and demand. From 1933, local authorities had been required to focus on slum clearance and the rehousing of people on low incomes, leaving private builders to provide for the majority. Pre-war economic conditions had fostered a boom in private house building, and had brought homeownership within the reach of a much wider proportion of the population, including growing numbers of the regularly employed skilled working class. The dominant view within Whitehall was that while this was the way forward in the longer run after the war, in the short term it would be necessary to rely on local authorities to build the majority of the new houses that would have to be built during the difficult transitional period.

In this context, the word transitional referred to the process of returning the economy from its highly-regulated wartime form, to a more normal peacetime mode; it was assumed that this would take two years. By the summer of 1942, officials in the Ministry of Health had drafted a paper about post-war policy, and this was incorporated into a more detailed paper approved by the war cabinet in May 1943 (Malpass, 2003). An interesting aspect of this plan was that despite the conservatism and complacency of the assumptions about the relative long-term roles of the public and private sectors, the 1943 proposals envisaged a radical renewal of Britain's housing stock, involving the construction of 3–4 million dwellings in the first post-war decade, and the replacement of 1.5–2.5 million existing older houses. However, as the war moved through its protracted closing phase, Ministers became alarmed at the damage inflicted on London and the southeast of England by Hitler's flying bombs, which started to arrive in the summer of 1944, but at the same time, with victory now assured, they also became more focused on the short-term problem of recommencing house building and how to achieve the targets for the transitional period.

Housing and the post-war welfare state

According to one historian of the 1940s, 'Housing ... deserves its honoured role in the saga of Labour's welfare state' (Morgan, 1985: 170). This claim rests on the record of the 1945–51 Labour Governments, which adopted a policy of concentrating house-building resources on the local authorities, limiting private building activity through a system of building licences, and the continuation of wartime controls on the use of materials. This approach was famously justified by the responsible minister, Aneurin Bevan, on the grounds that local authorities were 'plannable instruments' in a way that private builders were not. The result was that local authorities built 80 per cent of all new houses in the first six years after the war. The construction of a million houses in this period, in difficult post-war circumstances, was a considerable achievement, as was the high quality of the houses built by the local authorities. Yet this should not be confused or equated with the sorts of reforms being implemented at the same time in other areas of social policy. In housing, there was no systemic reform comparable with the measures taken elsewhere, notably in the creation of the National Health Service, and the extension of the social security system. For example, there was no attempt to nationalize the private rented sector (which still accounted for over 60 per cent of the total housing stock), nor the construction industry (a striking omission in the context of the programme of nationalization of key industries such as coal, railways, road transport and steel).

Accounts of the creation of the post-war welfare state emphasize the extension of public services to the whole population, and the importance of making essential services free at the point of use. Health and education are the exemplars of a model of service provision into which housing simply does not fit. There was never a realistic possibility of developing a free service, a fact that has been attributed to the way in which a nationalized free housing service would have been a much greater challenge to entrenched property interests in capitalist society than was the case in health or education (Harloe, 1995: 536). Another key difference between housing and the other public services is that its 'consumers' remained overwhelmingly working class. Whereas criticisms of the health service and the grammar schools in the 1950s centred on the way in which middle-class families had benefited more than the working class, the same could never have been said of council housing. This did not stop critics arguing that subsidized council rents were 'feather-bedding' affluent workers, but, significantly, the targets of attack were well-paid skilled factory workers and dual-income households, not the middle class, who showed no real interest in becoming council tenants.

The difficulty of fitting housing into orthodox accounts of the welfare state can also be seen in terms of the very slow development of an explicit focus on the least well-off. In other words, housing developed as a service that was neither universal nor residual. The least well-off are the least well served by the private market, and therefore precisely the group that might be expected to be targeted by a restricted public service, yet there was no attempt to construct housing policy in a way that would channel the new houses in their direction. On the contrary, the available evidence suggests that the main beneficiaries of the supply of good quality council housing after the Second World War were the rather better-off within the working class. It is also clear that rent rebate schemes designed to make council rents affordable to the least well-off, which had developed only slowly between the wars, actually began to decline in the late 1940s and early 1950s (Malpass, 1990: 83–5).

One way to make sense of all this is to recognize that the welfare state was not a product of joined-up thinking – it was not planned as a whole, and the term itself was not used by politicians to describe the post-war reforms until after the event (Lowe, 1993; Whiteside, 1996). The evidence from the official files suggests that post-war housing policy was planned in isolation from the reforms in other service areas, and it seems reasonable to conclude that housing was bracketed with the welfare state for what were essentially presentational reasons. Housing was such a pressing social and political issue after the war that it was perhaps inevitable that it was included alongside the other core services when the term welfare state came into more widespread use in the late 1940s. Nevertheless, looking back at these events half a century later, it now seems to be more sensible to see the welfare state as a kind of rhetorical overlay, and to recognize that housing policy was driven mainly by deeply ingrained assumptions about the long-term predominance of the market, and the role of the state and the public sector, in supporting and complementing private enterprise. The fact that housing developed as neither universal nor residual is hard to reconcile with the idea of housing as a service driven by welfare state thinking, but it sits quite comfortably with a perspective that sees housing policy responding to the changing pattern of supply and demand in a modernizing housing market.

The large post-war building programme of council houses can be seen as, on the one hand, an exercise in state-funded rehabilitation of the construction industry after the huge reduction

Table 6.1   House Building in Great Britain, 1945–64

	Local authorities	Private	Other	Total
1945	1,936	1,078	–	3,014
1946	25,013	30,219	168	55,400
1947	97,340	40,980	1,370	139,690
1948	190,368	32,751	4,497	227,616
1949	165,946	25,790	5,891	197,627
1950	163,670	27,358	7,143	198,171
1951	162,584	22,551	9,696	194,831
1952	193,260	34,320	12,342	239,922
1953	238,883	62,891	16,975	318,779
1954	234,973	90,636	22,196	347,805
1955	191,803	113,457	12,135	317,395
1956	166,267	124,161	10,197	300,625
1957	165,910	126,455	8,725	301,090
1958	140,519	128,148	5,028	273,695
1959	122,165	150,708	3,801	276,674
1960	124,738	168,629	4,451	297,818
1961	112,421	177,513	6,128	296,062
1962	124,090	174,800	6,538	305,428
1963	118,179	174,864	5,829	298,872
1964	148,624	218,809	6,958	373,676

Source: Annual Abstract of Statistics

in its capacity during the war – the local authorities were the developers, but private companies built the majority of the houses, thereby developing their strength in readiness for the return of 'normal' market conditions. On the other hand, it was a response to the political and economic power of workers in industries that were central to the reconstruction of the national economy. The demand for new houses was irresistible, but the people who received them were not necessarily those in the greatest need or the worst housing market position.

In terms of housing policy, the priority given to building by local authorities during the six years of Labour Government after 1945 represented no more than an extension of the two-year transitional period planned by the wartime coalition. However, the return of a Conservative Government in 1951 did not mark an immediate change of direction, largely because, in the short term at least, the only realistic way to redeem an electoral promise to build 300,000 houses per year was to continue building council houses. Thus we observe the irony that the two record years for council house building were years of Conservative Government, 1953 and 1954, when an aggregate of over 450,000 were completed (Merrett, 1979: 320–1). Yet private house building also increased, and as soon as the 300,000 target was reached, the local authorities' house building was reduced each year, so that their output in 1959 was only half the figure for 1953, as can be seen in Table 6.1.

The mid-1950s were thus a period of change in housing policy, marking the beginning of some important long-term trends. The first of these trends to be signalled was a clear policy commitment to the growth of owner-occupation (which, between the wars, had grown without obvious policy support). A White Paper of November 1953 stated that:

One object of future housing policy will be to continue to promote, by all possible means, the building of houses for owner occupation. Of all forms of saving, this is one of the best. Of all forms of ownership this is one of the most satisfying for the individual and the most beneficial to the nation. (Ministry of Housing and Local Government, 1953)

No government has since resiled from that position, and the impact of such policy continuity has helped to boost the owner-occupier sector from about 31 per cent in 1951 to nearly 70 per cent 50 years later. Rising living standards have played an important part in sustaining the growth of homeownership, supported in the period up until the mid-1970s by successive governments' commitment to maintaining full employment.

The second change of direction in housing policy concerned the public sector. One aspect of this was that, in 1954, local authorities were required to turn their attention once more to the problem of slum clearance, which had been in abeyance since 1939. Changes in the subsidy system in 1956 meant that local authorities were given clear incentives to abandon building for general needs, and to concentrate on rehousing people from clearance areas. Slum clearance should be seen as an activity allocated to local authorities because it was unprofitable for private enterprise, whose entrepreneurial instincts led to a preference for the more straightforward development of greenfield sites, without the complications of complex title claims nor the problems of arranging for the rehousing of people already in occupation. Slum clearance undoubtedly incorporated many low-income households into the public sector, but it should not be equated with a policy designed to provide for the least well-off in general, for many did not live in areas designated for redevelopment. Slum clearance was essentially about a commitment to the removal of what was seen as a historically specific and limited problem of old houses dating from the 19th-century period of urbanization.

The problem of older housing had been made worse by the impact of rent control since 1915, which had provided landlords with an incentive and excuse not to invest in repairs and improvements. In 1957, the Government decided that the housing shortage had eased sufficiently to justify a relaxation of rent control, in the hope that this would lead to a revival of investment, and a reversal of the long-term decline, in the private rented sector. However, it seems that the main outcome was an increase in the rate at which landlords disposed of their dwellings; the 1957 Rent Act made it easier for them to obtain vacant possession, which improved the sale price, whilst reducing security of tenure, which thus gave sitting tenants an incentive to buy when the opportunity arose.

The steady decline and diminution of the private renting sector meant that the least well-off were increasingly reliant on their local authority for housing. The second aspect of the change of direction for public housing, then, was that local authorities came under pressure, not only on the demand side, but also from central government, to be more accommodating towards low-income households and others who had not previously been given priority (including the growing numbers of newly and recently arrived people from the Caribbean and the Indian sub-continent). Among the problems to be overcome in this context was local resistance to widening the scope of the service. From the point of view of local stakeholders (including councillors, housing staff and existing tenants), there was little attraction in the recruitment of more tenants from among groups seen as undesirable or undeserving. Local control of the allocation of council houses was a cherished feature of the system, and one that central government was slow to tackle.

Another problem was how to make council housing more affordable to people on low incomes without making it even cheaper for the better-off. Rents policy was a key area of local autonomy, and again governments were reluctant to take on councillors in a direct challenge. However, in this case, a solution of sorts was readily at hand, and a brief discussion will reveal not only something of the nature of central–local relations in the period, but also the way in which the seeds of the 'residualization' of council housing were sown as long ago as the mid-1950s.

The solution was higher basic rents, and targeted rent rebates for the less well-off – a clever way of simultaneously making council housing more expensive for the better off (thereby encouraging them to consider the option of buying or renting privately), and more affordable for those deemed to be in need. However, neither higher rents nor rebates could be imposed on local authorities, for during the 1950s it was up to local councils to set their own rents, and central government carefully respected that right, albeit whilst adopting fiscal devices to put pressure on local policy makers. From 1955 onwards, central government deliberately allowed the level of subsidy on new houses to decline in real terms, whilst urging councils to compensate by increasing rents on existing houses (this can be seen as the redistribution of existing subsidies away from older, lower-cost houses to support new, high-cost houses). The following year councils were released from the obligation to make rate fund contributions to support housing; this was conceived as another incentive to encourage them to raise rents. In the case of rent rebate schemes, the Government confined itself to rhetorical encouragement, arguing that rebates were an integral feature of what it liked to call 'realistic' rents policies. It has been shown that there was a marked increase in the number of authorities operating rent rebate schemes in the late 1950s, and that they tended to have average rents about a fifth higher than other authorities (Malpass, 1990: 99).

Although the changes of the mid-1950s prompted or presaged certain long-term continuities in British housing policy, the high political profile of housing ensured that it remained a dynamic area. In the early 1960s, for example, the Conservative Government experimented with two new forms of provision, cost renting (which was unsubsidized and non-profit making) and co-ownership (which was intended to combine the advantages of both renting and owning: unsubsidized rental housing provided by not-for-profit societies which were collectively owned and controlled by the tenants themselves) (Malpass, 2000: 136–7.) Although neither of these innovations made much numerical impact, they were none the less deemed sufficiently successful to justify further investment, which gave rise to the Housing Corporation, which later became a major regulator and funder of a burgeoning housing association sector (Malpass, 2000: 134–41). In 1965, Harold Wilson's recently-elected Labour Government signalled how far the Party had travelled since losing power in 1951 by the apologetic terms in which it announced plans to increase public sector production:

> Once the country has overcome its huge social problem of slumdom and obsolescence and met the need of the great cities for more houses to let at moderate rents, the programme of subsidised council housing should decrease. The expansion of the public programme now proposed is to meet exceptional needs: it is born partly of a short-term necessity,

partly of the conditions inherent in modern urban life. *The expansion of building for owner occupation on the other hand is normal; it represents a long term social advance which should gradually pervade every region.* (Ministry of Housing and Local Government, 1965, emphasis added)

In the event, the expansion of new building was short lived, and the national economic crisis of 1967 was swiftly followed by the abandonment of high-output housing policy. Although it was not apparent at the time, 1968 heralded the end of an era in which successive governments had competed with each other in promising the electorate quantitative housing targets. Some commentators have seen this as a blessing, given the poor quality and unpopular high-rise, high-density layouts of much 1960s council housing. An alternative perspective, though, is to suggest that during a period of economic crisis, housing was recognized as a policy area where cuts in public expenditure could readily be imposed.

During the late 1960s, such cuts were justified partly on the basis that there was no longer an overall housing shortage, although some acute local shortages remained. Finance, rather than production, began to emerge as the central area of debate in housing policy. One factor in this development was the growing recognition that mortgaged homeowners were heavily subsidized through tax relief, and, furthermore, in a manner that gave most assistance to those on the highest earnings. Attention was focused on the housing market by a price spiral in 1971–2, raising questions about the role of mortgage lenders in fuelling rising house prices, and the knock-on effects in terms of the rising cost of tax relief. In the public sector there was also growing concern in some circles about the cost of subsidies and their distribution. The Labour Government of the late 1960s resisted pressure to reform rents and subsidy arrangements, although there was 'a crescendo of advice, demands and exhortations' calling for action on rent rebates (Merrett, 1979: 184).

However, in 1971, Edward Heath's Conservative Government published a White Paper, somewhat misleadingly called *Fair Deal for Housing* (Department of the Environment, 1971), outlining plans for a radical overhaul of public sector housing finance. This proposed the abandonment of the conventions that had operated in this area for several decades, and unleashed a great set piece political struggle over a cherished area of local autonomy (Malpass, 1990: Ch. 6). The controversy engendered by the 1972 Housing Finance Act and its troubled implementation contributed to the unpopularity of the Government itself at the election of February 1974, but by then Britain was engulfed in the wider political and economic crisis that is generally understood to mark the end of the long post-war economic boom which had been sustained by Keynesian techniques of macroeconomic management. Unemployment and inflation increased from the late 1960s, although according to Keynesian theory rising unemployment and rising prices and incomes should not have occurred together. However, it was the quadrupling of the price of oil in 1973 (in the wake of a brief Arab–Israeli war) that ensured that the world economy was tipped into recession. This single action, which 'sent shock waves of hitherto unimaginable dimensions through the system' (Pollard, 1983: 373), precipitated the major watershed of the second half of the 20th century.

Reshaping housing policy?

The world economic crisis of the mid-1970s is generally seen as marking a turning point for the governance of developed capitalist economies. The post-war confidence in the power of states to manage their economies for the well-being of their citizens was replaced by uncertainty in the face of market forces and globalization. In this changed environment, state welfare systems were more easily depicted in terms of their costs rather than their benefits. Once the long post-war boom began to falter and unemployment began to rise, it became more difficult to defend the economic and welfare policies adopted since the 1940s, and 'instead of sailing with the tide the welfare state was now battling against it' (Glennerster and Hills, 1998: 12). Whereas, for the previous 30 years, the welfare state had been generally (though not unanimously) regarded as part of the solution to social and economic problems, it now became targeted as very much part of the problem. Old Right-wing arguments about the burden of welfare and the incentive-sapping drawbacks of the welfare state were dusted off and given new credence by the emergent 'New Right'.

Housing policy was inevitably affected by these wider developments, although it can be difficult to ascertain how far it continued to march to its own logic. Indeed there is some credence in the argument that changes in the welfare state have brought it closer to the position occupied by housing all along. The mid-1970s crisis coincided with a prolonged and detailed review of housing policy, which, when it was finally published in 1977 (Department of the Environment, 1977), was widely regarded by commentators as a disappointment, and a missed opportunity to remove some of the inefficiency and inequity from the British housing system (Harloe, 1978; Lansley, 1979; Merrett, 1979: 268–74). It is clear that the mid-1970s did not mark a sharp change of direction in housing policy; rather, what we see in the ensuing years is an acceleration of existing trends, particularly in terms of the increasing tendency to see owner-occupation as the panacea for all housing problems, and the opposite stance in relation to council housing, which experienced a steep decline in investment and faster residualization. The election of a New Right-influenced Conservative Government in 1979, headed by the self-proclaimed conviction politician Margaret Thatcher, is often seen as the real turning point, but, again, it must be stressed that, radical as it was, Conservative housing policy after 1979 was explicable in terms of established trajectories, and as Michael Ball noted in 1985:

> Thatcherism has not changed the basic tenets of traditional Tory housing policy. Instead it has tried to bring them to reality in a time period so short that no previous government would have dared to try for fear of the outcry. (Ball, 1985: 16)

It is important to keep this observation in mind when examining housing policy after 1979. Policy developments in this period should be viewed against the long-established basic assumption that the market could and should provide for most people. Government policy throughout the 1980s was dominated by the objective of expanding owner-occupation, and this has remained a priority ever since. Consequently, owner-occupation in Britain has risen from 55 per cent in 1979 to 69 per cent in 2000 (Wilcox, 2002: 91). Almost a third of the growth in owner-occupation since 1980 has been due to the sale of council houses, and for several years during the housing market recession of the early 1980s, the sale of council houses was the main source of growth.

On one level, the introduction of a mandatory right for council tenants to buy their homes, coupled with severe cuts in capital available for new building by local authorities, was a stunning departure from past orthodoxies, whereby all governments (since 1919) had regarded local authorities as having a positive role to play in tackling housing problems. The council sector had grown continuously for 60 years; now that process was put into reverse, and over the next 20 years 1.8 million dwellings were sold to individual purchasers, helping to reduce local authority renting from 31 per cent in the mid-1970s to 14.6 per cent in 2000 (Wilcox, 2002). Council housing was presented by Ministers and some commentators (Coleman, 1985) as part of the problem, although there was an element of duplicity involved in this stance, because, of course, the enthusiasm of council tenants to buy their houses was itself a tribute to the success of local authorities in building dwellings that were seen as worth buying. On another level, however, it can be seen that, for decades, the growth of owner-occupation had been based on both new building, and the purchase of existing private rented houses, which were in diminishing supply by the early 1980s. Council housing was, therefore, the obvious next reservoir of existing supply for the continued growth of owner-occupation. Selling council houses was also a logical way of drawing into home-ownership the better-off working class (who, incidentally, were also more likely to vote Conservative than other sections of the working class), on whom the further growth of this sector relied to a considerable extent. The right-to-buy may have brought 60 years of growth in council housing to a sudden halt, but in terms of the long-standing bipartisan commitment to encouraging homeownership, it represented a kind of continuity.

Although cuts in investment in new house building by local authorities were emphasized and intensified after 1979, they had actually begun much earlier; apart from a brief revival in 1975 and 1976, new building by local authorities had been in decline since 1969. However, this cannot diminish the severity of the attack on housing expenditure by the first Thatcher Government: at least 75 per cent of all public expenditure cuts in the period 1980–4 were to come from the housing programme, which was cut by nearly half (House of Commons, 1980: v). During the next decade or more, new building by local authorities was reduced to negligible numbers, and between 1979 and 1997 total public expenditure on housing was cut by more than 80 per cent (Glennerster and Hills, 1998: 183).

However, the headline figure for net expenditure obscures some important changes. Firstly, throughout the period after 1980, the capital programme was underpinned by capital receipts from right-to-buy sales. Secondly, after 1990, changes in the council housing subsidy system generated growing revenue surpluses, which grew to outweigh subsidies after 1994 (Glennerster and Hills, 1998: 182). Thirdly, in the period after 1982, the long-established trend towards giving assistance with housing costs on a means-tested basis (referred to above in the discussion of rent rebates in the 1950s and 1960s) led to an accelerated switch of expenditure from housing subsidy into housing benefit (which counted as a form of social security expenditure). In practice, a significant proportion of the cost of housing benefit has come to be covered by surpluses on housing revenue accounts, reinforcing the view that local authority housing has become substantially self-financing.

During their first two terms in office (1979–87), the Conservatives' housing policy concentrated almost exclusively on expanding owner-occupation, both through the right-to-buy scheme, and a robust defence of the principle of mortgage interest tax relief (although its real value was allowed to fall). Housing was seen by the Conservatives as a vote winner for them in 1979, and it was a policy area in which they continued to have something positive to offer – for example, the 1987 general election took place during a period in which house prices were rising steadily, which encouraged existing homeowners to feel better off.

In 1987–8, the Conservative Government re-formulated its housing policy, introducing a bold new strategy for rented housing (Department of the Environment, 1987). This consisted of plans to deregulate the private rented sector (in the hope that this would stimulate investment), proposals further to erode local authority housing stocks, converting councils into 'enablers' rather than providers of housing, and a new financial regime for housing associations as the main suppliers of new accommodation at affordable rents. The deregulation of private renting has had a scarcely measurable impact on the proportion of the total supply of housing falling within this category (Wilcox, 2002: 91), and the specific devices unveiled in 1987 to reduce further the housing stock of local authorities had even less impact. However, such is the unpredictability of policy in this area that a number of local authorities responded to the perceived threat to social renting by initiating the transfer of their entire stocks of dwellings to newly-formed housing associations, and this has subsequently become a mainstream government policy. Another unforeseen outcome dating from 1987 was the emergence of the term 'social renting' as a way of bracketing together provision by local authorities and housing associations. In the 1987 White Paper, *Housing: The Government's Proposals* (Cm 214, 1987), the Cabinet tried to promote the idea of the 'independent rented sector', consisting of housing associations and private landlords, but this never seriously became established, largely because of the much greater synergy between housing associations and local authorities.

Housing associations can trace their origins back to at least the 19th century, but for most of the period covered by this chapter, they remained minor contributors, very much on the edge of policy debates, and marginalized by the post-war growth of council housing (Malpass, 2000), to the extent that, as late as 1987, the local authorities owned over 90 per cent of social rented housing in Britain. However, the combined effect of increased investment in housing associations, and the transfer of council housing stocks, has brought about a major realignment, to the extent that, in 2000, the Labour Government itself predicted that housing associations might provide the majority of 'social housing' by 2004 (Department of the Environment, Transport and the Regions, 2000: 61).

Increased output by housing associations in the early 1990s was facilitated by two factors. Firstly, the higher aggregate input of grants via the Housing Corporation (and its equivalents in Scotland and Wales), and second the re-introduction of private finance (historically associations had relied on raising capital from investors and banks, but they had never been very successful in volume terms, and after 1974 they had been able to rely on public funds). In the mid-1980s, several large housing associations began to explore the possibilities of raising capital from the money markets, and once this was seen to be feasible, the Government adopted it as official policy. From January 1989, changes to the system for setting rents made it easier for housing associations to raise private loans, which gradually came to cover a higher proportion of the costs of new schemes as central government reduced the rate of capital grant per dwelling. Using private finance was a way of securing more new units for a given outlay of public expenditure, but initially the level of production was further boosted by a trebling of the Housing Corporation capital programme between 1988–9 and 1992–3. However, this level of investment was short lived, and deep cuts were imposed from 1993–4, as part of the government's attempt to reduce the overall budget deficit, so that by the end of the century the Corporation's programme was smaller in cash terms than in 1988–9.

The growth of the housing association sector since 1989 has been mainly due to the transfer of stock from local authorities, although this is overwhelmingly due to activity in England rather than Wales or Scotland, where transfers have made less impact so far. In every year, bar two, since 1988, stock transfer in England has added more dwellings to the housing association sector than have resulted from new building, and the aggregate impact of such transfer is dramatic, adding over 680,000 dwellings to a sector that consisted of only 534,000 in 1988 (Wilcox, 2002). A large majority of transferred dwellings were taken over by newly-established associations, set up for the purpose by the local authority planning the transfer. These new organizations, carved out of the public sector bureaucracy, are clearly different from the traditional associations in many ways, not the least of which is the greater representation of tenants on their governing boards.

The indications are that transfer organizations will continue to be formed, and that they will therefore have an increasing impact on the changing character of the housing association sector as a whole. The prospect of housing associations becoming the second largest tenure category in the British housing system within the next few years, and the possibility of council housing disappearing altogether, are signs of the huge changes that have been put in train over the last 15 years. It is also the case that no one was seriously predicting this scenario at the time of the first large-scale transfer in 1988. The growth of stock transfer is a fascinating example of the way that a policy can emerge as an unintended consequence of other decisions. In this case, transfer began as a local-level reaction to a perceived threat from central government, but was soon taken over by central government as its own policy, and by the mid-1990s, central government was pressing local authorities to come forward with plans for transfer (Department of the Environment, 1995: 29; Malpass and Mullins, 2002).

Conclusion: a new paradigm for housing policy in the 21st century

One of the most striking features of housing policy since the election of 'New Labour' to Office in 1997 is the high degree of continuity with the trajectories established under the Conservatives during the previous 18 years (Department of the Environment, Transport and the Regions, 2000). Labour's conversion to the virtues of owner-occupation dates from the 1960s, but it has now added an enthusiasm for private renting that would have been anathema to previous 'Old Labour' Governments, and its commitment to the transfer of council houses to housing associations is also something that has surprised its more traditional supporters. This is consistent with the view underpinning this chapter, namely that in the history of housing policy (and, by extension, public policy in general) party politics and the party of government have strictly limited influence on the overall shape of policy development. It is clearly wrong to see British housing policy 'swinging drunkenly back and forth' in response to changes in political control at Westminster (Balchin and Rhoden, 2002: xv; Donnison and Ungerson, 1982). Governments are, in fact, constrained by previous policy actions – as indicated by Rose's notion of policy inheritance (Rose, 1990; Rose and Davies, 1994) – and by wider social, economic and political circumstances.

Yet things do change, and the argument to be developed in this section is that, within the continuing dominance of the underlying idea that the market will provide, a new paradigm for housing policy had emerged before the 1997 election, and New Labour in office is working within this framework. Four key indicators of this 'paradigm shift' will be considered. Firstly, Britain has moved from a period (after 1945) in which housing was subsidized in various ways, with few people paying the full market price for their accommodation, to a situation where the housing system is characterized more by taxation than subsidy. For more than 30 years after the war, British housing consumers were protected from the full effects of market forces, with rent control in the private sector and subsidized rents in the public sector, whilst in the owner-occupier sector, there was mortgage interest tax relief and artificially low interest rates resulting from the lenders' cartel agreement. All that has now changed: the private rental market is effectively deregulated, council housing revenue accounts are mostly in substantial surplus (the discussion now centres on the level of negative subsidy, i.e., a form of taxation) and mortgage interest tax relief was finally abolished in April 2000. The volumes of money are impressive: at its peak in 1990–1 tax relief cost the Exchequer £7.7 billion, and in 2001–2 the yield from stamp duty on residential transactions was £2.7 billion (up from just £280 million in 1992–3; Andrew et al., 2003: 10).

Secondly, it has been argued above that for much of the post-war period, housing policy in Britain was shaped in response to the market-driven restructuring of private housing consumption patterns, from renting to owning. It is now possible to view that process as substantially complete; owner-occupation may continue to grow slowly, mainly because of life-cycle and age cohort effects, while private renting seems to have reached a minimum level. At the start of the 21st century, the focus of attention is now on the restructuring of social renting, a process that is motivated by quite different forces, grounded in ideas about the role of the public sector in direct service delivery (the so-called new public management). The contrast with the 1940s could not be clearer: then local authorities were the main instruments of housing policy, charged with building at least 80 per cent of all new houses, but now they are not only prevented from building, but under pressure from central government to divest themselves of their housing management functions altogether.

Thirdly, housing policy in relation to social renting has changed, not just in terms of ideas about how it should be managed, but also in relation to what it does in the housing system. This refers to the shift from solution to problem, and from a position where council housing was seen as modern and attractive to working families, to one where it is associated with disrepair, crime and social exclusion. The residualization of social renting is a direct result of housing market restructuring and the tailoring of housing policy to support it. While it is possible to criticize housing policy in the past for the rather insouciant stance taken in relation to the least well-off, the concentration of low-income households, with low levels of formal employment and high rates of benefit dependency, within the social rented sector is a factor in the intractability of social exclusion.

Fourthly, the issue of demand has reappeared on the policy agenda, but in two quite different ways, both of which reflect the quantum shift in thinking about housing. In the mid-1990s, startling new estimates of household growth were produced, suggesting a need to build 4.4 million new dwellings between 1991 and 2016 (largely due to the increasing number of single-person households, a trend deriving from more people marrying later or remaining single, divorce, lone-parent families and longer life expectancy). Even allowing for subsequent downward revision of the figures, it appeared that Britain needed a house-building programme equivalent to that of the early post-war decades. One difference in the present period is that central governments have responded by cutting resources for new building by social housing organizations, preferring to rely on the private sector for the largest proportion of new supply. Another difference is that in contrast to the post-war policy of developing new towns, and other devices to reduce urban congestion, the current orthodoxy specifies an 'urban renaissance' by concentrating 60 per cent of new building on brownfield sites (i.e., redevelopment sites). The other way in which demand has re-emerged is in the context of the lack of demand in certain areas and for certain sorts of housing. This is mainly a problem in the economically less buoyant parts of the country, where it affects all tenures, but it has had a particularly strong impact in the social rented sector. For many years social housing organizations could assume that there was a demand for all the dwellings they could supply, but the slackening or, sometimes, complete collapse of demand has altered the balance of power and led to a recognition that consumers have choices.

Finally, returning to the relationship between housing and the welfare state, it is a curious feature of Prime Ministerial pronouncements about the reform of public services (Blair, 1998b; 2002) that housing gets barely a passing mention, because in many ways housing is at the heart of the new welfare state. The government itself has acknowledged that:

Our homes influence our well-being, our sense of worth, and our ties to our families, communities and work. If we live in decent housing we are more likely to benefit from good health, higher educational attainment and better-paid work. (Department of the Environment, Transport and the Regions, 2000: 15)

In the current era when the Government professes its commitment to 'joined-up policy', housing is central to strategies for tackling social exclusion and community regeneration and improving public health. Housing is also at the leading edge of the financial and organizational restructuring and modernization of the welfare state. In terms of the introduction of private finance, the fragmentation of service delivery and the targeting of public resources on those in greatest need, housing is clearly in tune with the way the welfare state is changing. Certainly, there is more clarity about housing policy now than in the early days of the post-war welfare state, when, as mentioned above, housing was neither universal nor residual, and as such, occupied an unclear position. Now, as Kleinman (1996) argues, there has been a split in housing policy, such that for the majority, it is treated in much the same way as any other marketed commodity. For the minority, social housing now provides a more focused, residual service. The fact that this is associated with deeply intractable problems should act as a warning for other services, and a reminder of Titmuss's observation that: 'Separate state systems for the poor, operating in the context of powerful private welfare markets, tend to become poor standard systems' (Titmuss, 1968: 143).

7 Industrial Relations Policy
Peter Dorey

Introduction

Trade unions in Britain today are a pale imitation of what they used to be, and industrial relations rarely registers as an issue on either the systemic or institutional policy agendas. Yet during the 1940s and 1950s, the trade unions were effectively viewed as 'estates of the realm', powerful bodies whose co-operation was essential to Britain's economic well-being, who were deemed to have a legitimate role to play in various aspects of economic and industrial policy, and whom most politicians assiduously sought to avoid coming into conflict with. During the 1960s and 1970s, though, the trade unions increasingly became, in Robert Taylor's phrase, 'scapegoats of national decline' (Taylor, 1993: 1–4), and the increasingly recognized 'trade union problem' moved from the systemic (policy) agenda to the institutional (policy) agenda. The 1980s and 1990s, though, heralded the decline of Britain's trade unions, partly as a conscious and wholly intended consequence of governmental policies to 'solve' the 'trade union problem' (entailing a major reform of industrial relations), and partly because of wider changes in the occupational character and structure of the British economy and its labour market, where the decline or increasing automation of heavy industry – car-manufacturing, coal-mining, ship-building, steel-making – resulted in the loss of millions of jobs, and thus union members, in precisely those industries and occupations where trade union membership had often been most extensive, and trade union strength at its greatest. The trade unions have never recovered, and no government would now wish to restore to them the power or influence they once enjoyed, least of all 'New Labour'.

It should be noted in passing, though, that there is a body of Marxist literature which challenges the notion that trade unions in Britain have ever possessed, even remotely, the degree of power attributed to them by their critics (see, for example, Miliband, 1973: 139–40; Westergaard and Resler, 1976: Part Three; Ch. 5; Anderson, 1977; Coates, 1980: Ch. 5; 1983; 1984: Ch. 5; Panitch, 1986: Chs. 5 and 7). This Marxist perspective argues that in a capitalist society, trade unions are generally defensive bodies which seek to afford some limited protection to workers who would otherwise be even more vulnerable to the caprice and connivance of employers, who are constantly seeking ways and means of 'getting more' out of their workers, in order to increase profits and/or undercut their economic rivals. More generally, Marxists argue, the alleged power of trade unions in a capitalist society can never match the power – and increasing international mobility – of 'capital': the power of the business community is invariably much greater than that of the organized working class, who always remain dependent on employers and big business for their jobs and wages.

Furthermore, Marxists argue, trade unions have always struggled ideologically compared to capital and big business, for the profit-seeking activities of the latter are usually deemed to be natural, sensible and, ultimately, in both the national interest, and also in the interests of the workers whose employment depends on continued business confidence and profitability. Certainly, the decisions taken by the business community are rarely publicly questioned or exposed to critical scrutiny in the media.

Conversely, the aims and activities of trade unions have almost invariably been portrayed or perceived as selfish, sectional and thus inimical to the national interest, and constantly subject to intense media scrutiny and condemnation. For example, those commentators who instinctively condemn 'irresponsible' workers for going on strike hardly ever castigate 'capital' when it effectively goes on strike (by withholding or withdrawing investment, and/or closing down factories or offices).

Moreover, Marxists have alleged that the legal and judicial system is heavily weighted in favour of 'capital', whereby the vast majority of court cases arising from legal disputes between business and trade unions, or employers and employees, are resolved in favour of business and employers; judges have rarely evinced much sympathy or understanding *vis-à-vis* the grievances of ordinary working people and their trade unions in dispute with management.

Fuller coverage and discussion of this particular perspective is beyond the remit of this chapter, however, and besides, whatever the merits may or may not be of this particular perspective of British trade unionism, it was the widespread perception, amongst the public and policy makers alike, that the trade unions *did* possess immense – excessive – economic and industrial power (and invariably exercised it in a negative or destructive manner) which provided most of the impetus for reforming industrial relations in Britain from the late 1960s onwards.

The three periods just referred to highlight three discrete approaches adopted by policy makers towards industrial relations and the trade unions. From 1945 to about 1960, the general policy adopted was that of *voluntarism*, whereby policy makers sought to avoid becoming directly involved in industrial relations, and declined to intervene (interfere) in the internal affairs and activities of the trade unions. The official stance was that employers and employees, and management and unions, ought to be permitted to resolve employment-related issues – including wage determination – between themselves, free from political interference. The state's role was deemed to be one of formal neutrality between management and organized labour. (For discussions of voluntarism as an industrial relations policy, see Rogin, 1962: 521–2; Flanders, 1974; 1975: 288–94).

In the 1960s and 1970s, however, industrial relations policy shifted towards two other strategies, namely a form of *neo-corporatism* or what Crouch has termed 'bargained corporatism' (Crouch, 1982: 212–22; see also Middlemas, 1979: *passim*; Cox, 1988a; O'Sullivan, 1988; Taylor, 1989: 111; Perkin, 1990: 328–31; Dorey, 1993a; McIlroy, 1995: 188–93), and two abortive attempts at *legalism* or legal regulation (discussed below). Neo-corporatism entailed policy makers actively seeking a closer and more regular partnership with the trade unions, and employers' organizations (the CBI being formed in 1965 from the merger of three separate bodies formerly representing employers), but was unable or unwilling to impose its political will on organized interests in the way that governments might do in the 'pure' form of corporatism sometimes found in authoritarian regimes.

Instead, the emphasis was on bargaining and negotiation, as well as general encouragement and exhortation to accept certain policies adjudged to be in the national interest. The adoption of this particular industrial relations strategy derived from growing political concern that the trade unions were not behaving 'responsibly', and were therefore a major cause of Britain's mounting industrial problems and relative economic decline. However, governments generally – with two notable exceptions – wished to avoid imposing legislative curbs and statutory controls on the trade unions, and so, instead, sought to elicit more 'responsible' behaviour from them by directly involving them in industrial and economic decision taking, and in some cases permitting them a say over aspects of social policy too (Cox, 1988b). Neo-corporatism also heralded a recourse to various incomes policies, in an increasingly desperate attempt at persuading the trade unions to reduce their pay claims and accept lower wage increases. This reflected the prevalent view during this period, that 'excessive' wage increases were the main cause of inflation. (For a study of incomes policies in post-war Britain, see Dorey, 2001.)

However, the third industrial relations strategy also made an appearance during the late 1960s and early 1970s, namely legalism, whereby policy makers sought to impose statutory curbs and controls on the trade unions, and subject relations between management and workers to much greater legal regulation. However, this early mode of legalism was not sustained when it encountered practical (implementation) problems and trade union opposition, whereupon the neo-corporatist strategy was pursued with even greater vigour and urgency.

It was during the 1980s and 1990s that the failure of both voluntarism and neo-corporatism (and the repeated breakdown of successive incomes policies) led to the adoption of legalism as the dominant industrial relations strategy in Britain. Industrial relations and trade union activities were subjected to an extensive range of legislative curbs and statutory restrictions, clearly intended to compel the trade unions to behave more 'responsibly', whilst also aiming to restore (labour market) discipline and managerial authority – 'management's right to manage' – in the workplace. Indeed, whilst legalism formally constitutes legislative regulation of relations between employers and employees, in practice, in Britain, the statutory restrictions and obligations were almost overwhelmingly placed on the trade unions and employees, rather than on employers. In other words, legislative restrictions on the rights and activities of trade unions and workers were fully intended *pari passu* to enhance or restore the rights and authority of management and employers.

If and when trade unions failed to adhere to the legal restrictions or requirements imposed upon them, they were liable to a variety of sanctions, punitive measures and financial penalties imposed via the courts. At the same time, from 1979 onwards, when industrial disputes did occur, Ministers usually made little pretence of impartiality, instead encouraging, directly or indirectly, employers to 'stand firm and not give in to trade union bully-boys'. Furthermore, legalism not only surpassed voluntarism, it also entailed the rejection of neo-corporatism, so that trade union representation on a plethora of advisory or policy-making bodies was steadily reduced, as was their contact with Ministers. This exclusion of trade unions from economic and industrial policy making was further reflected and reinforced by the abandonment, from 1979 onwards, of incomes policies, whereupon wages were to be determined by 'the market' and/or criteria such as affordability, efficiency, effort, merit, performance and productivity.

Laying the basis of voluntarism and partnership, 1945–51

The trade unions had acquired unprecedented respectability and legitimacy as a consequence of their role in the war effort during the first half of the 1940s. With the leader of the TGWU, Ernest Bevin, having been appointed Minister of Labour in Winston Churchill's 1940–5 Coalition Government, the trade unions had accepted considerable state intervention in industrial affairs, particularly with regard to the allocation of manpower to areas where there were labour shortages, or production urgently needed to be increased. Yet even when workers with particular skills were effectively conscripted (by Bevin) to work in a particular factory or industry, in order to perform 'essential work', they were granted

> ... important provisions which went some way to compensate the workers for the loss of their freedom of engagement. All undertakings classified as 'essential' were to satisfy minimum requirements of wages and conditions, and were to have adequate provision for the welfare of the employees; and while workers were forbidden to leave their employment without the permission of an officer of the Ministry of Labour, a similar restriction was placed upon the employer's right to dismiss any of his employees. (Pelling, 1963: 214–15)

The trade unions had also accepted the introduction, in July 1940, of Order 1305, which outlawed strikes, and imposed a system of compulsory arbitration in cases where management and trade unions were unable to reach agreement over terms and conditions of employment. However, Order 1305 was rarely invoked, even when strikes did occur, partly because Bevin preferred to rely on appeals to patriotism and regard for the national interest and the war effort (defeating Hitler and Nazism) when industrial stoppages did occur, but also because he was acutely aware that the problem of labour shortages, and the need to boost industrial production, were hardly likely to be served by sending recalcitrant workers to prison. Even at this stage, there was considerable Ministerial cognizance that compulsion and coercion against the trade unions were likely to make industrial relations worse, and hence there was a strong emphasis on exhortation and encouragement to persuade the trade unions to behave responsibly.

Meanwhile, trade union representatives were increasingly being appointed to a plethora of governmental bodies and advisory committees during the 1940s, thereby further ensuring that their views were often articulated at the highest levels, and over a range of policy areas. It has been estimated that whereas the trade unions had been formally represented on just 12 governmental committees at the outbreak of the Second World War in 1939, they were represented on no less than 60 such bodies by 1949 (Allen, 1960: 34; see also Taylor, 1993: 39).

Meanwhile, the exceptionally close organizational links between the Labour Party and the trade unions – the political and industrial 'wings' respectively of the British organized labour movement – meant that when a Labour Government was elected in July 1945, 120 Labour MPs were sponsored by trade unions, with 29 of these then appointed to Ministerial posts, of which six were of Cabinet rank. Among the senior trade unionists who were elected as Labour MPs in July 1945, and then given Cabinet posts, were Ernest Bevin, who was appointed Foreign Secretary, whilst George Isaacs, erstwhile chairman of the TUC, succeeded Bevin as

Minister of Labour. Aneurin Bevan, meanwhile, who was sponsored by the National Union of Miners (NUM), was appointed Secretary of State for Health, whereupon he presided over the introduction of the NHS (Pelling, 1963: 221–2; Taylor, 1993: 38; Howell, 1999: 124–6). As one historian of the Labour Party has noted, 'Attlee's recognition of the political–industrial alliance, reflected in the composition of his governments, helped to ensure for a considerable time the maintenance of harmonious relations' (Jefferys, 1993: 13).

One of the first legislative initiatives of the Labour Government was the repeal of the 1927 Trades Disputes Act (introduced by the Conservatives in the wake of the 1926 General Strike). This Act had placed a number of statutory limits on trade union activity and organization, and was, therefore, deeply despised by the trade unions, many of whom deemed it a draconian attack on the right of ordinary working people to organize and defend themselves *vis-à-vis* employers and management. One notable feature of the Labour Government's repeal of the 1927 Act was that 'contracting-into' the political levy was replaced by 'contracting-out'. This meant that trade union members who did not want a proportion of their membership fee to be paid into their union's 'political fund' had to specify this wish in writing, whereas, previously, the onus had been on members who did want to contribute towards their union's political fund to make their wishes known. The 'political levy' was controversial because many trade unions used part of their political levy to make donations to the Labour Party, yet many of their members voted Conservative or Liberal. However, the repeal of the 1927 Act effectively meant that, either through ignorance or apathy, many of these trade union members did not make the effort to 'contract-out', and so inadvertently contributed to the finances of the Labour Party (see, for example, Pelling, 1963: 222). Indeed, it has been calculated that during the two years immediately following the repeal of the 1927 Act, the number of trade unionists paying the political levy increased by nearly 2 million (Kavanagh and Morris, 1989: 53).

However, trade union gratitude towards the 1945–51 Labour Governments extended far beyond this legislative initiative, warmly welcome though it was. The organizational and personal connections between the Labour Party and the trade unions were buttressed, during this period, by a similar ideological outlook and a shared commitment to particular policy goals, particularly with regard to the pursuit of full employment, the establishment of the welfare state, and the nationalization of certain key industries and utilities, such as coal, gas, electricity and the railways – there was a tacit assumption that workers employed in 'publicly-owned' industries would somehow cease to be 'exploited', and would henceforth be working for the 'common good' or 'the community', whereas workers in private industry were deemed to be working for the benefit of profit-seeking employers and shareholders.

This is not to say that there were no conflicts or tensions between the 1945–51 Labour Governments and the trade unions, for the Cabinet's recourse to a 'wage freeze' – in response to serious economic problems – undoubtedly strained relations at the end of the 1940s. There were also occasional trade union complaints that Ministers were failing to consult them sufficiently over certain issues and policies (see, for example, Chester, 1975: 79). Furthermore, Ministers themselves were concerned about the incidence of unofficial strikes, and occasionally adopted a tough stance against this mode of industrial action, but they generally found trade union leaders themselves hostile to such strikes. This was partly because many trade union leaders were vehemently anti-Communist (this being the era in which the Cold War and concomitant concern about the alleged threat posed to the West by the Soviet Union were becoming established), and were sometimes inclined to attribute unofficial strikes to the subversive machinations of Communists on the factory floor. Yet even when such strikes were not blamed on Communists, national-level trade union leaders were still inclined to join Ministers in denouncing them, not least because unofficial industrial action undermined the authority and credibility of the union leaders themselves, and threatened to jeopardize their own rapport and relationship with 'their' Labour Government. In other words, there were ideological, organizational and personal reasons why many trade union leaders were as hostile towards unofficial strikes and other forms of industrial militancy as Cabinet Ministers.

In accounting for the high 'degree of industrial peace' which existed during this period, one commentator has noted that this:

> … was due less to Order 1305 [which was not formally rescinded until 1951] than to the closeness, both personally, and in terms of outlook, between Ministers and union leaders; the union leaders' sense of involvement in government, both formally and informally; and general contentment with a government which … delivered much of what the unions wanted. … The key demands of many unions … were … fulfilled. (Thorpe, 1997: 116)

In this context, the issue of industrial relations and trade union reform was not on the (institutional) agenda. To the extent that Ministers sought to influence the behaviour of the trade unions, the emphasis was very much on a judicious blend of private discussion and public exhortation.

Voluntarism maintained: the Conservative Governments, 1951–64

Having lost the 1945 election by such a wide margin, many Conservatives acknowledged the need to reconsider the Party's stance on a number of issues, not least of which were the dual policies of industrial relations and trade unionism. The scale of Labour's victory was seen by many Conservatives as clear evidence that the organized working class had finally 'arrived' in British politics, so that the Conservative Party had to accommodate itself to this fact, and ensure that at least some of its policies were expressly targeted at industrial workers. This, it was soon realized, would not be achieved without tackling popular (mis)conceptions that the Conservatives were 'anti-trade union', a view which had gained wide currency due to the Conservatives' stance *vis-à-vis* the 1926 General Strike, and the following year's 'revenge' Trades Disputes Act which, as noted above, placed a number of statutory restrictions on the trade unions.

The Industrial Charter

It was with such political and electoral considerations in mind that the Party leader, Winston Churchill, in 1946, established a Conservative industrial policy committee, comprising four backbenchers, and five members of the Shadow Cabinet. Their deliberations produced *The Industrial Charter*, published in May 1947, which was presented as the basis of modern Conservative approach to economic and industrial management, including relations between management and workers. For example, *The Industrial Charter* rejected economic *laissez-faire* (what would today be termed economic liberalism or neo-liberalism), arguing that a policy of 'go-as-you-please' was no longer credible in the modern world, so that much greater central guidance of economic activity would henceforth be required (Conservative Party, 1947: 10).

With regard to industrial relations and trade unionism, *The Industrial Charter* not only declared that the Conservative Party was in favour of trade unions, and believed that they could play an important part in ensuring the future success of the British economy, but that trade unions should aim for a high (but voluntary) and active membership, which would ensure that they were genuinely representative of as many workers as possible (Conservative Party, 1947: 21–2).

In the final section of *The Industrial Charter*, entitled 'The Worker's Charter', it was decreed that Conservative Party policy was to 'humanise' industry, not nationalize it. It therefore suggested ways in which employers should aim to make employees feel more secure in their employment, and valued for the work that they did. This, it was suggested, would do much to overcome feelings of 'them and us' in the modern workplace, and thereby eradicate the (mis)conception that there were 'two sides of industry' who had irreconcilable or mutually exclusive interests (Conservative Party, 1947: 28–34).

The 'human relations' approach

Underpinning much of this new and more positive stance towards industrial relations and trade unionism was a 'human relations' perspective concerning conflict in the workplace (for a detailed account of this approach during the 1950s, see Dorey, 2002a). This 'human relations' approach, enunciated by many senior Conservatives during this period – particularly those associated with the 'One Nation' or paternalist wing of the Party – held that many problems and conflicts in the workplace derived from workers' feelings that they were not appreciated or valued by management, or that they were somehow being 'exploited'. It was such feelings which often fuelled suspicion or resentment amongst workers, and which were then seized upon by the Left in the trade unions to foment industrial unrest and militancy; minor grievances flared up into major disputes (see, for example, Conservative Central Office, 1949: 23; Conservative Party Archives, Advisory Committee on Policy ACP 4(54) 34, 'Industrial Relations', 11 June 1954; Robert Carr MP, House of Commons Debates, 5th series, Vol. 568, col. 2127; Harold Watkinson MP, quoted in *The Times*, 20 October 1952).

The solution, according to Conservatives subscribing to this 'human relations' approach, was for management and workers to develop a sense of partnership, so that the 'two sides of industry' mentality could be replaced by the notions of a team, in which all played an important and mutually beneficial part, even though the employer would naturally remain 'team captain'. Such partnership would best be achieved, it was believed, through closer consultation and dialogue between employers and employees, thereby enabling each to appreciate the concerns of the other, and so respond accordingly. It was envisaged that through such partnership, management and workers would develop a greater mutual understanding, which would, in turn, foster greater confidence amongst employees that their views and anxieties were understood by management. At the same time, workers would become less susceptible to the anti-capitalist propaganda and agitation of the Marxist Left in the trade unions. Employers, meanwhile, would be better able to explain to their employees the reasoning behind certain decisions, such as those pertaining to proposed changes to working practices, employment, profit margins, etc. Many senior Conservatives shared the optimistic view of the then Minister of Labour, Walter Monckton, who was 'sure [that] the more workpeople are kept fully informed by the management about the business and the prospects of the undertaking in which they are engaged, the more there will grow up a feeling of common purpose and of confidence' (House of Commons Debates, 10 November 1952, col. 624).

Crucially, espousal of this 'human relations' approach meant a rejection by Conservative Ministers of legislation to regulate either industrial relations or trade unions. Throughout the 1950s, senior Conservatives consistently maintained that better relations and greater trust in the workplace could not be secured through passing Acts of Parliament; the law could not compel individuals to work more harmoniously together. As the Conservatives' own backbench parliamentary labour committee observed:

> … the law and its apparatus of injunctions, damages, fines, penal sanctions, etc., has little to contribute to the solution of the problems of industrial relations. Laws [to regulate or curb strikes] have been found from experience to be almost totally unenforceable, and do more harm than good. (Conservative Party Archives, PLC(64) 3, 'Trade Unions, Employers' Associations and the Law', 19 March 1964)

The role of government, therefore, was to encourage and exhort employers and employees to work more closely together, but without recourse to the statute book.

In this respect, the Ministry of Labour (the forerunner to the Department of Employment, and now itself replaced by the Department of Work and Pensions) enshrined a clear 'Departmental philosophy', seeing its role as being to promote greater trust and co-operation between 'the two sides of industry' (management and labour), whilst avoiding, as far as practicably possible, direct intervention or interference (see, for example, PRO PREM 11/3125, Macleod to Macmillan, 11 April 1957). In this sense, the Ministry of Labour became, during the 1950s, the institutional embodiment and bulwark of a voluntarist industrial relations strategy (by the time that later governments sought to dispense with voluntarism, by committing themselves to industrial relations legislation, the Ministry of Labour had been abolished).

There was one further argument occasionally used to reject these sporadic calls for legislation, particularly *vis-à-vis* unofficial strikes, or strikes called without a ballot of the workers involved, and this argument illustrates a key technique of agenda management. When, during his brief time (October 1959 to July 1960) as Minister of Labour, Edward Heath was faced with calls from some Conservative backbenchers for legislation to curb strikes and other forms of industrial disruption perpetrated by trade unions, he retorted that such legislation was neither desirable not necessary, because in comparative terms, Britain actually enjoyed a very low level of strikes. Heath was comparing the number of strikes in Britain to those in other advanced industrial countries at the time, and was thereby able to claim that, by comparison, Britain actually fared rather well. He also pointed out that the number of working days lost each year due to strikes was much fewer than days lost as a consequence of illness or industrial accidents. Placed in such a comparative context, therefore, Britain's strike record was not really deemed a problem at all, certainly not one which warranted legislative action. When and where industrial conflict did occur, Heath maintained, the best solution was likely to be more dialogue and closer partnership between management and labour, to overcome the misunderstandings and mutual suspicions which soured relations between the 'two sides of industry'.

Meanwhile, at the same time as the Conservative Governments of the 1950s and early 1960s were formally eschewing governmental intervention in industrial relations and trade union affairs, they none the less presided over the increasing co-option of trade union representatives onto a wide range of advisory bodies concerned with economic, industrial and social affairs: one historian has claimed that by 1958, for example, the TUC was represented 'on no less than 850 tripartite committees, alongside representatives of the government and the employers' (Perkin, 1990: 328). In other words, whilst maintaining that government should not involve itself in the affairs of the trade unions, Ministers were apparently happy to allow the trade unions to involve themselves in a wide range of policy discussions and decisions. This partly accorded with the (then) Conservative emphasis on industrial partnership, but it was also envisaged that by granting the trade unions membership of such an extensive range of bodies – particularly those of an economic or industrial character – they would acquire an appreciation of the economic realities facing Britain, and thus of the need to evince greater 'moderation' and responsibility in their actions and overall conduct.

Oscillating between neo-corporatism and legalism, 1961–78

Although the Inns of Court Conservative and Unionist Society published its own proposals for legislative curbs on the trade unions in 1958, entitled *A Giant's Strength* (clearly indicating that the leadership's conciliatory and paternalistic approach to industrial relations and trade unionism was not universally supported in the wider Conservative Party), it was not until the early 1960s that impatience with the unions became more widespread, and permeated the Party's Ministerial ranks. Right from the start of the decade, the trade unions began to be blamed for Britain's relative economic decline (awareness of which only really developed during this time, as Britain's economic performance lagged behind that of many of its competitors). That the Conservative Party finally resorted to an incomes policy in 1961, and, the following year, established the National Economic Development Council (NEDC), were indications that even the most conciliatory and paternalistic Ministers were recognizing the limits of the previous decades' 'hands-off' approach. However, the Conservatives still refrained from introducing legislation during the remainder of their period in Office, with Ministers hoping that closer partnership and dialogue – enshrined via the NEDC – would educate the trade unions about the 'economic facts of life', and thereby finally persuade them of the urgent need for more responsible behaviour and wage restraint.

However, the failure of the trade unions to respond accordingly exasperated even the most conciliatory Conservatives, not least the very personification of post-war 'one nation' Conservatism, Harold Macmillan himself (Macmillan, 1972: 375; 1973: 66). Consequently, as the 1964 general election loomed, the Conservative Party made it clear that if it won, there would be a review of trade union and industrial relations law, whereupon they could claim to have been given a mandate from the electorate for legislation in this sphere. Making specific recommendations prior to the election, though, would probably be seen as somewhat provocative, and might deter some working-class voters from supporting the Conservatives (see, for example, Conservative Party Archives, PLC(64) 3, 'Trade Unions, Employers' Associations and the Law', 19 March 1964).

In Place of Strife

Also concerned about the incidence and impact of unofficial strikes, particularly with regard to the undermining of their attempts at securing wage restraint through a series of incomes policies, were the 1964–70 Labour Governments, led by Harold Wilson. In 1965, therefore, Wilson appointed Lord Donovan to chair a Royal Commission on Trade Unions and Employers' Associations (although clearly it was the former who were the real focus of the inquiry). It seems that Wilson was quietly hoping for a report which would recommend radical reforms of trade unionism and industrial relations, whereupon he and his Ministerial colleagues could then win trade union support by proposing rather more modest measures instead. If this was indeed Wilson's strategy, it went woefully awry.

The Donovan Report, published in 1968, acknowledged that there were effectively two industrial relations systems in British industry: a formal system, based on official, industry-wide or national-level institutions which engaged in collective bargaining over terms and conditions of employment, most notably wages; and an informal system, derived from lower-level or local managers and trade union shop stewards, who would variously conduct their own relatively autonomous bargaining, and reach their own agreements accordingly. Consequently, the Donovan Report observed that: 'The formal and informal systems are in conflict. The informal system undermines the regulative effect of industry-wide agreements. ... Procedure agreements fail to cope adequately with disputes arising within factories' (Royal Commission on Trade Unions and Employers' Associations, 1968: 36).

However, the Commission's Report was emphatic that the British system of industrial relations was too complex to be placed under statutory regulation, and that attempting to introduce the law into the workplace would exacerbate the distrust between management and workers which often underpinned industrial disputes in the first place. Consequently, the Report merely recommended strengthening the existing voluntarist system of industrial relations, the primary aim being to make it work more effectively and smoothly, rather than attempting to replace it.

Not surprisingly, Wilson was somewhat disappointed by the modesty of the Donovan Report, and resolved to persevere with reform of Britain's industrial relations, insisting that 'the confessed failure of the Commission to find any short-term remedy for unofficial strikes could not be accepted' (Wilson, 1971: 591). Wilson's stance was undoubtedly strengthened by recognition that the Conservative Opposition was itself developing a new policy which aimed to place industrial relations in a statutory framework, with a view to fostering more 'responsible' trade unionism, and thereby lead to much greater order and stability in British industry. Alert to the possibility that the Conservatives' pledge to curb trade union 'irresponsibility' was likely to prove electorally popular, whilst also recognizing the extent to which his own Government's incomes policies were being undermined by the 'informal' system of industrial relations, Wilson resolved to pursue industrial relations reform regardless of the warnings of the Donovan Commission's Report.

Thus it was that in January 1969, with Wilson's encouragement, the Employment Secretary, Barbara Castle, published a White Paper entitled *In Place of Strife* (Department of Employment and Productivity, 1969). Not that Castle needed much encouragement, for she herself had been disappointed at the conservatism of the Donovan Commission's Report, and was determined to pursue the reform of industrial relations, even though she recognized that '[it] may be the political end of me with our own people. I'm taking a terrific gamble, and there is absolutely no certainty that it will pay off'. Castle's 'only comfort is that I am proposing something I believe in' (Castle, 1990: 296, diary entry for 7 January 1969). Castle herself survived, but *In Place of Strife* did not.

The White Paper comprised 25 specific measures, some of which were actually intended to bestow certain statutory rights on the trade unions and their members, but there were three other proposals within *In Place of Strife* which aroused the ire of the trade unions, namely:

- The Secretary of State for Employment to be empowered to order a 28–day 'cooling-off' period when an imminent unofficial strike was deemed likely to prove damaging to the British economy.
- The Secretary of State also to be empowered to order a trade union to ballot its members prior to calling a strike which might prove damaging to the British economy.
- A Commission for Industrial Relations (CIR) to be established, which would be empowered to conduct inquiries into inter-union disputes.

The trade unions were bitterly opposed to such proposals, believing them to confer too much power on the Employment Secretary and proposed CIR to 'interfere' in trade union affairs. Such opposition was to be expected, but what did surprise Castle (and Wilson), and eventually led to the abandonment of *In Place of Strife*, was the degree of opposition within the Parliamentary Labour Party, right up to Cabinet level. (For a study of the rise and fall of *In Place of Strife*, and the divisions it engendered both amongst and between Labour Ministers, backbench MPs and the trade unions themselves, see Dorey, forthcoming.)

There were two main sources of opposition within the Labour Party. Firstly, the Left, particularly those MPs associated with the Tribune Group, strongly opposed what they saw as an attack on the rights of ordinary working people and their trade unions to bargain freely with employers. Labour's Left also resented the manner in which the trade unions were being blamed for what were, ultimately, deemed to be problems emanating from, and intrinsic to, capitalism itself. The second main source of opposition to *In Place of Strife* from within the Parliamentary Labour Party emanated from those Labour MPs who were sponsored by trade unions. As such, when *In Place of Strife* was debated in the House of Commons, 50 Labour MPs voted against it, whilst a further 40 abstained: 'more than we had anticipated', Castle ruefully reflected (Castle, 1990: 99, diary entry for 3 March 1969).

Castle, fully supported by Wilson, resolved to persevere regardless. Not only were they convinced of the necessity of industrial relations reform, they were also concerned that if they abandoned *In Place of Strife* in the face of backbench opposition in the Parliamentary Labour Party, then Labour MPs would be emboldened to 'rebel' more often on a wider range of issues, at a time when intra-Party discipline and cohesion had already become a serious problem. This consideration was quite apart from the realization that backing-down at this stage would be a political gift to the Conservative Opposition, which would then be able to portray Wilson and his Ministerial colleagues as weak, and of being unable or unwilling to tackle Britain's increasingly serious industrial relations problems.

April 1969 therefore heralded the introduction of a short Industrial Relations Bill, intended to be a prelude to a more comprehensive Bill later in the autumn. The Short Bill was largely intended to persuade Labour's critics, as well as 'the City', that the Government was serious about tackling industrial relations problems and trade union 'irresponsibility'. It also reflected concern amongst some Labour Cabinet Ministers that if no legislation was introduced until the autumn, as originally intended, then the trade unions would effectively have up to 10 months in which to organize a campaign of opposition to industrial relations legislation. With these considerations in mind, Castle hoped that having introduced a short Industrial Relations Bill in the spring, she could then 'win over' the trade unions, through consultations to be conducted over the summer, prior to introducing a more comprehensive Bill in the autumn.

The Short Industrial Relations Bill comprised just five main provisions:

- A statutory right for any employee to belong to a trade union.
- The Employment Secretary to be empowered to order an employer to 'recognize' a trade union for bargaining purposes.
- Workers laid off due to a strike in which they were *not* directly taking part to be entitled to receive unemployment benefit.
- The Employment Secretary to be empowered to impose a settlement in an inter-union dispute, based on recommendations from the proposed Commission on Industrial Relations, with fines liable to be paid by the trade unions concerned if they refused to accept the decision.
- The Employment Secretary to be empowered to order a 28-day 'cooling off' period with regard to unofficial strikes, with fines liable to be imposed on trade unions who defied such an order.

Once again, the trade unions and many Labour MPs made clear their opposition to the proposed measures, particularly the last two, yet Wilson insisted that the Bill was 'essential to this Government's continuance in Office' (quoted in Jenkins, 1970: 134). However, he also hinted that the Bill could conceivably be withdrawn, if the trade unions were able to convince him that they would develop their own mechanisms for dealing effectively with unofficial strikes and inter-union disputes.

What ultimately compelled the abandonment of the Industrial Relations Bill – and, in effect, of *In Place of Strife* – was the opposition of many Labour MPs (PREM 13/2726, Report of PLP Meeting to Wilson, 7 May 1969; PRO PREM 13/2728, Houghton to Wilson, 16 June 1969; PRO PREM 13/2728, 'Note of a Meeting of the Management Committee', 17 June 1969), coupled with growing doubts around the Cabinet table, even amongst Ministers who had originally supported Barbara Castle's proposals (PRO CAB 128/44 Part One, CC(69) 26th Conclusions, 9 June 1969; PRO CAB 128/44 Part One, CC(69) 28th Conclusions, 17 June 1969).

Faced with such divisions and hostility, Wilson and Castle urgently sought some form of agreement with the TUC, which would provide the Government with a plausible reason for withdrawing the Bill. The breakthrough came on 18 June, when all-day discussions yielded a 'solemn and binding' (wryly referred to by many journalists subsequently as Mr Solomon Binding) undertaking by the TUC's General Council to adopt a much more active role in regulating and resolving unofficial strikes and disputes arising between trade unions, thereby obviating the need for the Government to legislate on such issues. Ministers themselves were sceptical about the TUC's ability or willingness to regulate its own members – affiliated trade unions – but the 'solemn and binding' agreement served its purpose in providing the Labour Government with a reason for not implementing the Industrial Relations Bill.

In return for this pledge, Castle and Wilson promised that the Government would not proceed with the short Industrial Relations Bill, nor would the 'penal clauses' be included in industrial relations legislation planned for the next Parliamentary Session, or, indeed, for the lifetime of the current Parliament, unless the TUC reneged on its side of this agreement (PRO PREM 13/2728, 'Note of a Meeting with Representatives of the Trades Union Congress', 18 June 1969). This 'solemn and binding' agreement, though, also enabled the Conservative Party to claim that Labour was totally beholden to the trade unions, and to insist that only a Conservative government would have the independence and political will to introduce the industrial relations legislation which Britain was deemed to need so urgently.

The 1971 Industrial Relations Act

Although much policy-making in Britain has tended to be reactive, responding to the sudden emergence or recognition of a particular problem by decision takers and political elites, or characterized by overall continuity and, at most, only incremental change, the 1971 Industrial Relations Act marked a departure from both of these general characteristics. It not only constituted a radical break with the hitherto voluntarist tradition in post-war industrial relations, it was also the product of almost six years of planning and preparation, mainly whilst the Conservatives were in Opposition, yet ultimately, this careful and lengthy gestation did not yield a correspondingly successful policy. The Industrial Relations Act does, however, provide examples of other aspects of the policy 'process' in Britain, most notably that of policy failure deriving from problems arising at the implementation 'stage'.

Having lost the 1964 election, after 13 years in Office, the Conservative Party elected, in 1965, a new leader (the first time that a Conservative leader had actually been elected, as opposed to 'appointed' by the so-called men in grey suits emerging from a smoke-filled room), Edward Heath, and embarked on a major internal policy review. A number of subject groups were established to develop proposals for particular areas of policy, including one on 'trade union law and practice'. Unofficial strikes were soon identified as the key industrial relations problem which needed to be tackled, although agreement on the primary problem did not prevent considerable disagreement, both amongst members of the policy review group on 'trade union law and practice', and more widely in the Conservative Party, over precisely how to tackle unofficial strikes, and to what extent invoking the law really would solve the problem. (For a flavour of such intra-party debates and disagreements, see

Figure 7.1   Main provisions of the 1971 Industrial Relations Act

- A statutory right to belong, or not to belong, to a trade union (thereby outlawing the closed shop).
- Establishing a new Registrar of Trade Unions and Employers' Associations, with which trade unions would need to register in order to retain their legal immunities.
- Legally enforceable collective agreements.
- Legal enforcement of certain procedural agreements.
- Narrowing the range of legal immunities enjoyed by the trade unions.
- Introducing a statutory right for trade unions to be 'recognized' by employers for the purposes of collective bargaining.
- Establishment of an Industrial Court to adjudicate in serious industrial disputes or alleged breaches of the Act.
- Statutory powers invested in the Secretary of State for Employment to apply to the Industrial Court to impose a 60-day 'cooling-off' period, and/or seek a strike ballot, in lieu of an industrial dispute deemed likely to be harmful to the British economy or likely to result in serious public disorder.

Conservative Party Archives, CRD, Policy Group on Industrial Relations, PG/20/66/130; Conservative Party Archives, Leader's Consultative Committee, various meetings and discussion papers, 1965–9; see also Sewill, 1967: 2; Moran, 1977: *passim*; Taylor, 1993: 177–86; Dorey, 1995b: Ch. 4.)

Having won the June 1970 election, the Conservatives swiftly gave legislative effect to the proposals which had finally been agreed in Opposition by the aforementioned policy review group on 'trade union law and practice', although some reservations remained (and were subsequently to be vindicated). The new Conservative Prime Minister, Edward Heath, and many of his Ministerial colleagues, however, deemed their legislative proposals for industrial relations reform to be 'rational, sensible and essentially modest' (Taylor, 1993: 184). After all, they were the product of five years of discussion and deliberation; they could hardly be depicted as a hasty, ill-considered, panic measure.

The ensuing 1971 Industrial Relations Act comprised eight main provisions, shown in Figure 7.1: the Conservatives' Employment Secretary, Robert Carr, explained that the Industrial Relations Bill was primarily intended to restore order and stability in British industry, these having increasingly been undermined by unofficial strikes and shopfloor militancy which undermined national-level agreements – particularly pay deals – reached by trade union leaders and employers. Indeed, Carr was adamant that far from constituting an attack on the trade unions – as the unions themselves claimed – the Bill would strengthen responsible trade unionism. Certainly, he and many of his Cabinet colleagues calculated that much trade union opposition to the Industrial Relations Bill was rather ritualistic and hyperbolical, and would therefore largely dissipate once it reached the statute book, whereupon the unions would begin to appreciate the Bill's alleged benefits.

This, however, proved to be a major miscalculation, as trade union opposition actually became stronger, more widespread and well-organized. Having been instrumental in compelling the previous Labour Government to abandon its Industrial Relations Bill based on *In Place of Strife*, the trade unions – with some unlikely assistance from the courts – similarly compelled the Heath Government to retreat. The trade unions' official response to the Conservatives' Industrial Relations Act was one of 'passive non-co-operation', entailing a refusal – *en masse* – to register with the new Registrar of Trade Unions and Employers' Associations, although whilst the Act had been proceeding through Parliament, there had also been a number of high-profile trade union marches and rallies demanding 'Kill the Bill'.

However, it was the judiciary – not traditionally known for its trade union sympathies – which effectively undermined the Industrial Relations Act, and precipitated a major change of approach towards the trade unions by the Heath Government. A series of court cases and decisions highlighted an ambivalence about precisely who should be held responsible when alleged breaches of the Act occurred: the trade union itself, or the individual union members involved? When the courts decided that it was individual trade union members themselves who were in breach of the Act, the members involved were occasionally imprisoned, or threatened with imprisonment, whereupon trade union militancy and solidarity increased. After the threatened imprisonment of five London dockers, in connection with breaches in defiance of the Act, a national docks strike was called, accompanied by 'sympathy' or 'solidarity' action by various other groups of workers. The Solicitor-General effectively spared the Heath Government from a deeply damaging national industrial dispute by quashing the convictions against the five dockers, but in so doing, also left the Government's industrial relations legislation in disarray. The manner in which such legal cases served to undermine the Industrial Relations Act has been described by a number of commentators as 'a farce' (Stewart, 1977: 127; Dorfman, 1979: 58; Taylor, 1993: 199).

Although the Government hurriedly sought to develop a new partnership with the trade unions – a return to neo-corporatism – whereby Ministers and trade union leaders, along with employers' representatives, would regularly meet to discuss economic and industrial affairs ('a trialogue', one of the Ministers involved, Peter Walker, called it), Heath's desire for reconciliation was insufficient to prevent two serious miners' strikes, one at the beginning of 1972, and one at the beginning of 1974: by calling the strikes during January and February, the two coldest winter months, when demand for coal was at its highest, the NUM could apply maximum pressure on Ministers, or, in the words of their critics, 'hold the country to ransom', in support of their pay claims. The latter strike prompted Heath to call a general election, the theme of which was 'Who runs the country – democratically elected government, or politically-motivated, militant trade unions?' To use modern parlance, the question was meant to be 'no brainer', with voters expected resoundingly to endorse government over unions. In fact, the outcome was not what Heath had envisaged, and a (minority) Labour Government was formed instead.

Labour's 'social contract', 1974–9

In spite of the problems which it had encountered over both incomes policies and *In Place of Strife* just a few year earlier, the Labour Party claimed, in the 1974 elections (a second election was held in October after the February poll had failed to give any party an overall majority, although Labour had formed a minority government), that only it could work harmoniously with the trade unions, whereas the re-election of Heath's Conservative Government would merely herald another five years of industrial conflict. Five years later, this claim would return cruelly to mock the Labour Government, for it too was effectively brought down after repeatedly clashing with the trade unions, but in 1974 there was hope that Labour and the trade unions could indeed work more harmoniously together.

Much of this cautious optimism derived from agreement, in 1972, between senior Labour politicians and trade union leaders, over a *social contract*. This was to establish a set of policy priorities – most notably in matters pertaining to industrial relations and the trade unions – for the next Labour Government, including repeal of the Conservatives' Industrial Relations Act, the establishment of an Advisory, Conciliation and Arbitration Service (ACAS) to mediate in the case of serious industrial disputes, 'employment protection' legislation, and improvement to the 'social wage' (i.e., welfare benefits and pensions). For their part, though, the trade unions were expected to exercise voluntary wage restraint.

Following its election to Office in 1974 – whereupon the veteran Left-wing Michael Foot was appointed Employment Secretary, in preference to Reg Prentice, who had been Labour's Employment spokesperson in Opposition, but who was viewed as less sympathetic or accommodating towards the trade unions[1] – the Labour Party swiftly implemented many of the measures enshrined in the *social contract*. The Industrial Relations Act was duly repealed, and replaced by the 1974 Trade Union and Labour Relations Act, which virtually restored to the trade unions the legal rights and immunities they had enjoyed until 1971. Indeed, this Act was replaced by an amended version in 1976, which provided the trade unions with additional legal immunities, and strengthened the closed shop (whereby employees had to join, or belong to, a trade union as a condition of employment).

Other legislation introduced by the Labour Government during the mid-1970s, under the auspices of the *social contract*, were the 1974 Health and Safety at Work Act and the 1975 Employment Protection Act. Measures were also implemented to strengthen existing legislation concerning racial and sexual discrimination. Meanwhile, ACAS was established in 1974, and strengthened the following year by being given statutory powers. Ultimately, though, although welcome by the trade unions, and constituting evidence that Labour was keeping its side of 'the bargain' as represented by the *social contract*, these measures failed to offset the increasing tensions occasioned by Ministerial recourse to incomes policies from 1975 onwards.

In many respects, the 1974–9 period can be viewed as the 'last gasp' of both voluntarism and neo-corporatism, for the Labour Government avoided legislative measures which sought to place legal curbs on either the internal affairs or wider industrial activities of the trade unions. There was no attempt at reviving *In Place of Strife*. Yet as Taylor (1993: 240) has noted, these final years of voluntarism did entail governmental legislation *vis-à-vis* trade union organization and activity, in so far as laws were introduced to grant the trade unions *more* rights and immunities. In this context, voluntarism was upheld by recourse to 'permissive' legislation, rather than being eroded by prescriptive legislation, as was to be the case from 1979 onwards.

Legalism: the weakening and marginalization of the trade unions, 1979–97

The first few months of 1979 provided a good example of what John Kingdon (1984) identifies as a 'policy window' providing a clear opportunity for policy change. As we noted in

---

1 Indeed, four years later, Prentice 'crossed the Floor' (of the House of Commons) to join the Conservative Party, claiming that the Labour Party was being taken over by Marxists.

Chapter 2 of *Policy Making in Britain: An Introduction* (Dorey, 2005), Kingdon identifies three discrete streams, namely a problem stream, a policy stream and a political stream, and explains how policy change generally occurs when the three streams flow together, an occurrence which is relatively rare, and usually short-lived. During such junctures, however, a change in existing policy can be effected, but if the opportunity is not seized, then circumstances are likely to change again – and the three streams flow apart – so that the 'policy window' closes.

With regard to the policy stream, many Conservatives and sympathizers, particularly in the media, academia and newly-formed 'New Right' think-tanks or organized interests, during the 1970s, were advocating various policies which they believed to be desirable, particularly such initiatives as pre-strike ballots, and also ballots for the election of trade union leaders, as well as curbs on both the closed shop (compulsory trade union membership in certain occupations or industries), and entitlement to social security benefits during strike action. However, to make such policy proposals more popular, or to imbue them with greater credence, they had to be 'attached' to a corresponding problem, in this instance, the spate of strikes which occurred in the 1970s, culminating in the notorious 'winter of discontent' during January and February 1979. That many of these strikes were called by trade union leaders without a ballot of the workers concerned highlighted a problem to which pre-strike ballots provided a solution. Furthermore, many of these strikes also drew attention to the problem of apparently unaccountable or politically-motivated or extremist trade union leaders, whereupon the 'solution' of ballots to elect trade union leaders also became more popular. Such ballots, it was argued, would render trade union leaders more accountable to their mass membership in their union, and would probably result in fewer strikes, due to the perceived greater moderation of ordinary trade union members compared to their more Left-wing union leaders. It was sometimes further argued that those on strike could too readily claim certain welfare benefits whilst not working, which meant that taxpayers were indirectly subsidizing those who were withdrawing their labour. Indeed, the alleged ready availability of certain social security benefits was seen by some critics as something of a partial incentive to go on strike: at the very least, it apparently made strike action financially viable.

Finally, and crucially, these problem and policy streams merged with the political stream in early 1979, this particular political stream comprising four discrete elements. Firstly, the scale and high visibility of the 'winter of discontent' shocked many ordinary British people, rendering them highly susceptible to newspaper claims that the trade unions (and 'bully boys' within them) were effectively declaring war on the British public, and/or were 'running the country'. These claims were lent added resonance by graphic television pictures of Britain apparently at a standstill, with public transport halted, schools closed, hospitals cancelling operations and sending people home, funerals postponed because of gravediggers on strike, and rubbish piled high in Britain's streets due to strikes by refuse collectors.

The 'winter of discontent' thus also entailed two of the characteristics which, according to Solesbury (1976), will usually help to push an issue to the top – or, at least, near to the top, of the policy agenda, namely *generality* (such as the large number of people affected, or who believe that they could be affected) and *particularity* (in terms of the issue being exemplified by a clearly visible or dramatic event, or series of closely-related events, whose profile was greatly increased by dramatic television pictures).

Table 7.1 Responses to the question: do you agree or disagree that 'trade unions have too much power in Britain today'?

	Agree (%)	Disagree (%)
October 1975	75	16
August 1977	79	17
September 1978	82	16

Source: MORI, reproduced in Taylor, 1993: 369

Table 7.2 Responses to the question: do you think the trade unions are becoming too powerful, or are not powerful enough?

	'Becoming too powerful' (%)	'Not powerful enough' (%)'
August 1973	52	13
August 1976	65	5
January 1979	84	3

Source: Gallup: reproduced in Taylor, 1993: 370

Certainly, by this time, as Tables 7.1 and 7.2 illustrate, opinion polls revealed that most British people had acquired a negative view of the trade unions, believing them to have become too powerful, and increasingly acting as self-serving, sectional bodies, selfishly pursuing their own short-term material or political interests, with scant regard for the wider, longer-term, national interest. Having originally been formed to provide protection for ordinary working people against employers, there was a growing belief that ordinary working people – and employers – now needed protection against the trade unions themselves as, indeed, did the British public.

Secondly, the winter of discontent seemed to herald the exhaustion of the Labour Party's hitherto claim that it alone could work harmoniously with the trade unions, and thereby ensure industrial peace. This had been a notable part of Labour's electoral appeal in 1974, but by 1979, the claim had lost its credibility. Indeed, the public hostility which was levelled against the trade unions in the wake of the 'winter of discontent' also rebounded fatally against the Labour Party itself, which appeared unable or unwilling to control the unions, due to its organizational links, financial dependency and ideological affinity. As the then Labour Prime Minister, James Callaghan, recalls – perhaps more in sorrow than in anger – the 'winter of discontent' fuelled a:

> … general tide of disillusionment and dislike that … swept the country. Both the Labour Government and the trade unions had become widely unpopular. … The serious and widespread industrial dislocation caused by the strikes of January 1979, short-lived though they were, sent the Government's fortunes cascading downhill, our loss of authority in one field leading to misfortune in others … (Callaghan, 1987: 540)

Thirdly, but following naturally from these two factors, the Conservative Party won the May 1979 general election, and thereby paved the way for a new, albeit cautious (in implementation), approach to industrial relations and trade union reform. The Conservative Party, led (since 1975) by Margaret Thatcher, skilfully exploited public exasperation with the trade unions, coupled with Labour's apparent inability to tackle the problem itself, and reaped the electoral dividends as consequence (although, of course, the trade union issue was certainly not the only issue which enabled the Conservatives to win the 1979 election). As William Whitelaw observed, though: 'It needed further hard experience culminating in the Winter of Discontent in 1978–9 ... before the British people were ready to give continuous backing to a Government for trade union reform' (Whitelaw, 1989: 75–6).

Although one can engage in endless conjecture about 'what if ...?', it is conceivable that had James Callaghan, the Labour Prime Minister, gone to the polls in the autumn of 1978 (as a number of his Ministerial colleagues had urged him to do) he might have secured re-election for the Labour Government, and either somehow pre-empted the 'winter of discontent' or alternatively, endured it, and then had a further four years or so (until the next election) during which to rectify the damage, and/or hope that it faded from people's memories (*viz.* the issue attention cycle). Delaying the general election beyond autumn 1978, and then being obliged to go to the polls so soon after a winter of widespread and deeply unpopular industrial action, was to prove fatal to the Labour Party, not merely costing them the 1979 election itself, but heralding 18 years in Opposition. The Conservative Party was the beneficiary of Callaghan's misjudgement – or political gamble.

The fourth and final element which constituted the political stream in early 1979 was that the Conservative Party was increasingly dominated, intellectually and ideologically, by the New Right (Dorey, 1996). This was crucial, because had the Party remained dominated by the 'one nation' paternalists who had prevailed for most of the 20th century, then its approach to industrial relations and the trade unions might have been rather different. The 'one nation' Conservatives certainly acknowledged that the trade unions had become too powerful during the 1970s, but they also tended to believe that only a small degree of legislation was needed, and that a Conservative government should be careful to avoid giving the impression of 'declaring war' on the trade unions, not least because this might well play into the hands of militants, and thus lead to even greater industrial conflict and disruption. (For an overview of the debate within the Conservative Party over future industrial relations and trade union policies during the latter half of the 1970s, prior to the 1979 election victory, see Dorey, 1995c.)

The 'one nation' Conservatives also tended to believe that once (limited) legislation had been invoked to curb the worst excesses of trade union 'irresponsibility', efforts ought to be made by Conservative Ministers to establish a new dialogue or partnership with the trade unions – to offer them an olive branch – in order to secure a more consensual and constructive approach to tackling Britain's economic and industrial problems (Gilmour, 1983: 206; Patten, 1983: 128–9; Baldry, 1985: 10–11; Pym, 1985: 160–2, 182).

However, the increasing ideological and intellectual influence – and confidence – of the New Right within the Conservative Party, and Margaret Thatcher's skill in appointing like-minded Ministers to key economic and industrial posts – most notably the Treasury, the Department of Trade and Industry, and (from September 1981 onwards) the Department of Employment – ensured that there was no relenting or backtracking in the determination to weaken British trade unionism irrevocably (Dorey, 2003). From 1980 to 1993, therefore, six laws were introduced to reform industrial relations and tackle trade union power, as summarized in Table 7.3.

Table 7.3 Trade union and industrial relations legislation, 1980–93.

Title	Year	Main provisions
Employment Act	1980	• New closed-shop agreements to be endorsed by at least 80% of workforce in a secret ballot. • Compensation payable to employees whose refusal to join a trade union, on grounds of conscience, leads to the loss of their job. • Government funds made available to finance pre-strike ballots, and ballots for union leadership elections. • Curbs on picketing. • Curbs on secondary or 'sympathy' action by one group of workers in support of another group of workers.
Employment Act	1982	• Existing closed-shop agreements to be approved by at least 80% of employees via a secret ballot. • Compensation increased to workers losing their jobs for refusing to join a trade union on grounds of conscience. • Definition of 'trade dispute' narrowed, thereby outlawing various forms of industrial action.
Trade Union Act	1984	• Strikes only deemed lawful (and thus immune from legal action) if supported by a majority of employees in a secret ballot. • Trade union members entitled to demand a ballot for union leadership contests. • Trade unions obliged to conduct a ballot, at least once every 10 years, to ensure that members wish to retain or establish a 'political fund', financed out of their subscriptions.
Employment Act	1988	• Unlawful for an employer to dismiss an employee for refusing to join a trade union (even if 80% of the workforce have previously voted in favour of operating a closed shop). • Trade unions prohibited from engaging in industrial action to enforce a closed-shop agreement. • Trade unions prohibited from taking disciplinary action against members who refuse to participate in a strike.

Table 7.3   (Continued)

Title	Year	Main provisions
Employment Act	1990	• Unlawful for an employer to reject job applicants merely because they are not trade union members. • All secondary and 'sympathy' industrial action outlawed.
Trade Union Reform and Employment Rights Act	1993	• Employers entitled to offer financial rewards or incentives to employees who give up their trade union membership. • Employees have to provide written approval, every three years, to authorize their trade union to deduct the union's membership fee, direct from their wage/salary. • Abolition of Wages Councils. • All pre-strike ballots to be postal, and subject to independent scrutiny. • Employers to be given seven days' advance notice of impending strike action. • Customers of public services entitled to seek injunctions against unlawful industrial action by public sector workers.

A number of factors are worth highlighting about these legislative reforms:

- They reflect a process of explicit policy learning by the Conservative Party under Margaret Thatcher's leadership, for her Governments carefully noted the problems engendered by the Heath Government's 1971 Industrial Relations Act, and framed the post-1979 legislation accordingly, in order to avoid making the same mistakes.
- One of the lessons thereby learned was the need to avoid doing too much, too soon, for a radical, all-out legislative assault was likely to prompt a 'closing of ranks' by the trade unions against the Government, as had occurred in 1971–2. Whilst the Thatcher (and then Major) Governments were determined to introduce long-lasting and far-reaching reforms, they none the less recognized that these would be more readily attained if introduced on an incremental basis. Hence the deliberate step-by-step approach towards trade union and industrial relations reform by the Thatcher–Major Governments (Dorey, 1993b), and the realization that a series of relatively modest reforms would appear fairly innocent and innocuous, thereby making it harder for trade union leaders to mobilize their members against such reforms.
- Another lesson learnt, which informed the presentation of, and discourse surrounding, the Thatcher-Major reforms, was to depict the legislation, not so much as restrictions on the trade unions *qua* institutions, but as measures to empower their members *vis-à-vis* trade union leaders and rule books. The language invoked by Conservative Ministers was of 'democratizing' the trade unions, and 'handing them back to their members', thereby seeking to win the support of ordinary trade union members who were apparently

being liberated from the tyranny of union leaders, militants and so-called 'bully boys' of the Left. Here was classic Thatcherite populism, aligning itself 'out there' with the people, in this case, 'downtrodden and exploited' ordinary trade union members, who were fed-up with being called out on strike, or afraid of crossing picket lines which exuded hatred and intimidation. This discourse depicted many trade union members living in fear, not of their employer, but of their trade union leaders.

- The Thatcher–Major Governments' legislation also deliberately invoked civil, not criminal, law. The effect of this was two-fold. Firstly, it meant that legal action would be instigated by employers or trade union members themselves, against a trade union deemed to be acting in breach of the law, and not by the Government. This was intended to ensure that industrial disputes, and ensuing legal action, did not become politicized by embroiling the Government itself, which would run the risk of bringing Ministers and trade unions into direct conflict with each other. Secondly, invoking civil, rather than criminal, law was intended to ensure that any proven breaches of the Acts would be punished by injunctions to desist, or/and fines against the recalcitrant trade union(s). Crucially, it meant that no trade union members would be liable to imprisonment, thereby preventing any opportunity for 'martyrs' to be created. Norman Tebbit, in spite of his public image as a 'union basher', was adamant during his time as Employment Secretary from 1981 to 1983, that no trade union leader would be able to get *into* prison as a result of defying the Thatcher Government's trade union and industrial relations laws (Tebbit, 1988: 182).

- That four of the first five laws were entitled Employment Acts derived from the Thatcherite claim that trade union behaviour was itself contributing towards rising unemployment, by pricing workers out of jobs through excessive pay demands, for example, or by deterring, through repeated strike action or restrictive practices, the investment on which new jobs depended. Conservative Ministers therefore claimed that as their legislation eradicated such destructive forms of trade union behaviour, a new climate of business confidence would develop, leading, ultimately, to the creation of new jobs. Hence the appellation of the Employment Act for four of the five legislative reforms introduced between 1980 and 1990 inclusive.

Other factors transforming industrial relations after 1979

Yet it was not only 'employment' legislation *per se* which weakened Britain's trade unions during the 1980s and 1990s, vitally important though this was. Other policies pursued by the Thatcher–Major Governments, coupled with wider economic trends, also played a notable part, and served to weaken and marginalize the trade unions and tilt the balance of power in industrial relations firmly back in favour of employers (see, for example, Marsh, 1992).

Firstly, whereas previous governments in post-war Britain had often sought a compromise settlement when faced with a serious industrial dispute, possibly involving a face-saving inquiry which then recommended a pay increase rather higher than the Government had originally offered or permitted, the Thatcher–Major Governments were generally inclined to 'stand firm', and wait for a strike to dissipate, particularly when faced with industrial action by public sector workers. Private sector employers, meanwhile, were similarly encouraged to stand firm, and praised for so doing by Conservative Ministers. To this end also, the police were often given great praise for their handling of picketing, and for defending the 'right to work' of those employees 'courageously' seeking to cross a picket line. This was particularly evident during the bitter 1984–5 miners' strike, although, curiously, neither

Conservative Ministers nor the police seemed overly concerned with the 'right to work' of those miners made redundant when their pits were subsequently closed down.

Secondly, as noted above, the Thatcher–Major Governments increasingly excluded the trade unions from economic and industrial policy making, insisting that decisions in these spheres were for Ministers and/or 'the market' to determine, not 'vested interests' like the unions. Consequently, during the 1980s and 1990s, trade union representation on a variety of tripartite bodies (comprising trade union officials, employers' representatives and civil servants or Ministers) was reduced or removed altogether. For example, in 1992, of the 1,136 representatives sitting on the Training and Enterprise Councils (TECs), only 82 (just 5 per cent) were trade unionists, whereas on the body which the TECs had relatively recently replaced, the Manpower Services Commission (MSC), the trade unions had enjoyed equal representation with employers (McIlroy, 1995: 207). However, it was the 1992 abolition of the NEDC which provided the starkest symbol of this marginalization of the trade unions. Needless to say, there was a steady decline in the number of meetings between trade union leaders and Ministers throughout the Thatcher–Major years (see, for example, Mitchell, 1987; Longstreth, 1988; McIlroy, 1995: 199–208; Dorey, 1999b: 189–90; 2002b).

Thirdly, the Thatcher–Major Governments were willing to tolerate and preside over record levels of post-war unemployment, sometimes exceeding 3 million people, insisting either that this was a necessary short-term price to pay for reducing inflation, in lieu of restoring economic growth, and thus generating new jobs in the longer term, or claiming that many of the unemployed had 'priced themselves out of work' by insisting on excessive pay increases. (Although, oddly enough, one never heard of any company directors or chief executives similarly pricing themselves out of work when they regularly received rather larger pay increases!) Certainly, high unemployment further weakened the trade unions, both by depleting their membership, and by ensuring that those who retained their jobs would be much more hesitant about supporting industrial action, lest this resulted in them too joining the dole queue.

However, whilst some of the unemployment of the 1980s and 1990s could be attributed either to the Conservative Governments' deflationary economic policies, and/or international recession, it was also a partial consequence of more general changes in the character of the labour market yielded by de-industrialization and globalization. During the 1980s and 1990s, the decline of Britain's manufacturing and extraction (i.e., coal mining) industries gathered pace, due either to significant advances in technology and automation, or to companies and industries relocating to other countries and continents, particularly in the so-called 'Third World' or newly industrializing countries (NICs), where unit labour costs, taxation, welfare expenditure and government regulation were invariably much lower, thereby facilitating much higher levels of profitability and competitiveness.

Back in Britain, new jobs did materialize during the 1980s and 1990s, but unfortunately for the trade unions most of these were in other sectors of the economy, most notably the service and tertiary sectors, not in manufacturing industry. What is significant here is that the sectors which did experience expansion and job creation during the 1980s and 1990s were precisely those sectors of the economy traditionally characterized by a low level of trade union membership and activity. Indeed, many of those who worked in the expanding service and tertiary sectors of the British economy were women and/or part-time

Table 7.4   The decline of trade union membership in Britain, 1979–98, by selected trade unions (membership rounded to the nearest 1,000)

Trade union	1979	1989	1998
Transport and General Workers' Union (TGWU)	2,086,000	1,271,000	891,000
General, Municipal and Boilermakers (GMB)	967,000	823,000	659,000
Union of Shop-Workers, Distributive and Allied Workers (USDAW)	470,000	376,000	300,000
Union of Construction, Allied Trades and Technicians (UCATT)	348,000	258,000	115,000
National Union of Railwaymen/Rail, Maritime and Transport Workers (RMT)*	180,000	103,000	60,000
National Union of Mineworkers (NUM)	253,000	n.a.	9,565

*RMT was formed in 1990 from a merger between the National Union of Railwaymen and National Union of Seamen.

Source: Dorey, 1999b: 49.

employees – two sectors of the labour force generally much less likely to belong to a trade union than male employees and full-time workers. To compound the problem for the trade unions, union membership is generally rather lower in new enterprises and companies than those which have been long-established. The decline of trade union membership is illustrated in Table 7.4 and Figure 7.2.

Dramatic though this decline has been, at least as worrying for the trade unions has been the decline in union density; that is, the proportion of workers belonging to a trade union. It is not just that overall trade union membership has declined dramatically, but also that fewer of those in employment are bothering to join a trade union, a trend illustrated by Figure 7.3.

It is evident that whereas somewhat over half of all employees belonged to a trade union in 1979, fewer than a third do so today. This partly reflects our earlier point, about the changing structure of the British economy and the concomitant changes in the character of the labour market, whereby the greatest job losses have been in those industries and sectors which previously enjoyed a high level of trade union membership, whereas since 1990 the sectors which have seen jobs created have been those traditionally characterized by low(er) levels of trade union membership anyway. For example, in the year of New Labour's first election victory, only 7 per cent of those employed in hotels and restaurants were trade union members, whilst 11 per cent of workers employed in wholesale and retail trades belonged to a trade union. Meanwhile, business services were characterized by a trade union membership rate of 12 per cent.

Figure 7.2   Decline of total trade union membership in Britain since 1979

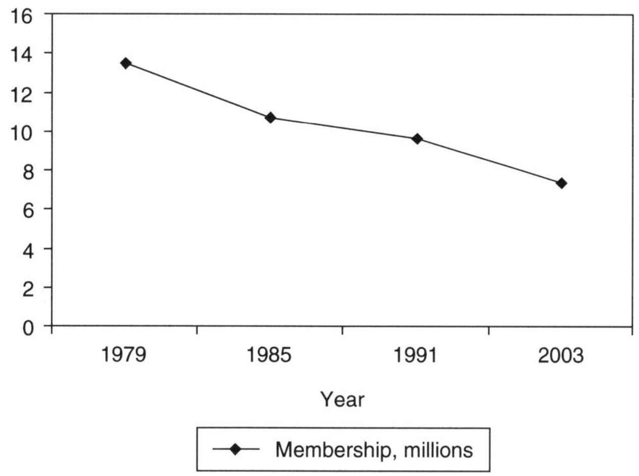

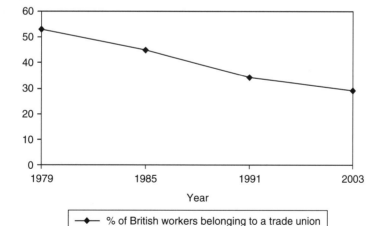

Source: Hicks and Palmer, 2004

Figure 7.3   Declining trade union density in Britain since 1979

Source: Hicks and Palmer, 2004

However, the trade unions are probably also perceived to be relatively ineffective after years of decline and legislative reform, so many employees do not see the point of joining them. Nor has their decline and weakness been reversed by the 1997 election of a Labour Government.

New Labour: 'fairness, not favours' for the trade unions

Neil Kinnock – via Labour's 1987–90 Policy Review – and John Smith, during his 1992–4 leadership of the Party, both acknowledged the need for a reappraisal of the Party's links with the trade unions, and recognized that some of the legislative reforms introduced by the Conservatives might need to be retained, not repealed. Such an acknowledgement was vindicated by private polling and surveys, conducted by Party officials in the immediate aftermath of Labour's 1992 election defeat, which revealed that many (potential or former Labour) voters felt disquiet or disapproval about the closeness of the close links between the Labour Party and the trade unions, and were thus sceptical about the ability of a Labour government to govern in the national interest, as opposed to being beholden to their 'trade union paymasters'. Such findings even prompted a few generally Left-inclined or broadly pro-Labour commentators to suggest that it might be in the interests of both the trade unions and the Labour Party to arrange a 'divorce' from each other (see, for example, Dewdney, 1992; Kellner, 1992; Walsh and Tindale, 1992; MacShane, 1993).

Certainly, when Tony Blair became Labour leader, in the summer of 1994, a much stronger emphasis was placed on loosening the links between political and industrial wings of the British labour movement. Indeed, for Blair, and other senior Party figures, such as Peter Mandelson, a looser – 'more grown-up' – relationship with the trade unions was to become a defining feature of 'New Labour' (see Mandelson and Liddle, 1996: 224–7).

As such, Blair himself was emphatic that under a New Labour government, there would be no repeal of the Conservatives' (anti-)trade union laws, nor a return to 'beer-and-sandwiches' at 10 Downing Street. Instead, the trade unions could expect 'fairness, not favours', and would be listened to just as any other legitimate organized interest: no more, no less (see, for example, Tony Blair cited in *The Times*, 23 July 1994: *The Sunday Times*, 23 April 1995; Blair, 1996: 132; Labour Party, 1996: 14). The popularity of Blair's stance and statements in this respect was confirmed by Labour's own internal pollsters, who informed him, in 1995, that: 'New Labour is defined for most voters by Tony Blair's willingness to take on and master the unions. … In focus groups, the switchers spoke of little else' (Gould, 1998: 257–8).

Having deliberately sought to dampen trade union expectations (whilst also assuaging the continuing concerns of the electorate about Labour's trade union links) of how they might benefit from Labour's return to Office after 18 years in the political wilderness, the Blair Governments have introduced two particular measures long-favoured by the trade unions: namely, the statutory minimum wage, and statutory trade union recognition. The former was introduced in 1999, with the hourly rate set at £3.60 – rather less than the £4.15 to £4.50 called for by many trade unions, but clearly much closer to the £3.50 which the CBI deemed reasonable and realistic. By 2004, the minimum wage had been increased to £4.85 per hour, with trade unions calling for it to be raised to £6.00 per hour by 2006.

Meanwhile, statutory trade union recognition was introduced via the 1999 Fairness at Work Act, which stipulated that when and where at least 40 per cent of employees (not just 40 per cent of those actually voting) in a workplace or industry voted in favour, employers would be legally obliged to recognize the trade union for bargaining purposes, although small firms with fewer than 20 employees were exempted.

Figure 7.4   Strikes in the UK, 1983–2003

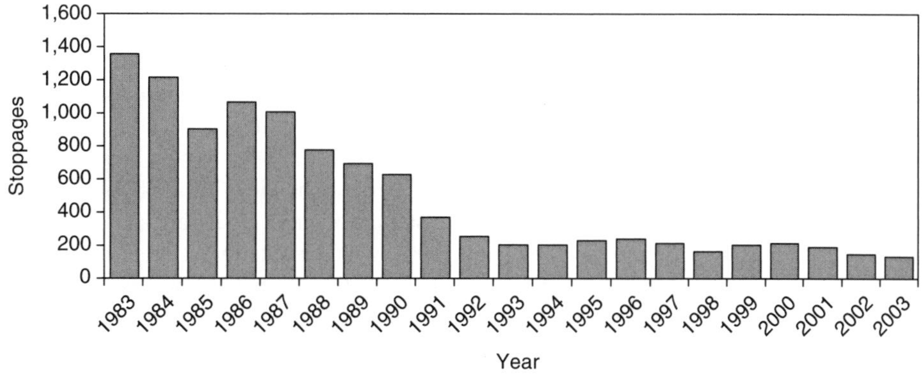

Source: Monger, 2004: 240

Beyond these measures, however, many trade unions have been dismayed or frustrated by the Blair Governments' apparent disregard of their views and grievances, believing that New Labour is too eager to heed the advice or demands of the business community (for an overview of the early years of the Blair government and the trade unions, see Dorey, 1999c). Although individual trade union leaders have found New Labour Ministers rather more willing than their Conservative predecessors to meet them, they have sometimes felt that such meetings are little more than a mere courtesy, in which they are listened to, but ultimately ignored. Certainly, meetings between trade union leaders and New Labour Ministers have tended to be ad hoc, rather than regular or institutionalized via the tripartite policy-making bodies of yore. For example, one study discovered that of more than 3,000 appointments to the first 259 'task forces' established by the Blair Government after its 1997 election victory, only 2 per cent were allocated to trade union representatives, compared to the 35 per cent awarded to business representatives (Barker et al., 2000: 26–7; Ludlam, 2004: 73).

Yet in spite of the trade unions' disappointment with aspects of the Blair Governments' stance on industrial relations and employment issues – such as the Ministerial dilution of various EU initiatives to enhance workers' rights and employment protection, and Blair's own strictures on increasing 'labour market flexibility' (often code for longer or more unsocial working hours and/or less job security) – strike activity remains extremely low. Of course, the paucity of strike action does not in itself mean that workers are more contented, or that relations in Britain's workplaces are joyous and harmonious – various studies and surveys have revealed growing concern and unhappiness amongst British workers about excessive working hours (the longest in Western Europe), employment-related stress, and excessive (and ever-increasing) targets and deadlines – but according to official statistics, the Blair Governments have presided over remarkably low levels of strike activity overall, as illustrated by Figure 7.4. Furthermore, in spite of employee anxiety over the employment conditions and trends just referred to, the overwhelming majority of industrial stoppages derived from disputes over pay (Monger, 2004: 244–5).

Conclusion

As we have seen, industrial relations policy has undergone major changes since 1945, to the extent that, in the context of wider economic and industrial changes since the 1980s, Britain's trade unions are a shadow of their former selves. The pendulum in the workplace has swung back firmly in favour of employers, and 'management's right to manage' has been restored. Having been courted as partners by governments – with occasional exceptions – until the late 1970s, and offered a significant role in economic and industrial policy making (although, even during the pre-Thatcher era, the views of the business community probably carried more weight with Ministers and senior civil servants), the trade unions were confronted, during the 1980s and 1990s, with a markedly different ideological and political climate, in which they were clearly identified by policy makers as a major problem, one which required a tranche of legislation to tackle. Coupled with an accelerating process of deindustrialization, which led to widespread job losses in precisely those sectors of the economy where trade union membership was highest, the unions experienced a virtually relentless decline in membership, and thus a dissipation in their former strength and influence. The balance of power in industry and the workplace swung decisively back towards management and employers, a process actively encouraged by policy makers.

Although the trade unions have been granted a few welcome concessions and measures following the return of a Labour Government in 1997, they remain in a weak position overall, with the Blair Government retaining all of the industrial relations laws introduced by the Thatcher–Major Governments, and insisting on the continued need for 'labour market flexibility' in a global economy. Whereas the trade unions, until the end of the 1970s, participated in regular and routine negotiations with Ministers over a wide range of policies, at the beginning of the 21st century, they are merely consulted on an ad hoc basis.

Indeed, such has been the transformation in British industrial relations since the 1980s that Digby Jones, the director-general of the employers' representative body, the Confederation of British Industry (CBI), recently alleged that the trade unions were becoming irrelevant (*The Guardian*, 3 September 2004). The claim was undoubtedly mischievous, maybe even provocative – such a cavalier or contemptuous attitude on the part of any employer itself proves the continued need for trade unions – but one cannot imagine any employer making such a claim back in the 1960s or 1970s. Meanwhile, just days after the Blair Government had been re-elected for a third term, one of Britain's leading trade unions, Amicus, was complaining that British workers were amongst the easiest (in Europe) to sack, due to their lack of statutory employment rights and protection. As the union's General Secretary, Derek Simpson, observed: 'Unless we have employment protection parity with other European countries, UK workers will continue to be the soft touch when it comes to slashing jobs' (*The Guardian*, 16 May 2005).

These two observations, one from an employers' leader, and one from a trade union leader, clearly indicate just how much industrial relations have changed in Britain since the 1980s, and how the trade unions have been weakened as a consequence.

8 Pensions Policy
Stephen Thornton

Introduction

It has been argued that, compared with other areas of policy making in Britain, social policy is rather unusual. Jordan and Richardson previously described the 'normal' British policy style as one of 'bureaucratic accommodation', by which they meant that the preferred style of policy making in Britain is one in which conflict is avoided in 'a system in which the prominent actors are groups and government departments and the mode is bargaining rather than imposition' (Jordan and Richardson, 1982: 81). However, with regard specifically to social policy, Jordan and Richardson highlighted a partial exception to this usual 'pattern of relatively predictable policy communities' (Jordan and Richardson, 1982: 96). Taking note of Banting's research on poverty, they suggest that social policy provides an example where traditionally the accommodation of organized interests is of secondary importance. Rather, social policy is deemed to be largely a matter of interdepartmental conflict – with the Treasury playing a significant role – and is also to be regarded as a policy area in which 'thinkers and writers' such as William Beveridge and Richard Titmuss have proved strikingly influential (Banting, 1979: 5).

Following a summary of the post-war development of pensions policy in Britain, it will be argued that Jordan and Richardson were indeed correct to suggest that social policy – or at least that pertaining to retirement pensions policy – has failed to conform fully to the 'normal' consultative, incremental style associated with the British policy process. Moreover, it will be argued that, in the 23 years since Richardson's (1982) classic text on national policy styles was published, British pension policy-makers have continued to dance to their own tune. One further goal of this chapter will be to provide a graphic illustration of a phenomenon Pressman and Wildavsky (1973) highlighted 32 years ago, namely that the gap between policy-makers' intentions and the actual outcomes of policy can be very wide indeed.

Post-war pensions policy: Beveridge and universal pension provision

Much to his initial chagrin, in 1941, former civil servant and academic administrator Sir William Beveridge was pushed into chairing a committee with the goal of sorting out state social security provision in Britain (Harris, 1997: 363). It was, at this stage, in a mess. For example, just before the Second World War started, state pensions came in three different categories. Some pensioners, aged 70 and older, received the original non-contributory, means-tested pension based on legislation from 1908. Some others, also 70 and over, received a non-contributory pension by virtue of the 1908 Act, but did so through contribution rights laid out in the 1925 legislation, and thus could therefore forgo the need for means tests. Others, aged between 65 and 70, received an untested contributory pension by virtue of legislation introduced in 1925. To confuse matters still further, in 1940 the Government reduced the pensionable age for insured women and wives of contributors to 60, and introduced a means-tested supplementary pension for the poorest claimants (Macnicol, 1998: 340–1).

In response to this situation, Beveridge consulted bodies such as friendly societies, pensioners' groups, employers and local authorities. However, in a process to be repeated in later years, it was clear that – despite the appearance of debate – policy was being led, by Beveridge himself, down a largely predetermined path (Harris, 1997: 365–412). Having expanded his Committee's remit, Beveridge published his famous Report on Social Insurance and Allied Services in December 1942. Its main proposal was the creation of a 'national minimum' with the aim that no one should live below a level of subsistence – to be accomplished by the universal provision of benefits, including pensions, to be paid '[w]ithout means test ... from a Social Insurance Fund built up by contributions from the insured persons, from their employers, if any, and the state', with both benefits and contributions to be set at a flat rate, and with a means-tested safety-net to be provided merely to meet 'abnormal subsistence needs' (Beveridge, 1942: 11, 86).

This report – with its heroic talk of slaying the five giants of disease, idleness, ignorance, squalor and want – 'came to symbolize the widespread hopes for a different, more just world' (Thane, 1996: 237). This unusual position for an official document on welfare reform was partially achieved through propitious timing – coming a little after the Allied victory at El Alamein – and also what today would be called 'spin'. However, for all Beveridge's exciting references to revolutions, the heart of his reform was a consolidation of earlier measures; in particular the retention of the Treasury's preferred funding method, the insurance system – a concept not altogether compatible with the idea of universal coverage (Macnicol, 1998: 384). Thus, though sometimes thought of as a rational blueprint for social reform, the Beveridge Report can also be regarded as an untidy compromise. Indeed, for Lowe, this report '[f]ar from being a revolutionary and logical document', was rather 'conservative, illogical and ultimately impractical' (Lowe, 1993: 134).

Much – though, significantly, not all – of Beveridge's Report was translated into legislation. Clement Attlee's 1945–50 Labour Government introduced the 1946 National Insurance Act, which did establish a universal system of flat-rate benefits, and the companion National Assistance Act, passed in 1948, supported the whole scheme with a means-tested National Assistance safety-net provision. However, one significant break from Beveridge's original proposals was the abandonment of his financially prudent, but politically unwise, suggestion that full pensions would not be available until recipients had contributed for 20 years to the Social Fund. Instead, under the terms the 1946 Act, full pensions were to be paid immediately to those insured since 1925, whilst for those who had joined after that date, full pensions would be available after only 10 years' contributions. This serious breach of actuarial propriety was deemed a political inevitability, but it did seriously weaken the financial foundation of the whole scheme (Macnicol, 1998: 390–1). It also guaranteed that the 'Social Insurance Fund', as such, remained a 'fiction' (Lowe, 1994b: 123), in that employees' contributions went to pay existing pensioners' benefits rather than into a 'pot' from which their own retirement would eventually be financially secured.

A second departure from Beveridge's original proposals was the rejection of the goal of attaching benefits, including pensions, to subsistence levels. The Treasury, in particular, thought this pledge to be financially unsustainable (Macnicol, 1998: 391). One result of this departure from a fundamental aspect of Beveridge's vision was that National Assistance came to play a much greater role in future welfare provision than many had hoped. It also led to the situation where subsequent governments faced mounting pressure from pensioners to increase their inadequate flat-rate benefit (Fawcett, 1996: 22).

Whilst on the topic of consequences for future governments, it is also worth highlighting what is arguably the most significant legacy bequeathed by Beveridge and the other early pensions policy actors, namely an expanding industry in private pension provision. During the first half of the 20th century, the number of occupational pension schemes – many run by the private sector – had increased gently, having been given the odd prod of encouragement by the state, notably through the 1921 Finance Act's provision of some tax relief on pension fund contribution (Hannah, 1986: 47–8). By the time of the Beveridge Report, it was noted that the number with pension provision independent of the state was 'substantial in itself though small in proportion to the total numbers of persons of pensionable age' (Beveridge, 1942: 93). The flat-rate scheme Beveridge proposed 'really presented no serious rivalry or alternative to good occupational schemes' (Atkinson, 1977: 220) and, as a result, this small but significant industry continued to expand.

The frustrating tale of state earnings-related pension provision

As suggested above, although the introduction of a universal system of state retirement pensions was indeed a major step in the development of pensions policy in Britain, the regime which the 1946 National Insurance Act inaugurated was inherently unstable. O'Higgins (1986: 103) notes two 'flaws' which 'meant that reform and change were inevitable'. One of these was the lack of subsistence-level pensions, which encouraged the expansion of both the means test and of the state-subsidized occupational pension industry. The second problem was the flat-rate contribution system which, because contributions had to be set at a level that poorly-paid workers could afford, was hardly the ideal set-up to address the almost incessant calls to increase the rate of benefit – particularly as the subsidy from the Exchequer remained at a level lower than Beveridge had recommended.

In addition to these 'flaws', there was also serious concern – keenly felt at the Treasury – that the gap between future income and future liabilities would widen (Bridgen and Lowe, 1998: 96). One response to this concern was the 1953 appointment, by Churchill's Conservative Government, of the Phillips Committee. The following year's report gave official notice that Beveridge's objective – that a state scheme should offer adequate standard pensions for all – had finally bitten the dust. The Phillips Committee declared that '[a] contributory scheme cannot, in our view, be expected to provide a rate of benefit which would enable everybody, whatever their circumstances, to live without other resources, either by their own providing or by way of national assistance' (Phillips Committee, 1954: 56). The

Committee also lauded the principle – and recommended the expansion – of occupational pension schemes. In short, the Phillips Committee rationalized existing post-Beveridge developments in pensions policy.

The Conservative Government accepted the main thrust of this report – indeed, the growth in occupational pensions was encouraged still further by the Finance Act 1956 – but others, typically on the political Left, did not. At this time, the near-legendary Professor Richard Titmuss, of the London School of Economics, began a number of attacks on what he dubbed 'the problem of two nations in old age', reflected and reinforced by 'the greater inequalities in living standards after work than in work', and, in particular, '[t]he generous provision which society is earmarking for the future benefit of the professional, executive, and salaried classes' – largely through tax concessions for certain private pension schemes – when compared to '[t]he relatively meagre National Insurance pension, fast becoming the new Poor Law' (*The Times*, 30 December 1953).

However, it was not Titmuss but two promising young researchers at the London School of Economics (LSE) who placed on the British policy agenda a concept to solve the 'two nations' problem; an idea that had proved successful elsewhere. In a 1953 Fabian pamphlet, Brian Abel-Smith argued that if an insurance-based state pension system was deemed inevitable, then the flat-rate system should be abandoned, and replaced by one modelled on the Swiss model, which included 'variable contributions and variable benefits connected to them' (Abel-Smith, 1953: 25). With Peter Townsend, Abel-Smith extended this proposal to suggest, as a possible future development, 'a compulsory insurance scheme, [in which] benefits should be related to past earnings, with an appropriate minimum and maximum'. This they called 'National Superannuation', with the explanation that the state will 'make the principles of private superannuation fulfil the needs of a national social service' (Abel-Smith and Townsend, 1955: 27, 25).

Though it was ostensibly odd for socialists to argue for a system that appeared to perpetuate differentials and inequalities in earnings during working years into retirement – it was hardly egalitarian – the system which Abel-Smith and Townsend recommended did include a significant degree of redistribution. Besides, they argued that

> [i]f earnings in working life were absolutely equal, only then would flat-rate provision for old age be a sacrosanct corollary. The least we can do is ensure that there are not more inequalities in old age than in working life. (Abel-Smith and Townsend, 1955: 23)

Moreover, Abel-Smith, quoting Barbara Wootton, argued that '[r]eal equality is only achieved when all classes not only can, but do, use the same services' (Abel-Smith, 1953: 40). Thus, whilst enshrining a redistributive element was undoubtedly important, for Abel-Smith, the overriding characteristic of a fair pension system was solidaristic ambition.

Fate played a part in taking the hesitantly-expressed, half-formed suggestions of the two junior academics to the top of the policy agenda. According to the personal account of the politician who subsequently became associated with national superannuation for much of his career, Richard Crossman serendipitously stumbled across Abel-Smith and Townsend's work the evening before he had to make a potentially embarrassing speech to Labour's 1955 annual conference, in which he was due to explain why the Party should not commit itself to demands for a large increase in the flat-rate pension. By persuading delegates to postpone committing the Labour Party to the flat-rate increase until it had had chance to examine 'this new marvellous idea' (Crossman, 1972: 12), Crossman turned potential humiliation into a surprising triumph and, in so doing, attached the Labour Party to the concept of earnings-relation.

Once the decision had been made by the Labour Party Conference to explore the idea of a solidaristic, earnings-related, state pension scheme, momentum steadily gathered pace. The 'Study Group on Security and Old Age', a sub-committee of the Home Policy Committee of the National Executive, was established to develop the concept. The membership of this body was limited to Labour Party politicians, trade union representatives and – most significantly – the academics Titmuss, Abel-Smith and Townsend (Labour Party Archives, Study Group on Security and Old Age, minutes, 4 July 1956 and *passim*). By 1957, this body had produced the policy document *National Superannuation: Labour's Policy for Security in Old Age*. The main proposal was to provide a state pension to satisfy nearly all – with the promise of 'half-pay on retirement' for the average-paid worker (Labour Party, 1957: 21). This was to be achieved through a 50 per cent increase in the basic pension, buttressed by a new level of earnings-related pension to be financed through the establishment of a 'National Pensions Fund'.

Fawcett stresses the significance of National Superannuation, and argues that it proved 'rare amongst opposition party policy papers in being a fully worked out blueprint rather than a statement of general principles and desirable objectives' (Fawcett, 1996: 21). Many in the higher echelons of the Labour Party were certainly pleased with it, and the core 'half-pay on retirement' message was projected prominently in Labour's 1959 general election campaign, where Crossman had hopes of it proving a 'marvellous vote winner' (Morgan, 1981: 581). Instead, the Labour Party suffered its third successive general election defeat.

However, this did not sound the death-knell for the earnings-related pensions concept, for it strongly influenced subsequent Labour Party attempts at reforming pensions, and, more immediately, it also affected Harold Macmillan's Conservative Governments' own plans for reform. As a 'one nation' Conservative, Macmillan proved rather more interested in social reform than Churchill and Eden, his immediate predecessors. Consequently, in response both to prompts from the Treasury – anxious about the future financial implications of an ageing population – and to the impact made by Labour's National Superannuation, Macmillan declared, '[w]hy should we not make a scheme of our own? It would not be put forward as an economic scheme to save the fund etc. … It would be put forward as an imaginative scheme of social reform' (quoted in Bridgen and Lowe, 1998: 105). In essence, Macmillan thought it possible to accomplish the tricky feat of demonstrating to the electorate the more social progressive side of Conservatism in response to Labour's efforts, yet, at the same time, attempt to address the traditional Conservative concern regarding 'excessive' public expenditure.

However, the eventual path to legislation was tortuous (Bridgen and Lowe, 1998: 104–12). Iain Macleod, the (Conservative) Minister of Labour, began the debate that reverberated around Whitehall – if nowhere else at this stage – by suggesting a bold scheme whereby employers would be compelled to take out pension schemes for their employees.

Interestingly, this debate continues to rage to this day. Back in the 1950s, prominent amongst opponents of this scheme was the Treasury, with officials there distrustful both of the private sector, and of any measure that would lose the Exchequer revenue – the potential result of the proposed tax allowances on private pension contributions (Bridgen, 2000: 95–8). It was the Treasury's counter-proposal that included an element of 'earnings-relation', though only for a narrow band of contributors, in order to provide a (pretty miserable) state supplement to the standard pension. This 'graduated' pension was proposed largely because such a scheme offered the opportunity to raise contributions immediately, with the payback of higher returns only necessary sometime in the future. Treasury officials saw this as a short-term means to plug the perceived hole in the National Insurance Fund (Bridgen, 2000: 96).

In the end, it was the Treasury-inspired line that largely won the day. The compulsory occupational scheme idea was abandoned. Instead employees, earning between £9 and £15 a week – in a period when average male earnings were about £13 a week – were to pay additional contributions based on these earnings, this securing for them so-called 'bricks' of extra state pension (Ministry of Pensions and National Insurance, 1958: 15). However Macleod and John Boyd-Carpenter – the Minister for Pensions and National Insurance – did manage to convince enough of their Cabinet colleagues at least to tack a limited contracting-out facility on to this proposed graduated scheme; whereupon an individual did not have to contribute to the graduated pension if an adequate alternative was provided by the occupational pensions sector. As Boyd-Carpenter explained, contracting-out was seen as a device with which 'to encourage the private sector occupational pension schemes' (Boyd-Carpenter, 1980: 135) and this – solidly in the Conservative tradition of supporting market solutions wherever and whenever possible – was supported in Cabinet.

The resultant piece of legislation, the 1959 National Insurance Act, was an unloved compromise. Indeed Macleod – after witnessing his ambitious reform wither and die – dubbed the eventual pension plan 'a little mouse of a scheme' (quoted in Timmins, 2001: 192). It did nothing to help existing pensioners, nor did the system it established prove any more stable than that which it replaced. Yet the 1959 National Insurance Act was still a highly significant chapter in the story of British pensions policy, for as Lowe argues, the introduction of the graduated pension, which included the potential for individuals to 'opt-out' of part of the state scheme, pulled the social insurance system even further away from Beveridge's original vision (Lowe, 1994b: 123). Furthermore, through a combination of generous contracting-out terms, and the lack of competition from the mean graduated state scheme, the occupational sector was given a significant boost. Occupational pension scheme membership increased by over 4 million between 1956 and 1967, meaning that by the mid-1960s, around half of Britain's workforce were contributing towards an occupational pension (Hannah, 1986: 145).

This increase in the numbers with a stake in the private pension market was one factor that created problems for the Labour Party when it returned to power in 1964, having retained the manifesto commitment to introduce a comprehensive state earnings-related pension scheme (Fawcett, 1996: 38). Other problems were caused by: poor planning during the final years in Opposition; economic difficulties, exacerbated by a large increase in the standard pension rate announced soon after the election; unsettled organization; and a lack of coherence regarding social policy priorities (see Crossman, 1972; Webb, 1975: 444–52; Bridgen, 1999: 12–16; Thornton, forthcoming). On this last point, it is worth emphasizing that the 1960s witnessed the so-called 'rediscovery of poverty'. Somewhat ironically, Abel-Smith and Townsend (1965) were central to this development, in which attention became focused on 'relative' poverty experienced in a variety of pockets of socio-economic deprivation throughout society, not least amongst children. This did little to abate the pressure in the labour movement for measures that more directly improved the condition of existing pensioners (Fawcett, 1996: 35–6). Consequently, other reforms, such as the unsuccessful income guarantee – which was specifically designed to help the poorest – jostled with the state superannuation for supremacy on Labour's social security policy agenda during the first critical months of Harold Wilson's 1964–6 Labour Government. In the end, the Government's initial pension reform was merely to increase the basic state benefit.

Despite the Wilson Government's re-election with a comfortable parliamentary majority in March 1966, for a number of years pensions reform remained conspicuous only by its absence. It was only in 1969 that a major piece of pensions legislation was introduced into the House of Commons, one which promised to abolish the flat-rate standard pension altogether, and replace it with a single tier of earnings-related benefit, paid for through earnings-related contributions, using the established pay-as-you-earn system. Unfortunately, it had taken the Minister responsible, Richard Crossman, so long before being in a position to be able to introduce such a radical reform, that when the Labour Government fell in the general election of June 1970, the National Superannuation and Social Insurance Bill fell with it.

Consequently, as Ellis notes, '[t]he Conservatives who took office in 1970 found a vacuum where a large Pensions Bill had been' (Ellis, 1989: 37). With nature abhorring a vacuum, it was filled with the 1973 Social Security Act. Although the flat-rate pension was maintained, the existing mixed flat-rate and graduated contributions system made way for a fully earnings-related one, with the result that people would pay at differing rates, according to the size of their income, but would eventually receive the same benefit – an oddly 'Socialist plan' according to one confused actuary (Kerr, 1974: 10). It was also proposed that the state would provide an earnings-related second pension, but unlike Labour's scheme, this particular pension was designed merely as a 'safety-net', to cater for those who would have difficulty obtaining a reasonable second pension from the private sector. Indeed, it was hoped that, in time, the private sector would increasingly bear the brunt of pensions provision. As declared in the White Paper *Strategy for Pensions*, '[i]t is by personal enterprise and foresight, and not by reliance on an ever-widening extension of state commitments, that better living standards in the later years of life will be secured' (Department of Health and Social Security, 1971: 27).

One interesting aspect of the 'Joseph scheme' – the Conservatives' 1970–4 Secretary of State for Health and Social Security being Keith Joseph – was the proposal to build up an independent Reserve Scheme Fund to cover the proposed state second pension. However, this unusual form of nationalization, along with other aspects of this scheme (such as the reserve pension itself), suffered a similar terminal fate to that inflicted on Crossman's previously attempted pension reform. Between the passing of the 1973 Social Security Act, and the planned operating date of April 1975, the Conservatives lost the February 1974 general election, and the incoming (minority) Labour Government had little desire to finish the process the Conservatives had begun. Another pension scheme had fallen at an early fence.

Thus, despite the intense efforts of a number of policy makers from both parties of government, pensions policy during the early 1970s remained largely a product of legislation from the 1940s and 1950s. To some extent, this changed in 1975 when – in the year following Labour's return to government – the new political head of the DHSS, Barbara Castle, was, at long last, able to conclude a 20-year unconsummated relationship with the passing of the Social Security Act, legislation which introduced the State Earnings-Related Pension Scheme (SERPS). Though it has since been suggested that SERPS was 'the only one measure of permanent value [from the 1974–9 period] that might be regarded as having about it the tinge of socialism' (Dell, 2000: 469), this scheme was, in essence, a fusion of the wreckage from both the Crossman and Joseph schemes, and, moreover, was passed with bipartisan support.

Before providing some details about SERPS, it is worth briefly noting a couple of short-term measures which the Labour Government introduced in 1974 in order to appease existing pensioners hit hard during a period of extremely high inflation (peaking in 1975 at a phenomenal 24 per cent). One such short-term measure was an unprecedented 29 per cent increase in the standard rate of pensions, whilst the other notable innovation was the statutory guidance that future annual pension uprating reviews would take into account increases in both national earnings and prices, and then match the new benefit to whichever had risen the greater amount. This innovation was not fated to last too long.

Regarding the 1975 Act, Joseph's two-tier model was followed, with a base-level flat-rate pension introduced, but supplemented by an earnings-related element provided by the state through SERPS. Contracting-out was to remain permissable but, unlike the Conservative proposal, SERPS was not designed merely as a reserve scheme. This additional pension was based on the accrual of an indexed-linked one-eightieth of earnings each year, for 20 years, to a maximum pension equivalent of 25 per cent of earnings in the additional pension range. One generous touch was that, once 20 years of contributions had elapsed, the top-up pension would be derived from a worker's best 20 years' earnings. This evaded the problem that Crossman had faced, whereby for some – typically in manual occupations where final working years often meant reduced wages – the calculation of contributions worked out over a whole-life basis, or on a final salary basis, could result in a reduced earnings-related entitlement. It also, as Castle (1993: 465) proudly recalled, made it easier for women to build up a reasonable contribution record.

This second pension tier was designed to rise with inflation – in contrast to the flat-rate pension which, as noted earlier, was to rise with either inflation or earnings, whichever displayed the greater increase. Contributions for the weekly pension were designed to 'represent £1 for every £1 of average weekly earnings up to a base level and a quarter of the earnings between the base level and the ceiling' (Department of Health and Social Security, 1974: 5). The whole scheme was to be phased in over 20 years, and was to continue to be financed using the established pay-as-you-earn system.

Surpassing the last two attempts at major pension reform, SERPS came into force in April 1978, whereupon 'for the first time in twenty years pensions and their future was off the agenda' (Ellis, 1989: 56). With SERPS, the idea of earnings-relation had finally become an integral aspect of the British pensions' regime. Indeed, earnings-relation had proved a very flexible device, able to adapt the different ambitions of both Labour and Conservative Governments, and thus had become a common theme of all major attempts at pension reform during the period from the late 1950s to the 1970s.

This happy consensus was not to last. As Hill observes, what Ellis might have added to his aforementioned statement was that pension reform was off the agenda 'only until 1984 when Norman Fowler started questioning whether the nation could afford SERPS' (Hill, 1993: 112). By this stage, earnings-relation had been cast back into the primeval (policy) soup, whilst a fresh pensions idea wended its way to the top of the agenda.

The impact of personal pensions

Before examining the arrival on the policy agenda of an important new idea in pensions policy, it is worth noting that soon after the Conservatives' May 1979 election victory, Margaret Thatcher's Government made a quiet, but highly significant, alteration to the existing pensions system. From 1980 onward, annual increases in standard pension rates – which had been linked to rises in prices or earnings, whichever was the higher – were instead merely indexed to price rises, the typically less generous linkage (given the propensity for average annual earnings generally to increase at a somewhat higher rate than inflation). This somewhat technical measure has inevitably made – and continues to make – the standard pension an increasingly less generous package in comparison to the average rate of earnings. In addition, the severance of the earnings link put the future of SERPS into question, because – as the legislation then stood – a future government would have to balance the decline in basic pension rates with an increase in the supplementary pension, thus removing some of the savings the original measure was supposed to create.

The next step towards a pensions future with reduced state provision was the establishment, in November 1983, of an Inquiry into Provision for Retirement, to be chaired by the then Secretary of State for Health and Social Security, Norman Fowler. One of the Inquiry's first tasks was to study the potential role of personal pensions – an idea that had risen rapidly up the pensions policy agenda. This ascent had been boosted by some eager advocacy from New Right 'think-tanks'; indeed the Centre for Policy Studies (CPS) is credited with the creation of the concept of 'personal and portable pensions' (Centre for Policy Studies, 1983; see also Araki, 2000: 608). Nesbitt also highlights the continuing importance of this area of influence into the pensions policy process, arguing that, during the Inquiry, the CPS – and Downing Street's Central Policy Unit (CPU) – 'were probably the only two organisations to possess influence in their own right rather than by virtue of the personal status of their members' (Nesbitt, 1995: 146). Incidentally, the representatives of these bodies on the Inquiry were two senior Conservative politicians of the future: David Willetts and John Redwood, of the CPS and the CPU, respectively.

Obviously, for an idea to rise quickly up the policy agenda, and/or move from the systemic to the institutional agenda, not only requires keen advocacy (by 'policy entrepreneurs', for example), but also a receptive audience – and the idea of individual, portable pensions being provided by the private sector was enthusiastically embraced. There were a number of reasons for this. It was clear from an early stage that the Thatcher

Governments wanted a private sector replacement for SERPS, with the state scheme being judged as financially unsustainable in the 21st century (Fowler, 1991: 211). However, whereas previous Conservative Governments had looked to the occupational sector to shoulder most of the burden of those outside the state scheme, by the 1980s, occupational pensions had rather fallen out of favour, marked as they were by 'the smack of corporatism and the job for life' (Evason, 1999: 122). This put personal pensions firmly in the frame, not least because they were much more in tune with the Conservatives' ideological emphasis and discourse on individual rights and responsibilities. Certainly, they appeared more suited (than occupational pensions) to a changing labour market that requires flexible pensions as a counterpart to frequent job changes (itself a feature of what neo-liberals somewhat euphemistically refer to as 'labour market flexibility').

As Timmins (2001: 394) notes, there was also a personal element to all this. Norman Fowler himself had not been treated well by the occupational pensions sector. As Fowler's memoirs (1991: 203) elucidate, his father had died before he had been able to collect his company pension, leaving his mother with returned contributions but no widow's pension. Fowler's understandable sense of injustice was compounded by outrage that the occupational pension he himself had earned as a journalist early in his working life, would, if collected, have become – like that of many 'early leavers' – frozen in value to the point of near worthlessness.

Anyway, although the Inquiry produced little of substance, the next stage in the policy process – the Green Paper *The Reform of Social Security* (Department of Health and Social Security, 1985) – signalled clearly the direction to be taken, by proposing the abolition of SERPS. In its stead, all workers would be compelled to join an occupational pension scheme or, for the first time, be permitted to take out a personal pension. As it happened, the Treasury suddenly spotted that the proposal, as it stood, would cause a significant loss in revenue. Thus, after a heated debate between Norman Fowler at the DHSS and Nigel Lawson at the Treasury (Fowler, 1991: 214–22; Lawson, 1992: 586–98) – and against the backdrop of considerable consternation from an insurance industry worried about the prospect of thousands of low-paid workers seeking pension cover – SERPS was temporarily reprieved.

Instead, in the 1986 Social Security Act, SERPS was made much less generous: the replacement value of 25 per cent of earnings was reduced to just 20 per cent, whilst the celebrated '20 Best Years' formula was replaced with a calculation based over the lifetime average. Furthermore, widows lost half their husbands' pension rights. Moreover, whilst making the state scheme less attractive, to make doubly sure that the private pension market flourished legislation was passed to make business easier. 'Money purchase' schemes were allowed to contract out. These schemes – unlike those based on final-salary calculations – do not guarantee a set amount of pension on the date of retirement; rather, the pension is dependent on the state of the equity market at that time. Furthermore – and this is where the preference for personal pensions was made very plain – financial incentives were made to those thinking of leaving SERPS or occupational schemes to take out approved personal pensions. Thus, though SERPS did survive, in a form, overall, the 1986 Act remained a significant piece of legislation, with Bonoli suggesting that it constituted 'one of the most radical departures from the traditional West European post-war approach to pension policy' (Bonoli, 2000: 52).

Measures from the 1986 Act were implemented in 1988, alongside an expensive advertising campaign to promote personal pensions. The impact of this piece of legislation was such that the 1990s were to be dominated by its fallout, in particular by a number of what Araki delicately describes as 'unanticipated policy outcomes' (Araki, 2000: 614). Regarding personal pensions, one unexpected turn of events was that these products were taken up, as one former Chancellor noted, on a 'positively embarrassing scale' (Lawson, 1992: 370), this 'embarrassment' generated by the fact that the financial inducements offered to encourage people to transfer to personal pension schemes effectively transformed a policy partially designed to save money into one that actually cost billions of pounds. More discomfiture followed for Conservative Ministers in the mid-1990s, when it was discovered that 2.5 million people who had transferred to personal pensions would have been better advised to remain in either SERPS, or their original occupational scheme; they had, in Hutton's words, 'been sold a pup' (Hutton, 1995: 202). In the midst of all this, confidence in the occupational pension sector evaporated when, following the death of publishing tycoon, Robert Maxwell, it was discovered that his companies' pension funds had been plundered.

John Major's Government (John Major had replaced Margaret Thatcher as Conservative Prime Minister in November 1990) reacted to the last of these events with the appointment of the Goode Committee, which reported in 1993, and some of whose recommendations were enshrined in the 1995 Pensions Act. Though supposedly seeking to improve the statutory regulation of company pension schemes, the terms did little to provide greater protection. Certainly, as Evason (1999: 124) pointedly notes, the scheme would not have protected the Maxwell pensioners. Instead, the Conservative Government's focus remained on encouraging the private sector, partially through the relaxation of certain statutory guarantees on non-money purchase pension products. A further reform was to remove the disparity between women's and men's retirement ages that had existed since 1940, with this levelling inevitably being upwards, with women's pensionable age gradually to rise to 65 by 2020. In 1997, the Conservatives had plans to cement fully the dominance of the private sector as the nation's chief pensions provider by introducing the 'Basic Pension Plus'. In this scheme, state provision would eventually, it was claimed, become largely redundant, as workers would have been compelled to contribute to private pension funds (Conservative Research Department, 1997: 87–102).

New Labour, new idea – similar result

Not unusually for this story, a fateful election result brought an abrupt end to plans for radical pension reform. After 18 years in Opposition, the Labour Party – having been re-branded under Tony Blair's leadership (since 1994) as New Labour – won the 1997 general election by a landslide. This new – and New – Labour Government entered Office with what appeared to be another fresh pension idea. However, as the reader might expect by this stage, the path from idea to implementation was not a smooth one, nor were the policy outcomes those envisaged.

Prior to New Labour's 1997 victory at the polls, successive election defeats had led senior figures in the Party to become somewhat sensitive about Labour's persistent 'tax and spend' image. This negative image was deemed crucial in explaining the 1992 election defeat, when Labour had apparently snatched defeat from the jaws of (electoral) victory. As part of the ensuing modernization process, the Labour leader from 1992 to 1994, John Smith, appointed a Commission on Social Justice, a body which suggested that the brightest future lay on a path between the unfettered free market and traditional state-centred socialism (although the concept of the 'Third Way' had not yet become common currency amongst Labour modernizers). The goal in mind was an 'Investors' Britain', one which combined 'the ethics of community with the dynamics of a market economy', and where the state should 'offer a hand-up, not just a hand-out' (Commission on Social Justice, 1994: 4, 8). With regard to pensions, the Commission suggested that the traditional policy of raising basic state pension to a level that would eradicate pensioner poverty was simply too expensive. Instead, a new 'pension guarantee' was proposed, targeting the poorest, together with suggestions for the universal provision of a second pension.

Once Tony Blair had become leader, following John Smith's sudden death in 1994, the Labour Party began to distance itself even more from profligate images of the past. Indeed, the Shadow Chancellor, Gordon Brown, pledged that if Labour won the next general election, it would adhere firmly to Conservative spending plans for the first two years in Office. This obviously limited still further the number of 'goodies' the Labour Party could promise to pensioners. In Labour's 1997 manifesto, there was a vague suggestion of more means-tested support, but no pledge was made to re-attach the earnings link to the basic pension, nor to restore SERPS. Instead, a new concept was offered to the British electorate – the 'stakeholder' pension. Introduced in a policy document in 1996, these stakeholder pensions were described in the manifesto as 'a new framework', and were to be developed in partnership with 'financial service companies, employers and employees' – with the aim of securing a decent second pension for those on low and modest incomes (Labour Party, 1997: 27).

To give a little context, assisted by publications such as Will Hutton's *The State We're In* (1995), the term 'stakeholder capitalism' – and 'stakeholding' in general – began to gain popular currency during the dog days of John Major's Conservative Government. For Hutton, the term suggested a reform of companies and institutions whereby more attention would be paid to employees, consumers and affected communities – the so-called 'stakeholders'. At the same time, Frank Field – Labour MP for Birkenhead and 'iconoclastic thinker on welfare policy' (Evans, 2002: 247) – was developing his own stakeholding idea in respect to pension reform. Field proposed a mandatory scheme whereby all citizens could enjoy a stake in the nation's prosperity, by being able to claim a second pension based on a national fund invested in stocks and shares (Field, 1996: iii–viii).

Though he had not been on Labour's front-bench in Opposition, it was Field whom Blair appointed as Minister for Welfare Reform, his brief being 'to think the unthinkable'. In one sense, that is exactly what Field did. It has been suggested that Blair was unfamiliar with Field's ideas – not least the latter's support of the concept of universalism (Rawnsley, 2001: 110; Blackburn, 2002: 303) – and, apparently, the Prime Minister was somewhat taken aback when Field explained that his plans for a universal stakeholder pension would, despite expected savings in the long term, initially cost £8 billion per year. Field only lasted 15 months in government, with much of that time apparently spent feuding with Harriet Harman, the Secretary of State at Social Security (Rawnsley, 2001: 118–19).

In December 1998 – after both Field and Harman had left the Department of Social Security (DSS) – the Government's long awaited pension proposals were published in the Green Paper *A New Contract for Welfare: Partnership in Pensions* (Department of Social Security, 1998). These complicated proposals retained elements of Field's ideas, but they were combined, rather uneasily, with ideas proposed by others with different priorities. The whole scheme was, as Evason dubs it, 'a curious amalgam' (1999: 130).

A number of tiers of pension provision were proposed. To underpin the hugely complicated scheme was the Minimum Income Guarantee (MIG), a measure intended to replace means-tested Income Support for pensioners. This signalled New Labour's – and the Treasury's – dislike of universal provision, and its desire to find, instead (in Blair's words) 'more sophisticated and better targeted ways' of helping pensioners (*Daily Record*, 2 September 2000). Though its status as the bedrock of state pension provision was threatened by the MIG, that old survivor, the basic state pension was to continue. However, as before, through being linked to prices (rather than earnings, which continued usually to increase at a faster or higher rate), this pension was destined to continue to 'wither on the vine'. This disappointed Barbara Castle who, at the time of the Green Paper's publication, was still campaigning vigorously for the earnings link, as well as for the restoration of SERPS. Regarding SERPS, Castle was again disappointed with the proposal to phase out her scheme, to be replaced with a State Second Pension. Unlike SERPS – but with echoes of Keith Joseph's Reserve Scheme – this new tier was designed for those, typically the very low-paid and carers, who would have difficulty in gaining a second pension from the private sector.

At the heart of the reform was the ambition that, by 2050, state schemes would contribute to only 40 per cent of overall pension provision in the UK, compared with 60 per cent at the end of the 20th century (Department of Social Security, 1998: 14). To fulfil this objective, it was necessary to help bolster the expansion of the private sector into the middle-income market – initially regarded as those earning between £9,000 and £18,500. This is where a new level of stakeholder pension provision was to come in. These 'stakeholder' pensions were very different to those Field had originally proposed – indeed, were merely 'a muffled echo' (Blackburn, 2002: 307). In *Partnership in Pensions*, it was proposed that stakeholder pensions should be voluntary, that they should be state subsidized through tax and National Insurance relief, and that existing commercial providers should manage them. The enthusiasm which these commercial providers initially evinced for stakeholder pensions was curbed somewhat by the proposed imposition of a tight cap on the fund management costs on these products. From a different perspective, Barbara Castle's team campaigning for the restoration of SERPS were even less enthused by the scheme, dubbing stakeholder pensions 'little more than modified Personal Pension schemes' (Castle et al., 1998: 16).

In the wake of *Partnership in Pensions* came the 1999 Welfare and Pension Reform Act, and the following year's Child Support, Pensions and Social Security Act. However, as is so often the case with public policy, the implementation 'stage' quickly began to reveal deficiencies in the Government's strategy and associated legislation. Frank Field – with a touch of 'I told you so' – noted that, because the MIG was designed to rise with earnings, in a manner that the stakeholder pension could not, most savers in the very income bracket that stakeholder pensions were designed for would be better served by not saving at all (*Financial Times*, 3 August 2000). Realization of this led to the subsequent – hasty –

introduction of the Pension Credit, another means-tested device, albeit one, unlike the short-lived MIG, that does not penalize those with modest savings. However, this measure does little to persuade those who can claim benefit, but do not. The Government estimated – too conservatively, according to pensioner groups – that of the 5.5 million entitled to claim Pension Credit, 1.8 million would not do so (*The Times*, 8 March 2003). The scheme's complexity, and the stigma attached to claiming means-tested benefits, are regarded as the key factors contributing to this situation.

The continued downgrading of the basic state pension has also led to embarrassment for the Blair Governments, for in accordance with the policy of up-rating the basic state pension in line with inflation (rather than earnings), April 2000 heard the Chancellor of the Exchequer, Gordon Brown, announce a basic state pension increase that amounted to a 75 pence a week. Though in line with a two-decade-old policy, on this particular occasion it appeared to be the action of a truly miserly administration, and it became a very effective stick with which critics could – and certainly did – beat the Government. Indeed, this beating hurt so much – particularly as most of it was from its own side – that, though the earnings-link was not restored, Brown did announce later that year, a break from existing policy, in the guise of an inflation-busting increase in the basic state pension. That, since autumn 2003, the Conservatives have joined the campaign to restore the earnings link (which they broke in the first place) is another interesting irony in this tale.

The cornerstone of the Blair Governments' pensions policy, stakeholder pension provision, has also not developed in the manner that many policy makers expected. By August 2003, 1.4 million stakeholder pensions had been sold since their launch in 2001, yet most of these were not taken out by the low-to-middle income earners, for whom the scheme had primarily been designed. Many of those sold were merely transfers from other forms of pension provision, whilst others were taken out by '[w]ealthy men – who never let an opportunity for tax relief pass them by – ... keen to take out stakeholder pensions for their wives and children' (*The Times*, 9 August 2003). In addition, another device designed to persuade the target group to invest in the stock market – the Individual Pension Account – has 'simply flopped' (*Financial Times*, 8 January 2002).

To make matters even worse, the Blair Governments' ambition to get young people saving for their future was undermined by 'a series of pension related scandals' (*The Scotsman*, 14 March 2002), one of the most notable being the near-collapse of the venerable private pensions' provider Equitable Life. Another 'scandal', of potentially more long-term significance, has been the worrisome exodus of firms fleeing from that former cornerstone of occupational pension provision, the final-salary scheme. Instead, companies have tended to offer the alternative of money-purchase schemes, the sort of pension provision where, typically, firms contribute much less. Moreover, these products cannot, by their very nature, provide a guarantee to employees about their eventual benefits.

Though a depressed stock market has assisted in the creation of this unfortunate situation, some of the Government's own actions have, unwittingly, proved rather detrimental. One of Gordon Brown's earliest measures, as Chancellor of the Exchequer, was to withdraw tax relief on pension fund dividend income, an action that removed billions of pounds from pension funds at what proved to be an unfortunate time. Another, slightly bizarre, factor was the imposition by the Accounting Standards Board of a new accounting code, FRS17, which compels companies to disclose whether their defined benefit pension funds – such as those designed to finance final-salary schemes – include enough assets to meet their obligations to exiting and future beneficiaries. Though designed with the entirely worthy intention of enhancing the transparency of occupational funds, the main result of this policy has been to encourage further the flight from defined benefit schemes (Blackburn, 2002: 331).

Yet another issue has been the growing problem of pension scheme members losing part or all of their pension entitlement after their employers became insolvent – a trend illustrated by the steel group Allied Steel and Wire which went bankrupt in 2002, consequently leaving over 1,000 former employees to face financially uncertain retirements. The Government has established an assistance scheme for such victims, but this has not restored faith in the system (*Daily Telegraph*, 20 October 2004).

In the light of mounting criticism, the Government responded with the publication of another Green Paper – one optimistically entitled *Simplicity, Security and Choice: Working and Saving for Retirement* (Department for Work and Pensions, 2002). One result of the Green Paper has been the establishment of a Pensions Commission, chaired by the former director-general of the Confederation of British Industry, Adair Turner. This has been seen as an attempt – prompted by Blair against the wishes of Brown – to open the pension debate (*Financial Times*, 8 September 2004). However, in contrast, Frank Field reckoned the establishment of the Pensions Commission was merely an attempt 'to knock the issue into the long grass' (*Financial Times*, 12 October 2004). Certainly, as noted in Chapter 2 of this book's companion text, *Policy Making in Britain* (Dorey, 2005), governments will sometimes deploy commissions and committees of inquiry in order to take advantage of the 'issue attention cycle', reckoning that by the time a report is eventually published, public interest – if not the problem itself – will have dissipated, thereby obviating the need for Ministerial action.

However, whatever the reason for its creation, the Pension Commission has actually pushed the pension issue further into the spotlight. An interim report, published in October 2004, was critical of current Government policy, suggesting that

> [t]he UK pensions system appeared in the past to work well because one of the least generous state pension systems was complemented by the most developed system of voluntary private funded pensions. This rosy picture always hid multiple inadequacies relating to specific groups of people, but on average the system worked. ... But the state plans to provide decreasing support for many people in order to control expenditure in the face of an ageing population and the private system is not developing to offset the state's retreating role. Instead it is in significant decline. (Pensions Commission, 2004: x)

At the time of writing, the Government had not responded in earnest to this stark challenge.

Pensions policy style

Before highlighting aspects of the British pensions policy style it is worth noting that there exist a number of potent explanations that attempt to explain the overall development of post-war pensions policy in Britain; that is, from a largely state-dominated system to one in which the private sector is set to become the country's dominant pensions provider. For example, Myles and Pierson (2001: 305–33), in an account involving the concept of 'path dependency', have argued that, particularly since the 1980s, economic and demographic pressures have driven pensions policy across the world towards a model of pension provision in which the state plays an increasingly residual role, with this course being made easier in Britain than in many other countries because of the absence of an entrenched earnings-related, pay-as-you-earn public pension system. That Conservative governments were in power throughout the 1980s, ideologically responsive to neo-liberalism and largely unfettered by Britain's unusual constitutional structure, is a key feature of other explanations (Araki, 2000: 599–621; Bonoli, 2000: 52–83). These accounts are important in understanding the evolution of the British pension regime. However, for this chapter, it is certain smaller-scale features of the pensions policy process that remain the focus. Though these features do not, in themselves, explain the overall direction of pension reform, they do suggest reasons why this journey has not been a smooth one.

As suggested in the introduction, social policy has not been regarded as a typical aspect of the British policy process, with Jordan and Richardson arguing, more than 20 years ago, that social policy was a partial exception to their assertion that a process of 'bureaucratic accommodation' shaped most public policy in Britain. In terms of pensions policy at least, this exception appears justified, for consultation with interested parties was – and has remained until very recently – a secondary aspect of the policy process.

From 1945 until the late 1970s, it is clear that pensions policy making was a very closed process. Indeed, during his period in charge of social services, Richard Crossman described the officials working on social security as a 'tight little group of people, a rather monastic collection of inward-looking experts' (Crossman, 1977: 380, diary entry for 24 February 1969). Outsiders, such as the insurance industry, were included in discussions, but typically only to determine details after substantive decisions had already been made. As Nesbitt has argued, by the early 1980s, this situation appeared to have changed; pensions policy making 'had become a pluralist process with a number of organisations and individuals all contributing policy ideas' (Nesbitt, 1995: 146). However, the pensions policy process soon reverted to type. Although Norman Fowler's 1983 establishment of the Inquiry into Provision for Retirement appeared to open the policy process to various organized interests, the proposals the Inquiry produced were not adopted, because 'Fowler already knew what policies he was going to adopt', leading Nesbitt to conclude that 'despite appearances, the actual policy making process was as elitist as that employed by Barbara Castle in 1974' (Nesbitt, 1995: 147).

This insular policy process appears to have continued into the Blair era. Despite the publication of various Green Papers, the number of key decision makers has remained very small, and debate tends to be invited only after the significant decisions have been made (Blackburn, 2002: 309). It has, really, only been since the establishment of the Pensions Commission that debate has broadened out – an occurrence that has been described as 'several decades too late' (*Financial Times*, 13 October 2004). This is not to argue that groups have played no role in the post-war evolution of British pensions policy. The insurance industry, in particular, has been very active. For example, following the publication of Labour's 1957 superannuation scheme, the insurance industry unleashed a 'barrage of opposition to the plan' (Hannah, 1986: 56), whilst 28 years later, Nigel Lawson faced 'the most astonishing lobbying campaign of my entire career' (Lawson, 1992: 368) when he appeared to be ending tax relief on lump-sum payments in 1985. From the side of state pensioners, the angry response of groups such as Age Concern and Help the Aged to the 75 pence pension rise in 2000 did much to rattle the government (Blackburn, 2002: 316–26). All these examples of organized (group) pressure did make a difference, although, significantly, these campaigns were reactions to decisions already made.

The pensions policy process has remained, fundamentally, a 'Whitehall-driven process' (Blackburn, 2002: 309). The major post-war debates have occurred between whichever ministry has been responsible for pensions policy – from the Ministry of Pensions and National Insurance to the current Department of Work and Pensions – and the Treasury. Whilst the Treasury's traditional reluctance to countenance all of the funding desired by the pensions' Ministry/Department has been one constant (and unsurprising) theme, there have been others. The Treasury's consistent hostility to compulsory private pension schemes has caused the failure of a number of proposals – including Iain Macleod's scheme in the late 1950s, and Norman Fowler's in the 1980s. Furthermore, the Treasury was, until recently, the obstacle that blocked a plethora of proposals to use the tax system for social security purposes. However, it was not until 1998 that this interdepartmental tension received its most memorable public expression, when Frank Field, having suggested that a personal battle over pensions reform was being fought against those who 'see a limited operation as desirable, with a major role for means-tested provision', then pointedly argued, in his resignation speech to the House of Commons, that progress was only possible if 'the entire Cabinet, especially the Chancellor, shares beliefs about that common endeavour' (House of Commons Debates, Vol. 317 (No. 215), col. 344, 29 July 1998). More recently, the Treasury has clearly become the dominant department in terms of pensions policy. One problem with this situation, identified by former Pension Minister, John Denham, is 'that the Treasury dominates pensions and doesn't really understand pensions' (*Financial Times*, 15 October 2004).

Meanwhile, it is clear that the 'thinkers and writers' identified by Banting (1979: 5) have variously contributed significantly to the pensions policy process (see also Heclo, 1974: 308–10). As was noted earlier, Beveridge was indeed the central figure proposing the universal social security system in 1942, and Abel-Smith and Townsend were clearly responsible for introducing the earnings-relation concept to the British pensions policy process in the 1950s. Abel-Smith also played a major role as (in Townsend's words) 'probably the most influential political adviser appointed by successive Labour Governments, first in 1968 to Crossman, and then, in turn, to Barbara Castle, David Ennals and finally Peter Shore' (*The Independent*, 9 April 1996). It could be argued that successors in this role have included figures such as David Willetts, of the CPS, and John Redwood, of the CPU, with the creation and advocacy of the concept of personal private pensions in the early 1980s. In the 1990s, it would appear that Frank Field took over this mantle, with the arrival of the stakeholder pension on the policy agenda.

Having noted the importance of these figures in introducing particular concepts to the pensions policy process, it is also worth highlighting, at this point, the unpredictable changes that have occurred to many initial ideas for pension reform, once they became involved in the policy process. Typically, the process of transformation from idea into practical legislation has involved some serious 'stretching' of the original concept, and implementation has tended to mutate still further the original policy makers' concept. This phenomenon was noted in the very first post-war pensions' reform. Beveridge's original scheme involved creating a 'national minimum' that would drastically reduce means-testing. However, as noted, legislation based on the Beveridge scheme did not include the very proposal to make that goal possible – subsistence-level benefits – and, in practice, dependence on the means test expanded rapidly.

There are many further examples of this type of mutation along the various stages of the policy process. Abel-Smith's original goal for earnings-related pensions was to reduce the disparity between the 'two nations in old age'. However, the concept was initially corrupted, by Harold Macmillan's Conservative Government, into a device for plugging the hole in the National Insurance Fund. Moreover, the first legislation that included an element of earnings-relation – the National Insurance Act 1959 – actually encouraged the take-up of private sector pensions, thus exacerbating the very issue Abel-Smith wished to resolve. Moving forward more than 20 years, whilst personal private pensions were designed as a means of leading workers away from excessive reliance on state provision, a major consequence of the mis-selling fiasco has been that the private pensions sector came to be viewed with increased suspicion. Finally, the stakeholder pension concept was transformed, in the course of becoming legislation, from being a device designed to provide a universal second pension into one with the primary goal of enticing middle-income earners into the private sector. Moreover, following implementation, these pensions appear to have largely developed into a tax-perk for the wealthy.

Developing the theme that the pensions policy process is characterized by considerable unpredictability – unlike, perhaps, policies shaped by 'bureaucratic accommodation' – it is worth noting a point made by Jones and Lowe. When introducing the quiet, early change to the up-rating rule made by the first Thatcher Government – a seemingly minor reform that, over time, has drastically weakened the state basic pension – these authors remark that '[m]ajor changes in social security policy have typically been effected by technical changes to the small print of legislation' (Jones and Lowe, 2002: 54). In the case of this particular reform, it could be argued that the outcome was wholly intentional. However, some such technical changes have yielded less predictable results, one of the most recent being the imposition, by the Accounting Standards Board, of the new accounting code, FRS17, a move which has unexpectedly exacerbated the problem associated with the closure of defined benefit schemes.

Conclusion

British pensions policy constitutes an unusual case, with the consultative nature associated with a process of bureaucratic accommodation largely absent. One result has been that British pensions policy has not developed in a smoothly incremental fashion. A general policy path from a state-dominated system towards a largely privatized model has been followed, but it has been a bumpy ride. Indeed, at certain junctures since 1945, Britain has appeared, to some, to be at the cutting edge of the reform process. The Beveridge 'revolution' itself was one such period (Baldwin, 1994: 40), as was the premiership of Margaret

Thatcher four decades later (Pierson, 1994: 53–73). In contrast, at other times it has been suggested that British pensions policy has been bringing up the rear in comparison to other more 'advanced' states. A stagnant period during the 1960s was one such era (Lynes, 1969: 31), and – despite the frantic efforts at reform – the 'turn of the century' Blair premiership has also been subject to similar accusations (Arthur, 2001: 41). Overall, it appears that the pensions policy process in Britain has been a messy one, and one that has resulted in a system regarded as 'incomprehensible, inequitable and inadequate' (*Financial Times*, 13 October 2004). Remarkably, at the start of the 21st century, the British pension system is even less coherent than the one Beveridge was asked to sort out in 1941.

9 Transport Policy

Nick Robinson

Introduction

> Winter in the Great Smokies would shortly be upon us, the winter that would see us into the next century and the new millennium. Other things were on their way to us as well, things we never anticipated nor, in some cases, could even imagine. This is the story of how we met them and were changed by them. (Goodwin, 1999: 3)

Since the mid-1990s it has been impossible to ignore the importance of transport within British politics. A series of fatal rail crashes led to serious questioning of transport safety; concerns about the impact of inadequate transport provision on economic efficiency have risen; public alarm over the impact of vehicle emissions on public health has increased, and direct action protests have grabbed media attention, initially in protesting against road building, and more recently and most spectacularly, against fuel prices when protesters in September 2000 temporarily destabilized the government. Such happenings reflect a pattern of increasing volatility surrounding transport policy making in Britain.

This chapter analyses the changing nature of British transport policy since 1945, arguing that it can be best explained by a cyclical model of the policy process, whereby the status quo, which was relatively closed and stable, and based on a dominant market-based 'predict and provide' (P&P) ethos, has given way to a relatively open policy process in which the dominant ethos has been challenged by two rivals based on 'encourage and provide' (E&P) or 'restrict and provide' (R&P), before returning once more to the status quo (see Figure 9.1). In order to explore this changing politics of transport, this chapter is divided into four sections.

Firstly, it provides an overview of Anthony Downs' 'issue attention cycle' (IAC) in which he argues that issues rise and fall on the policy agenda in a stage-based policy cycle (Downs, 1973). Thinking of the policy process in this way significantly aids understanding of the changing nature of post-war transport policy in Britain.

Secondly, the core of the chapter provides an overview of the changing nature of transport since 1945, arguing that transport policy in the post-war period has gone through two complete policy cycles, with recent events suggesting that a third will begin in the near future.

The period until the mid-1980s demonstrates the initial ascendancy within central government thinking of the P&P orthodoxy which served to stabilize policy around the interests of a market-based model of transport provision, and which allowed the road lobby to dominate the policy process.

Figure 9.1   Changing transport orthodoxies over time

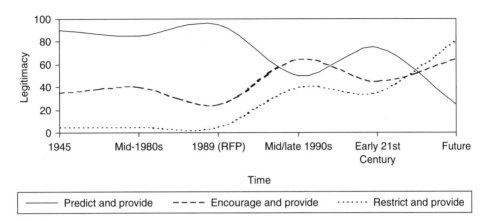

However, since then, two key periods during the mid-1980s, and then the mid-1990s, saw public concern over the impact of transport on the environment and public health destabilize the policy process. These concerns coincided with the onset of the two IACs, the second of which, in particular, challenged both the ethos and the constellation of actors historically dominant within the sector. At first glance, as Downs' framework predicts, such challenges have been relatively short-lived, rapidly giving way to the previous pattern of policy making. Yet the apparent stability which presently exists is largely illusionary: the hitherto dominant P&P ethos has been heavily discredited, and experts have increasingly advocated policies explicitly designed to restrict mobility, despite strong opposition from the public. Thus, in the short term at least, the prospect is for a continuing pattern of IACs as transport policy continues to be dominated by conflict and volatility.

Finally, the chapter seeks to explain how and why this cyclical pattern of policy has occurred, addressing three key questions – Why do the cycles begin? Why do they move on? Why do they return to the status quo? Insights into these questions are used not only to develop a model to explain the cyclical nature of British transport policy, but also to offer some important suggestions as to how Downs' original framework may best be modified to provide a more comprehensive explanation of the policy process.

The issue attention cycle

This chapter argues that in order to understand the ebb and flow of British transport policy since 1945, we need to make use of a cyclical model of policy making. The model developed later in this chapter draws on insights from Anthony Downs' issue attention cycle (IAC), which is designed to explain the rise and fall of issues such as transport which Joppke (1991: 45–6) has termed 'collective issues'. According to Downs (1973: 64–5), issues rise and fall in a policy cycle made up of five clearly separable stages: a *pre-problem stage*, in which specialists or interest groups are captivated by a problem which has yet to grab the public's attention; *alarmed discovery and euphoric optimism*, in which the public becomes aware of a problem and demands a response from government, often resulting in over-ambitious promises of quick-fix solutions from political leaders; *realizing the cost of significant progress*, in which experts, and later the public, realize that any serious attempt to solve the problem would require considerable financial costs and changes to the power relations between actors and institutions which the majority are unwilling to pay; *gradual decline of intense public interest*, which almost inevitably follows, finally; *the post-problem stage*, which is 'a sort of prolonged limbo' (Downs, 1973: 65).

The completion of the IAC, and the entering into the post-problem stage, marks a significant change to the situation prior to the onset of the IAC, in two key ways. Firstly, any policies, institutions or programmes which were created during the IAC are likely to have an enduring impact on the issue, ensuring that it is attended to even when it is not of public concern. Secondly, once a problem has completed an IAC it is likely to sporadically reoccur, either attached to another problem or propelled there by one of the vested interests which were created when the problem previously enjoyed high political salience (Downs, 1973: 65–6; see Walker, 1977: 432–7, for a discussion of this in relation to road safety legislation in the USA).

The remainder of this chapter builds on Downs' work and utilizes a stage-based account of policy making as a framework to discuss the changing nature of British transport policy since 1945. Using this framework, we will argue that transport policy has gone through two clear policy cycles, peaking in the mid-1980s and mid-1990s respectively. Following these policy cycles, it may seem that the policy process has returned once more to relative stability, but this is likely to prove short-lived. Thus the future holds the prospect of an increasingly frequent pattern of IACs as the policy process once more enters a period of growing volatility.

Transport history, 1945 to the early 1970s: the 'unpolitics' of transport

This first period of the history of transport policy runs from 1945 until the early 1970s and covers the period before the onset of the first IAC. During this period, transport policy reflected an almost totally dominant, market-based, predict-and-provide ethos, with the policy process centred on the interests of the road lobby.

The ideas paradigm: the domination of market orthodoxy

> A generation hence, people won't ask what the Government is doing to meet increased demand for transport, any more than they now ask what the Government is doing to meet the increased demand for chocolate. (Paul Channon, then Secretary of State for Transport, cited in Hanna and Mogridge, 1992: 102)

The words of the then Minister for Transport in April 1989 capture the essence of the so-called 'predict and provide' (P&P) orthodoxy which dominated transport policy throughout the post-war period, without coherent institutional or political opposition until the mid-1980s.[1] This paradigm operated consistently regardless of changes of government, and had three bases: that an efficient transport system was essential for economic prosperity, as it enabled the free movement of produce and the expansion of the macro-economy; that transport policy ought to be market-based and respond to the demands of transport consumers; that transport policy should not aim to incorporate the impact of external costs such as congestion, accidents or environmental effects (externalities). The practical effect of this was that transport policy became almost totally synonymous with roads policy.

Government documents published in the 1960s and 1970s demonstrate the key aspects of this policy orthodoxy, and its prioritization of road transport (see, for example, Cmnd 3057 and Cmnd 4369). Firstly, they show that both Labour and Conservative Governments had a very positive image of the motor car at that time, with the Labour Government's 1966 *Transport Policy* White Paper, for example, viewing it as bringing 'immense benefits to millions of people: increased mobility, a fuller social life, family employment, new experiences' (Cmnd 3057: para. 1).

Secondly, while Governments did identify some environmental concerns related to the impact of road vehicles, and outlined the importance of a multi-modal transport strategy, the thinking behind policy at that time was almost totally car-centric, being designed to 'come to terms with the motor car, while not allowing it to ruin our environment. This meant an expanded road programme to relieve the growing congestion' (Castle, 1984: 154; see also the 1970–4 Conservative Government's *Roads for the Future* White Paper (Cmnd 4369: para. 29)). It is perhaps unsurprising that of all of the proposals in the 1966 White Paper only those centred on expanding the road network were successfully implemented.

Throughout the 1960s and 1970s, transport policy in Britain remained motivated by the P&P orthodoxy, with governments unwilling to advance proposals to restrict either road use or the growth of road vehicle ownership. Thus, throughout this period, the interests of both existing and future transport users were to be served by a combination of an unparalleled expansion of the road network, and by cuts to those services (particularly rail) for which demand was falling. The concerns which later emerged about the environmental impact of road transport, and the benefits of its alternatives, were simply not an issue at that time: road building was seen as broadly beneficial to the environment (Cmnd 4369: para. 22).

In this climate, the structural interests of the road lobby were assured. As the beneficiary of what Dowding (1991: 137–8) has termed 'systematic luck', the road lobby's interests

---

1 Even though P&P was dominant at this time, there were still some actors which advocated rival philosophies (see Wistrich, 1983: 62–70). Yet it was not until the mid-1990s that these rival philosophies were able seriously to challenge the pre-eminence of P&P.

Figure 9.2   Location of actors on a policy network continuum (pre-Major period)

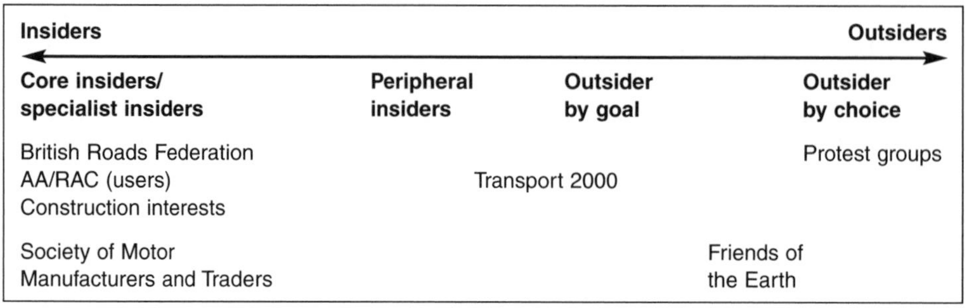

Insiders			Outsiders
Core insiders/ specialist insiders	Peripheral insiders	Outsider by goal	Outsider by choice
British Roads Federation AA/RAC (users) Construction interests		Transport 2000	Protest groups
Society of Motor Manufacturers and Traders			Friends of the Earth

were served not as a result of its lobbying activity, but rather because they coincided with the priorities of central government.

The unchanging nature of the transport policy network: 1945 to the early 1970s

Academic studies of the post-war power of the road lobby, such as those by Finer (1958), Plowden (1971) and Dudley (1983), have shown that, historically, the Department of Transport and the pro-roads interests have formed a structurally quiescent policy network which did not 'have to fight for recognition or support, but rather enjoyed it because of its structural position in the economy' (Marsh, 1983: 15).

Until the onset of the first IAC during the mid-1980s, the pattern of transport policy making accorded with these studies, with the dynamics of the conflict over policy described well by a network metaphor. Figure 9.2 provides a diagrammatic representation of that transport policy network, illustrating that the pro-roads groups were well organized and formed 'an integral part of the "policy community"', enjoying frequent contact with Ministers and having representatives serving on a number of Department of Transport advisory committees (Dudley, 1983: 109).

During this time, the interests of the road lobby and those of central government were virtually indistinguishable, with the predict-and-provide philosophy dominating the thinking of both, and the road lobby deriving insider status from its structural linkage to economically powerful interests and industrial competitiveness. This meant that, in practical terms, no distinction existed between core and specialist insiders: governments treated the British Roads Federation (BRF) and its constituent actors both as policy experts, with specialist knowledge, and as generalists, qualified to advise on policy at a strategic level (see Maloney et al., 1994, for an overview of the insider–outsider typology; see Grant, 2000: 18–35, for a review).

The strength of central government's commitment to the road lobby's objectives meant that it was very difficult for any anti-roads groups to gain even peripheral insider status. Transport 2000, in particular, tried to pursue an insider strategy during this period, but failed because its goals were seen as completely incompatible with the goals of central government.

At the other end of the spectrum were protest groups, which undertook a series of campaigns designed to disrupt the highway inquiry process:

> ... what the actual roads protesters did was they accepted that they would campaign against a road through the given channels; public consultation, public enquiry. They made elegant, and in their case, noisy arguments at public enquiries and they all lost. Now that's because they were campaigning on the territory set out by the Department of Transport, by officialdom. (Interview, lead campaigner, ALARM UK, November 1995)

At this time, therefore, the opposition to the roads programme was relatively limited. As Figure 9.2 illustrates, the anti-roads groups were restricted to those representing the 'traditional' arm of the movement: groups such as Transport 2000, and the protest groups opposing roads through the highway inquiry process, had not yet been joined by either 'quasi-insiders', such as the National Trust, or 'radical' outsiders in the form of the direct action movement, neither of which had a significant impact until the mid-1990s.

It might be expected that the pre-eminence of P&P alongside the advantageous position of the road lobby would lead to widespread road building throughout the period (see, for example, Hamer, 1987). Yet this was not the case: historically UK investment has been relatively low compared to other European states, due both to the limited support for it within the Cabinet and with the electorate (Finer, 1958: 54) and the Treasury's considerable control over all central government spending (see Plowden, 1971).

Thus even when investment in the trunk roads sector expanded significantly in the 1960s and 1970s (Cmnd 7132: 31), extending the motorway network in England and Wales from 130 miles in 1961 (Ministry of Transport, 1962: 19) to 1,185 miles by 1976 (Cmnd 7132: 34), it was not due to the activities of the road lobby; the fact of rising congestion was undermining a central element of the ideas orthodoxy that had dominated government thinking, namely that freedom and liberty should be promoted by the usage of the motor car.

Transport history, early 1970s to 1983: exogenous pressure on the road lobby and the first issue attention cycle

The second stage of the history of transport policy corresponds to the period between the early 1970s and the mid-1980s when, for the first time, the car became linked to public and environmental health problems, thereby damaging its hitherto positive policy image. The pressure groups which had been engaged in disrupting the highway inquiry process were joined by a number of environmental groups, such as the 'Campaign for Lead Free Air' (CLEAR) and Friends of the Earth. In addition, the emergence of new information concerning the environmental impact of lead in petrol attracted the attention of 'institutional' environmental interests, such as the statutory standing Royal Commission on Environmental Pollution (RCEP) (see Figure 9.3). These developments combined to instigate the first IAC and pose an unprecedented challenge to the road lobby.

Figure 9.3   Location of actors on a policy network continuum (early 1980s)

Insiders			Outsiders
Core insiders/ specialist insiders	Peripheral insiders	Outsider by goal	Outsider by choice
British Roads Federation AA/RAC (users)		Transport 2000 Friends of the Earth	
Construction interests		Royal Commission on Environmental Pollution	ALARM UK Campaign for Lead Free Air
Society of Motor Manufacturers and Traders			

The issue attention cycle and transport policy: the lead in petrol case[2]

As outlined earlier, the issue attention cycle is made up of five clearly separable stages, which transport policy followed in the early 1980s with regard to lead pollution: the pre-problem stage; alarmed discovery and euphoric optimism; realizing the cost of significant progress; gradual decline of intense public interest; and the post-problem stage.

In the transport case, the first stage corresponded to the period from the late 1970s until the early 1980s, before road vehicles were identified as 'a major source of the lead pollution implicated in the damage to human health' (McCormick, 1991: 136). Lead in petrol first emerged as a specialist issue in 1971 when the Government's Chief Medical Officer recommended that atmospheric lead levels should not be allowed to increase any further, whereupon Ministers agreed to a phased reduction of lead in petrol from 0.84 grams per litre to 0.4 grams per litre over a 10-year period (McCormick, 1991: 136–7). At this time, though, the issue remained under the control of a core policy community and public interest was limited.

The second stage focused on the publication of the Ninth Report of the statutory Royal Commission on Environmental Pollution in April 1983 (Cmnd 8852), entitled *Lead in the Environment*. This Report had two primary functions: providing a comprehensive study of the effect of lead in the environment, covering the effect on human health and the natural environment; and evaluating the methods which could be adopted in order to reduce lead emissions. The Royal Commission identified the road transport sector as the most

---

2 For a detailed summary of the controversy surrounding the role of different actors in this case refer to McCormick (1991, Ch. 7).

significant source of lead in the environment at that time, and so concluded that any policy designed to reduce lead in the environment should focus on removing lead from petrol. The Royal Commission's strategy to offer a technical solution as its principal policy recommendation was based on the view that 'if you take the lead out of petrol then you arrive at 100 per cent of the solution. In such a climate there is no need to offer a lifestyle solution [i.e. one which is centred on reducing car usage]' (interview, Chair of the RCEP, August 1997).

The Royal Commission's Report marked a watershed as, for the first time, the previously positive policy image of road transport was subjected to exogenous pressure and *alarmed discovery* by the public. Within half an hour of the publication of the Royal Commission's Report, the Government had announced that it would begin negotiations with the European Commission to remove the minimum permitted levels of lead in petrol, and ultimately to lobby for the introduction of cars which would run on unleaded petrol. Meanwhile, pressure groups such as Transport 2000 and CLEAR used scientific reports in order to foster a new, negative policy image for the car.[3]

The satisfaction of the immediate demands of the anti-roads groups contributed to the decline of public interest in the issue of lead in petrol. With the Government agreeing to phase out the use of lead in petrol by the end of the decade, and with the cost to the average motorist only £10 per year, the impetus for further change evaporated (Vogel, 1986: 68; see Cm 552: 2–3, for details of the Government's initiatives).

During stage three, realizing the cost of significant progress, the Government thus ensured that the problem remained defined in such a way that it only required a 'quick fix' technical solution. Consequently, they were able to instigate the fourth stage, the gradual decline of public interest, and contain the demands of those elements of the environmental movement which saw the removal of lead in petrol as only the first step in a process which should result in significant reductions in road transport use. Thus, no actors were able to provoke a strategic rethink of the future of transport policy or to capture the public's imagination and the issue rapidly progressed through stages three and four of the cycle.

Finally, the issue attention cycle was completed and the transport issue entered the post-problem stage. As we have seen, Downs argues that once a problem has completed an issue attention cycle it is likely to reoccur sporadically, either attached to another problem or propelled there by one of the vested interests which were created when the problem previously enjoyed issue salience (1973: 65–6). This pattern of events indeed developed during John Major's premiership (1990–7), although not until after the implementation of the initial stages of a significantly expanded roads programme which the Thatcher Government had announced in 1989, through the *Roads for Prosperity* White Paper (Cm 693).

---

3 There is considerable dispute within the literature concerning how the agenda was set in this case. Des Wilson (1984) identifies the role of the single-issue campaigning group CLEAR. Richard Southwood, Chairman of the RCEP, claims that the RCEP's report was the key (cited in McCormick, 1991: 138). Other scholars identify the crucial role of the EU at a systemic level and of developments in the German political system (see McCormick, 1991: 136–40, for a summary of this discussion).

Issue attention cycle two: eroding predict and provide and the end of roads for prosperity?[4]

The third phase in the history of British transport policy since 1945 centres on the launch of the so-called 'Roads for Prosperity' programme in 1989:[5]

> Effective transport is a vital element of economic growth and prosperity. The continuing advance of our economy requires progressive development of the motorway and trunk road network. Now is the time for a large step forward. A major extension of the Government's programme for building and improving inter-urban roads is being put in hand to meet the forecast needs of traffic into the next century. The Government is committed to taking the programme forward as a matter of urgency. (Cm 693: para. 52)

Responding to the Government's own forecasts of congestion in the *National Road Traffic Forecasts* of 1989 – which predicted that traffic levels would grow by between 83 and 142 per cent by the year 2025 (Department of Transport, 1989) – *Roads for Prosperity* (Cm 693) represented the Government's attempt to present itself as providing a solution to the problems of congestion.

The programme seemed to symbolize a return to a pattern of apparent stability, with central government reasserting a strong commitment to the predict-and-provide orthodoxy, demonstrated by the active consideration of rail privatization (Thatcher, 1993: 686), the implementation of deregulation within the bus industry and a return to a focus on strategic road building. But the apparent stability of the policy sector at this time was misleading: *Roads for Prosperity* was in fact instrumental in increasing the pressure that would ultimately lead to the onset of the second IAC.

This was because it became clear almost immediately that the scale of the congestion problem outlined by the Government's own traffic projections could not be solved by the proposed programme (see Cm 2674: paras 6.25–6.35). The simultaneous publication of the *National Road Traffic Forecasts* and the Government's *Roads for Prosperity* initiative was thus a public policy disaster (Dunleavy, 1995a), raising real concerns within the expert community, not only as to the general worth of strategic road building, but also the long-term viability of the predict-and-provide ethos more fundamentally:

---

4 Much of the information contained within this section is based on interviews conducted with a wide range of policy makers, including members of the road lobby (e.g., the AA, RAC, BRF and Road Hauliers), their opponents (e.g., FoE, CPRE, Transport 2000) and 'other actors' such as media commentators, MPs and civil servants. For a book-length discussion of the changing nature of UK transport from the early 1990s until 2000, see Robinson (2000).

5 The principal focus of this discussion is centred on consideration of the politics of the car for three reasons: it was the government's primary priority; the car most clearly demonstrates the competition which ultimately develops over predict and provide, and conflict over the car provides the clearest and most important indicator of change to the constellation of actors centred on transport.

Roads for Prosperity was the last symbol of the old orthodoxy. It appeared to be justified by the 1989 road traffic forecasts which preceded it, but actually the 1989 forecasts, having as it were launched roads for prosperity, then immediately undermined it. (Interview, senior member of Standing Advisory Committee on Trunk Roads Assessment (hereafter SACTRA), June 1997)

The second stage, alarmed discovery and euphoric optimism, developed during the early 1990s when the public became acutely aware of, and alarmed by, the 'problems of transport', which manifested themselves in many different forms simultaneously, and established transport for the first time as an emotive, public issue rather than a technical, specialist one.

The radical direct action tactics of new groups of anti-roads protesters helped to focus widespread media attention on the problems of transport and the failings of the Government's solution (Doherty, 2000). Transport, and protests against it, became news – aided by increasing public concern over the wider health and environmental consequences of transport policy. Within Britain, transport was identified as a significant contributor to deteriorating public health (Cm 2674: paras 3.20–3.30; Cm 3587: 43), with public attention focused in particular on perceived links between vehicle emissions and increasing levels of asthma (Grant, 1995a: 172–3).[6] Globally, awareness of the impact of transport on transnational or global problems such as acid rain and global warming increased dramatically in the early 1990s, damaging still further the policy image of road transport in general and the car in particular (Button, 1995).

In such circumstances, the prospect of a massively expanded roads programme was already a cause for concern, even before the publication of the quasi-governmental Standing Advisory Committee on Trunk Roads Assessment's 1994 report *Trunk Roads and the Generation of Traffic* (SACTRA, 1994) which served to undermine the very rationale behind *Roads for Prosperity* by suggesting that road building would actually increase transport activity and ultimately congestion, rather than reduce it (SACTRA, 1994: paras 7–9; for an overview see Robinson, 2000: 94–100).

The cumulative effect of the second stage of this IAC was felt in two key ways: there were significant changes to the nature of the policy process and an unprecedented challenge to the coherence of the hitherto dominant P&P orthodoxy.

The transport policy process

During the mid-1990s, the transport policy process changed radically (see Figure 9.4). Firstly, the number of actors actively involved in the conflict over transport policy increased considerably during the 1990s, affecting both the scale and the nature of the

---

6 It is important to emphasize that the public's concern with the impact of transport as causally responsible for deteriorating public health, particularly in terms of asthma, was heavily disputed by a number of reports by scientific experts who emphasized the primary role of poor indoor air quality (household dust mites, wall-to-wall carpeting and central heating) but also of stress and diet (see Robinson, 2000: 83–8 for a review).

Figure 9.4   Location of actors on a policy network continuum (Major period)

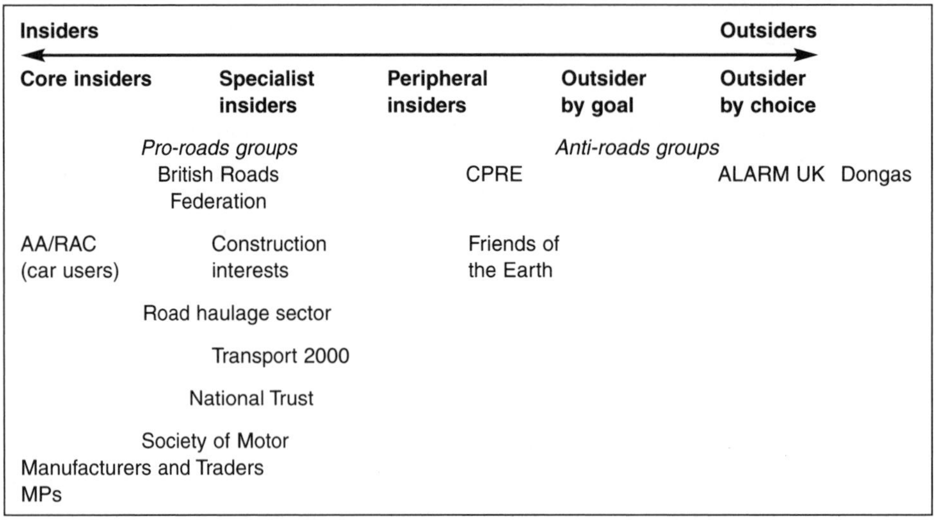

Insiders				Outsiders
Core insiders	Specialist insiders	Peripheral insiders	Outsider by goal	Outsider by choice
	Pro-roads groups		*Anti-roads groups*	
	British Roads Federation	CPRE		ALARM UK Dongas
AA/RAC (car users)	Construction interests	Friends of the Earth		
	Road haulage sector			
	Transport 2000			
	National Trust			
	Society of Motor			
Manufacturers and Traders				
MPs				

opposition to road building. At one end of the spectrum, the growing involvement of quasi-insider groups such as the Council for the Protection of Rural England (CPRE) and the National Trust (who have historically had good links to policy makers), sat alongside the vocal opposition to particular road-building schemes of several Conservative MPs (concerned to retain electoral support in marginal constituencies), served to broaden the anti-roads agenda to much more important political strata. At the other end, as we have seen, direct action enabled anti-roads groups to exploit the opportunities presented by extra-legal activity. In the resultant media limelight, moderate groups such as Transport 2000 were able to gain a public forum for their proposals.

Paralleling this growth and change in the nature of the anti-roads lobby, commentators have suggested that during the early 1990s, the road lobby itself became increasingly fragmented (interview information (multiple respondents), summer 1996).[7] Fault lines began to emerge between users and constructors, and between user groups – essentially between road freight and car users (interview information, senior policy adviser, RAC, June 1996).

The division between road users and construction interests was the most fundamental, centring on the continuing legitimacy of the predict-and-provide ethos. While user groups began to acknowledge that it would not be possible to accommodate the projected increases in traffic through road-building, and thus pragmatically re-orientated their objectives towards ensuring

---

7 Whilst it is true that the road lobby did indeed show some signs of becoming increasingly divided at this time, it is important not to overstate the impact of this division. As I have demonstrated elsewhere (Robinson, 2000: Ch. 5), the road lobby was still more unified than the anti-roads 'coalition' which was lined up against it.

that the existing network operated more efficiently, the constructors failed to adjust to the challenge represented by the SACTRA Report, and continued to emphasize the link between extensions to the road network and economic growth (interview information, senior policy adviser, BRF, and senior policy adviser, RHA (Road Haulage Association), both August 1996).

Given the extensive changes to the nature of the transport policy network, it might be expected that there would have been potential for a significant reorientation of the policy process towards alternatives to road transport, centred in particular on the interests of the rail industry. However, as we later illustrate, a combination of the enduring legacy of pre-dict and provide, and the overwhelming focus of central government on rail privatization, served to continue marginalizing such interests, thereby ensuring that they had little pos-sibility of moving towards insider status.

Competing philosophies

In addition to these changes to the policy network, a coherent challenge to the hitherto dominant transport orthodoxy also emerged. Transport policy, it was argued, should follow the broader aim of government policy, focusing on 'development that meets the needs of the present without compromising the ability of future generations to meet their own needs' (Cm 2426: para. 26.18). For the first time, the potential for the development of policy on the basis of a rival orthodoxy, centred on either 'encourage and provide' or 'restrict and provide', seemed possible.

The 'encourage and provide' (E&P) ethos describes a pro-active pattern of government intervention in which a principal objective of policy is actively to encourage behavioural change by transport consumers through providing genuine transport alternatives (subsi-dized if necessary) in order to influence the market. By providing improved cycling, public transport and high-speed rail facilities, for example, as alternatives to the car, and improved air and rail facilities, for example, as a rival to road freight, governments can seek to mani-pulate the market. (See below for the different impact which E&P had within the thinking of the Conservative and Labour Governments.)

The 'restrict and provide' (R&P) ethos moves beyond this, referring to measures designed to restrict the behaviour of transport users which are matched by the provision of improved transport alternatives as outlined above.[8] Fiscal instruments which affect the rel-ative cost of competing transport modes, such as road pricing, or the use of physical restrictions, such as reductions in parking provision or a freeze on airport capacity, are used by government to force changes in behaviour. This approach acknowledges that it is neither possible nor desirable to provide sufficient infrastructure to accommodate the pre-dicted growth in traffic, so network access must be restricted to *essential users* (i.e., those who can pay). At the same time, with knowledge of the environmental and social costs of

---

8 The use of the term 'restrict and provide' is preferable to Owens's (1995) term 'predict and pre-vent', because 'predict and prevent' only offers an emphasis on the restrictive aspect of policy (i.e. the stick) whereas in fact all proposals with a restrictive aspect have contained a package of mea-sures combining restrictions alongside the provision of alternatives (the so-called 'carrot and stick' approach) – so the term 'restrict and provide' is preferable.

transport activity increasing (e.g., noise, greenhouse gas emissions, health effects and accidents), it also calls for market-based changes to account for such costs. However, as we show later, such a focus is highly controversial: it inevitably means forcing some transport users to change their behaviour, and move from private transport onto public transport.

During the mid-1990s, as the issue attention cycle passed through stage two, these alternatives to P&P gained increasing influence on the thinking of a growing array of policy actors. Transport experts who had always been aware of the potential importance of E&P and R&P were joined by a wide range of actors, with little previous interest in such debates, who began to question the implications of the P&P orthodoxy for the future development of transport policy (see, for example, Royal Society for the Protection of Birds, 1995; National Trust, 1995).

The third stage, realizing the cost of significant progress, developed during the mid-to-late 1990s when first the Government, and later the public, became acutely aware of the 'costs' of action which challenged the existing focus on predict and provide. This third stage can itself be divided into three phases.

The first phase ran from December 1994 until the general election of May 1997, coinciding with the last years of John Major's Conservative Government. Policy was centred on launching a consultation process over transport: the 'Great Debate' was launched by Brian Mawhinney in December 1994, inviting contributions from all groups in six key areas ranging from 'transport and the environment' to 'the importance of choice' (speeches reproduced in Mawhinney, 1995). It might at first appear that this period marks the first time at which the P&P approach was undermined, as the debate coincided with significant cuts to the road programme – between March 1994 and November 1996 over 250 schemes were withdrawn, reducing the road programme by almost two-thirds (Department of Transport, 1994: 25–7; 1995a: 21–2; 1996). However, the Major Government's commitment to rail privatization belies this; and the Great Debate itself, together with the halt in road building that accompanied it, can in fact be seen as an exercise by the Government both to save money (Dudley and Richardson, 1996: 79–80) and to manage an electorally unpopular policy area in the run-up to the general election which was due in 1997 (Robinson, 2000: 134–8). Mawhinney's speeches, which set out the debate's parameters, continued clearly to articulate the importance of P&P to central government (Department of Transport, 1995b).

Overall, therefore, the 'Great Debate' must primarily be seen as an exercise designed by the Government to help it to manage the policy agenda. It did not reflect either a desire to achieve genuine consensus between the road lobby and the anti-roads groups, or a desire to entertain seriously the possibility of change of the basis of an alternative ethos to the hitherto dominant P&P orthodoxy. The motives for attempting to move the transport issue through the issue attention cycle at this time were not in fact driven, as Downs suggests, by public hostility to change – in fact they reflected the Government's understanding that any *significant change would involve costs which were unacceptable to it*, being perceived as posing a fundamental challenge to its core commitments to liberalism, free markets and choice.

The second phase of the third stage ran from May 1997 to the late 1990s, coinciding with the initial years of Tony Blair's 'New Labour' Government. At this time, the Labour Party demonstrated, at least at a rhetorical level, a serious commitment to tackling the problem of transport, with John Prescott asserting that:

Figure 9.5 Location of actors on a policy network continuum (Blair Period)

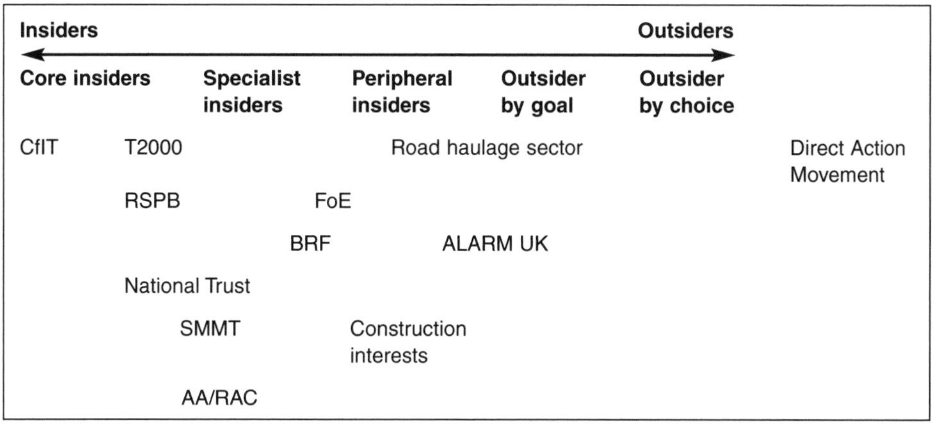

Insiders					Outsiders
Core insiders	Specialist insiders	Peripheral insiders	Outsider by goal	Outsider by choice	
CfIT	T2000		Road haulage sector		Direct Action Movement
	RSPB	FoE			
		BRF	ALARM UK		
	National Trust				
	SMMT	Construction interests			
	AA/RAC				

> I will have failed in this if in five years' time there are not many more people using public transport and far fewer journeys by car. It is a tall order but I want you to hold me to it. (*The Guardian*, 6 June 1997)

As with its predecessor, the newly-elected Labour Government also launched a consultation process which, it claimed, was designed to find solutions to the transport problem (see, for example, Department of the Environment, Transport and the Regions, 1997; 1998). In contrast to Mawhinney's 'Great Debate', however, it is clear that the debate was initially intended to be a genuine one, aiming to achieve real change through consensus among a wide range of actors. This is evidenced by the Government's positioning of previous moderate anti-roads outsider groups as now integral to the debate and formulation of policy, as shown in Figure 9.5.

Moderate anti-roads groups such as Transport 2000 and the CPRE were increasingly incorporated within the core policy community, serving on a number of Department of the Environment, Transport and the Regions (DETR) advisory committees; their incorporation within the newly formed Commission for Integrated Transport (CfIT) symbolized this change in status (interview information (multiple sources), autumn 2000).

The creation of the DETR also evidenced this shift in the Government's intention, as it served to reduce the links between the pro-roads groups and what had historically been their client department (see Dudley, 1983, for an overview). In an interview in 1996, a senior policy adviser of the BRF foresaw the danger which a merger between the two departments would present for the road lobby:

> I'm sure the Department of the Environment would like Transport to be back. I think we would be very concerned by that and we would be lobbying as hard as we could to ensure that it didn't [become merged within the DoE]. ... I think we would be concerned that it would, within the DoE, lose the ability to recognize the commercial, or the industrial

importance, of transport. ... I think it would change things, I think we would struggle even more to get attention. Transport would become just one other thing that the DoE handled. (Interview, August 1996)

Underlying these changes in the policy network were the different beliefs of the Labour Government, which in terms of transport were much closer to the moderate anti-roads groups than to the pro-roads groups. The Government accepted as fact that cars cause fundamental damage (Department of the Environment, Transport and the Regions, 1998: paras 1.2–1.3), and identified that 'the mood is for change' (Cm 3950: para 1.3). In contrast to the Major era, Labour aimed to use science, and to work at both national and EU levels, through consensus, in order to formulate a long-term strategy for responding to that need. Such thinking was historically unheard of in the British context.

Overall, these efforts by the first Blair Government to construct a consensus between organized interests, expert opinion and the EU were largely successful, resulting in a significant change of emphasis between the Major and Blair administrations. The 1998 White Paper on the Blair Government's proposed transport policy developed a multifaceted framework designed to solve the problem of transport. This framework contained aspects of both an E&P ethos, centred on the significant expansion of resources for local public transport schemes and the rail network and the creation of the strategic rail authority, and an R&P ethos, centred on the serious discussion of implementing local road pricing and work-based parking schemes but also on the consideration of national trunk-road-based road pricing.

Yet the ways in which these measures were to be implemented also reveals a desire on the part of the Labour Government to avoid bearing what they quickly realized would be – as the IAC model suggests – the *significant political costs* of their introduction (see also Dowding, 1991: 137, on the 'law of anticipated reactions').

Firstly, in spite of the rhetorical commitment to change, the Government continued the pattern of using technical fixes to reduce road vehicle emissions, thus mirroring the pattern of the lead in petrol case, which whilst positive in terms of local emissions, also served to make the possibility of solutions centred on reducing usage of the car much less likely.

Secondly, the Government's proposed policies to implement road pricing and work-based parking charges placed important restrictions on their introduction and operation by local authorities, ensuring that any introduction would be made piecemeal, and slowly, and not be perceived as a national initiative. Road pricing would not be permitted 'as a general revenue raising device' (Cm 3950: para. 4.111), but could only be used for transport improvements; the revenues could only be retained by local authorities 'provided that there are worthwhile transport-related projects to be funded', after which point the revenues would revert to the Exchequer as part of general taxation (Department of the Environment, Transport and the Regions, 1998: para. 3.13). At the same time, the conditions to be met by local authorities before being granted the legal entitlement to implement road pricing were made more stringent, pushing back the date at which any road pricing scheme was likely to be formally introduced until 2005 (*The Guardian*, 30 November 1999). It was further suggested that the local authority 'would have to consult the electorate, through a referendum if necessary, before introducing congestion charging' (*The Guardian*, 30 November 1999; see also Commission for Integrated Transport, 1999: paras 29–35, for the

CfIT's view that public consultation ought to be comprehensive, encompassing all stages of the policy formulation process).

Thirdly, the Government rapidly realized that the development of policies on the basis of E&P would also entail significant financial costs: the public sector would have to pay heavily in terms of general taxation and the private sector would also have to make huge commitments to modernize what was essentially a decrepit infrastructure network, particularly in the rail sector (Department of Transport, 2002a: 26–7, 105–15). Such concerns became linked with a fear that E&P would not deliver the benefits predicted, with road transport continuing to rise regardless of public transport improvements (Department of Transport, 2002a: 87).

The third and final stage of the third phase of the IAC centres on the period from the late 1990s until the early years of the 21st century, when the public became increasingly alarmed by (and hostile to) the implications of widespread policy change. The key event which raised public awareness was the publication of the *Transport Bill* (HC Bill 8, 1999) in the autumn of 1999, which contained proposals for the introduction of urban road pricing and work-based parking charges.

The public, and Right-wing newspapers, such as the *Daily Telegraph* and the *Daily Mail*, reacted strongly to the proposals. The Conservative Party, in turn, sought to use this shift in public opinion as the basis for attacks on the Labour Government, arguing that it was 'pursuing a vicious vendetta against the motorist' and suggesting, instead, a return to an expanded roads programme in order to accommodate projected congestion (John Redwood, then Shadow Transport Secretary, cited in *The Guardian*, 30 November 1999; for an overview of Conservative proposals for an expanded roads programme see *The Guardian*, 13 July 1999).

A series of rail accidents (beginning with Paddington, in October 1999) – and media reaction to them – also undermined public faith that trains could provide a safe alternative to road transport, even though rail travel is considerably safer than road travel (Clarence, 2003: 456–7). This, combined with increasing negative reporting of inefficiency, lack of reliability and poor profitability, served to erode further the previously positive view of E&P.

Finally, the rise in petrol prices in the autumn of 2000, and the subsequent fuel tax protests, in which hauliers and farmers blockaded oil refineries and depots, seriously disrupting the economic and political system, provides a further explanation for the public's growing sense of 'alarm' over the perceived failure of the Government's transport policy. The public's opposition to R&P (which at this time manifested itself in opposition to rising fuel prices, seen as part of the Labour Government's policy to restrict car use) was very clearly demonstrated by their overwhelming support for the fuel protests, in spite of the disruption caused and the strident opposition of Ministers to the protesters' actions (Robinson, 2002).

As Downs' model predicts, this combination of governmental ambivalence and public hostility did indeed facilitate the IAC entering phase four, the gradual decline of public interest. This process was accelerated by the fact that a number of other issues gained significant public and media attention during this period: ongoing preoccupations with asylum seekers (Schuster, 2003) and crime were initially joined, for example, by widespread alarm centred on genetically modified crops (for food production) during the late 1990s (Toke, 2002) before giving way to further food scares centred on the foot-and-mouth crisis which began in February 2001 (McConnell and Stark, 2002). Such issues displaced transport from the public policy agenda, thereby leading to a decline of government and public interest in tackling the ongoing problems in this area.

Finally, the second IAC was completed with transport entering the post-problem stage; as Downs suggests, this showed significant differences from the position at the pre-problem stage.

The changes which had occurred in the transport policy community were decisive in two key ways. On the one hand, the incorporation of groups such as the CPRE and Transport 2000 as insiders within the newly constituted CfIT ensured that this quasi-governmental body continued to deliver policy initiatives which challenged the Government, even as it appeared to retreat from the previously agreed consensus. On the other hand, the marginalization of the previously dominant road lobby was decisive in the collapse of their umbrella organization, the BRF (interview information (multiple sources), autumn 2003), and also in undermining faith in dialogue with the Government, which ultimately led to the fuel protests of September 2000 (Robinson, 2002: 61–4).

In addition, conflicts between the different transport policy philosophies continued to be felt in a number of contradictory ways. At one level, the ambiguous status of E&P resulted in conflicting legacies, pointing both to continued expansion of investment in public transport on the one hand, but also to a reduction in such spending on the other, as its cost, lack of reliability and inability to stem the rise in road transport became increasingly clear. Facing the collapse of Railtrack, for example, the Government was clearly unable to decide whether or not to invest still further in a public transport system which seemed incapable of improvement.

At another level, the increasing legitimization of R&P has also had a powerful legacy. It provided the impetus, first to Durham City Council, and then to London, for implementation of local road pricing schemes, both of which have proven to be highly successful and – perhaps surprisingly in the context of negative national media campaigns – popular with their local electorates (Transport for London, 2003: 41). Its increased legitimacy has also enabled the ongoing investigation of more widespread local and national road pricing schemes, with road pricing for lorries on trunk roads already due for implementation from 2006 (Department of Transport, 2003a: 1).

Finally, whilst it might seem that P&P had been totally delegitimized during this IAC, this was in fact not the case: the hostility of the public and the ambiguous commitment of the Government to the implications of policy on the basis of R&P; the perceived failure of policy on the basis of E&P, and the continued growth of road traffic all provided considerable policy space for actors still committed to P&P to advance projects on such a basis. This is important because a number of the UK regions, much of the old Department of Transport and a number of transport experts, still remain committed to increasing road building – which, while no longer seen as the only priority, could still be justified on the basis of P&P, as we will now demonstrate.

The third issue attention cycle: the end of the road for roads but the beginning of air for prosperity?

Last week, a statement was attributed to me, made in 1997: 'I will have failed if in five years' time there are not many more people using public transport and far fewer journeys by car.' I did not say that. And rather like the alleged Jim Callaghan words, 'Crisis, what crisis?', wide reporting of them does not make them true. ... So let me set the record straight. I have never believed that the amount of traffic could be reduced in absolute terms within five years. (John Prescott, quoted in *The Independent on Sunday*, 9 June 2002)

At the beginning of the 21st century, transport policy appears to be on the verge of entering two different, yet interrelated, issue attention cycles. The first of these is likely to see a return to conflict centred on road building, with two announcements in December 2002 (Department of Transport, 2002b) and July 2003 (Department of Transport, 2003b) amounting to a £9 billion programme of road building, which may well lead once more to widespread opposition developing as protesters try to prevent the implementation of these schemes.

Opposition might also be expected to increase from groups such as Transport 2000 – which have recently enjoyed insider status, particularly if the expanded programme reflects a substantive change to the ethos underpinning governmental policy (for example, a return to P&P) combined with a change to their position within the policy community which returns them to their historical status as policy outsiders.

Superficially, there seems to be a convincing case to be made that the basis of policy has indeed reverted to the P&P orthodoxy. The new roads programme was justified by reference to regional surveys of transport provision which argued that road building, and road-based transport, were essential for regional development (statement by Alistair Darling, Transport Secretary, to House of Commons, cited in *The Guardian*, 10 December 2002), and the discourse accompanying its launch was reminiscent of that accompanying the roads for prosperity initiative:

> This new investment in our major transport corridors will deliver real improvements for people and business across the country. The improvements are essential to tackling congestion on major routes – particularly the widening of the M25 and M1. They will add vital capacity to the strategic road network and support economic growth. (Alistair Darling, Transport Secretary, cited in Department of Transport, 2003b)

As in the 1960s and 1970s, congestion has once again provided its own impetus. Transport policy is once more developing on the basis of predict and provide, regardless of the fact that this ethos was fundamentally undermined in the mid-1990s.

The suspicion that we could be entering into another IAC on this basis is further demonstrated by the change to the nature of the policy community surrounding transport, which appears to be gradually reorienting itself around the Government's new priorities. On the one hand, changes to governmental policy reflect the interests of pro-roads groups such as the RAC, the AA and the CBI, whose campaigns have increasingly emphasized road transport's crucial role as a facilitator of economic prosperity (see Automobile Association, 2002, for a summary). On the other hand, the CfIT and its dual focus on multi-modal transport and restrict and provide seem to have been marginalized by the new road programme. Thus anti-roads groups, newly denied their status as insiders, may once more join forces with outsiders such as the direct action campaigners, to mount a sustained campaign against the Government's policy, returning once more to the pattern which existed in the mid-1990s.

However, this superficial view obscures an important alternative reading of contemporary developments, which requires us to place this newly announced road programme within the context of the now ongoing debate over road pricing. This alternative view suggests that the Government's primary aim is in fact to develop policy on the basis of R&P, with an unprecedented review announced in July 2003 of the implications of introducing national road pricing on all trunk roads for all car users, following the already scheduled introduction for road freight users (*The Guardian*, 10 July 2003):

> Our objective must be to provide a better deal for the motorist. Road Pricing would be a radically different approach. But it could have huge potential to reduce congestion, to allow faster more reliable journeys. Giving motorists a better choice about how and when they travel. We'd be failing future generations if we did not test its feasibility and examine the gains that could come from it. (Alistair Darling, Transport Secretary, Speech to House of Commons cited in *The Guardian*, 10 July 2003)

From this perspective, the present road programme is merely the initial stage of a long-term framework based on R&P, with the aim of filling in 'missing links' in the trunk road network before the implementation of road pricing.

Even if such a view were correct, opposition to the Government's policy, based on road building, is unlikely to diminish. Whilst it suggests that the changes to the policy network are relatively minor, with groups such as the CPRE and Transport 2000 retaining their status as insider groups, there is still likely to be considerable opposition from the public and direct action groups, centring on both the environmental aspects of road building and also the subsequent implementation of road pricing. Thus there remains a strong likelihood of the development of a future IAC which would most closely reflect the pattern of the 1990s; transport is likely to remain a politically salient issue, at least until the middle of the next decade.

Air transport

The second key reason for suggesting that we may be on the brink of entering a second IAC centres on analysis of the politics of air transport, which has, for the first time, become an issue of serious potential conflict in Britain.[9] Facing a massive projected growth in demand for air travel, the Government is presently undertaking a consultation process, aimed at finding ways of meeting that demand, and its discourse is full of the rhetoric of a P&P-based approach to policy:

> Aviation is a great British success story, and one of the major strengths of the UK economy, both now and for the future. Flying is today part of the ordinary lives of most people in the UK. In 2001 alone almost 50 per cent of the UK population made at least one

---

9 Whilst airport protesting can in fact be traced back to the early 1990s with the campaign against the expansion of Manchester airport centring initially, in 1995, on opposition within the highway inquiry process, before the direct action began in January 1997 designed to prevent the runway construction, a strong argument can be made that the government's present consultation process is unprecedented in terms of its unequivocal exposition of the predict-and-provide ethos, and with it the potential of a significant expansion of airport capacity nationwide (see Griggs et al., 1998, for an overview).

journey by air. In London and the South East around 60 per cent of people did so. It seems likely that in the future, people will want to fly more, and expect to be able to fly more, as their prosperity continues to increase. (Department of Transport, 2003c: 14)

We would argue that the primary aim of this consultation process is to find a politically expedient way of providing increased airport capacity to meet this projected demand. Looking back to the history of road transport, we can trace a similar pattern of policy now developing in the air transport sector to that which developed in the late 1980s when the government used similar arguments to justify a huge expansion of road building.

Reading the politics of air transport in this way leads us towards a highly probable scenario for the future development of the policy, in which the policy process will indeed follow the pattern which was set in the earlier IAC centred on *Roads for Prosperity*. From this perspective, one would expect the public to become increasingly alarmed about the environmental impact of increased air travel, associated in particular with noise pollution, but also with greenhouse gas emissions, and local effects centred on the huge amounts of traffic generated by people travelling to and from the airport. This disquiet may manifest itself in widespread opposition to the physical construction of additional airport capacity, which will then lead to a reconsideration of the basis on which air travel policy is being formulated, and the extent to which it is sensible and sustainable for society to continue to provide for that projected growth in air travel.

Having begun for such reasons, however, the IAC is then likely to move on through its third and fourth stages as it becomes apparent that the perceived costs of restrictions in air travel are more than the public is willing to bear. In particular, the British public is now accustomed to the idea of low-cost air travel and holidays to continental Europe, made possible in part through the deregulated nature of the air transport sector, and the huge subsidy which is given to all air travellers in the provision of tax-free aviation fuel. So we are likely to see a pattern in which the development of air transport policy on the basis of meeting huge demand for growth initially faces vociferous popular opposition, until public realization that provision for such growth is essential if low-cost air travel is to continue, results in that opposition dissipating again.

It is therefore possible to predict two possible, and distinct, futures for transport policy in Britain at the start of the 21st century. On the one hand, there remains deep disagreement over the road programme, and uncertainty about the Labour Government's aims. On the other hand, a significant IAC in the air transport sector is about to start developing. If nothing else, these two developments mean that transport issues will continue to be as interesting politically in the next 20 years as they have been in the last 60.

Theorizing transport policy

This chapter has shown that transport policy in the post-war period has become increasingly volatile. The status quo, a relatively closed policy process based on the dominant P&P ethos, has succumbed with increasing regularity to a relatively open process in which that ethos has come under threat, before re-exerting its hold once more. In order to understand this cycling of policy over time, we have made use of Anthony Downs' work; this section now outlines a modified version of his model which works to explain more fully such a cyclical process of policy making.

Downs' IAC offers insights into three key questions which are essential in understanding the development of British transport policy in the post-war period: How and why do policy cycles start? Why do they move on from stage to stage? Why do they return to the status quo? Here, we outline the answers to these questions suggested by the IAC, before presenting a modified model which we argue better accounts for the increasing volatility of Britain's transport policy in the post-war period.

In looking first at the question, 'how and why do policy cycles start?' Downs argues that the conceptualization of an issue as a policy problem is decisive in gaining media and public attention, so giving it prominence on the agenda:

> Public perceptions of most crises in American domestic life do not reflect changes in real conditions as much as they reflect the operation of a definite and systematic cycle of heightening public interest and then boredom with major issues. This issue attention cycle is rooted in both the nature of certain domestic problems and the way major communication media interact with the public. (Downs, 1973: 63)

The inference here is that issues tend to come to prominence because of changes to the nature of the problem itself, often occurring independently of the actions of actors (i.e. the issue is 'free-floating'). A developing sense of political crisis – caused either by an 'act of God' (or some other form of disaster) or due to increasing awareness of the negative impact of existing practices – leads to demands for action.

The analysis of British transport policy offered above clearly shows considerable similarities with Downs' model: the onset of the two issue attention cycles discussed coincided with periods in which transport increasingly came to be seen as a policy problem in terms of damaging the environment (e.g., the contribution of road transport to global warming), having a negative effect on public health (e.g., the perceived effect of vehicle emissions) and undermining the economy (e.g., the impact of congestion on economic growth).

In addition, as Downs suggests, the media's role in communicating such concerns to the public was vital, resulting in public alarm centred, in particular, on the perceived link between rising vehicle emissions and growing levels of asthma, and on the impact of road building on the quality of rural and urban life.

However, in order to better explain the case of transport policy in Britain since 1945, the model developed here draws three subtle differences from Downs's work. Firstly, in contrast to Downs' focus on 'free-floating policy problems', we have seen that the conflict over the definition of problems has been absolutely crucial to the conceptualization of transport as a policy problem and hence to the onset of IACs. As Diane Stone has argued:

> Problem definition is a process of image making, where the images have to do fundamentally with attributing cause, blame, and responsibility. Conditions, difficulties, or issues thus do not have inherent properties that make them more or less likely to be seen as problems or to be expanded. Rather, political actors deliberately portray them in ways calculated to gain support for their side. [Political actors do not, in fact, accept the

definition of the problem that is advanced by] ... science, popular culture or any other source. [Rather they] ... compose stories that describe harms and difficulties, attribute them to actions of other individuals or organisations, and thereby claim the right to invoke government power to stop the harm. (Stone, 1989: 282)

Secondly, we have argued that the creation of 'policy disasters' was absolutely crucial to the onset of the second IAC. Central government and the pro-roads groups together demonstrated, albeit unwittingly, that proposals for a much expanded road programme would ultimately fail to solve the problem of transport congestion, thus significantly contributing to the emerging conceptualization of transport as a policy problem – a factor which Downs' work ignores.

Thirdly, the onset of an IAC has also been influenced by the impact of actors. At one level, the onset of both IACs has coincided with an explosion in the number and diversity of actors involved in the conflict over the transport issue, with a combination of direct action groups, 'mainstream' pressure groups and even backbench MPs posing a challenge to the dominant policy community. The simple fact that more actors were involved in the conflict thus increased the public's sense that there was a developing policy problem. At another level, the onset of the second IAC coincided with the growth of innovative activity by the opponents of road building with the direct action groups, in particular, succeeding in infiltrating a number of institutional venues such as the media and the construction sites, so shifting the conflict into arenas in which the pro-roads groups were not dominant.

In looking secondly at the inter-related questions 'why do the policy cycles move on from stage to stage?' and 'why do they return to the status quo?' Downs offers two key explanations. Firstly, some problems move through the cycle because they are effectively 'solved' by the utilization of a technical fix. This can be clearly seen in the early phase of British transport policy, in which a proposal to remove lead from petrol was used to address public concerns about the impact of pollution on public health, so completing the first IAC. Secondly, those issues which cannot be solved by a technical fix move on through the IAC due to public concern over the costs of actually solving the problem:

The public thus begins to realize that the evil itself results in part from arrangements that are providing significant benefits to someone – often to a great many people. ... [I]n reality, the very nature of our most pressing social problems involves either deliberate or unconscious exploitation of one group in society by another or the prevention of one group from enjoying something which another wants to keep for itself. (Downs, 1973: 64–5)

Once such a realization becomes widespread, a combination of public hostility and/or boredom, and the fact that another issue is almost inevitably entering into the public consciousness forces the cycle into its final stage, and with it a return to the status quo.

In looking at the transport case one can see that on the surface there is much evidence to support Downs' analysis. Since the late 1990s, when a widespread debate developed over the future development of transport policy in Britain, the public has become increasingly hostile to the sacrifices required for the implementation of a transport package centred

Figure 9.6   Benson's model of a policy sector

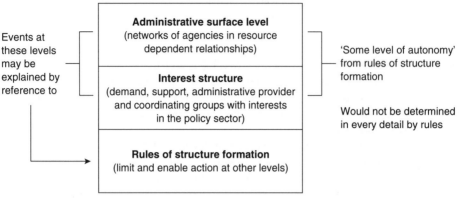

Source: Parsons (1995: 149)

on offering alternatives to road building. During the Blair era, in particular, the media and public have vociferously opposed action designed to restrict car usage (such as road pricing) in spite of the fact that it is acknowledged as essential for any coherent transport programme. This is unsurprising: car ownership has important aspirational values, being associated with coming of age and the satisfaction of one's basic material needs. It is an important element of the perceived material development of many citizens: when they own a car they are well on the way to economic emancipation. Thus any attack on car ownership and usage is likely to meet considerable opposition.

In order to fully address the questions 'why do the policy cycles move on from stage to stage?' and 'why do they return to the status quo?', however, the model developed here also adds an extra dimension to Downs' analysis, arguing for the inclusion of two additional (and essential) aspects: the role of government priorities and what Benson (1982) has termed 'the rules of structure formation', both of which decisively shape the policy process.

The discussion of transport policy in Britain since 1945 has clearly shown that the government has always had strong priorities for transport which it has clearly articulated. Furthermore, and crucially, these priorities have been decisive in both shifting the balance of power within the transport networks – changing actors from insiders to outsiders and vice versa – and in shaping the conflict which has developed over the rival ethoses used to legitimate policy. Government actions have thus been a vital factor in the progression of the IACs, determining the pace at which the cycles have moved from stage to stage.

However, Benson's work suggests that we need to look beyond the actions of government to further extend the workings of Downs's model. Benson (1982: 160) argues that the operation of the policy process takes place within three interlinked levels: rules of structure formation, interest structure and the administrative surface level, with the rules of structure formation providing a baseline which constrains the operation of the higher levels, as illustrated by Figure 9.6.

Parsons (1995: 149) argues that the rules of structure formation level

> shapes the way in which issues are brought into the realm of decision-making and others are kept outside the decisional processes. ... In terms of agenda setting, Benson's framework stresses how the analysis of administrative and interest structures in given policy sectors are shaped by 'deep rules' which operate to ensure that some demands are excluded from the decision making process, and which limit the choices and behaviour of policy makers.

Such insights are very important for understanding the cyclical nature of post-war transport policy in Britain. In particular, Benson's work suggests an alternative explanation for the movement of issues through the policy cycle and their return to the status quo, emphasizing that issues which challenge the rules of structure formation will rapidly move through the IAC before returning to the status quo.

The conflict over road pricing in the Blair era, symbolizing as it does a conflict over measures to restrict the usage of the car, can, we argue, be explained with reference to this framework.

Road pricing, with its focus on restricting the usage of the car, poses a challenge to a number of deeper values which are connected to the core values of the capitalist state. As we have argued elsewhere, in Britain the car has become interlinked with core values such as liberty, freedom and self-realization (see Robinson, 2000). Such values are not merely those of advertising executives and car enthusiasts, but are ingrained in the structural imperatives of the state. The problem for road pricing is that it is seen as an attack on such core values. It poses a fundamental challenge to the right of certain citizens (i.e., marginal motorists) to own a car, forcing them away from individualistic solutions towards collectivist ones in the form of public transport.

Ironically, the perception that road pricing is an attack on personal liberty and challenges the structural imperatives of the state is only enhanced by the proposal to hypothecate road pricing to public transport investment. The link of the imposition of the charge with investment in public transport sends two clear signals to transport consumers: you are being forced out of your car, and you are being forced onto public transport. The latter could not be provided without the former, so it appears that the attack on individuality and freedom is being mounted in order to promote a collectivist approach to policy (such a view is particularly well articulated in Mawhinney, 1995).

This is not to suggest that the popular opposition to road pricing has been motivated by such structural imperatives; they may indeed just be motivated by self-interest. But a policy such as road pricing which poses an unprecedented challenge to the near core imperatives of the state will, we suggest, always meet real difficulties in being successfully implemented.

Overall, therefore, whilst Downs' work on IACs does provide a useful starting point for understanding the changing nature of British transport policy since 1945, it has clear limitations. This account therefore suggests a number of changes to the IAC which enable us to offer a more comprehensive answer to the key questions posed earlier, namely, 'how and why do policy cycles start?', 'why do they move on from stage to stage?' and 'why do they return to the status quo?', and by doing so, offer a more sophisticated explanation for the increasing volatility of British transport policy since 1945.

Conclusion

This chapter has sought to provide an explanation for the changing nature of transport policy in the post-war period. It has argued that we can begin to explain the increasingly volatile nature of policy over time through reference to Anthony Downs' IAC, which suggests that policy issues go through 'a definite and systematic cycle of heightening public interest and then boredom with major issues' (Downs, 1973: 63), resulting in a cyclical pattern of policy.

The study of post-war British transport policy suggests that conceiving of policy in a cyclical way is highly useful. We have shown that policy has gone through two complete IACs, with the prospect of further policy cycles for the future, which have served to destabilize the nature of the network of actors centred on transport, and pose unprecedented challenges to the coherence of the dominant 'predict and provide' ethos, used historically as the basis for policy.

Yet this chapter has also argued that, whilst useful, Downs' framework requires modification in two ways. Firstly, acknowledging the importance of the conflict over the definition of issues, the role of policy disasters and the importance of actors helps us to more fully understand how cycles begin in the first place. Secondly, understanding the importance of government intervention together with what Benson terms 'the structural imperatives of the state' helps to clarify 'how and why policy cycles move on from stage to stage' and 'why they return to the status quo'. Insights from such a framework combined with the discussion of the transport issue presented above, enable us to predict that transport is certain to remain a heavily contested issue in the near future, with a pattern of increasing volatility and uncertainty lasting well into the next decade. Whilst this may be unwelcome for policy practitioners, it ensures that for students of British politics and public policy, it will continue to remain a rich source of study.

10 Developments in British Public Policy
Peter Dorey

Introduction

Many of the areas of public policy examined in this book can be divided, at least for analytic purposes, into two general periods, the first being from 1945 until 1979, and the second from 1979 onwards. Even if particular policies did not suddenly start *de novo* in 1945, or end suddenly in 1979 (for example, as we will note below, Thain has shown that Keynesianisn was increasingly being supplanted by monetarism *during* the 1970s, prior to being pursued with ideological conviction during the early 1980s), to be replaced by a new policy, these two dates do provide useful 'shorthand' for political scientists and policy analysts seeking to make sense of developments in British public policy since the end of the Second World War. Certainly, this particular periodization is extremely useful in aiding our understanding, and providing examples, of particular features of public policy in Britain.

For example, in several areas of public policy, the period preceding 1979 was characterized by the prevalence of discrete policy paradigms, whereby the relevant actors broadly accepted particular goals and objectives pertaining to their policy, to the extent that changes of government did *not* normally result in a corresponding change of policy, whatever the ostensibly 'adversarial' nature of electoral competition and parliamentary politics in Britain might imply.

These dominant policy paradigms often reflected and reinforced the crucial role of government departments, senior civil servants and their 'client' organized interests – collectively constituting policy communities – in particular policy areas, such as agriculture, health and transport, whereupon these key actors tended to share an operational ideology or in-house philosophy about the primary purpose and priorities of public policy in their domain. With senior (Cabinet) Ministers often adopting a predominantly managerial or overseer role, this meant that the various policy paradigms often continued relatively unchecked, thereby further contributing to overall policy community prior to 1979. On those occasions when reform-minded Ministers were appointed with the clear intention of introducing new policies, they often found that the strength of the extant policy paradigm, and the extent to which it was upheld by other key policy actors in that sphere, obliged them to dilute, or even abandon, their proposed reforms, thereby further contributing, in effect, to overall policy continuity. This, in turn, ensured that particular policies – and the paradigms underpinning them – became further embedded and entrenched, and thus generally accepted as 'the way things are done'. Over time, this meant that each new government or Minister inherited a greater number of policies and programmes, which, in turn, reduced further their scope for choice and change (Rose, 1990; Rose and Davies, 1994).

All of these characteristics were themselves an integral part of a broader political consensus – they both reflected and reinforced it – in which successive governments, Labour and Conservative, generally pursued largely similar goals and objectives, whilst also accepting the political 'rules of the game'. Indeed, the degree of continuity in many areas of public policy in Britain prior to 1979, coupled with the role played by key policy actors, and the emphasis placed on consultation, dialogue and negotiation between them, led Jordan and Richardson (1982) to refer to a distinct 'British policy style', whilst Richard Rose (1990; Rose and Davies, 1994) – as we have just noted – emphasized the degree of 'inheritance in public policy'.

Whilst aware of the danger of over-simplification, 1979 does seem none the less to provide an analytically convenient 'point of departure', heralding a new phase in many spheres of British public policy. From 1979 onwards, not only were a number of previously dominant policy paradigms challenged, but so too was the privileged role which certain actors had been accorded in the policy process. During the 1980s and 1990s, a series of ideologically-motivated and intellectually-confident Conservative Governments – inadvertently aided by the weakness of the opposition, both within the Conservative Party itself (most Conservative MPs were *not* Thatcherites (Norton, 1990), and some of them deemed much of Thatcherism to be singularly un-Conservative) and on the Opposition benches in the House of Commons – succeeded in challenging many of the assumptions of post-war policy makers, and thereby managed to introduce new policies and policy goals in a number of key areas.

However, to do so, these Conservative Governments deemed it necessary to challenge and thus change the ways in which public policy tended to be 'made' in Britain. In so doing, the Thatcher–Major Governments provided further examples of concepts and characteristics which are of great importance to policy analysts. For example, as we will discuss a little more fully below, the 1980s and 1990s witnessed such phenomena as the destabilizing or dismantling of various policy communities and/or the incorporation of new – more ideologically-compatible – policy actors, a downgrading of the role of senior civil servants in proffering policy advice (as Ministers increasingly looked and listened to Special Advisers and politically sympathetic think-tanks, as well as resorting to 'policy transfer' in some areas), and a trend whereby more Ministers adopted an 'activist' or agenda-setting role *vis-à-vis* their Departments, in order to overcome the resistance to new ideas and policies by entrenched Departmental philosophies and their dominant policy paradigms. More Ministers therefore became willing to invoke 'despotic power' to impose changes, either to particular policies, or to the process by which policies were 'made' (or, in many cases, both, for the latter was often a prerequisite of the former).

In some instances, though, policy communities were weakened not so much by conscious Ministerial action – vitally important though this often was – but by exogenous factors, such as crises, or developments and discoveries in medical or scientific knowledge, which served to discredit the operational norms and policy paradigms which had previously sustained those policy communities, and which had thereby excluded other (potential) policy actors, whilst also precluding the adoption of new policies.

Before looking a little more fully at these developments, however, we need firstly to summarize – based on the findings of the chapters in this book – the factors and features which contributed towards relative continuity and stability in public policy in Britain prior to 1979. We will then extrapolate from these chapters the main sources of change in British public policy since 1979, although in the 'exceptional' case of foreign policy, we will be obliged to explain why policy change in this period was either limited, or, rather, entailed the continuation of changes which had begun somewhat earlier, to the extent that 1979 does not mark a clear 'point of departure'.

Sources of relative continuity in British public policy prior to the 1980s

For long periods since 1945, many areas of public policy in Britain either exhibited considerable continuity, or changed only slowly and incrementally, in accordance with Rose's notion of a 'moving consensus' (Rose, 1984: 87–91). Indeed, so strong and widespread did the prevalence of policy continuity appear, that Rose argued that, in the short-term (less than eight years, or two consecutive terms of Office), political parties and governments did not generally make much difference to public policy (Rose, 1984).

Rose subsequently developed this theme further, noting the extent to which much of the 20th century had been characterized by 'inheritance' in public policy, whereby many policies and programmes became 'embedded' and/or supported by organized interests or sections of the electorate, who effectively became their beneficiaries or 'clients'. This compounded the difficulties which new governments or Ministers experienced in seeking to repeal or significantly change existing policies and programmes, so that irrespective of the size of a government's parliamentary majority and apparent mandate from the voters, their degree of (policy) choice and room for manoeuvre were, in practice, seriously constrained and limited (Rose, 1990; Rose and Davies, 1994). The ensuing trend towards policy continuity, or only incremental change, was both reflected and reinforced by a range of factors prior to the 1980s.

The wider ideological and political context

One important reason for the high degree of continuity or gradualism in many areas of public policy in post-war Britain derives from the dominance of a social democratic consensus until about 1979. As we observed in Chapter 2 of *Policy Making in Britain* (Dorey, 2005), with the notable exception of the first two years of Edward Heath's 1970–4 Conservative administration, governments from 1945 to the mid-1970s, be they Conservative or Labour, broadly subscribed to similar policy goals, and generally adopted the same means of achieving them. Certainly, as Thain explains in Chapter 2, the period from 1945 until the early 1970s was dominated by the paradigm of Keynesian social democracy, whereby successive governments – Labour and Conservative – accepted a range of new economic roles and responsibilities, most notably with regard to the conscious and active pursuit of 'high and stable levels' of employment (which soon came to be viewed as the goal of full employment). This new macroeconomic policy paradigm thereby entailed unprecedented – at least in peace-time – governmental regulation of, and intervention in, industry and the economy (leading, in the 1960s, to experiments in economic planning), although these represented an attempt at protecting and stabilizing capitalism, not supplanting it. Policy makers pursued various policies and economic techniques to avoid a slump, entailing not only a judicious blend of fiscal and monetary measures, but also greater co-operation and partnership between governments, trade unions and employers, culminating in the 1960s development of a form of corporatism, in which incomes policies were ascribed a significant role in the growing battle against inflation (reflecting another dominant policy perspective at this time, namely that inflation was largely derived from 'excessive' wage increases fuelling the cost of living, as employers increased prices in order to offset higher labour costs and protect profit margins).

These economic policies, and the objectives they were intended to achieve, yielded considerable overall policy continuity from 1945 to 1979, and not only reflected the existence of a significant degree of political bipartisanship, but also, in turn, helped to underpin it. In other words, the existence of a broad political consensus and bipartisan commitment to the policy objectives which we have just noted, themselves facilitated and fostered relative continuity of many public policies and programmmes, and often close relationships between the various actors (Ministers, Departments, senior civil servants and organized interests) in many policy areas.

Until the 1970s, when the Keynesian social democratic framework crumbled (paving the way for a new – neo-liberal – economic paradigm to become established during the 1980s), its apparent success meant that there was little necessity for policy makers to abandon or question it. To the extent that problems were identified or acknowledged – most notably Britain's relative economic decline – the policy response was invariably to strengthen or supplement existing macroeconomic policy through additional techniques of regulation or intervention: adapting it, not abandoning it.

Dominant paradigms

From the 1940s through to the 1970s at least, the close relationships which existed between key actors in various policy subsystems often served to sustain 'dominant paradigms', entailing a prevalent perspective or philosophy concerning Departmental or sectoral goals in their particular sphere of policy. For example, as Wyn Grant explained in Chapter 1, agricultural policy was – until the 1990s – characterized by a 'productionist' paradigm, whereby a primary policy goal was the maximization of domestic food production, entailing the payment of significant subsidies to British farmers. So prevalent was this 'productionist paradigm, Grant notes, that it largely survived the neo-liberalism of the Thatcher Governments, when other industries were repeatedly exhorted to be less reliant on taxpayers' subsidies, and, instead, become more competitive, profitable and self-reliant.

Meanwhile, in Chapter 9, Nick Robinson explains how transport policy, until the mid-1980s, was largely shaped by a 'predict-and-provide' paradigm, whereby the emphasis was on 'a market-based model of transport provision' which was highly responsive to the interests of consumers (road-users) and thereby 'allowed the road lobby to dominate the policy process'. This particular policy paradigm held cars and lorries (road haulage) to be the most important modes of transport in Britain, which effectively meant that public passenger transport – buses and trains – was treated as secondary. This perspective, in turn, meant that the response to increased car usage and traffic congestion was to expand the number or range of roads, as evinced, for example, by the building of various motorways (M1, M4, M62, etc.) throughout the length and breadth of Britain.

Elsewhere, as Jones explains in Chapter 5, health policy was shaped by a perspective which privileged curative medical treatment and health care via hospitals and general practitioners (GPs), rather than preventative medicine aligned with a concomitant recognition of the socio-environmental factors influencing people's health. This paradigm also meant that proposals to improve health care in Britain usually focused on building more hospitals (or modernizing and expanding existing ones) and recruiting more nursing staff. Within this particular policy paradigm, the NHS was the fulcrum or lode star of most health policy in Britain, to the extent that improving the nation's health was assumed *a priori* to necessitate improving the NHS *per se*: the two were inextricably linked.

In another key area of the welfare state, namely pensions, Thornton shows, in Chapter 8, how the prevailing ethos for much of the post-war period was to provide a universal system of old-age pensions financed primarily through National Insurance Contributions. However, it was also widely accepted by pension policy makers that this alone would not provide an adequate income for all pensioners, and so there was also an acceptance, reflected in the policies of successive governments throughout this period, of the need to devise a system of 'top-up' pensions provided through occupational or private pension schemes. However, whilst the need to provide such 'supplementary' pensions was widely acknowledged, policy makers found it extremely difficult to devise a policy which was fair and effective, not least because low-paid workers would be precisely those employees least able to make additional contributions to an occupational or private pension scheme. Similarly, government-inspired schemes to top-up the flat-rate state pension with a second pension linked to earnings merely replicated into old age the inequalities which had prevailed, due to vastly differing incomes, prior to retirement.

With regard to housing policy, as Malpass notes in Chapter 6, the dominant ethos from the 1940s through to the 1970s was that of promoting a mixed economy of housing, whereby the promotion of homeownership, facilitated by house-building via the private sector, in the context of 'the market', was pursued in tandem with the provision of rented public housing, provided by local authorities (council houses), primarily for those on low incomes, who could not afford to buy their own property. Within this mixed economy of housing, though, there was a clear assumption about the desirability of homeownership, with one practical manifestation of this being the availability of a subsidy, in the form of mortgage tax relief, in order to make buying their own home more affordable to more people. However, for those who could still not afford to become homeowners, subsidies were also provided in the form of means-tested rent rebates and/or housing benefit.

Overall, though, this period entailed a steady increase in homeownership – clearly facilitated by rising living standards and incomes – and this was widely viewed as both natural and desirable by governments (including Labour administrations) and policy makers. However, this bipartisan agreement on the desirability of homeownership did not yet extend to the selling of council houses.

In the sphere of industrial relations policy prior to 1979, as discussed in Chapter 7, a voluntarist perspective prevailed, whereby management and trade unions were to be left, as far as practicably possible, to determine terms and conditions of employment between them, free from interference by policy makers. The Ministry of Labour during this period, along with successive Ministers of Labour, assiduously sought to refrain from becoming embroiled in industrial disputes, unless directly requested to do so via arbitration and conciliation procedures. Instead, the Ministry, and the Ministers who headed it during the 1950s, relied heavily on exhortation and encouragement, believing that greater communication and dialogue between the 'two sides of industry' would foster greater trust and co-operation, and thereby lead to a gradual diminution of distrust and concomitant disruption in the workplace. Ultimately, it was believed, good industrial relations could not be achieved by invoking Acts of Parliament and statutory stipulation.

These dominant paradigms often reflected (and, in turn, served to reinforce) the prevalence of Departmentalism in various policy subsystems, whereby particular Departments evinced a discernible philosophy or ethos, and which itself significantly shaped its perspective *vis-à-vis* issues and problems (and, indeed, what were defined as problems). This, in turn, effectively sustained an institutional agenda frequently sceptical of new ideas or policy initiatives. Having spent most, if not all, of their working lives in a particular Department, senior civil servants tended to acquire a set of values and views which strongly shaped their approach to policy issues, and this Departmental philosophy was then inculcated into younger civil servants as they too rose through the ranks.

Where Departmentalism was particularly pronounced or prevalent, it often exerted a notable impact on Ministers appointed to head the Department in question, to the extent that many Ministers 'went native', becoming inculcated with the views and values of 'their' Department, even when these seemed to contrast or conflict with their own previously expressed political outlook, or even the goals of their government itself. Certainly, as we noted in Chapter 3 of *Policy Making in Britain*, many senior Ministers until the 1980s could be classified as 'managers' *vis-à-vis* their Departments (rather than 'agenda-setters' or 'innovators'), and this served further to entrench the prevalence of a particular philosophy or paradigm within the Department. This often meant, in effect, that the Departments would adhere to, and continue with, a broadly similar approach to issues and problems, irrespective of the Secretary of State officially heading the Department, and the political hue of the governing party.

It was only really from the 1980s onwards that more Ministers began to adopt an 'activist' or agenda-setting role, thereby enabling them to challenge extant Departmental philosophies, and associated policy paradigms. This development will be discussed below, when we turn our attention to sources of change in contemporary British public policy.

Meanwhile, in many instances, Departmentalism and dominant policy paradigms were further reinforced by the prevalence, at least until the 1980s, of policy communities in particular policy subsystems.

Policy communities

As we noted in Chapter 5 of *Policy Making in Britain*, several policy areas or subsystems in post-war Britain were characterized by policy communities, whereby a very close – and closed – relationship existed between the key actors in that domain, most notably Departments, their senior civil servants, and the dominant organized interest (or pressure group) in that sphere of policy. These policy communities entailed a symbiotic relationship between their constituent members, with Departmental officials heavily reliant on the 'client' organized interest(s) both for specialist or technical advice when formulating or modifying policies, and for assistance in implementing the ensuing policies. In return, the organized interest(s) sought to influence and shape public policy in a manner beneficial to their – or their members' – interests. In general, such a reciprocal relationship was mutually beneficial, with individual Departments and their 'client' organized interest(s) engaged in an ongoing exchange relationship, and also characterized by considerable resource dependency.

These relationships, in turn, played a major role in shaping and sustaining the afore-mentioned dominant paradigms in various policy sectors, and thus in largely determining the institutional agenda much of the time. Organized interests seeking to articulate alter-native perspectives or recommend significantly different policies were usually deemed to be 'unrealistic', 'unrepresentative' or even 'irresponsible', thereby remaining 'outsiders', and therefore part of the systemic agenda.

Certainly, policy communities usually served to 'de-politicize' many, if not most, policy issues, to the extent that much decision taking was largely administrative, specialist or technical. The shared values and interests which were intrinsic to policy communities effectively precluded ideological or partisan disagreements. Instead, with the 'ends' or goals of public policy generally agreed or accepted by the actors in a policy community, negoti-ations were normally about the means of achieving them, or on the most appropriate – feasible, practicable or realistic – response to a particular problem which may have been identified. In these respects, policy communities were central to a predominantly incre-mental style of policy making in many policy areas from 1945 to the 1980s. This sought to ensure that the impact of any change was kept to an absolute minimum, and that where changes or modifications to existing policies were unavoidable, they were pursued on the basis of the fullest possible agreement or consent, whilst also ensuring that the actors themselves retained as much control over the policy as possible. The actual goals of exist-ing public policy were rarely questioned or explicitly considered by the participants, but, rather, were generally taken as given, to the extent that dialogue between the relevant policy actors was mainly about the means and methods of achieving these goals.

The policy sphere which was characterized by the best example of a policy community was agriculture. As Grant shows in his chapter on agriculture, from 1945 right through until the 1990s, an extremely close and mutually supportive relationship existed between the Ministry of Agriculture, Fisheries and Food (MAFF) and the National Farmers' Union (NFU). This agricultural policy community effectively regulated the institutional agenda, and sustained the dominant paradigm, which ensured that agricultural policy in Britain prioritized the maintenance and maximization of domestic food production, via routine subsidies to British farmers, thereby guaranteeing prices and incomes for them. This productionist paradigm was intended to prevent food shortages, for these would lead either to a return to food rationing (as had been the case during the Second World War) or to rising food prices (in accordance with the laws of supply and demand, whereby the price of a commodity increases if demand outstrips supply), neither of which would have been popular with the electorate. In this context, this productionist paradigm could be defended politically as being in the interests of producers (farmers) and consumers alike.

Another good example of a policy community until the 1990s was provided by the sphere of transport. As Robinson's chapter explains, throughout much of the post-war period, there existed a strong transport policy community in Britain, comprising the Department of Transport and the 'road lobby', namely the British Road Federation, the AA and RAC, the construction industry, and the Society of Motor Manufacturers and Traders. Although the number of organized interests was somewhat larger than in most policy communities, their commonality of interests – in promoting policies favourable to private transport and road-building – normally ensured a strong degree of cohesion and unity between them. Certainly, those who sought to promote public transport and/or highlight the environmental consequences of building more roads to cope with an increasing number of cars and lorries found themselves largely marginalized or excluded altogether.

Elsewhere, as Clyde Chitty's chapter illustrates, education policy in Britain, prior to the 1980s, entailed a close relationship between central government (via the Department of Education), local government (through local education authorities), individual schools and colleges, and the teaching unions. As such, there was a strong emphasis on partnership between these various bodies in the formulation and implementation of education policy.

In the sphere of health policy, meanwhile, as illustrated by Jones's chapter, the Department of Health and the British Medical Association (BMA) were generally characterized by a very close relationship until the 1980s, thereby constituting a health policy community. Certainly, one writer has asserted that on many issues, until the 1980s, there existed 'a partnership between the medical profession and the DH [Department of Health] equivalent to those that exist[ed] in the educational and agricultural policy communities between the relevant Departments and their client groups' (Ham, 1999: 130). Consequently, the BMA and the Department of Health

> excluded other actors who did not share their perceptions of health policy. This exclusion occurred through institutional arrangements – when making policy the Ministry gave formal recognition to the doctors – and through ideology – the notion of clinical autonomy meant that it was the doctors alone who had responsibility for health policy in the last instance. (Smith, 1993: 175)

This clearly indicates the extent to which policy communities and dominant (policy) paradigms tend to be interlinked and mutually reinforcing, thereby frequently militating against policy change.

The predominance of the 'Departmental manager' role adopted by Ministers

Prior to the 1980s, many senior (Cabinet) Ministers adopted a mainly managerial role *vis-à-vis* the Departments to which they were variously appointed. The prevalence of this managerial role – confirmed by Headey's (1974) seminal study of Cabinet Ministers – tended to entail the maintenance of existing Departmental policies, rather than the pursuit of significantly new policy initiatives. This was, of course, partly derived from the apparent efficacy, and thus widespread acceptance by most policy makers, of the wider ideological and political context noted above, and then reinforced by both the dominant (policy) paradigms or departmental philosophies, and the prevalence of the sundry policy communities. With the senior echelons of the Conservative Party strongly influenced by 'one nation' Conservatism, and senior Labour politicians effectively upholding a social democratic or revisionist approach, many Ministers from 1945 until the end of the 1970s generally sought to make existing policies work, to the extent that Ministerial attempts at introducing markedly new policies were the exception rather than the rule, with many seemingly concerned, first and foremost, with conflict avoidance. In an apparently non-ideological era of consensus politics, there was little desire or apparent need to change policies which appeared to be largely effective or electorally popular. Even if policies did seem to evince certain problems, the usual Ministerial response was to redouble efforts at making the policy more effective, rather than abandoning it altogether.

This, in turn, often entailed even closer or more frequent interaction with the relevant organized interests or other professional bodies who, along with the Department itself, constituted the policy community in the particular subsystem. Certainly, the pre-1980 prevalence of policy communities in certain areas of public policy, most notably agriculture, health and transport (but to some extent, education and housing too), ensured that only the most ideologically-motivated or politically-determined Minister would have been inclined to introduce new policies, and there were very few of these. Instead, most Cabinet Ministers seemed content 'merely' to manage their Departments, and ensure, as far as they could, that existing policies and programmes functioned effectively and smoothly. This further militated against a pro-active or agenda-setting role for most Cabinet Ministers.

Finally, with regard to the predominantly managerial role adopted by most senior Ministers until the 1980s, we need briefly to note the greater policy making and policy-determining role ascribed to senior civil servants until the 'Next Steps' reforms of the 1980s. This ensured not only that many Ministers were heavily reliant on the advice of their senior Departmental officials – who were themselves an integral component of any policy community in that particular policy subsystem, and often conducted routine negotiations with the leaders of the key organized interest(s), rather than the Minister *per se* – but that Ministers often delegated a considerable degree of the work to the senior civil servants, thereby reinforcing the latter's scope for shaping many aspects of public policy. Senior civil servants were therefore able, it seems, to influence many of their Department's policies, either through the advice they proffered to Ministers – as 'gatekeepers' of information, they could decide what the Minister needed to know, and/or subtly present the 'evidence' or policy options in such a manner as to steer their Minister towards a particular decision – or through their subsequent role in administering the policies and programmes formally approved by their Minister or/and the Cabinet. With many Cabinet Ministers only able to spend a limited amount of time actually in their Departments, due to the need to attend numerous meetings and committees elsewhere, a considerable volume of Departmental work was effectively delegated to senior civil servants. This, in turn, further reinforced the prevalence of Departmental philosophies and dominant policy paradigms, particularly when the Department was also part of a policy community, whereupon its senior civil servants – rather than the senior Minister – would be regularly and routinely involved in negotiations with the leaders of the Department's 'client' group(s).

A 'British policy style'

As we noted in Chapter 9 of *Policy Making in Britain*, prior to the 1980s at least, writers such as Jordan and Richardson (1982) discerned a discrete 'British policy style', comprising: clientelism, consultation, sectorization, institutionalization of compromise, and the development of exchange relationships. These five characteristics reflected the extent to which public policy in Britain was often 'made' within particular relatively autonomous (of each other) policy subsystems, in which Government Departments and their 'client' organized interest(s), jointly developed public policy between them, via regular discussion and dialogue – the 'logic of negotiation', which, in turn, fostered 'bureaucratic accommodation'. These negotiations were largely conducted in the context of shared values, whereby each Department and its client organized interest(s) broadly agreed on the overall aims and objectives of public policy in their particular sphere.

This general agreement itself reflected and reinforced the prevalence of 'policy paradigms', and ensured that discussions within the policy communities were often largely administrative or technical, to the extent that policy making – or, in many cases, piecemeal policy modification – was de-politicized. These features were themselves instrumental in fostering relative continuity and stability in many areas of public policy prior to the 1980s, for the members of a policy community would normally desire to maintain the status quo as far as practicably possible, because this reflected the outcome of previous bargaining and negotiation, and shared values or goals. As such, policy communities would not normally wish to see significant departures from existing policies, unless they could be persuaded that reform was absolutely vital, and in their interests. However, such instances were very few and far between, particularly during an era of consensus politics in general, and when many, if not, most Cabinet Ministers, adopted a 'manager' role *vis-à-vis* their Departments (rather than an agenda-setting or innovator role).

Sources of change in British public policy since the 1980s

In most of the policy areas examined in this book, significant changes did not occur until the 1980s and 1990s, many of which have been maintained into the early 21st century. The 1970s had been characterized by serious and recurring economic, industrial relations and social problems, which, in turn, served to raise questions about whether Britain was becoming 'ungovernable' or/and was experiencing an 'overload of government' (King, 1976; see also Clutterbuck, 1978; Hutber, 1978; Kavanagh, 1980; Gamble, 1981; Beer, 1982). In this context, some academics, journalists and (Conservative) politicians – the nascent New Right – began to query the continued viability of various policies and programmes which had prevailed or been introduced (with bipartisan support) since the 1940s, along with the principles and values which had underpinned them.

Furthermore, the involvement of sundry organized interests in policy making, particularly via the various policy communities, was also called into question, for not only were such groups held, in large part, responsible for the apparent 'overload of government', or the manner in which Britain was becoming 'ungovernable', they were also deemed, as a consequence, to be a major impediment to policy change. Some critics believed that the emphasis on 'bureaucratic accommodation' and associated features of a consultative, consensual mode of policy making had led to a form of 'institutional sclerosis' (Olson, 1982), with an ossification of policy programmes and policy making processes. Overcoming these alleged problems, and devising new policies to replace those which appeared to be failing – intellectually, and quite possibly financially, bankrupt – would entail confronting many policy communities and the privileged 'insider' status which they accorded to various organized interests, as well as challenging the associated 'policy paradigms' prevalent in a number of Departments, and inculcated by their senior civil servants. In short, the pursuit of new policies would also necessitate new forms of policy making. This, in turn, would mean that some policy actors would need to be marginalized or downgraded (trade unions, along with various other organized interests and professional bodies), or, at the very least, their roles significantly transformed (most notably senior civil servants), whilst new actors were incorporated into the policy-making process (Special Advisers and think-tanks), and some extant policy actors adopted new roles (such as Cabinet Ministers becoming 'proactive' or 'agenda-setters' *vis-à-vis* their Departments, rather than acting primarily as 'mere' managers).

The wider ideological and political context

Certainly, the Conservative Governments of Margaret Thatcher and John Major (from 1979 to 1997) were characterized by a significantly different ideological perspective compared to pre-1979 Conservative Governments (indeed, Conservatives hitherto had proudly defined themselves as being non-ideological). As Thain explains in Chapter 2, Keynesian social democracy crumbled during the 1970s, and was increasingly supplanted by variants of monetarism – enthusiastically subscribed to by many senior Conservatives, as well as sympathetic (New Right) think-tanks, academics and journalists – whereby control of the money supply and curbing inflation were prioritized over the maintenance of full employment, and the emphasis shifted decisively towards controlling, if not actually cutting, public expenditure. At the same time, the previous emphasis on governmental intervention or public provision to rectify alleged market failure was totally transformed, so that policy failures were increasingly attributed to excessive or unwarranted governmental intervention, which could only be rectified and obviated by restoring market mechanisms. (Sir Keith Joseph – a major intellectual and ideological influence on Margaret Thatcher, and one of her Cabinet Ministers in the 1980s – had once declared that capitalism in Britain had not failed; it had never been allowed to flourish, and thereby prove its virtues, due to incessant political interference, and the pernicious effects of an anti-enterprise culture.) In this context, the 1980s and 1990s witnessed an increasing emphasis on deregulation, liberalization and privatization (all inextricably linked to the avowed objective of 'rolling back the state'), coupled with the promotion of consumer choice – and thus a degree of competitiveness – in those parts of the public sector where outright privatization was not deemed feasible or electorally acceptable.

Committed to 'the market' (economy), the renaissance of private enterprise, greater competition, consumer (over producer) interests, much more rigorous control of public expenditure, reform (retrenchment) of the welfare state and public services, and challenging the role and influence of 'vested' organized interests – both to promote consumer sovereignty and restore the authority of government – the post-1979 Conservative

Governments sought to challenge many policies, programmes or policy objectives during the 1980s and 1990s, which, in turn, frequently entailed confronting, destabilizing or marginalizing the organized interests who had previously been intimately involved in policy making in 'their' policy subsystem.

This was most evident with regard to the trade unions and associated professional bodies or representative organizations, both at a general level, but also at the sectoral level. At the general level, trade unions were increasingly excluded from policy making by Conservative Ministers, with bodies like the National Economic Development Council (NEDC) meeting less frequently as the 1980s progressed, and with senior Ministers (Secretaries of State and the Chancellor) increasingly sending their Junior Ministers or civil servants to the meetings instead. Eventually, in 1992, the NEDC was finally abolished. Other bodies on which the trade unions had formerly enjoyed representation comparable to that of employers' organizations, such as the Manpower Services Commission (MSC), were either abolished too, or radically reformed and restructured in a manner which significantly reduced the trade unions' representation, and thereby left them with far fewer seats around the decision-taking table (whilst employers' representatives found themselves being granted rather more seats).

The increasing exclusion of the trade unions from a range of decision-taking bodies concerned with economic and industrial policy making, reflected both ideological precepts, and the commitment to a certain governing style. Ideologically, the post-1979 Conservative Governments' commitment to reviving the role of 'the market', and relying on 'supply and demand' to determine what was produced (and what wages would be paid to those involved in production), in response to consumer demand and profitability, meant that the trade unions were increasingly excluded from economic and industrial policy making.

The New Right's view was that employers – responding to 'market forces', and ultimately accountable to their companies' shareholders – should enjoy sovereignty over the day-to-day management of their firms or enterprises, and not have to concern themselves with what the trade unions wanted (or did not want). This, of course, was also part of the Conservatives' emphasis on restoring 'management's right to manage', aligned with the revival of 'labour market discipline'. Meanwhile, the primary role of government was to maintain the right framework in which 'the market' could thrive, with particular emphasis on curbing inflation through control of the money supply, whilst also seeking to reduce public expenditure. These perspectives left little room for the involvement of trade unions in economic and industrial policy making in the 1980s and 1990s, and hence they found themselves being increasingly marginalized.

However, this ideological perspective was also buttressed by the Thatcher Governments' style of governing, which often entailed imposing changes on particular policy subsystems – what has been referred to as 'despotic power' (Smith, 1993: 95–6). When Conservative Ministers sought to introduce significant reforms into policy areas such as education and health during the late 1980s, they did so in spite of inevitable trade union opposition. Given that many Conservatives viewed the trade unions as part of the problem with regard to making certain industries or public services more dynamic, efficient and responsive to consumer choice, and deeming the leaders of many trade unions to be self-serving oligarchies, it was hardly surprising that some Ministers pursued policy change without seeking trade union advice or consent. As we will note below, reforms of the education system and the health service were introduced in spite of strong and vocal opposition from teaching unions and the BMA respectively. This opposition, of course, was then deemed by Ministers to vindicate their original decision not to consult the 'representative bodies' in the first place.

Besides, whilst the Thatcher Governments waxed lyrical about their determination to 'roll back the state' – even though in many public services, the state actually became more directive and intrusive, via various reforms, targets, performance indicators, audits and funding mechanisms – they were also concerned to restore the authority of government. (On the rise of the regulatory state, see Moran, 2000; 2001; on the concomitant rise of the 'audit society', see Power, 1994; 1997.) As it was the trade unions who were deemed to have played a major part in undermining the authority of government in the 1970s, rendering Britain increasingly ungovernable, many Conservative Ministers in the 1980s felt little obligation to seek trade union approval prior to introducing reforms in the public sector. Trade union opposition was deemed to be entirely predictable and self-interested, and further reflected the extent to which the trade unions were apparently 'selfish vested interests' whose activities were inimical to the wider 'national interest'.

However, the Conservative Governments, particularly during John Major's premiership in the 1990s, invariably found it necessary to solicit the advice or co-operation of certain trade unions and professional 'representational' bodies at the implementation stage, when problems with the original policy or reform became apparent. Indeed, in the sphere of education especially, some of the ensuing problems derived from non-cooperation or non-compliance by those representative institutions which had been marginalized or bypassed when the policy was originally being formulated. In such circumstances, some trade unions or professional bodies found themselves being incorporated back into the policy process, albeit on new terms, and possibly alongside other bodies and sources of advice.

Yet this also illustrated the extent to which the 'implementation stage' is actually an integral and ongoing part of the policy-making process – rather than an entirely separate and final stage – whereby public policy is often modified in accordance with problems which only become apparent during the implementation 'stage'. This means that representative bodies and 'street-level bureaucrats' who may have had little or no input or influence *vis-à-vis* the original formulation of the policy can subsequently play a notable role in modifying it, in order to render it more practicable and effective.

The re-incorporation of various representative bodies seems to have continued apace under the Blair Governments since 1997, although the trade unions have not regained their pre-1979 input into economic and industrial policy making. What does seem to have continued since 1997, though, is the renewed emphasis on consultation with 'interested parties' in various policy areas or subsystems, even though this may be consultation over reforms which the Blair Governments have already resolved to pursue, and whose principles or objectives are thus non-negotiable. This return to consultation has been evident on the Blair Governments' penchant for establishing a range of advisory bodies, task forces and working parties. There has also been a notable trend towards seeking the advice of sundry experts, which itself has reflected a trend towards more evidence-based policy making. These developments, of course, have emerged alongside the increased use of Special Advisers in the core executive.

Paradigm shifts

Many aspects of public policy in Britain have been subject to a 'paradigm shift' since the 1980s, either due to the Thatcher–Major Governments' new ideological framework and eschewal of traditional modes of consultation, or as a result of various crises in particular policy systems. In either case, a major consequence was the undermining of the normative and operational paradigm which had hitherto strongly shaped policy making and public policy 'outputs' in the policy sector concerned, and which had constituted a powerful force for (relative) policy continuity. In such instances, 'despotic power' and/or new issues have provided a challenge to the norms and policy goals which had previously prevailed in key policy subsystems, and which had effectively sustained (and thus protected) the institutional agenda from the wider systemic agenda.

For example, Jones's chapter on health policy shows how the Thatcher–Major Governments placed greater emphasis on modes and sources of health care other than traditionally provided by NHS hospitals. In particular, private medical (and related insurance) schemes were explicitly promoted, and although the majority of people continued to rely on – or choose – the NHS for their medical treatment, there was an increasing emphasis on the rights and preferences of patients themselves. This, of course, constituted something of a challenge to the medical profession, and doctors in particular, whose medical opinion had hitherto been widely viewed as sacrosanct. Instead, the rights and choices of patients were supposed to be granted much greater weight in health care (although these choices and preferences were obviously contingent on resource constraints).

Meanwhile, whereas improved health treatment had previously been inextricably linked to increased health expenditure and hospital building programmes, funded primarily by general taxation, the period since the 1980s has heralded a much greater emphasis on such criteria as efficiency, cost-effectiveness and value-for-money. In other words, there emerged a much greater concern to gain improvements and increases in health 'outputs' from existing expenditure on the NHS, rather than automatically assuming that 'outputs' could only be increased by additional expenditure.

Of course, government expenditure on the NHS has increased during this period, but even the Blair Governments, with Gordon Brown as Chancellor, have insisted that all additional resources allocated to the NHS must be linked to, or subsequently evince, improved performance, and the attainment of specified targets.

Meanwhile, although a commitment remains to building new hospitals (or modernizing existing ones) as a means of improving health care and meeting increased demand, the emphasis has shifted towards private sector provision of infrastructure, most notably through the Private Finance Initiative (PFI). Elsewhere, there has been an increasing emphasis on preventative health care, and public health campaigns, with policy makers increasingly promoting measures and life-style changes which ought to reduce the likelihood of diseases and illnesses in later life (and which ought to prevent further demands on an over-stretched NHS).

Elsewhere, as Grant's chapter on agricultural policy explains, the various crises which have beset the farming industry since the mid-1990s, have challenged – albeit with varying degrees of success – some of the principles and precepts which previously constituted the dominant (productionist) paradigm in agricultural policy in post-war Britain. It has become apparent that intensive (often industrialized) and large-scale farming methods, with high densities of cattle often kept in very close proximity (yielding problems pertaining to hygiene and the spread of harmful bacteria), and sometimes fed cheap – but unsafe – animal feed, can seriously compromise the safety of food produced for human consumption. Various crises, such as the salmonella-in-egg-production episode, the BSE crisis of the mid-1990s (and the consequent concern over the link between BSE and variant Creutzfeldt–Jakob Disease (vCJD) which could – and in a few cases, did – fatally affect humans), and the 2001 foot-and-mouth epidemic, have therefore pushed food safety to the top of the institutional policy agenda, thereby weakening the former agricultural policy paradigm in which maximizing food production was an over-riding priority, and automatically assumed to be a good policy *per se*.

Similarly, the increased use of agri-chemicals and pesticides, to maximize crop production, has become associated with various environmental problems, most notably the pollution of rivers (near to farms) and the poisoning of various forms of wildlife in the countryside. This is quite apart from concomitant concerns about whether such chemicals, as applied to crops, vegetables and fruit, are also a threat to human health and safety.

Consequently, concerns over food safety have been conjoined with concerns about the environmental impact of modern intensive farming methods, derived from the goal of maximizing production in order to maintain a cheap and ready supply of food, and therefore reduce reliance on imports of food. The productionist paradigm has thus been seriously challenged since the 1990s, and weakened further by an increased questioning of why agriculture – unlike other industries – should continue to be so heavily subsidized. Although it would, perhaps, be an exaggeration to say that the productionist paradigm has been completely destroyed, it is clear that other considerations and criteria now shape agricultural policies and food production, as symbolized by the 2001 abolition of the Ministry of Agriculture, Fisheries and Food (MAFF), and its replacement by the Department of the Environment, Food and Rural Affairs (DEFRA).

Similarly, Robinson shows how environmental concerns – and, to some extent, health concerns too – have yielded something of a paradigm shift in the sphere of transport policy since the 1990s. Such concerns have led to a questioning of the 'predict and provide' model of a market-based, pro-private transport policy which prevailed until the 1990s, by which time there was increasing opposition – from a range of sources and social groups – to the policy of constantly building new roads and motorway bypasses as a means of reducing traffic congestion. It was variously argued that as the volume of traffic seemed to increase in proportion to the road space available, simply building more roads would ultimately do little to reduce traffic congestion: it might actually exacerbate and increase it.

In tandem with this argument against the 'predict and provide' paradigm which had prevailed in the sphere of transport policy throughout the post-war era, it was also alleged that increases in both road-building and the volume of traffic were themselves a significant cause of various environmental and health problems in contemporary Britain, allegations supported by a growing body of medical and scientific evidence. Consequently, although various road-building schemes have continued, there has also been consideration of alternative transport strategies actually intended to reduce the volume of traffic on Britain's roads, with congestion-charging (a form of 'restrict-and-provide') in central London providing perhaps the most obvious example – an originally controversial policy which several other cities in Britain are now proposing to adopt. There has also been a greater willingness by transport policy makers to consider 'road pricing' and 'motorway tolls', whereby motorists would be charged for using certain roads, although for political and electoral reasons, Ministers are invariably anxious about allegations of being 'anti-car', or adding to business costs (and thus undermining competitiveness).

The new sources of knowledge or scientific evidence which have sometimes served to challenge – sometimes to the point of discrediting – the dominant paradigm in particular policy domains, have also played a notable part in destabilizing various policy communities during the 1980s and 1990s.

Destabilization of policy communities

As we noted in Chapter 5 of *Policy Making in Britain*, policy communities can be challenged or destabilized in various ways. Economic circumstances might prove detrimental to a policy community, necessitating (or being used as a means of legitimizing) a significant change of policy which effectively weakens the policy community. A government pursuing a new ideological approach might similarly serve to challenge and undermine a policy community. Indeed, during the 1980s, significantly altered economic circumstances, and the particular ideological perspective of the Thatcher Governments – the free economy and the strong state, as Gamble characterized it (Gamble, 1988) – combined to challenge the hitherto dominance and stability of various policy communities in Britain.

As we noted above, this was certainly the case with the Thatcher Governments' pursuit of education reform during the late 1980s, which entailed defying the teaching unions and ignoring their opposition to major reforms of primary and secondary education. Furthermore, the teaching unions increasingly found that their traditional representation, on various bodies concerned with the governance of education, was reduced. Instead, their places – particularly on school governing bodies – were increasingly allocated to parent-governers, headteachers, and members of the (local) business community. Of course, this also served greatly to reduce the role and representation of local education authorities in the governance of education.

Similarly, with regard to industrial relations and labour market policy, the role of the trade unions was greatly reduced by the Thatcher–Major Governments, and their representation on various advisory or policy-influencing bodies diminished accordingly (whereas employers frequently saw their representation markedly increased). Conservative Ministers invariably justified such marginalization of the trade unions on the grounds this was a prerequisite of rendering the British economy more competitive, and providing business with the type of workforce it needed at the end of the 20th century and into the 21st. This economic rationale, though, was also yoked to the Thatcher–Major Governments' ideological antipathy to trade unions (the latter also deemed to be wedded to an outdated and debilitating collectivist ethos, as well as being inherently and instinctively anti-enterprise), and thereby provided a powerful means of bypassing trade unions who were already seriously weakened due to the combined impact of Conservative trade union legislation and the loss of jobs – and thus of trade union members – derived from de-industrialization.

However, we noted that policy communities can also be challenged or undermined by new knowledge or scientific evidence which calls into question the former goals of public policy, and/or the practices of policy making, in a particular subsystem. Thus, for example, the transport policy community has been weakened somewhat since the 1990s partly as a consequence of new evidence about the detrimental environmental and health impacts of increased car usage and road-building, whilst the agricultural policy community has similarly been weakened or destabilized somewhat following a growing body of evidence about the environmental and health problems arising from modern methods of intensive farming and the extensive use of agri-chemicals and pesticides. Some of these were deemed to pose a threat to animals and wildlife on the one hand, and to humans on the other.

In both cases, the organized interests who formerly constituted an integral part of a close – and closed – policy community, subsequently found themselves obliged to 'share' the policy domain with other, previously excluded, bodies. In both cases, the policy community has been destabilized or opened-up somewhat, so that other groups or organized interests have also been granted involvement and, presumably, greater influence, in policy making. For example, with regard to policies concerning food production, the National Farmers' Union has increasingly found itself seeking to influence policy makers alongside medical experts and the British Medical Association, the Department of Health, nutritionists and consumer groups (Smith, 1991: 251). This, in turn, further challenges the hegemony of hitherto dominant paradigms, as the incorporation of new(er) groups both reflects and reinforces the advocacy of alternative policies or priorities.

Another means by which some policy communities have been challenged since the 1980s – albeit in the context of the other factors just noted – is that of 'despotic power', entailing an 'activist' or agenda-setting Minister imposing change in a particular sphere of policy. Such imposition of policy change sometimes entailed confronting or bypassing the key organized interest(s) who normally enjoyed privileged insider status *vis-à-vis* a particular government department. The spheres of both education and health are good examples of this phenomenon, for in the late 1980s and early 1990s, the relevant Conservative Secretaries of State 'took on' or largely ignored the teaching unions and medical profession respectively, in order to introduce significant changes of policy which were generally opposed by these bodies. In so doing, the Ministers destabilized the education and health policy communities, and sought the advice of other – more politically sympathetic – individuals and bodies instead. More recently, following its re-election in June 2001, the Blair Government effectively defied the National Farmers' Union (NFU) by abolishing the Ministry of Agriculture, Fisheries and Food (with whom the NFU had previously enjoyed a very close and beneficial relationship for more than 50 years), and replacing it with the more eclectic Department of the Environment, Food and Rural Affairs. Such a move hardly endeared the farming community to a Labour administration, which they already blamed for many of the ills afflicting British agriculture.

Changes to the 'British policy style'

All of the above developments both reflected and reinforced a discernible change to what Jordan and Richardson (1982) had characterized as the dominant 'British policy style'.

Many changes in British public policy since the 1980s have either arisen from, or themselves caused, changes to the manner in which policy is 'made'. As we discussed in Chapter 9 of *Policy Making in Britain*, the former emphasis on *clientelism* and relatively autonomous, closed policy communities, in which public policy was often determined through a process of 'bureaucratic accommodation', has been superseded somewhat by the involvement, in many areas of public policy, of a wider range of organized interests, such as groups who were previously 'outsiders', as well as think-tanks, and various individuals, of whom Special (Ministerial) Advisers are, perhaps, the most notable example.

This eclecticism has been compounded by the greater emphasis on co-ordination between departments, especially since 1997 – 'joined-up government' – reflecting the fact that many problems are now acknowledged to be multi-causal in origin, and therefore require greater co-operation between different Ministers and their Departments, as well as an input from a wider range of outside bodies and experts. This trend clearly undermines 'sectorization', which was another of the features of the British 'policy style' identified by Jordan and Richardson (1982).

However, what has also enhanced these trends is the transformation from government to governance, whereupon many policies in Britain today are not only shaped by a wider range of actors, but also determined at different levels, beyond Westminster and Whitehall, of which central government is now only one. Of course, even in the halcyon days of Jordan and Richardson's British 'policy style', sub-national actors – most notably local government – often played an important role in the policy process, particularly at the implementation 'stage'. However, since the 1980s, although local government itself has been considerably weakened, a variety of other organizations have acquired a new or enhanced policy role, most notably the hundreds of agencies established via the Next Steps reform of the civil service (initiated by the third – 1987–90 – Thatcher Government, and continued apace by the subsequent Major and Blair Governments), and the plethora of bodies in both the private and voluntary sectors who have been ascribed various roles in the policy process since the 1980s.

Post-1999 devolution has also introduced new policy actors in the guise of the Scottish Parliament, the National Assembly for Wales, and the Regional Development Agencies in England. Many of these devolved bodies themselves place considerable emphasis on partnership schemes in public policy, entailing consultation with, and co-ordination between, organizations from the public, private and voluntary sectors.

Of course, the process of European integration has itself added a major dimension to the trend from government to governance, constituting another level at which policies are increasingly determined, with EU member states, via their national and sub-national policy actors, expected to implement them. However, as we noted in Chapter 8 of *Policy Making in Britain*, the process and impact of Europeanization have been uneven, with some policy areas and departments more involved or affected by others. Moreover, in spite of Britain's 'awkward partner' reputation, some departments have actually developed a more positive view of the EU, due to shared agendas or objectives in certain areas of policy. In such cases, the departments have often been able – and willing – to develop a more constructive engagement with the EU, and viewed it as an ally, rather than a threat.

The exceptional case of British foreign policy

If there is one exception to the trend for policies or the policy-making process in Britain to have undergone notable changes since the 1980s, it is foreign policy. Indeed, as Marsh illustrated in Chapter 4, foreign policy has been characterized by considerable continuity throughout the post-war period, right up until the present day. The 1980s' 'point of departure' which can analytically be applied to most other areas of British public policy is not readily applicable to foreign policy. This is not to say that foreign policy has not witnessed changes – the decline of empire and Commonwealth is clearly a major post-war development – but many such changes occurred relatively gradually, during the 1950s and 1960s, rather than after 1979.

Of course, the dramatic collapse of the Soviet Union at the very end of the 1980s, heralding the end of the Cold War – which had dominated much of British foreign (and defence) policy since 1946 – might be cited as a clear example of a major change occurring after 1979, but the crucial point here is that it did not significantly alter the general features of British foreign policy. During the 1990s (through to the beginning of the 21st century), as in the 1950s and 1960s, British foreign policy sought to retain a global role for Britain, in spite of relative decline, the dissipation of the empire, and the emergence of the United States as a world superpower and hegemon of the (Western) neo-liberal capitalist international order. Indeed, it was precisely these developments which underpinned the determination of Britain's foreign policy makers to secure a continued role for Britain in global affairs, and this has most clearly manifested itself through the cultivation of the 'special relationship' with the United States (US), whereby Britain and the US perceive and portray themselves as the bulwark of Western values and interests. Prior to the 1990s, the Soviet Union was axiomatically assumed to be the major threat to these values and interests, whilst since the 1990s (and more particularly during the early 21st century), global terrorism and 'rogue states' have underpinned the 'special relationship' between Britain and the US. As Condoleezza Rice asserted, during a brief visit to Britain in early 2005, following her appointment as US Secretary of State:

> ... we [the US] have no better friend, we have no better ally. We deeply value the close relationship between our two countries, and, of course, we share so much, but we, of course, also share a global agenda as well. ... We have done so much together, and we still have so much to do together. (*The Guardian*, 5 February 2005)

Like any close partnership, the Anglo-American 'special relationship' has occasionally been subject to disagreements, with a corresponding cooling of relations, but these have never been sufficiently deep or damaging to undermine the overall commonality of interests between the two countries, and which has been the linchpin of British foreign policy to such a large extent since 1945.

Of course, the privileging of the 'special relationship' with the US is also a major reason (but by no means the only one) why Britain has never been an enthusiastic or wholehearted member of the European Community/Union, acquiring, instead, a reputation for being an 'awkward partner'. Although Britain's relationship with its European partners became particularly strained during the 1979–97 Thatcher–Major Governments, British lack of enthusiasm for European integration and the concomitant pooling of sovereignty – coupled with the aforementioned concern to maintain a global role far beyond Europe – predated the Thatcher–Major years, to the extent that Britain declined to involve itself in the original creation of the European Economic Community in the 1950s. Even then, Britain saw its interests primarily in terms of the 'special relationship' with the US, and continued ties and trade links with the Commonwealth. Europe was the least important of the 'three circles' of British foreign policy delineated by Churchill. Even though the dissipation of the Commonwealth did prompt Britain – partly under pressure from the US – to turn towards Europe from the 1960s onwards, the 'special relationship' between Britain and the US remained paramount throughout, and remains so today.

Conclusion

With the notable exception of foreign policy, most of the key developments in British public policy have occurred since the 1980s, although the emergence of neo-liberalism in the realm of economic policy emerged from the wreckage of the 1970s collapse of Keynesian social democracy. Thereafter, various key policies underwent varying degrees of change, not only in terms of objectives and content, but also in terms of the discourses associated with them, with notions such as 'accountability', 'choice', competition', 'consumer sovereignty', 'efficiency', 'responsiveness to service users' and 'value-for-money' frequently cited as the purpose of reform in many policy areas, particularly those which might be deemed core components of the welfare state. Certainly, these values have become particularly prominent in policy areas such as education and health, where reforms have often been couched in terms of empowering parents and patients respectively.

Another concomitant development in British public policy since the 1980s has been the increasing promotion of 'the market', and involvement of the private sector in areas of public policy in which the state had previously played a major – if not the dominant – role. In the sphere of health policy, for example, not only was private health care and medical insurance promoted during the 1980s; since the 1990s, private capital has increasingly been used to finance the building of new hospitals (or modernize existing ones), even though politicians insist that the NHS remains free to patients at the point of access or need. In other policy areas where there has long been a 'mixed economy', entailing a combination of public and private provision, the period since the 1980s has evinced a conscious shift in the balance towards the private sector, with public provision increasingly becoming 'residualized'. This changing shift towards a greater role for private provision has been most apparent with regard to pensions and housing policy.

Other policy areas, such as agriculture and transport, have undergone changes partly as a consequence of increasing concerns over environmental issues and public health. Such concerns have themselves been fuelled by a growing body of well-publicized medical and scientific evidence identifying certain environmental and health risks arising from intensive farming methods (including the use of agri-chemicals and pesticides) and increased volumes of traffic. In the case of agriculture, in particular, public anxiety has been greatly exacerbated by a number of crises concerning British farming since the late 1980s, all of which served to push food safety (and to some extent, animal welfare) firmly onto the policy agenda.

In many areas of British public policy, such developments have either arisen from, or themselves prompted, changes to the style of policy making and/or the involvement of new actors in the policy process. For example, the 1980s witnessed various policy communities – most notably those of education and health – being by-passed or destabilized by Ministers determined to introduce significant changes to extant policies and practices. Other policy communities – most notably agriculture and transport – were undermined somewhat either by new knowledge and scientific evidence, which effectively called into question the assumptions and practices on which policy had hitherto been based, or by the entrance (into what had formerly been a closed policy community) of hitherto 'outsiders' who succeeded in changing the terms of debate, and challenged the dominant discourses, thereby altering the institutional agenda, and necessitating consideration of new issues by policy makers.

Changes, both to particular policies and the style of policy making, are also attributable to changes within the core executive, most notably the downgrading of the policy advice role previously fulfilled by senior civil servants, as Ministers have increasingly adopted an agenda-setting or activist role. At the same time, Ministers have increasingly looked to additional or alternative sources of advice, most notably from Special Advisers, and think-tanks, whilst the Prime Minister, Tony Blair, has both strengthened the role of his Downing Street Policy Directorate (formerly the Policy Unit), whilst enhancing the co-ordinating role of the Cabinet Office. He has also evinced a penchant for establishing a plethora of advisory groups and working parties, which often include sundry experts from particular policy areas.

These developments have been further accompanied by increasing recourse to such innovations as 'pilot schemes' to test and evaluate new policy initiatives (and thereby gauge potential implementation problems), policy transfer and evidence-based policy making. Such innovations have themselves been made more viable by the transition to governance, for this itself facilitates greater policy divergence at different levels of the polity, with different regions and cities increasingly learning from each others' experiences in devising new policies, whereupon policies can then be adopted, but adapted, as appropriate for a particular city or region in another part of the country.

As such, British public policy in the early 21st century is in a state of considerable flux, whilst the policy 'process' itself is more variegated, and involves a greater number of actors and influences. The core executive, therefore, finds itself simultaneously seeking both to relinquish and retain control, whilst public policy is increasingly prone to various tensions arising from divergence and diversity. Consequently, policy making in Britain is now rather more 'messy' than it used to be. By the same token, however, it is also considerably more interesting to study.

Bibliography

Abel-Smith, Brian (1953) *The Reform of Social Security*, Fabian Research Series No. 161. London: Fabian Publications/Victor Gollancz.

Abel-Smith, Brian and Townsend, Peter (1955) *New Pensions for the Old*, Fabian Research Series No. 171. London: Fabian Publications.

Abel-Smith, Brian and Townsend, Peter (1965) *The Poor and the Poorest*, LSE Occasional Papers on Social Administration No. 17. London: Bell & Sons.

Alden, E. (2002) 'Europe freezes terrorist assets worth $35 million', *The Financial Times*, 8 April 2002.

Allen, V.L. (1960) *Trade Unions and the Government*. London: Allen & Unwin.

Anderson, Perry (1977) 'The limits and possibilities of trade union action', in Tom Clarke and Laurie Clements (eds), *Trade Unions under Capitalism*. London: Fontana.

Andrew, Mark, Evans, Alan, Koundouri, Phoebe and Meen, Geoffrey (2003) *Residential Stamp Duty: Time for a Change?* London: CML.

Araki, Hiroshi (2000) 'Ideas and welfare: the Conservative transformation of the British pension regime', *Journal of Social Policy*, 29 (4): 599–621.

Arthur, Terry (2001) 'UK pension policy: world leader turning laggard?', *Economic Affairs*, December: 41–5.

Ashby, Eric and Anderson, Mary (1981) *The Politics of Clean Air*. Oxford: Clarendon Press.

Atkinson, John (1977) 'The developing relationship between the state pension scheme and occupational pension schemes', *Social and Economic Administration*, 11 (3): 216–25.

Auld, Robin (1976) *William Tyndale Junior and Infants Schools Public Inquiry: A Report to the Inner London Education Authority by Robin Auld, QC*. London: Inner London Education Authority.

Automobile Association (2002) *The 10-Year Transport Plan – Will We Ever Get There? What the Key Players Say About the Plan*. Basingstoke: Automobile Association.

Baker, Kenneth (1993) *The Turbulent Years: My Life in Politics*. London: Faber & Faber.

Balchin Paul and Rhoden, Maureen (2002) *Housing Policy: An Introduction*, 4th edn. London: Routledge.

Baldwin, Peter (1994) 'Beveridge in the *longue durée*', in J. Hills, J. Ditch and H. Glennerster (eds), *Beveridge and Social Security*. Oxford: Clarendon Press.

Baldry, Tony (1985) 'Time to talk', *Reformer* (Tory Reform Group Quarterly), Summer.

Ball, Michael (1985) 'Coming to terms with owner occupation', *Capital and Class*, 24: 15–24.

Ball, Stephen (1984) 'Introduction: comprehensives in crisis?', in Stephen Ball (ed.), *Comprehensive Schooling: A Reader*. Lewes: Falmer Press.

Bank of England (1997) 'Changes at the Bank of England', *Bank of England Quarterly Bulletin*, 37 (3): 241–7.

Banting, Keith (1979) *Poverty, Politics and Policy*. Basingstoke: Macmillan.

Barker, Tony, Byrne, Iain and Veall, Anjuli (2000) *Ruling by Task Force*. London: Politico's/Democratic Audit.

Barling, David and Lang, Tim (2003) 'A reluctant food policy? The first five years of food policy under Labour', *Political Quarterly*, 74 (1): 8–18.

Barnett, Correlli (1987) *The Audit of War: The Illusion and Reality of Britain as a Great Nation.* Basingstoke: Macmillan.

Batteson, C.H. (1999) 'The 1944 Education Act reconsidered', *Educational Review*, 51 (1): 5–15.

Baylis, John (1984) 'Britain, the Brussels pact and the continental commitment', *International Affairs*, 60 (4): 615–29.

Baylis, John (1989) *British Defence Policy: Striking the Right Balance.* Basingstoke: Macmillan.

BBC2 (1996) *Safe With Us*, September.

Beer, Samuel (1982) *Britain Against Itself.* London: Faber & Faber.

Bell, Coral (1964) *The Debatable Alliance: An Essay in Anglo-American Relations.* Oxford: Oxford University Press.

Benn, Tony (1994) *Years of Hope: Diaries, Papers and Letters, 1940–1962.* London: Hutchinson.

Benson, J. (1982) 'A framework for policy analysis', in D. Rogers, and D. Whetten & Associates (eds), *Interorganizational Coordination: Theory, Research and Implementation.* Ames, IA: Iowa State University Press.

Berridge, Virginia (2003) 'Postwar smoking policy in the UK and the redefinition of public health', *20th Century British History*, 14 (1): 61–82.

Beveridge, William (1942) *Social Insurance and Allied Services*, Cmd 6404. London: HMSO.

Black Report (1979) *Inequalities and Health.* London: DHSS.

Blackburn, Robin (2002) *Banking on Death.* London: Verso.

Blair, Tony (1996) *New Britain: My Vision of a Young Country.* London: Fourth Estate.

Blair, Tony (1998a) *The Third Way: New Politics for the New Century*, Fabian Pamphlet 588. London: Fabian Society.

Blair, Tony (1998b) *Leading the Way: A New Vision for Local Government.* London: Institute for Public Policy Research.

Blair, Tony (1999) 'Speech to the Lord Mayor of London's Banquet', 22 November (available at http://www.fco.gov.uk).

Blair, Tony (2002) *The Courage of Our Convictions: Why Reform of Public Services is the Route to Social Justice.* London: Fabian Society.

Blank, Stephen (1982) 'Britain: the politics of foreign economic policy, the domestic economy and the problem of pluralist stagnation', in Peter Katzenstein (ed.), *Between Power and Plenty.* Madison, WI: University of Wisconsin Press.

Blinken, A.J. (2001) 'The false crisis over the Atlantic', *Foreign Affairs*, 80 (3): 35–48.

Blinkin, Antony (1987) *Ally versus Ally: America, Europe and the Siberian Pipeline Crisis.* New York: Praeger.

Blumenthal, S. (1997) 'Along the Clinton–Blair axis', *The Times*, 5 May.

Board of Education (1943) *Educational Reconstruction.* London: HMSO.

Bogdanor, Vernon (1979) 'Power and participation', *Oxford Review of Education*, 5 (2): 157–68.

Bonoli, Giuliano (2000) *The Politics of Pension Reform.* Cambridge: Cambridge University Press.

Bosanquet, Nicholas (1983) *After the New Right.* London: Heinemann.

Boyd-Carpenter, John (1980) *Way of Life*: *The Memoirs of John Boyd-Carpenter.* London: Sidgwick & Jackson.

Bridgen, Paul (1999) 'Remedy for all ills: earnings-relation and the politics of pensions 1950s/1960s'. Unpublished paper given at the conference 'Relative Decline and Relative Poverty: Signposts to the Sixties?', at the University of Bristol, 13 May 1999.

Bridgen, Paul (2000) 'The one nation idea and state welfare', *Contemporary British History*, 14 (3): 83–104.

Bridgen, Paul and Lowe, Rodney (1998) *Welfare Policy under the Conservatives.* London: Public Record Office.

Brittan, Samuel (1971) *Steering the Economy*. Harmondsworth: Penguin.

Brittan, Samuel (1983) *The Role and Limits of Government: Essays in Political Economy*. London: Temple Smith.

Buiter, Willem and Miller, Marcus (1983) *Macroeconomic Consequences of a Change of Regime: The UK under Mrs Thatcher*, Centre for Labour Economics Discussion Paper 179. London: London School of Economics.

Bullock, Alan (1983) *The Life and Times of Ernest Bevin. Volume 3: Foreign Secretary, 1945–1951*. London: Heinemann.

Bulpitt, Jim (1986) 'The discipline of the new democracy: Mrs Thatcher's domestic statecraft', *Political Studies*, 34 (1): 19–39.

Burk, Kathleen and Cairncross, Alex (1992) *'Goodbye Great Britain': The 1976 IMF Crisis*. New Haven, CT: Yale University Press.

Butler, David and Sloman, Anne (1980) *British Political Facts 1900–1979*, 5th edn. Basingstoke: Macmillan.

Button, Kenneth (1995) 'UK environmental policy and transport', in T.S. Gray (ed.), *UK Environmental Policy in the 1990s*. Basingstoke: Macmillan.

Cahill, Michael (1994) *The New Social Policy*. Oxford: Blackwell.

Cairncross, Alex (1985) *Years of Recovery: British Economic Policy 1945–51*. London: Methuen.

Calder, Angus (1969) *The People's War: Britain 1939–45*. London: Jonathan Cape.

Callaghan, James (1987) *Time and Chance*. London: Collins/Fontana.

Campbell, C. and Rockman, B.A. (2001) 'Third way leadership, old way government: Blair, Clinton and the power to govern', *British Journal of Politics and International Relations*, 3 (1): 36–48.

Campbell, Duncan (1984) *The Unsinkable Aircraft Carrier: American Military Power in Britain*. London: Michael Joseph.

Carson, Rachel (1962) *Silent Spring*. London: Hamish Hamilton.

Castle, Barbara (1984) *The Castle Diaries, 1964–70*. London: Weidenfeld & Nicolson.

Castle, Barbara (1990) *The Castle Diaries, 1964–1976*. Basingstoke: Papermac (Macmillan).

Castle, Barbara (1993) *Fighting All The Way*. Basingstoke: Macmillan.

Castle, Barbara, Davies, Bryn, Land, Hilary, Townsend, Peter, Lynes, Tony and Macintyre, Ken (1998) *Fair Shares for Pensioners*: *Our Evidence to the Pensions Review Body*. London: Security in Retirement for Everyone.

Centre for Policy Studies (1983) *Personal and Portable Pensions for All*. London: Centre for Policy Studies.

Chalmers, Malcolm (1985) *Paying for Defence: Military Spending and British Decline*. London: Pluto Press.

Chamberlain, Muriel (1999) *Decolonization*, 2nd edn. Oxford: Blackwell.

Cheshire, Paul (1975) 'Management of the market: the economic aim of agricultural policy', in D. Murray, R. Thomas, W. Grant and N. Smith (eds), *Decision Making in Britain III: Agriculture, Parts 1–5*. Milton Keynes: Open University Press.

Chester, Norman (1975) *The Nationalization of British Industry, 1945–1951*. London: HMSO.

Chitty, Clyde (1989) *Towards a New Education System: The Victory of the New Right?* Lewes: Falmer Press.

Chitty, Clyde (2002) 'The role and status of LEAs: post-war pride and *fin de siècle* uncertainty', *Oxford Review of Education*, 28 (2&3): 261–73.

Chouraqui, Jean-Claude and Price, Robert (1984) 'Medium-term financial strategy: the co-ordination of fiscal and monetary policy', *OECD Economic Studies*, 2: 7–50.

Churchill College, University of Cambridge. Willink papers Box 2 file IV. Unpublished autobiography.

Clarence, Emma (2003) 'Railways: a policy derailed?', *Parliamentary Affairs*, 56 (3): 456–70.

Clarke, Peter (2002) *The Cripps Version: The Life of Sir Stafford Cripps 1889–1952*. London: Allen Lane.

Clarke, Roger, Davies, Stephen, Dobson, Paul and Waterson, Michael (2002) *Buyer Power and Competition in European Food Retailing*. Aldershot: Edward Elgar.

Clutterbuck, Richard (1978) *Britain in Agony*. London: Faber & Faber.

Cm 214 (1987) *Housing: The Government's Proposals*. London: HMSO.

Cm 552 (1988) *Air Pollution: The Government's Reply to the First Report from the Environment Committee Session 1987–88, HC 270–1*. London: HMSO.

Cm 693 (1989) *Roads for Prosperity*. London: HMSO.

Cm 2426 (1994) *Sustainable Development: The UK Strategy*. London: HMSO.

Cm 2674 (1994) *Royal Commission on Environmental Pollution, Eighteenth Report – Transport and the Environment*. London: HMSO.

Cm 3587 (1997) *The United Kingdom National Air Quality Strategy*. London: HMSO.

Cm 3950 (1998) *A New Deal for Transport: Better for Everyone (The Government's White Paper on the Future of Transport)*. London: HMSO.

Cm 5776 (2003) *UK Membership of the Single Currency: An Assessment of the Five Economic Tests*. London: The Stationery Office.

Cmd 6527 (1944) *Employment Policy*. London: HMSO.

Cmnd 1249 (1961) *Agriculture: Reports on Talks between the Agricultural Departments and the Farmers' Unions, June–December 1960*. London: HMSO.

Cmnd 2764 (1965) *The National Plan*. London: HMSO.

Cmnd 3057 (1966) *Transport Policy*. London: HMSO.

Cmnd 4369 (1970) *Roads for the Future: The New Inter-Urban Plan for England*. London: HMSO.

Cmnd 7132 (1978) *Policy for Roads: England 1978*. London: HMSO.

Cmnd 8852 (1983) *Royal Commission on Environmental Pollution, Ninth Report – Lead in the Environment*. London: HMSO.

Coates, David (1980) *Labour in Power? A Study of the Labour Government 1974–1979*. London: Longman.

Coates, David (1983) 'The question of trade union power', in David Coates and Gordon Johnston (eds), *Socialist Arguments*. Oxford: Martin Robertson.

Coates, David (1984) *The Context of British Politics*. London: Hutchinson.

Coker, Christopher (1986) *A Nation in Retreat?* London: Brassey's.

Coker, Christopher (1992) 'Britain and the new world order: the special relationship in the 1990s', *International Affairs*, 68 (3): 407–21.

Cole, Ian and Furbey, Robert (1994) *The Eclipse of Council Housing*. London: Routledge.

Coleman, Alice (1985) *Utopia on Trial*. London: Hilary Shipman.

Colville, John (1985) *The Fringes of Power: Downing Street Diaries, 1939–1955*. London: Hodder & Stoughton.

Commission for Integrated Transport (1999) *Guidance on Provisional Local Transport Plans – Advice by the Commission for Integrated Transport*. London: Commission for Integrated Transport.

Commission on Social Justice (1994) *Social Justice – Strategies for National Renewal*. London: Vintage.

Congdon, Tim (1989) *Monetarism Lost and Why it Must Be Regained*, Policy Study No. 106. London: Centre for Policy Studies.

Conservative Central Office (1949) *The Right Road for Britain*. London: Conservative Central Office.

Conservative Party (1947) *The Industrial Charter: A Statement of Conservative Industrial Policy*. London: Conservative Central Office.

Conservative Party (1979) *The Conservative Manifesto*. London: Conservative Central Office.

Conservative Research Department (1997) 'Security in retirement', *Politics Today*, 3: 87–102.

Cope, Helen (1999) *Housing Associations: Policy and Practice*, Basingstoke: Macmillan.

Corbett, A. (1969) 'The Tory educators', *New Society*, 22 May: 785–87.

Cox, Andrew (1988a) 'Neo-corporatism versus the corporate state', in Andrew Cox and Noel O'Sullivan (eds), *The Corporate State: Corporatism and the State Tradition in Western Europe*. Aldershot: Edward Elgar.

Cox, Andrew (1988b) 'The failure of corporatist state forms and policies in post-war Britain', in Andrew Cox and Noel O'Sullivan (eds), *The Corporate State: Corporatism and the State Tradition in Western Europe*. Aldershot: Edward Elgar.

Cox, Brian and Boyson, Rhodes (eds) (1975) *Black Paper 1975: The Fight for Education*. London: Dent.

Cox, Brian and Boyson, Rhodes (eds) (1977) *Black Paper 1977*. London: Maurice Temple Smith.

Cox, Brian and Dyson, Anthony (eds) (1969a) *Fight for Education: A Black Paper*. London: Critical Quarterly Society.

Cox, Brian and Dyson, Anthony (eds) (1969b) *Black Paper Two: The Crisis in Education*. London: Critical Quarterly Society.

Cox, Brian and Dyson, Anthony (eds) (1970) *Black Paper Three: Goodbye Mr Short*. London: Critical Quarterly Society.

Cox, Graham, Lowe, Philip and Winter, Michael (1986a) 'Agriculture and conservation in Britain: a policy community under siege', in Graham Cox, Philip Lowe and Michael Winter (eds), *Agriculture: People and Policies*. London: Allen & Unwin.

Cox, Graham, Lowe, Philip and Winter, Michael (1986b) 'The state and the farmer: perspectives on agricultural policy', in Graham Cox, Philip Lowe and Michael Winter (eds), *Agriculture: People and Policies*. London: Allen & Unwin.

Cox, Graham, Lowe, Philip and Winter, Michael (1990) *The Voluntary Principle in Conservation: The Farming and Wildlife Advisory Group*. Chichester: Packard.

Critchley, Julian (1990) *The Palace of Varieties*. London: Faber & Faber.

Crook, D. (2002) 'Local authorities and comprehensivisation in England and Wales, 1944–1974', *Oxford Review of Education*, 28 (2&3): 247–60.

Crossman, R. (1972) *The Politics of Pensions*, Eleanor Rathbone Memorial Lectures No. 19. Liverpool: Liverpool University Press.

Crossman, R. (1977) *The Diaries of a Cabinet Minister. Volume 3: Secretary of State for Social Services 1968–70*. London: Hamish Hamilton and Jonathan Cape.

Crouch, Colin (1982) *The Politics of Industrial Relations*, 2nd edn. London: Fontana.

Dahrendorf, Ralf (1982) *On Britain*. London: BBC.

Danchev, Alex (1998) 'On friendship: Anglo-America at the *fin de siècle*', in Alex Danchev (ed.), *On Specialness; Essays in Anglo-American Relations*. Basingstoke: Macmillan.

Darby, Philip (1973) *British Defence Policy East of Suez, 1947–68*. Oxford: Oxford University Press.

Darwin, John (1988) *Britain and Decolonisation: The Retreat from Empire to the Post-War World*. Basingstoke: Macmillan.

Deighton, Anne (1990) *The Impossible Peace: Britain, the Division of Germany and the Origins of the Cold War*. Oxford: Clarendon Press.

Dell, Edmund (2000) *A Strange Eventful History: Democratic Socialism in Britain*. London: HarperCollins.

Denman, Roy (1996) *Missed Chances: Britain and Europe in the Twentieth Century*. London: Cassell.

DeNovo, J.A. (1976–7) 'The Culbertson economic mission and Anglo-American tensions in the Middle East, 1944–1945', *Journal of American History*, 63.

Department of Education and Science (1965) *The Organisation of Secondary Education*, Circular 10/65. London: HMSO.

Department of Education and Science (1967) *Children and their Primary Schools* (2 vols), The Plowden Report. London: HMSO.

Department for Education (1992) *Choice and Diversity: A New Framework for Schools*, Cmnd 2021. London: HMSO.

Department for Education and Employment (1997) *Excellence in Schools*, Cmnd 3681. London: HMSO.

Department for Education and Skills (2001) *Schools Achieving Success*, Cmnd 5230. London: HMSO.

Department for Education and Skills (2004a) *Five Year Strategy for Children and Learners*, Cmnd 6272. London: HMSO.

Department for Education and Skills (2004b) *14–19 Curiculum and Qualifications Reform: Final Report of the Working Group on 14–19 Reform*. London: HMSO.

Department for Education and Skills (2005) *14–19 Education and Skills*, Cmnd 6476. London: HMSO.

Department of Employment and Productivity (1969) *In Place of Strife*, Cmnd 3888. London: HMSO.

Department of the Environment (1971) *A Fair Deal for Housing*, Cm 4728. London: HMSO.

Department of the Environment (1977) *Housing Policy: A Consultative Document*, Cmnd 6851. London: HMSO.

Department of the Environment (1987) *Housing: The Government's Proposals*, Cm 214. London: HMSO.

Department of the Environment (1995) *Our Future Homes: Opportunity, Choice, Responsibility*, Cm 2901. London: HMSO.

Department of the Environment, Transport and the Regions (1997) *Roads Review – What Role for Trunk Roads in England?*, consultation paper. London: DETR.

Department of the Environment, Transport and the Regions (1998) *Breaking the Logjam: The Government's Consultation Paper on Fighting Traffic Congestion and Pollution Through Road User and Workplace Parking Charges*. London: DETR.

Department of the Environment, Transport and the Regions (2000) *Quality and Choice: the Housing Green Paper*. London: The Stationery Office.

Department of Health (1991) *On the State of the Nation's Health*. London: Department of Health.

Department of Health (1992) *The Health of the Nation: A Strategy for Health in England*. London: Department of Health.

Department of Health (1994) *On the State of the Nation's Health*. London: Department of Health.

Department of Health (1997) *The New NHS: Modern. Dependable*. London: The Stationery Office.

Department of Health (1998a) *The Government's Expenditure Plans 1998–99: Departmental Report*. London: The Stationery Office.

Department of Health (1998b) 'Dobson unveils cross-government drive to improve public Health'. Press release, 98/051.

Department of Health (1998c) *Our Healthier Nation*, publication of Green Paper on Public Health. Press release, 98/050.

Department of Health (1998d) *Public Services for the Future: Modernisation, Reform, Accountability, Comprehensive Spending Review. Public Service Agreements 1999–2002*, Cm 4181. London: The Stationery Office.

Department of Health (2000) *The NHS Plan: A Plan for Investment, A Plan for Reform*, Cm 4818–1. London: The Stationery Office.

Department of Health (2002) *Delivering the NHS Plan: Next Steps on Investment, Next Steps on Reform*, Cm 5503. London: The Stationery Office.

Department of Health (2004) *Choosing Health*. London: The Stationery Office.

Department of Health and Social Security (1971) *Strategy for Pensions*, Cmnd 4755. London: HMSO.

Department of Health and Social Security (1974) *Better Pensions*, Cmnd 5713. London: HMSO.

Department of Health and Social Security (1985) *The Reform of Social Security*, Cmnd 9517. London: HMSO.

Department of Social Security (1998) *A New Contract for Welfare: Partnership in Pensions*, Cm 4179. London: The Stationery Office.

Department of Transport (1989) *National Road Traffic Forecasts (Great Britain) 1989*. London: HMSO.

Department of Transport (1994) *Trunk Roads in England – 1994 Review*. London: HMSO.

Department of Transport (1995a) *Managing the Trunk Road Programme*. London: HMSO.

Department of Transport (1995b) 'National transport policy should not ignore individual choice – Mawhinney: Department of Transport press release 357 (28 March 1995)' (available at http://www.newsrelease-archive.net/coi/depts/GDT/coi5410a.ok) (accessed 10 October 2003).

Department of Transport (1996) 'Government committed to £6bn trunk roads programme: Department of Transport press release 357 (26 November 1996)' (available at http://www.newsrelease-archive.net/coi/depts/GDT/coi4277c.ok) (accessed 10 October 2003).

Department of Transport (2002a) *Delivering Better Transport: Progress Report*. London: HMSO.

Department of Transport (2002b) '£5.5 billion package of transport improvements: Department of Transport press release 354 (10 December 2002)' (available at http://www.dft.gov.uk/pns/DisplayPN.cgi?pn_id=2002_0354) (accessed 22 October 2003).

Department of Transport (2003a) *Lorry Road User Charge (Modernising the Taxation of the Haulage Industry)*. London: Department of Transport.

Department of Transport (2003b) '£7 billion blitz on Britain's most congested roads: Department of Transport press release 85 (9 July 2003)' (available at http://www.dft.gov.uk/pns/DisplayPN.cgi?pn_id=2003_0085) (accessed 22 October 2003).

Department of Transport (2003c) *The Future Development of Air Transport in the United Kingdom: South East (A National Consultation – Second Edition, February 2003)*. London: Department of Transport.

Department for Work and Pensions (2002) *Simplicity, Security and Choice: Working and Saving for Retirement*, Cm 5677. London: HMSO.

Devereux, David (1989) 'Britain, the Commonwealth and the defence of the Middle East, 1948–56', *Journal of Contemporary History*, 24: 327–45.

Devereux, David (1990) 'Britain and the failure of collective defence in the Middle East, 1948–53', in Anne Deighton (ed.), *Britain and the First Cold War*. Basingstoke: Macmillan.

Dewdney, Kim (1992) 'Who runs Labour?', *Fabian Review*, 104 (4).

Dickie, John (1994) *'Special' No More. Anglo-American Relations: Rhetoric and Reality*. London: Weidenfeld & Nicolson.

Digby, A. (1989) *British Welfare Policy: Workhouse to Workfare*. London: Faber & Faber.

Dobson, Alan (1995) *Anglo-American Relations in the Twentieth Century: Of Friendship, Conflict and the Rise and Decline of Superpowers*. New York: Routledge.

Dobson, Alan (2002) *US Economic Statecraft for Survival, 1933–1991*. New York: Routledge.

Dobson, Alan and Marsh, Steve (2001) *US Foreign Policy since 1945*. New York: Routledge.

Doherty, Brian (2000) 'Manufactured vulnerability: protest camp tactics', in Benjamin Seel, Matthew Paterson and Brian Doherty (eds), *Direct Action in British Environmentalism*. London: Routledge.

Dolowitz, David and Marsh, David (2000) 'Learning from abroad: the role of policy transfer in contemporary policy-making', *Governance*, 13 (1): 5–24.

Donnison, David and Ungerson, Clare (1982) *Housing Policy*. Harmondsworth: Penguin.

Donoughue, Bernard (1987) *Prime Minister: The Conduct of Policy under Harold Wilson and James Callaghan*. London: Jonathan Cape.

Dorey, Peter (1993a) 'Corporatism in the UK', *Politics Review*, 1 (2): 24–7.

Dorey, Peter (1993b) 'One step at a time: the Conservatives' approach to the reform of industrial relations', *Political Quarterly*, 64 (1): 24–36.

Dorey, Peter (1995a) *British Politics since 1945*. Oxford: Blackwell.

Dorey, Peter (1995b) *The Conservative Party and the Trade Unions*. London: Routledge.

Dorey, Peter (1995c) 'Between principle, pragmatism and practicability: the development of Conservative trade union policy in Opposition, 1974–1979', in David Broughton, David Farrell, David Denver and Colin Rallings (eds), *British Elections and Parties Yearbook 1994*. Ilford: Frank Cass.

Dorey, Peter (1996) 'Exhaustion of a tradition: the death of "one nation Toryism"', *Contemporary Politics*, 2 (4): 47–65.

Dorey, Peter (1999a) 'The 3 Rs – reform, reproach and rancour: education policies under John Major', in Peter Dorey (ed.), *The Major Premiership: Politics and Policies under John Major, 1990–1997*. Basingstoke: Macmillan.

Dorey, Peter (1999b) 'No return to "beer and sandwiches": industrial relations and employment policies under John Major', in Peter Dorey (ed.), *The Major Premiership: Politics and Policies under John Major, 1990–1997*. Basingstoke: Macmillan.

Dorey, Peter (1999c) 'The Blairite betrayal: New Labour and the trade unions', in Gerald Taylor (ed.), *The Impact of New Labour*. Basingstoke: Macmillan.

Dorey, Peter (2001) *Wage Politics in Britain: The Rise and Fall of Incomes Policies since 1945*. Brighton: Sussex Academic Press.

Dorey, Peter (2002a) 'Industrial relations as "human relations": Conservatism and trade unionism, 1945–1964', in Stuart Ball and Ian Holliday (eds), *Mass Conservatism: The Conservatives and the People, 1867–1997*. Ilford: Frank Cass.

Dorey, Peter (2002b) 'Britain in the 1990s: the absence of policy concertation', in Stefan Berger and Hugh Compston (eds), *Policy Concertation and Social Partnership in Western Europe*. Oxford: Berghahn.

Dorey, Peter (2003) 'Margaret Thatcher's taming of the trade unions', in Stanislao Pugliese (ed.), *The Legacy of Margaret Thatcher: Liberty Regained?* London: Politico's.

Dorey, Peter (2005) *Policy Making in Britain: An Introduction*. London: Sage.

Dorey, Peter (forthcoming) 'Industrial relations imbroglio', in Peter Dorey (ed.), *The 1964–1970 Labour Governments*. London: Routledge.

Dorfman, Gerald (1979) *Government versus Trade Unions in British Politics since 1968*. Basingstoke: Macmillan.

Dow, J. Christopher (1964) *The Management of the British Economy 1945–61*. Cambridge: Cambridge University Press.

Dowding, Keith (1991) *Rational Choice and Political Power*. Aldershot: Edward Elgar.

Downs, Anthony (1973) 'The political economy of improving our environment', in Joe Bains (ed.), *Environmental Decay: Economic Causes and Remedies*. Boston, MA: Little, Brown.

Dudley, Geoff (1983) 'The road lobby: a declining force?', in David Marsh (ed.), *Pressure Politics*. London: Junction Books.

Dudley, Geoffrey and Richardson, Jeremy (1996) 'Why does policy change over time? Adversarial policy communities, alternative policy arenas, and British trunk roads policy 1945–95', *Journal of European Public Policy*, 3 (1): 63–83.

Dumbrell, John (2001) *A Special Relationship: Anglo-American Relations in the Cold War and After*. Basingstoke: Macmillan.

Dunleavy, Patrick (1995a) 'Policy disasters: explaining the UK's record', *Public Policy and Administration*, 10 (2): 52–70.

Dunleavy, Patrick (1995b) 'Reinterpreting the Westland affair: theories of the state and core executive decision making', in R.A.W. Rhodes and Patrick Dunleavy (eds), *Prime Minister, Cabinet and Core Executive*. Basingstoke: Macmillan.

Ellis, Bryan (1989) *Pensions in Britain 1955–1975*. London: HMSO.

English, Richard and Kenny, Michael (eds) (2000) *Rethinking British Decline*. Basingstoke: Macmillan.

Enthoven, Alain (1985) *Reflections on the Management of the NHS*. London: Nuffield Provincial Hospitals Trust.

Evans, Brendan (2002) 'Frank Field', in John Ramsden (ed.), *The Oxford Companion to Twentieth-Century British Politics*. Oxford: Oxford University Press.

Evason, Eileen (1999) 'British pensions policies', in John Ditch (ed.), *Introduction to Social Security*. London: Routledge.

Fawcett, Helen (1996) 'The Beveridge strait-jacket: policy formation and the problem of poverty in old age', *Contemporary British History*, 10 (1): 20–42.

Fearne, A. (1997) 'The history and development of the CAP 1945–1990', in Christopher Ritson and David Harvey (eds), *The Common Agricultural Policy*, 2nd edn. Wallingford: CAB International.

Fforde, J. (1983) 'Setting monetary objectives', *Bank of England Quarterly Bulletin*, 32 (2): 200–8.

Field, Frank (1996) *How to Pay for the Future: Building a Stakeholders' Welfare*. London: Institute of Community Affairs.

Finer, S.E. (1958) 'Transport interests and the road lobby', *Political Quarterly*, 29 (1): 47–58.

Flanders, Allan (1974) 'The tradition of voluntarism', *British Journal of Industrial Relations*, 12: 352–70.

Flanders, Allan (1975) *Management and Unions: The Theory and Reform of Industrial Relations*. London: Faber & Faber.

Foot, M. (1973) *Aneurin Bevan: A Biography. Volume 2: 1945–1960*. London: Davis-Poynter.

Forrest, Ray and Murie, Alan (1988) *Selling the Welfare State: The Privatisation of Public Housing*. London: Routledge.

Fowler, Norman (1991) *Ministers Decide*. London: Chapmans.

Gaddis, John (1982) *Strategies of Containment: A Critical Appraisal of Post-War American National Security Policy*. New York: Oxford University Press.

Gallagher, John (1982) *The Decline, Revival and Fall of the British Empire*. Cambridge: Cambridge University Press.

Gamble, Andrew (1981) *Britain in Decline: Economic Policy, Political Strategy and the British State*. Basingstoke: Macmillan.

Gamble, Andrew (1988) *The Free Economy and the Strong State: The Politics of Thatcherism*. Basingstoke: Macmillan.

Gamble, Andrew (1994) *Britain in Decline: Economic Policy, Political Strategy and the British State*, 4th edn. Basingstoke: Macmillan.

Gardner, Richard (1980) *Sterling–Dollar Diplomacy in Current Perspective: The Origins and Prospects of our International Economic Order*. New York: Columbia University Press.

Garner, Robert (2000) *Environmental Politics*, 2nd edn. Basingstoke: Macmillan.

Gelb, Leslie (1988) *Anglo-American Relations, 1945–49: Toward a Theory of Alliances*. New York: Garland Publishers.

George, Stephen (1998) *An Awkward Partner: Britain in the European Community*. Oxford: Oxford University Press.

Giddens, Anthony (1998) *The Third Way: The Renewal of Social Democracy*. Cambridge: Polity Press.

Gilmour, Ian (1983) *Britain Can Work*. Oxford: Martin Robertson.

Ginsburg, Norman (1999) 'Housing', in Robert Page and Richard Silburn (eds), *British Social Welfare in the Twentieth Century*. Basingstoke: Macmillan.

Glees, A. (1994) 'The diplomacy of Anglo-German relations: a study of the ERM crisis of September 1992', *German Politics*, 3 (1): 75–90.

Glennerster, Howard and Hills, John (eds) (1998) *The State of Welfare: The Economics of Social Spending*, 2nd edn. Oxford: Oxford University Press.

Goodhart, Charles (1989) *Money, Information and Uncertainty*, 5th edn. Basingstoke: Macmillan.

Goodwin, Gail (1999) *Evensong: A Novel*. New York: Ballantine Books.

Gormly, J.L. (1984) 'The Washington Declaration and the "poor relation": Anglo-American atomic diplomacy, 1945–46', *Diplomatic History*, 8: 125–45.

Gould, Philip (1998) *The Unfinished Revolution: How the Modernisers Saved the Labour Party*. Boston, MA: Little, Brown.

Gowing, Margaret (1974) *Independence and Deterrence: Britain and Atomic Energy, 1945–52*. Basingstoke: Macmillan.

Grant, Wyn (1981) 'The politics of the green pound', *Journal of Common Market Studies*, 19: 313–29.

Grant, Wyn (1995a) *Autos, Smog and Pollution Control: The Politics of Air Quality Management in California*. Aldershot: Edward Elgar.

Grant, Wyn (1995b) 'Is agricultural policy still exceptional?', *Political Quarterly*, 66 (3): 156–69.

Grant, Wyn (2000) *Pressure Groups and British Politics*. Basingstoke: Palgrave Macmillan.

Greenleaf, W.H. (1987) *The British Political Tradition. Volume Three: A Much Government Nation, Part One*. London: Methuen.

Greer, Alan (1996) *Rural Politics in Northern Ireland*. Aldershot: Avebury.

Greer, Alan (2003) 'Countryside issues: a creeping crisis', *Parliamentary Affairs*, 56 (3): 523–42.

Griggs, C. (1985) *Private Education in Britain*. Lewes: Falmer Press.

Griggs, Steven, Howarth, David and Jacobs, Brian (1998) 'Second runway at Manchester', *Parliamentary Affairs*, 51 (3): 358–69.

Guillebaud Committee (chairman C.W. Guillebaud) (1956) *Report of the Committee of Enquiry into the Cost of the NHS*, Cmd 9663. London: HMSO.

Gwyn, William and Rose, Richard (eds) (1980) *Britain: Progress and Decline*. Basingstoke: Macmillan.

Hall, Peter (1993) 'Policy paradigms, social learning and the state: the case of economic policy-making in Britain', *Comparative Politics*, 25 (3): 275–96.

Ham, Adrian (1981) *Treasury Rules: Recurrent Themes in British Economic Policy*. London: Quartet Books.

Ham, Christopher (1999) *Health Policy in Britain*, 4th edn. Basingstoke: Macmillan.

Hamer, Mick (1987) *Wheels Within Wheels*. London: Routledge & Kegan Paul.

Hanna, J. and Mogridge, M. (1992) 'Market forces and transport choices', in J. Roberts, J. Cleary, K. Hamilton and J. Hanna (eds), *Travel Sickness: The Need for a Sustainable Transport Policy in Britain*. London: Lawrence & Wishart.

Hannah, Leslie (1986) *Inventing Retirement: The Development of Occupational Pensions in Britain*. Cambridge: Cambridge University Press.

Harloe, Michael (1978) 'The Green Paper on housing policy', in M. Brown and S. Daldwin (eds), *The Year Book of Social Policy in Britain 1977*. London: Routledge & Kegan Paul.

Harloe, Michael (1981) 'The recommodification of housing', in Michael Harloe and Elizabeth Lebas (eds), *City, Class and Capital*. London: Edward Arnold.

Harloe, Michael (1985) *Private Rented Housing in the United States and Europe*. Beckenham: Croom Helm.

Harloe, Michael (1995) *The People's Home? Social Rented Housing in Europe and America*. Oxford: Blackwell.

Harris, José (1997) *William Beveridge*. Oxford: Clarendon Press.

Harris, Nigel (1972) *Competition and the Corporate Society*. London: Methuen.

Harris, R. (2001) 'Blair's "ethical" policy', *The National Interest*, 63 (Spring): 25–36.

Headey, Bruce (1974) *British Cabinet Ministers*. London: Allen & Unwin.

Healey, Denis (1989) *Time of My Life*. London: Michael Joseph.

Health Education Council (1988) *Inequalities in Health: The Health Divide*. Harmondsworth: Penguin.

Heath, Edward (1998) *The Course of My Life*. London: Hodder & Stoughton.

Heclo, Hugh (1974) *Modern Social Politics in Britain and Sweden*. New Haven, CT: Yale University Press.

Hennessy, Peter (1986) *Cabinet*. Oxford: Basil Blackwell.

Hennessy, Peter (1989) *Whitehall*. London: Secker & Warburg.

Hennessy, Peter (1993) *Never Again: Britain 1945–1951*. London: Vintage.

Hicks, Stephen and Palmer, Tom (2004) 'Trade union membership: estimates from the autumn 2003 Labour Force Survey', *Labour Market Trends*, March: 99–102.

Hill, Michael (1993) *The Welfare State in Britain*. Aldershot: Edward Elgar.

Hill, Michael (1997) *The Policy Process in the Modern State*. Hemel Hempstead: Prentice Hall/Harvester Wheatsheaf.

Hogan, Michael (1987) *The Marshall Plan: America, Britain and the Reconstruction of Western Europe, 1947–52*. Cambridge: Cambridge University Press.

Holland, R.F. (1984) 'The imperial factor in British strategies from Attlee to Macmillan, 1945–63', *Journal of Imperial and Commonwealth History*, 12.

Holmans, Alan (1987) *Housing Policy in Britain: A History*. Beckenham: Croom Helm.

Holt, Richard (2002) *Second Amongst Equals: Chancellors of the Exchequer Since the Second World War*. London: Profile Books.

House of Commons (1980) *Enquiry into Implications of the Government's Expenditure Plans 1980–81 to 1983–84 for the Housing Policies of the Department of the Environment*, First Report of the House of Commons Select Committee on the Environment, Session 1979–80, HC 714. London: HMSO.

HC (House of Commons) Bill 8 (1999) *Transport Bill (Session 1999–2000)*. London: HMSO.

Howe, Geoffrey (1994) *Conflict of Loyalty*. Basingstoke: Macmillan.

Howell, David (1999) '"Shut your gob!": trade unions and the Labour Party, 1945–64', in Alan Campbell, Nina Fishman and John McIlroy (eds), *British Trade Unions and Industrial Politics. Volume One: The Post-War Compromise, 1945–64*. Aldershot: Ashgate.

Howorth, J. (2000) 'Britain, France and the European Defence Initiative', *Survival*, 2 (1): 33–55.

Howorth, J. (2002) ' CESDP after 11 September: from short-term confusion to long-term cohesion?', *EUSA Review*, 15 (1): 1–4.

Hutber, Patrick (ed.) (1978) *What's Wrong with Britain?* London: Sphere.

Hutton, Will (1995) *The State We're In*. London: Jonathan Cape.

Ingersent, Ken and Rayner, A.J. (1999) *Agricultural Policy in Western Europe and the United States*. Cheltenham: Edward Elgar.

Inns of Court Conservative and Unionist Society (1958) *A Giant's Strength*. London: Inns of Court Conservative and Unionist Society.

Institute of Public Policy Research (2001) *A New Contract for Retirement: An Interim Report*. London: Institute of Public Policy Research.

Jackson, Brian (1961) 'Notes from two primary schools', *New Left Review*, 11: 4–8.

James, Harold and Stone, Maria (eds) (1992) *When the Wall Came Down: Reactions to German Unification*. New York: Routledge.

James, Oliver and Lodge, Martin (2003) 'The limitations of "policy transfer" and "lesson drawing" for public policy research', *Political Studies Review*, 1 (2): 179–93.

Jefferys, Kevin (1987) 'British politics and social policy during the Second World War', *Historical Journal*, 30: 123–44.

Jefferys, Kevin (1991) *The Churchill Coalition and Wartime Politics 1940–45*. Manchester: Manchester University Press.

Jefferys, Kevin (1993) *The Labour Party since 1945*. Basingstoke: Macmillan.

Jenkins, Peter (1970) *The Battle of Downing Street*. London: Charles Knight.

Jenkins, Roy (1998) *The Chancellors*. Basingstoke: Macmillan.

Jones, Helen (1994) *Health and Society in Twentieth-Century Britain*. London: Longman.

Jones, Helen (1998) 'The people's health', in Helen Jones and Susanne MacGregor (eds), *Social Issues and Party Politics*. London: Routledge.

Jones, Margaret and Lowe, Rodney (2002) *From Beveridge to Blair*. Manchester: Manchester University Press.

Joppke, Christian (1991) 'Social movements during cycles of issue attention: the decline of the anti-nuclear movements in West Germany and the USA', *British Journal of Sociology*, 42 (1): 43–60.

Jordan, Grant and Richardson, Jeremy (1982) 'The British policy style or the logic of negotiation', in Jeremy Richardson (ed.), *Policy Styles in Western Europe*. London: Allen & Unwin.

Kavanagh, Dennis (1980) 'Political culture in Britain: the decline of the civic culture', in Gabriel Almond and Sidney Verba (eds), *The Civic Culture Revisited*. Boston, MA: Little, Brown.

Kavanagh, Dennis and Morris, Peter (1989) *Consensus Politics: From Attlee to Thatcher*. Oxford: Blackwell.

Kavanagh, Dennis and Seldon, Anthony (1999) *The Power Behind the Prime Minister: The Hidden Influence of No. 10*. London: HarperCollins.

Keegan, William (1984) *Mrs Thatcher's Economic Experiment*. London: Allen Lane.

Keegan, William (1989) *Mr Lawson's Gamble*. London: Hodder & Stoughton.

Keegan, William (2003) *The Prudence of Mr Gordon Brown*. Chichester: John Wiley.

Kellner, Peter (1992) 'Time for Labour to bid goodbye to the trade unions', *The Independent*, 12 June.

Kennan, George (1968) *Memoirs, 1925–50*. London: Hutchinson.

Kerckhoff, Alan, Fogelman, Ken, Crooke, David and Reeder, David (1996) *Going Comprehensive in England and Wales: A Study of Uneven Change*. Portland, OR: Woburn Press.

Kerr, Michael (1974) 'Some thoughts on the future of state pensions in the United Kingdom', *Benefits International*, June: 9–15.

King, Anthony (ed.) (1976) *Why Is Britain Becoming Harder to Govern?* London: BBC Books.

King, Anthony (1985) 'Margaret Thatcher: the style of a Prime Minister', in Anthony King (ed.), *The British Prime Minister*, 2nd edn. Basingstoke: Macmillan.

Kingdon, John (1984) *Agendas, Alternatives and Public Policies*. New York: HarperCollins.

Klein, Rudolf (1983) *The Politics of the National Health Service*. London: Longman.

Kleinman, M. (1996) *Housing, the State and Welfare in Europe*. Cheltenham: Edward Elgar.

Knight, Christopher (1990) *The Making of Tory Education Policy in Post-War Britain, 1950–1986*. Lewes: Falmer Press.

Kogan, Maurice (1971) *The Politics of Education: Edward Boyle and Anthony Crosland in Conversation with Maurice Kogan*. Harmondsworth: Penguin.

Labour Party (1957) *National Superannuation: Labour's Policy for Security in Old Age*. London: Labour Party.

Labour Party (1976) *Labour Party Conference Report 1976*. London: Labour Party.

Labour Party (1996) *New Labour: New Life for Britain*. London: Labour Party.

Labour Party (1997) *Because Britain Deserves Better*. London: Labour Party.

Lang, Tim, Millstone, Erik, Raven, Hugh and Rayner, Mike (1996) *Modernising UK Food Policy: The Case for Reforming the Ministry of Agriculture, Fisheries and Food*. Slough: Centre for Food Policy, Thames Valley University.

Lansley, Stewart (1979) *Housing and Public Policy*. Beckenham: Croom Helm.

Lawson, Nigel (1992) *The View from Number 11: Memoirs of a Tory Radical*. London: Corgi.

Leffler, Melvyn (1972) *A Preponderance of Power: National Security, The Truman Administration and the Cold War*. Stanford, CA: Stanford University Press.

Leigh, David and Linklater, Magnus (1986) *Not With Honour: The Inside Story of the Westland Scandal.* London: Sphere.

Lieber, R.J. (2000) 'No transatlantic divorce in the offing', *Orbis*, 44 (4): 571–84.

Longstreth, Frank (1984) 'The dynamics of disintegration of a Keynesian political economy: the British case and its implications'. Unpublished paper, University of Bath.

Longstreth, Frank (1988) 'From corporatism to dualism: Thatcherism and the climacteric of British trade unions in the 1980s', *Political Studies*, 36 (3): 413–32.

Lord, Christopher (1996) *Absent at the Creation: Britain and the Formation of the European Community.* Aldershot: Dartmouth.

Louis, William Roger and Owen, Roger (eds) (1989) *Suez 1956: The Crisis and its Consequences.* Oxford: Clarendon Press.

Lowe, Philip, Clark, J., Seymour, Susanne and Ward, Neil (1997) *Moralizing the Environment: Countryside Change, Farms and Pollution.* London: UCL Press.

Lowe, Rodney (1993) *The Welfare State in Britain since 1945.* Basingstoke: Macmillan.

Lowe, Rodney (1994a) 'Lessons from the past: the rise and fall of the classic welfare state in Britain, 1945–76', in Ann Oakley and A. Susan Williams (eds), *The Politics of the Welfare State*. London: UCL Press.

Lowe, Rodney (1994b) 'A prophet dishonoured in his own country? The rejection of Beveridge in Britain, 1945–1970', in John Hills, J. Ditch and Howard Glennerster (eds), *Beveridge and Social Security*. Oxford: Clarendon Press.

Ludlam, Steve (2004) 'New Labour, "vested interests" and the union link', in Steve Ludlam and Martin J. Smith (eds), *Governing as New Labour: Policy and Politics under Blair*. Basingstoke: Palgrave.

Lukes, Steven (1974) *Power: A Radical View.* Basingstoke: Macmillan.

Lynes, Tony (1969) *Labour's Pension Plan*, Fabian Tract 396. London: Fabian Society.

Macmillan, Harold (1972) *Pointing the Way, 1959–1961.* Basingstoke: Macmillan.

Macmillan, Harold (1973) *At the End of the Day, 1961–1963.* Basingstoke: Macmillan.

Macnicol, John (1998) *The Politics of Retirement in Britain, 1878–1948.* Cambridge: Cambridge University Press.

MacShane, Dennis (1993) 'State of the unions', *New Statesman and Society*, 22 May.

Maier, Charles (ed.) (1996) *The Cold War in Europe: Era of a Divided Continent.* Princeton, NJ: Marcus Weiner.

Major, John (1999) *The Autobiography.* London: HarperCollins.

Maloney, W.A., Jordan, G. and McLaughlin, A.M. (1994) 'Interest groups and public policy: the insider/outsider model revisited', *Journal of Public Policy*, 14 (1): 17–38.

Malpass, Peter (1990) *Reshaping Housing Policy: Subsidies, Rents and Residualisation.* London: Routledge.

Malpass, Peter (2000) *Housing Associations and Housing Policy: A Historical Perspective.* Basingstoke: Macmillan.

Malpass, Peter (2003) 'The wobbly pillar? Housing and the postwar British welfare state', *Journal of Social Policy*, 32 (4): 589–606.

Malpass, Peter (2005) *Housing and the Welfare State: The Development of Housing Policy in Britain.* Basingstoke: Palgrave Macmillan.

Malpass, Peter and Mullins, David (2002) 'Local authority housing stock transfer in the UK: from local initiative to national policy', *Housing Studies*, 17 (4): 673–86.

Malpass, Peter and Murie, Alan (1999) *Housing Policy and Practice*, 5th edn. Basingstoke: Macmillan.

Mandelson, Peter and Liddle, Roger (1996) *The Blair Revolution: Can New Labour Deliver?* London: Faber & Faber.

Manderson-Jones, R.B. (1972) *The Special Relationship: Anglo-American Relations and the Western European Unity, 1947–56.* London: London School of Economics.

Marsh, David (1983) 'Introduction: interest groups in Britain', in David Marsh (ed.), *Pressure Politics: Interest Groups in Britain.* London: Junction Books.

Marsh, David (1992) *The New Politics of British Trade Unionism.* Basingstoke: Macmillan.

Marsh, Steve (2001) 'HMG, AIOC and the Anglo-Iranian oil crisis: in defence of Anglo-Iranian', *Diplomacy and Statecraft,* 12 (4): 143–74.

Marsh, Steve (2003) *Anglo-American Relations and Cold War Oil.* Basingstoke: Palgrave.

Marsh, Steve and Mackenstein, Hans (2005) *The International Relations of the European Union.* Harlow: Pearson/Longman.

Marwick, Arthur (1991) *Culture in Britain Since 1945.* Oxford: Blackwell.

Mason, S. (1965) 'Leicestershire', in Stuart Maclure (ed.), *Comprehensive Planning.* London: Councils and Education Press.

Maw, J. (1988) 'National curriculum policy: coherence and progression?', in D. Lawton and C. Chitty (eds), *The National Curriculum,* Bedford Way Paper No. 33. London: Institute of Education, University of London.

Mawhinney, Brian (1995) *Transport: The Way Ahead.* London: HMSO.

May, E.R. (ed.) (1993) *American Cold War Strategy: Interpreting NSC 68.* New York: Bedford Books.

McConnell, Allan and Stark, Alastair (2002) 'Foot and mouth 2001: the politics of crisis management', *Parliamentary Affairs,* 55 (4): 664–8.

McCormick, John (1991) *British Politics and the Environment.* London: Earthscan.

McCormick, J. (2002) *Understanding the European Union.* Basingstoke: Palgrave.

McGhie, S. (2002) 'UK leads security assistance force', *Janes Defence Weekly,* 37 (1): 2.

McIlroy, John (1995) *Trade Unions in Britain Today,* 2nd edn. Manchester: Manchester University Press.

McPherson, Andrew and Raab, Charles (1988) *Governing Education: A Sociology of Policy since 1945.* Edinburgh: Edinburgh University Press.

Meat and Livestock Commission (1997) 'The debate on the need for new thinking on how to develop, control and regulate food policy in the UK'. Typescript discussion paper.

Mee, Charles (1984) *The Marshall Plan: The Launching of Pax Americana.* New York: Simon & Schuster.

Meikle, James and Wintour, Patrick (2004) 'Compromise on smoking ban', *The Guardian,* 12 November.

Merrett, Stephen (1979) *State Housing in Britain.* London: Routledge & Kegan Paul.

Middlemas, Keith (1979) *Politics in Industrial Society: The Experience of the British System since 1911.* London: André Deutsch.

Miliband, Ralph (1973) *The State in Capitalist Society.* London: Quartet.

Ministry of Education (1944) *Education Act, 1944.* London: HMSO.

Ministry of Housing and Local Government (1953) *Houses – The Next Step,* Cmd 8996. London: HMSO.

Ministry of Housing and Local Government (1965) *The Housing Programme 1965–70,* Cmnd 2838. London: HMSO.

Ministry of Pensions and National Insurance (1958) *Provision for Old Age,* Cmnd 538. London: HMSO.

Ministry of Transport (1962) *Roads in England and Wales: Report by the Minister of Transport for the Year 1961–2.* London: HMSO.

Mitchell, Neil (1987) 'Changing pressure group politics: the case of the TUC 1976–84', *British Journal of Political Science,* 17 (4): 509–17.

Monger, Joanne (2004) 'Labour disputes in 2003', *Labour Market Trends,* June: 235–47.

Moran, Lord (1966) *Winston Churchill: The Struggle for Survival, 1940–1965*. London: Constable.

Moran, Michael (1977) *The Politics of Industrial Relations*. Basingstoke: Macmillan.

Moran, Michael (2000) 'From command state to regulatory state', *Public Policy and Administration*, 15 (4): 1–13.

Moran, Michael (2001) 'The rise of the regulatory state in Britain', *Parliamentary Affairs*, 54 (1): 19–34.

Morgan, Janet (ed.) (1981) *The Backbench Diaries of Richard Crossman*. London: Hamish Hamilton and Jonathan Cape.

Morgan, Kenneth O. (1985) *Labour in Power, 1945–51*. Oxford: Oxford University Press.

Morgan, Kenneth O. (1990) *The People's Peace: British History 1945–1989*. Oxford: Oxford University Press.

Mosley, Paul (1985) *The Making of Economic Policy: Theory and Evidence from Britain and the US since 1945*. Brighton: Wheatsheaf.

Murphy, Roger (2001) *Challenges from Within*. Aldershot: Ashgate.

Myles, John and Pierson, Paul (2001) 'The comparative political economy of pension reform', in Paul Pierson (ed.), *The New Politics of the Welfare State*. Oxford: Oxford University Press.

Nachmani, A. (1983) '"It is a matter of getting the mixture right": Britain's post-war relations with America in the Middle East', *Journal of Contemporary History*, 18: 117–40.

National Trust (1995) *Open Countryside – Access and Recreation on National Trust Land (Report of the Access Review Working Party)*. London: National Trust.

Naughtie, James (2001) *The Rivals: The Intimate Story of a Political Marriage*. London: Fourth Estate.

Nesbitt, Steven (1995) *British Pensions Policy Making in the 1980s*. Aldershot: Avebury.

Newby, Howard (1979) *Green and Pleasant Land?* Harmondsworth: Penguin.

Newhouse, J. (1997) *Europe Adrift*. New York: Pantheon.

Newman, J. (2002) 'Putting the "policy" back into social policy', *Social Policy and Society*, 1 (4).

Norton, Philip (1990) 'The lady's not for turning, but what about the rest? Margaret Thatcher and the Conservative Party, 1979–1989', *Parliamentary Affairs*, 43 (1): 41–58.

Nye Jr, J.S. (2000) 'The US and Europe: continental drift?', *International Affairs*, 76 (1): 51–60.

OECD (1979) *Monetary Targets and Inflation Control*, OECD Monetary Studies Series. Paris: OECD.

OECD (1987) *Medium-Term Macroeconomic Strategy Revised*, Economics and Statistics Working Paper No. 48. Paris: OECD.

O'Higgins, Michael (1986) 'Public/private interaction and pension provision', in M. Rein and L. Rainwater (eds), *Public/Private Interplay in Social Protection: A Comparative Study*. Armonk, NY: M.E. Sharpe.

Oliver, Dawn and Austin, Rodney (1987) 'Political and constitutional aspects of the Westland affair', *Parliamentary Affairs*, 40 (1): 20–40.

Oliver, Michael (1997) *Whatever Happened to Monetarism? Economic Policy-Making and Social Learning in the United Kingdom since 1979*. Aldershot: Ashgate.

Olson, Mancur (1982) *The Rise and Decline of Nations: The Political Economy of Economic Growth, Stagflation and Social Rigidities*. New Haven, CT: Yale University Press.

O'Sullivan, Noel (1988) 'The political theory of neo-corporatism', in Andrew Cox and Noel O'Sullivan (eds), *The Corporate State: Corporatism and the State Tradition in Western Europe*. Aldershot: Edward Elgar.

Ovendale, Ritchie (1994) *British Defence Policy since 1945*. Manchester: Manchester University Press.

Owen, David (1979) 'Britain and the United States', in W.E. Leuchtenburg et al. (eds), *Britain and the United States: Four Views to Mark the Silver Jubilee*. London: Heinemann.

Owens, Susan (1995) 'From "predict and provide" to "predict and prevent"? Pricing and planning in transport policy', *Transport Policy*, 2 (1): 43–9.

Panitch, Leo (1986) *Working Class Politics in Crisis*. London: Verso.

Parkinson, Michael (1970) *The Labour Party and the Organisation of Secondary Education, 1918–1965*. London: Routledge & Kegan Paul.

Parsons, Wayne (1995) *Public Policy: An Introduction to the Theory and Practice of Policy Analysis*. Cheltenham: Edward Elgar.

Patten, Chris (1983) *The Tory Case*. London: Longman.

Patten, John (1992) 'Who's afraid of the "S" word?', *New Statesman and Society*, 17 July: 20–1.

Pelling, Henry (1963) *A History of British Trade Unionism*. Harmondsworth: Penguin.

Pensions Commission (2004) *Pensions: Challenges and Choices*. London: The Stationery Office.

Perkin, Harold (1990) *The Rise of Professional Society: England since 1880*. London: Routledge.

Peston, Robert (2005) *Brown's Britain: How Gordon Runs the Show*. London: Short Books.

Phillips Committee (1954) *Report of the Committee on the Economic and Financial Problems of Old Age*, Cmd 9333. London: HMSO.

Pierre, Andrew (1972) *Nuclear Politics: The British Experience with an Independent Strategic Force, 1939–1970*. Oxford: Oxford University Press.

Pierson, Paul (1994) *Dismantling the Welfare State: Reagan, Thatcher, and the Politics of Retrenchment*. Cambridge: Cambridge University Press.

Pimlott, Ben (1992) *Harold Wilson*. London: HarperCollins.

Plowden, William (1971) *The Motor Car and Politics: 1896–1970*. London: Bodley Head.

Plumb, H. (Lord Plumb of Coleshill) (2001) *The Plumb Line: A Journey through Agriculture and Politics*. London: Greycoat Press.

Pollard, Sidney (1982) *The Wasting of the British Economy*. Beckenham: Croom Helm.

Pollard, Sidney (1983) *The Development of the British Economy 1914–1980*, 3rd edn. London: Arnold.

Power, Michael (1994) *The Audit Explosion*. London: Demos.

Power, Michael (1997) *The Audit Society: Rituals of Verification*. Oxford: Oxford University Press.

Pressman, Jeffrey and Wildavsky, Aaron (1973) *Implementation*. Berkeley, CA: University of California Press.

Pym, Francis (1985) *The Politics of Consent*. London: Sphere.

Pym, Hugh and Kochan, Nicholas (1998) *Gordon Brown: The First Year in Power*. London: Bloomsbury.

Rawnsley, Andrew (2001) *Servants of the People*, rev. edn. Harmondsworth: Penguin.

Rees, Wyn (2001) 'Britain's contribution to global order', in Stuart Croft, Andrew Dorman, Wyn Rees and Matthew Uttley, *Britain and Defence, 1945–2000: A Policy Re-evaluation*. Harlow: Pearson.

Renwick, Sir Robert (1996) *Fighting with Allies*. New York: TimesBooks.

Reynolds, David (1986) 'A "special relationship"? America, Britain and the international order since the Second World War', *International Affairs*, 62.

Reynolds, David (1988–9) 'Rethinking Anglo-American relations', *International Affairs*, 65 (1).

Reynolds, David (1991) *Britannia Overruled: British Policy and World Power in the 20th Century*. London: Longman.

Richards, David and Smith, Martin J. (2002) *Governance and Public Policy in the UK*. Oxford: Oxford University Press.

Richardson, Jeremy (ed.) (1982) *Policy Styles in Western Europe*, London: Allen & Unwin.

Richardson, Louise (1996) *When Allies Differ: Anglo-American Relations during the Suez and Falklands Crises*. Basingstoke: Macmillan.

Ridley, Nicholas (1991) *My Style of Government*. London: Hutchinson.

Robinson, Mike (1992) *The Greening of British Party Politics*. Manchester: Manchester University Press.

Robinson, Nick (2000) *The Politics of Agenda Setting: The Car and the Shaping of Public Policy*. Aldershot: Ashgate.

Robinson, Nick (2002) 'The politics of the fuel protests: towards a multi-dimensional explanation', *Political Quarterly*, 73 (1): 58–66.

Robinson, Piers (1999) 'The CNN effect: can the news media drive foreign policy?', *Review of International Studies*, 25 (2): 301–9.

Rogin, Michael (1962) 'Voluntarism: the political foundations of an anti-political doctrine', *Industrial and Labour Relations Review*, July: 521–3.

Rose, Richard (1984) *Do Parties Make a Difference?* 2nd edn. Basingstoke: Macmillan.

Rose, Richard (1990) 'Inheritance before choice in public policy', *Journal of Theoretical Politics*, 2 (3): 263–91.

Rose, Richard (1993) *Lesson Drawing in Public Policy*, Chatham, NJ: Chatham House.

Rose, Richard and Davies, Philip (1994) *Inheritance in Public Policy: Change without Choice in Britain*. New Haven, CT: Yale University Press.

Routledge, Paul (1998) *Gordon Brown: The Biography*. New York: Simon & Schuster.

Royal Commission on Trade Unions and Employers' Associations (1968) *Report*, Cmnd 36234. London: HMSO.

Royal Society for the Protection of Birds (1995) *Braking Point: The RSPB's Policy on Transport and Biodiversity*. Sandy, Bedfordshire: RSPB Publications.

Sanders, David (1990) *Losing an Empire, Finding a Role: British Foreign Policy since 1945*. Basingstoke: Macmillan.

Schuster, Liza (2003) 'Asylum seekers: Sangatte and the tunnel', *Parliamentary Affairs*, 56 (3): 506–22.

SED (Scottish Education Department) (1965) *Reorganisation of Secondary Education on Comprehensive Lines*, Circular 600. Edinburgh: Scottish Education Department.

Seitz, R. (1998) *Over Here*. London: Weidenfeld and Nicolson.

Self, Peter and Storing, H.J. (1962) *The State and the Farmer*. London: Allen & Unwin.

Sewill, Brendon (1967) *A New Incomes Policy*. London: Conservative Research Department.

Shephard, Gillian (2000) *Shephard's Watch*. London: Politico's.

Sherwin, M.J. (1994) 'The atomic bomb and the origins of the Cold War', in Melvyn Leffler and David Painter (eds), *Origins of the Cold War: An International History*. London: Routledge.

Shoard, Marion (1980) *The Theft of the Countryside*. London: Temple Smith.

Shonfield, Andrew (1958) *British Economic Policy since the War*. Harmondsworth: Penguin.

Short, Anthony (1975) *The Communist Insurrection in Malaya, 1948–60*. London: Muller.

Shultz, G.P. (1993) *Turmoil and Triumph*. New York: Scribner's.

Silberstein, Sandra (2002) *War of Words. Language, Politics, and 9/11*. London: Routledge.

Simon, Brian (1955) *The Common Secondary School*. London: Lawrence & Wishart.

Simon, Brian (1991) *Education and the Social Order, 1940–1990*. London: Lawrence & Wishart.

Singh, Anita Inder (1993) *The Limits of British Influence: South Asia and the Anglo-American Relationship, 1947–56*. New York: St Martin's Press.

Skidelsky, Robert (1979) 'The decline of Keynesian politics', in Colin Crouch (ed.), *State and Economy in Contemporary Capitalism*. Beckenham: Croom Helm.

Skidelsky, Robert (1992) *John Maynard Keynes. Volume Two: The Economist as Saviour 1920–1937*. Basingstoke: Macmillan.

Skidelsky, Robert (2000) *John Maynard Keynes. Volume Three: Fighting for Britain 1937–1946*. Basingstoke: Macmillan.

Smith, David (1987) *The Rise and Fall of Monetarism: The Theory and Politics of an Economic Experiment*. Harmondsworth: Penguin.

Smith, Martin J. (1991) 'From policy community to issue network: *salmonella* in eggs and the new politics of food', *Public Administration*, 69: 235–55.

Smith, Martin J. (1993) *Pressure, Power and Policy: State Autonomy and Policy Networks in Britain and the United States*. Hemel Hempstead: Harvester Wheatsheaf.

Smith, Martin J. (1999) *The Core Executive in Britain*. Basingstoke: Macmillan.

Smith, Martin J., Richards, David and Marsh, David (2000) 'The changing role of central government departments', in R.A.W. Rhodes (ed.), *Transforming British Government. Volume 2: Changing Roles and Relationships*. Basingstoke: Macmillan.

Snyder, William (1964) *The Politics of British Defence Policy, 1945–62*. Columbus, OH: Ohio State University Press.

Solesbury, William (1976) 'The environmental agenda', *Public Administration*, 54: 379–97.

Standing Advisory Committee on Trunk Roads Assessment (1994) *Trunk Roads and the Generation of Traffic*. London: HMSO.

Stephens, Philip (1997) *Politics and the Pound: The Tories, The Economy and Europe*. Basingstoke: Macmillan.

Stewart, Michael (1977) *The Jekyll and Hyde Years*. London: J.M. Dent.

Stone, Diane (1989) 'Causal stories and the formation of policy agendas', *Political Science Quarterly*, 104 (2): 281–300.

Strange, Susan (1971) *Sterling and British Policy: A Political Study of an International Currency in Decline*. Oxford: Oxford University Press.

Taylor, Andrew J. (1989) *Trade Unions and Politics: A Comparative Introduction*. Basingstoke: Macmillan.

Taylor, Robert (1993) *The Trade Union Question in British Politics*. Oxford: Blackwell.

Tebbit, Norman (1988) *Upwardly Mobile*. London: Weidenfeld & Nicolson.

Thain, Colin (1985) 'The education of the Treasury: the medium-term financial strategy 1980–84', *Public Administration*, 63 (2): 261–85.

Thain, Colin (2004) 'Treasury rules, OK? The further evolution of a British institution', *British Journal of Politics and International Relations*, 6: 123–30.

Thain, Colin and Wright, Maurice (1995) *The Treasury and Whitehall: The Planning and Control of Public Expenditure, 1976–1993*. Oxford: Clarendon Press.

Thane, Pat (1996) *Foundations of the Welfare State*, 2nd edn. London: Longman.

Thatcher, Margaret (1993) *The Downing Street Years*. London: HarperCollins.

Thornton, Stephen (forthcoming) 'Towards public–private partnership: Labour and pensions policy 1964–1970', in Peter Dorey (ed.), *The 1964–70 Labour Governments*. London: Routledge.

Thorpe, Andrew (1997) *A History of the British Labour Party*. Basingstoke: Macmillan.

Timmins, Nicholas (2001) *The Five Giants*, rev. edn. London: HarperCollins.

Titmuss, Richard (1950) *Problems of Social Policy*. London: HMSO.

Titmuss, Richard (1968) *Commitment to Welfare*. London: Allen & Unwin.

Toke, Dave (2002) 'UK GM crop policy: relative calm before the storm?', *Political Quarterly*, 73 (1): 67–75.

Tomlinson, Jim (1985) *British Macroeconomic Policy since 1940*. Beckenham: Croom Helm.

Torgersen, U. (1987) 'Housing: the wobbly pillar under the welfare state', in Bengt Turner, Jim Kemeny and Lennart Lundqvist (eds), *Between State and Market: Housing in the Post-Industrial Era*. Stockholm: Almqvist & Wiksell.

Tracy, Michael (1989) *Government and Agriculture in Western Europe, 1880–1998*, 3rd edn. Hemel Hempstead: Harvester Wheatsheaf.

Transport for London (2003) *Congestion Charging: Six Months On*. London: Mayor of London & Transport for London.

Treasury (1997) *UK Membership of the Single Currency: An Assessment of the Five Economic Tests.* London: HM Treasury.

Treasury (1998) *Modern Public Services for Britain: Investing in Reform. Comprehensive Spending Review: New Public Spending Plans 1999–2002*, Cm 4011. London: The Stationery Office.

Treasury (2002) *Reforming Britain's Economic and Financial Policy: Towards Greater Economic Stability*, Ed Balls and Gus O'Donnell (eds). Basingstoke: Palgrave.

Treasury and Civil Service Select Committee (1992) *The 1992 Autumn Statement and the Conduct of Economic Policy, First Report, 1992–3*, HC 201. London: HMSO.

Vital, David (1968) *The Making of British Foreign Policy.* London: Allen & Unwin.

Vogel, David (1986) *National Styles of Regulation: Environmental Policy in Great Britain and the United States.* Ithaca, NY: Cornell University Press.

Walker, J.L. (1977) 'Setting the agenda in the US Senate: a theory of problem selection', *British Journal of Political Science*, 7 (4).

Wallace, William (1975) *The Foreign Policy Process in Britain.* London: Royal Institute of International Affairs.

Walsh, T. and Tindale, S. (1992) 'Time for divorce', *Fabian Review*, 104 (4).

Walt, S.M. (1998–9) 'The ties that fray: why America and Europe are drifting apart', *The National Interest*, 54: 3–11.

Walters, Alan (1990) *Sterling in Danger: The Economic Consequences of Pegged Exchange Rates.* London: Fontana.

Warner, G. (1997) 'Foreign, defence and European affairs: commentary', in Brian Brivati and Tim Bale (eds), *New Labour in Power: Precedents and Prospects.* New York: Routledge.

Wass, Douglas (1978) 'The changing problems of economic management', in Central Statistical Office, *Economic Trends*, 293: 97–104.

Webb, Adrian (1975) 'The abolition of national assistance: policy changes in the administration of assistance benefits', in Phoebe Hall, Hilary Land, Roy Parker and Adrian Webb (eds), *Change, Choice and Conflict in Social Policy.* London: Heinemann.

Webster, Charles (1988) *The Health Services since the War. Volume 1: Problems of Health Care: The National Health Service before 1957.* London: HMSO.

Webster, Charles (1998) *The National Health Service: A Political History.* Oxford: Oxford University Press.

Weinberger, Casper (1991) *Fighting for Peace: Seven Critical Years at the Pentagon.* New York: Warner Books.

Westergaard, John and Resler, Henrietta (1976) *Class in a Capitalist Society.* Harmondsworth: Pelican Books.

Wexler, Imanuel (1983) *The Marshall Plan Revisited: The European Recovery Program in Economic Perspective.* Westport, CT: Greenwood Press.

Whitelaw, William (1989) *The Whitelaw Memoirs.* London: Aurum Press.

Whiteside, Noel (1996) 'Creating the welfare state in Britain, 1945–1960', *Journal of Social Policy*, 25 (1): 83–103.

Wilcox, Steve (2002) *UK Housing Review 2002/2003.* London: CIH/CML.

Williams, J. (1987) 'ANZUS: a blow to Britain's self-esteem', *Review of International Studies*, 13: 243–63.

Williams, T. (Lord Williams of Bamburgh) (1965) *Digging for Britain.* London: Hutchinson.

Wilson, D. (1984) *Pressure: The A to Z of Campaigning in Britain.* London: Heinemann.

Wilson, Harold (1971) *The Labour Government 1964–1970.* London: Weidenfeld & Nicolson/ Michael Joseph.

Winter, Michael (1996) *Rural Politics: Policies for Agriculture, Forestry and the Environment.* London: Routledge.

Winter, Michael (2003) 'Responding to the crisis: the policy impact of the foot-and-mouth epidemic', *Political Quarterly*, 74 (1): 47–56.

Wistrich, Enid (1983) *The Politics of Transport.* London: Longman.

Woodhead, Chris (2002) *Class War: The State of British Education.* London: Little, Brown.

Yergin, Daniel (1977) *Shattered Peace: The Origins of the Cold War and the National Security State.* Boston, MA: Houghton Mifflin.

Young, Hugo (1989) *One of Us: A Biography of Margaret Thatcher.* Basingstoke: Macmillan.

Young, Hugo (1990) *One of Us: A Biography of Margaret Thatcher.* London: Pan.

Young, John W. (2000) *Britain and European Unity, 1945–1999*, 2nd edn. Basingstoke: Macmillan.

Young, Stephen (1974) *Intervention in the Mixed Economy: The Evolution of British Industrial Policy.* Beckenham: Croom Helm.

Index

Abel-Smith, Brian, 164–7, 177–8
abortion, 103
Acheson, Dean, 83
Adam Smith Institute, 35
Adonis, Andrew, 66
Advisory, Conciliation and Arbitration Service (ACAS), 148
Afghanistan, 84–91 *passim*
ageing population, 3, 5, 104
agricultural policy, 1, 5, 7–23, 208, 211, 213, 218–19, 221, 224–5
AIDS, 109
air transport, 198–9
alcohol abuse, 114–16
Alexander, Sir William, 49
Amicus, 160
Amsterdam Treaty, 87
Araki, Hiroshi, 171
Assisted Places Scheme, 60
Atkinson, John, 163
Attlee, Clement, 26, 28, 43, 46, 51, 68, 75, 96–7, 120, 137, 162

Baker, Kenneth, 61
balance of payments, 10–11, 26, 33–4, 77
Ball, Michael, 127
Ball, Stephen, 57
Balls, Ed, 41
Bank of England, 26, 28, 34, 39–45
Batteson, C.H., 47
Battle, John, 89
Beckett, Margaret, 23
Benn, Tony, 28, 51
Benson, J., 202, 204
Berridge, Virginia, 102–3
Bevan, Aneurin, 61, 92, 96–8, 121, 137
Beveridge Report (1942), 94–5, 120, 161–3, 166, 177–9
Bevin, Ernest, 68, 71, 77, 80, 136–7
binge drinking, 114–16
Black Papers, 57
Black Report (1979), 109
Blackburn, Robin, 173

Blair, Tony, 5, 18, 25, 28–9, 40–3, 63, 83–9, 110–15, 132, 158–60, 171–6, 179, 192, 194, 202–3, 217–18, 221–2
Blunkett, David, 64, 66
Bogdanor, Vernon, 49–50
Bonoli, Guiliano, 170
bovine spongiform encephalopathy (BSE), 18–19, 86, 219
Boyd-Carpenter, John, 166
Boyle, Edward, 53, 56–7, 98
Bretton Woods system, 29, 31, 74, 76
British Medical Association (BMA), 3, 93, 96–101, 106–7, 212, 217, 221
'British policy style', 6, 214
    changes to, 221–2
British Roads Federation (BRF), 184, 193, 196, 212
Brown, Gordon, 26, 29, 39–45, 92, 112, 172–5, 218
Brussels Treaty Organization, 79
Bulpitt, Jim, 36
Bush, George H., 82–3, 87
Bush, George W., 88–9
Butler, R.A., 30, 46, 98

Cabinet Office, 72, 225
Cahill, Michael, 93
Callaghan, James, 2, 28–9, 34, 50, 57–9, 75, 85, 150–1, 196–7
Campaign for Lead-Free Air (CLEAR), 185, 187
Campbell, R.J., 78
Campbell-Bannerman, Sir Henry, 63
care in the community, 101
Carlisle, Mark, 60
Carr, Robert, 146
Carson, Rachel, 16
Castle, Barbara, 143–5, 168, 173, 176–7, 183
Casualty, 105
Centre for Policy Studies, 35, 57, 169
Champion, Bob, 108
Channon, Paul, 10, 182–3
child-centred learning, 3, 57–8
Chirac, Jacques, 87

Churchill, Winston, 3, 28, 67–77, 83, 90, 136, 138, 163, 165, 224
Chuter Ede, J., 48
city technology colleges and city academies, 62–3, 65
civil service and civil servants, 6, 28, 60–1, 69, 93, 95, 120–1, 205–15 *passim*, 222, 225
Clarke, Charles, 66
Clarke, Kenneth, 24, 42–5, 92, 106–7
Clarke, Roger, 21
Clean Air Act (1956), 101–2
Clinton, Bill, 86–9
'CNN effect', 72
Cold War, 3, 8, 69–82, 85, 104, 137–8, 223
Cole, Ian, 119
collectivist policies, 25, 104, 203, 220
Commission for Integrated Transport (CfIT), 193, 196–7
Common Agricultural Policy (CAP), 7, 11–15, 19–20, 22, 73, 81, 85
Common Foreign and Security Policy (CFSP), 72, 84–7
Commonwealth countries, 3, 11, 13, 25, 67, 76–84, 90–1, 223–4
comprehensive schools, 2, 48–64 *passim*
Confederation of British Industry (CBI), 32, 134, 158, 160, 197
congestion charging, 5, 194, 219–20
consensus, political, 5, 206–8, 213–16
conservation, 16–17, 22
Conservative Party, 15–16, 50–1, 56–7, 63, 66, 85, 96–100, 104, 106, 111–13, 138–53, 195, 206, 213–15, 221
continuity in public policy, 205–8, 218
contraception, 94, 99, 103
Cook, Robin, 83
corporatism, 2, 26, 31, 134, 170, 208
Council for the Protection of Rural England (CPRE), 17, 190, 193, 196, 198
council houses
   building and allocation of, 4, 122–31, 209
   sales of, 4, 113, 118–20, 127–8, 209
Country Landowners' Association (CLA), 8, 22
Countryside Commission, 16
Cox, Graham, 8, 16–17
Crequer, Ngaio, 61
Creutzfeldt-Jakob disease, 18–19, 219
Cripps, Sir Stafford, 28, 43
Crook, David, 53, 56
Crosland, Anthony, 54
Crossman, Richard, 9, 164–8, 176–7
Crouch, Colin, 134

Currie, Edwina, 18
Curry Commission, 21

Dalton, Hugh, 28, 45
Darling, Alistair, 197–8, 198
Davies, Philip, 97
Dearing, Ron, 62, 65
decline, economic, 2–3, 24–6, 30, 32, 35, 67–9, 133, 208
deficiency payments, 11–14
Dehaene, Jean-Luc, 86
Dell, Edmund, 168
Denham, John, 177
Department of the Environment, Food and Rural Affairs (DEFRA), 1, 7, 19–23, 73, 219, 221
Department of the Environment, Transport and the Regions (DETR), 193–4
Department (formerly Ministry) of Health, 3, 93, 95, 99, 101, 106, 112, 114, 212, 221
deregulation, 4, 15, 36–7, 40, 85–6, 129, 188, 199, 215
devaluation of sterling, 26, 31, 38
devolution, 222
Dickie, John, 85
dietary trends, 115
Dobson, Alan, 75
Dobson, Frank, 113
Dr Finlay's Casebook, 99
Doll, Richard, 102
dominant paradigms, 208–12
Don't Wait Up, 105
Donoughue, Bernard, 59
Donovan Report (1968), 142–3
Dorrell, Stephen, 110
Dowding, Keith, 183
Downing Street Policy Directorate (formerly Policy Unit), 59–60, 66, 169, 225
Downs, Anthony, 180, 187, 191–204 *passim*
Durham City Council, 196

Eastenders, 104–5
Eccles, David, 50
economic policy, 1, 24–45
   foreign, 25–6
Eden, Sir Anthony, 165
Education Act (1944), 2, 46–50
education policy, 2–3, 46–66, 212–13, 217, 220–1, 224–5
Education Reform Act (1988), 60–2
11–plus examination, 51–6, 64
Ellis, Bryan, 167–9
'encourage and provide' (E&P) ethos, 191–6 *passim*

Ennals, David, 177
Enthoven, Alain, 106–7
environmental issues, 5, 7–10, 16–18, 21–3, 101–2,
    181–92, 198–200, 212, 219, 221, 224
Equitable Life, 174
euro currency, 25, 40, 44, 86
European Central Bank, 44
European Court of Auditors, 13
European Free Trade Area, 81
European Union (formerly European Economic
    Community), 7, 11–15, 25, 32, 36–42, 69,
    72, 80–91, 159, 187, 194, 222–4
Evans, Brenda, 172
Evans, Stanley, 9
Evason, Eileen, 170–1, 173
evidence-based policy-making, 110–11, 225
Exchange Rate Mechanism (ERM), 25–6, 37–9, 44

Falklands War, 75, 83
family values, 101, 109
Farmers for Action, 21–2
Fawcett, Helen, 165
Fearne, A., 13
Field, Frank, 172–7 *passim*
fiscal policy, 42–3, 208
flying pickets, 14
Fontainebleau agreement (1984), 15, 81
food labelling, 115
food retailers, 21
food safety, 18–19, 22–3, 102, 116, 195, 219, 224–5
food security, 7–8, 11, 20
Foot, Michael, 148
foot-and-mouth disease (FMD), 19–22, 195, 219
Foreign and Commonwealth Office (FCO), 69, 72
foreign policy, 3, 67–91, 223–4
Forrest, Ray, 119
Fowler, Norman, 169–70, 176–7
France, 14, 25–30 , 38–40, 68–9, 75, 78–82, 86–7
Friedman, Milton, 32
Friends of the Earth, 16–17, 185
FRS17, 174–5, 178
fuel price protests (September 2000), 180, 195–6
full employment, 1–2, 29–31, 34, 30, 94, 117, 124,
    137, 207, 215
fundholding GPs, 107, 111
Furbey, Robert, 119

G8 countries, 84, 86
Gaitskell, Hugh, 51, 53–4
Gamble, Andrew, 220
Gardner, Richard, 74
Garner, Robert, 16–17

de Gaulle, Charles, 12, 81
General Agreement on Tariffs and Trade (GATT),
    29, 72, 74, 78
genetically-modified (GM) crops, 17–18,
    22–3, 116, 195
Germany 26, 28, 41, 68, 70, 79–86 *passim*
Ginsburg, Norman, 119
Glennerster, Howard, 127
global warming, 189, 200
globalization, 3, 67, 71, 88, 90, 127, 155
'golden rule' of British public finance, 42
Goode Committee report (1993), 171
Gould, Sir Ronald, 49
Gourlay, Sir Simon, 15
Gowing, Margaret, 73
grammar schools, 50–7, 63–4, 122
grant-maintained (GM) schools, 62, 65
Green Party, 102
'green pound' system, 13, 15
Greer, Alan, 9
Grenada, 75–6
growth, economic, 2, 25–7, 32–5, 38, 45, 155,
    191, 197
Growth and Stability Pact, 42
Guillebaud Report (1956), 98, 100
Gulf War (1990–91), 84, 87, 89
Gummer, John, 19

Ham, Christopher, 104, 107–8, 212
Hannah, Leslie, 177
Harman, Harriet, 172–3
Harriman, Averell, 80
Headey, Bruce, 212
Healey, Denis, 26, 33–5, 39
Health Education Council, 109
health policy, 3–4, 92–116, 122, 209, 217–18,
    221, 224–5
Heath, Edward, 13, 25, 31–2, 57, 59, 75, 81, 126,
    140–1, 145–7, 153, 207
Hennessy, Peter, 59
Hill, Michael, 92, 169
Hills, John, 127
Hogan, Michael, 80
Home Office, 114
Horsbrugh, Florence, 50
horticulture, 12
House of Commons select committees, 21, 41
housing associations, 4, 129–30
Housing Corporation, 125, 129–30
housing policy, 117–32, 209, 213, 224
Howe, Geoffrey, 29, 35
Howorth, J., 89

human relations theory of industrial relations, 139
Hurd, Douglas, 83
Hussein, Saddam, 87–8
Hutton, Will, 171–2

In Place of Strife, 143–7
incomes policies, 135, 141–3, 147–8, 208
India, 78
industrial relations policy, 133–60, 209–10, 220
　legalism in, 4, 134–5
inflation, 2, 13, 26, 31–41, 44–5, 60, 83, 126,
　135, 155, 168, 208, 215
Ingersent, Ken, 8, 10–11
Inns of Court Conservative and Unionist
　Society, 141
Institute of Economic Affairs, 35
'institutional sclerosis', 215
interest groups, 210–17, 221–2
internal markets, 106–7, 110–11
International Monetary Fund (IMF), 29, 33, 35,
　38, 75, 78, 84
Iran, 69, 72, 77
Iraq War (2003), 83, 89–91
Isaacs, George, 136–7
issue attention cycle (IAC), 180–203 *passim*
Italy, 79, 86

Jackson, Brian, 52
Jefferys, Kevin, 96
Jenkins, Roy, 37
Johnson, Harry, 32
'joined-up government', 111–16, 132, 222
Jones, Digby, 160
Jones, Margaret, 178
Jopling, Michael, 15
Joppke, Christian, 181
Jordan, Grant, 6, 161, 176, 206, 214, 221–2
Joseph, Sir Keith, 35, 57, 60, 167–8, 173, 215

Kelly, Ruth, 66
Kennan, George, 73
Kennedy, John F., 74
Kerr, Michael, 167
Keynesianism, 1–2, 24, 29–35, 126, 205–8,
　215, 224
Kingdon, John, 148–9
Kinnock, Neil, 43, 158
Klein, Rudolph, 99
Kleinman, M., 132
Kogan, Maurice, 54
Kohl, Helmut, 83
Kyoto Protocol, 89

Labour Party, 51–4, 57, 63, 66, 88, 100, 109–13,
　133, 136–8, 143–4, 147, 150–1, 158–9,
　164–6, 171–3, 192, 213
Lamont, Norman, 37, 43
Lang, Tim, 18
Lawson, Nigel, 29, 35, 37–8, 106, 170–1, 177
lead in petrol, 186–7, 194, 201
Lewinsky, Monica, 87
Libya, 81–2
Lloyd, Selwyn, 31
Lloyd George, David, 119
local education authorities, 2–3, 50–6 *passim*,
　60, 212, 220
London County Council, 50, 53
Longstreth, Frank, 29, 31
Lowe, Rodney, 162, 166, 178
Lukes, Steven, 93

Maastricht Treaty, 36, 38, 42, 82, 86
McCormick, John, 186
Macleod, Iain, 98, 100, 165–6, 177
McMahon, Brian 74
Macmillan, Harold, 12, 26, 28, 30, 53, 74, 76, 78,
　81, 85, 98, 120, 141, 165, 178
MacSharry, Ray, 19
Major, John, 4, 16, 24–8, 35, 38, 62–3, 66, 83–9,
　153–5, 171–2, 187, 192, 194, 206, 215–24
Malaya, 76–7
Mandelson, Peter, 158
Marsh, David, 184
Marshall Aid, 73, 80
Marxism, 133–4, 139–40
Mason, Stewart, 52
Maudling, Reginald, 31
Mawhinney, Brian, 192–3, 203
Maxwell, Robert, 171
means-testing, 162, 172–4, 177–8, 209
Meat and Livestock Commission, 18
Medical Research Council, 102
Medium-Term Financial Strategy, 26, 35–40, 45
mental health treatment, 100–1
Millan, Bruce, 56
Millett, Anthea, 64
miners' strikes, 14, 147, 154–5
Minimum Income Guarantee (MIG), 173–4
minimum wage, 113, 158
Ministers, activist role of, 6, 206, 212–15,
　221, 225
Ministry of Agriculture, Fisheries and Food
　(MAFF), 1, 7–10, 15–22, 73, 211, 219, 221
Ministry of Labour, 140, 210
Monckton, Walter, 98, 140

monetary policy and monetarism, 2, 24, 28–42
  passim, 205, 208, 215–16
Monetary Policy Committee, 41
Moore, John, 106
Morgan, Kenneth O., 121
Morris, Estelle, 66
Morrison, Herbert, 96
mortgage tax relief, 4, 126, 128, 131, 209
Mugabe, Robert, 84
Murie, Alan, 119
Myles, John, 176

National Audit Office, 42
National Curriculum, 3, 60–5
National Economic Development Council (NEDC),
  31, 141, 155, 216
National Farmers' Union (NFU), 1, 7–9, 12–16,
  20–2, 211, 221
National Health Service (NHS), 3–4, 61, 92–112
  passim, 121, 137, 209, 218, 224
National Trust, 185, 190, 192
nationalization, 30, 121, 137, 139
Nature Conservancy Council, 16
neo-corporatism, 4, 134–5, 147
neo-liberalism, 7, 14, 23, 61, 83, 90, 139, 170,
  208, 223–4
Nesbitt, Steven, 169, 176
New Labour *see* Labour Party
new public management, 131
New Right thinking, 81, 104–9, 127, 149, 151,
  169, 214, 216
Newby, Howard, 17
'Next Steps' reforms, 213, 222
Nice Treaty, 87
Nixon, Richard M., 75
Nkrumah, Kwame, 76
North Atlantic Treaty Organization (NATO), 70,
  74, 79–90 *passim*
nuclear weapons, 70–4, 79, 84

obesity, 115–16
Office for Standards in Education (Ofsted), 64, 115
O'Higgins, Michael, 163
oil prices 126; *see also* fuel price protests
One Flew Over the Cuckoo's Nest, 100
organic farming, 18, 102
Owen, David, 85
owner-occupation, 4, 118–31, 209

Pakistan, 84
paradigm shifts, 6, 32, 61, 131, 206–8, 218–21
Parkin, Michael, 32

Parkinson, Michael, 51
Parsons, Wayne, 203
path dependency, 176
Patten, John, 63
peacekeeping operations, 84
Peart, Fred, 9
Pelling, Henry, 136
Pension Credit, 173–4
Pensions Commission, 175–6
pensions policy, 5, 161–79, 209, 224
Percy Commission report (1957), 101
Perkin, Harold, 141
Phillips Committee report (1954), 163–4
Picture Post, 95
Pierson, Paul, 176
Plowden Report (1967), 57–8
Plumb, Sir Henry, 12–14
policy communities, 6, 161, 205–6, 210–15, 222
  destabilization of, 5, 220–1
  for agriculture, 1, 5, 7, 16–18, 20, 211, 213,
    221, 225
  for education, 3, 213, 225
  for health, 3–4, 93, 99, 101, 106–8, 212, 225
  for housing, 213
  for transport, 5, 102, 184, 186, 190–201,
    212–13, 221, 225
policy transfer, 26, 206, 225
policy windows, 148–9
Pollard, Sidney, 25, 126
pollution, 101–3, 113, 116, 185–6, 199, 201, 219
poverty, 5, 94–5, 98, 111, 113, 167
'predict and provide' ethos, 5, 180–92 *passim*,
  196–9, 204, 208, 219
Prentice, Reg, 148
Prescott, John, 192–3, 196–7
prescription charges, 98
Pressman, Jeffrey, 161
Prime Ministers, roles played by, 28, 105
Private Finance Initiative, 110, 218
privatization, 36, 101–4, 110–12, 188–92, 215
productionist policy paradigm, 1, 7, 10–11, 16,
  22, 208, 211, 218–19
public goods, 7, 20
public opinion, 95–7, 102, 150, 195
public sector borrowing requirement (PSBR), 33–9
purchaser-provider split, 107, 111

Qualifications and Curriculum Authority, 64

radio programmes, 20, 150
rail transport, 188, 191–6
Rayner, A.J., 8, 10–11

Reagan, Ronald, 75–6, 81, 88
'realist' foreign policy, 67, 71
Redwood, John, 169, 177, 195
religious schools, 47
rent control, 4, 124, 131
rent rebates, 4, 125–6, 209
Renwick, Robert, 76
reproductive health, 103
'restrict and provide' (R&P) ethos, 191–8, 219
Reynolds, David, 76
Rhodesia *see* Zimbabwe
Rice, Condoleezza, 223
Richardson, Jeremy, 6, 161, 176, 206, 214, 221–2
Ridley, Nicholas, 82
Ries, Charles P., 88–9
road-building, 5, 183–99, 208–9, 212, 219, 221
road pricing 191, 194–8, 202–3, 220
Roosevelt, Franklin D., 69
Rose, Richard, 30, 97, 130–1, 206–7
Royal College of Physicians, 114
Royal Commission on Environmental Pollution, 185–7
Royal Society for the Protection of Birds, 17, 192

salmonella, 18, 219
school leaving age, 46–7
Scotland, 7, 9, 46–9, 55–6, 61–2, 117, 119, 129–30, 222
Second World War, 68, 93–6, 119–22, 136, 162, 211
secondary modern schools, 52–3
Securities and Investment Board, 42
Self, Peter, 8–9, 11
Shephard, Gillian, 9–10, 16
Sherman, Alfred, 57
Shinwell, Emmanual, 51
Shoard, Marion, 16
Shore, Peter, 177
Shultz, George, 75
Simon, Brian, 47, 53
Simpson, Derek, 160
Smith, Ian, 79
Smith, John, 43, 158, 172
Smith, Martin J., 18, 61
smoking, 102–3, 113–15
social contract, 148
social democracy, 207–8, 213, 224
social exclusion, 113, 131–2
social housing, 4, 117–19, 129–32
social security, 94, 121, 128, 149, 177–8
social services, 105
'solemn and binding' agreement (1969), 145

Solesbury, William, 102, 149
Soviet Union, 67–71, 79, 82, 104, 138, 223
Spain, 82
special advisers to Ministers, 6, 206, 217, 222, 225
stakeholder pensions, 172–4, 177–8
Stalin, Joseph, 69
State Earnings-Related Pension Scheme (SERPS), 168–73
Sterling Area, 77–8, 82
Stone, Diane, 200–1
Storing, H.J., 8–9, 11
Strachey, John, 9
strikes, 14, 136–49, 154, 159
subsidies, 4, 10–15, 19–23, 124–31 *passim*, 191, 199, 208–11, 219
Suez Canal and Suez crisis (1956), 75–80 *passim*
supply-side measures, 2, 30–1, 35–6, 38

target-setting, 109, 112–13
tariffs, 9, 89
Tate, Nicholas, 64
Taylor Robert, 148
Teacher Training Agency, 64
Tebbit, Norman, 154
technology colleges, 62–3
television programmes, 20, 93, 99, 103–6, 109–10, 115
Temple, William, 47
terrorism, 20, 88–9, 223
Thane, Pat, 162
Thatcher, Margaret (and Thatcherism), 2, 4, 14–16, 25–38, 43, 57–62, 75–6, 81–3, 87–8, 92, 104–12, 118, 127–8, 151–5, 169–71, 178–9, 187, 206, 208, 215–24
'Third Way' policies, 24, 40, 43, 88, 110–11, 172
Thorneycroft, Peter, 28
Thorpe, Andrew, 138
Timmins, Nicholas, 170
Titmuss, Richard, 93–4, 132, 161, 164–5
Tomlinson, Mike, 65–6
Townsend, Peter, 164–7, 177
Tracy, Michael, 13
trade liberalization, 19, 22
trade unions, 2–4, 13, 26, 30–3, 36, 60, 104, 133–60, 208, 215–17, 220
  membership of, 155–7, 160
  recognition of, 158
Trades Disputes Act (1927), 137–8
Trades Union Congress (TUC), 32, 141, 145
transport policy, 5, 180–204, 208, 212–13, 219, 221, 224–5
Transport 2000, 184–98 *passim*

Treasury, the 9–10, 28–9, 33–45, 103, 107, 112, 151, 161–6, 170, 173, 177, 185
tripartism, 26, 31, 45, 155
Truman, Harry, 73, 75
Turner, Adair, 175

unemployment, 2, 33–8, 41, 57, 113, 126–7, 154–5
United Nations, 69, 74, 84, 87–9
United States 13, 18–19, 22, 25–32, 35, 41, 67–91, 98
    Britain's special relationship with, 3, 73–6, 79–88, 223–4

Wales, 7, 9, 14, 117, 119, 129–30, 222
Walker, Peter, 147
Walston, Oliver, 10
Walters, Alan, 29, 32
Warner, G., 85
weapons of mass destruction, 70–1
Webster, Charles, 95
welfare state regime, 119, 122, 127, 132, 137, 215, 224

welfare-to-work policies, 113
Western European Union, 83–7
Whitelaw, William, 151
Wilby, Peter, 61
Wildavsky, Aaron, 161
Wildlife and Countryside Act (1981), 17
Willetts, David, 169, 177
William Tyndale Junior School, 58
Williams, Tom, 8–9
Willink, Henry, 96
Wilson, Harold, 11–12, 26, 28–9, 32, 45, 54, 59, 81, 125, 142–5, 167
Winter, Michael, 17, 19, 21
'winter of discontent' (1979), 149–51
Woodhead, Chris, 64
Wootton, Barbara, 164
World Trade Organization, 72, 84
Wragg, Ted, 66

Zimbabwe, 79, 84

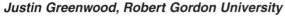